I AM DYNAMITE

Writer and Auschwitz witness Primo Levi; refugee and engineer Ben Glaser; artist Stanley Spencer; Israeli ceramicist Rachel Silberstein; Friedrich Nietzsche, the dynamic philosopher. Who are they? What have they seen? What do they share?

Freedom. Individuality. Existential power. The capacity and desire to live a life-project: to make one's life one's work. *I Am Dynamite* ignites an alternative theory of the self and will, wrapped up in a combustible assault upon scholarly convention. Asking why the real effort of constructing and living within an identity is so often overlooked, it examines the subjective experience of existing in the world, with the power to define and transform oneself.

Nietzsche famously claimed that 'an uninjurable, unburiable force is in me, something that gallops over rocks: it is called my Will'. Today, in contrast, we are taught to believe that social institutions determine the circumstances and scope of individual lives. But can we really write people out of the social power-equation, or subscribe to a dominant Foucauldian analytics that denies access to genuine truths and freedoms? Considering the trials and triumphs of five very different modern subjects, Nigel Rapport asks: can consciousness of being a self in the world enable control over one's life within it?

Calling for a renewed appreciation of the extraordinary within us all, this richly inventive work seeks to restore knowledge to its essential practical and moral aims – aiding and informing the lives we actually live.

Nigel Rapport holds the Chair in Anthropological and Philosophical Studies in the Department of Social Anthropology at the University of St Andrews. His books include *Social and Cultural Anthropology: The Key Concepts* (Routledge, 2000), *The Trouble with Community* (2002) and *Transcendent Individual* (Routledge, 1997). He has received awards from the Royal Anthropological Institute and the Royal Society of Edinburgh.

'A brilliant summation of his arguments for bringing the individual closer to the centre of our anthropological concerns. ... It is individuals – not society or history or circumstance – who make and unmake the world.'

Michael Jackson, from the Foreword

'An important and contentious book. ...It could stimulate a cult.'
Anthony Cohen, Principal of
Queen Margaret University College, Edinburgh

I AM DYNAMITE

An alternative anthropology of power

Nigel Rapport

LONDON AND NEW YORK

First published 2003
by Routledge
11 New Fetter Lane, London EC4P 4EE

Simultaneously published in the USA and Canada
by Routledge
29 West 35th Street, New York, NY 10001

Routledge is an imprint of the Taylor & Francis Group

© 2003 Nigel Rapport

Typeset in Bembo by Taylor & Francis Ltd
Printed and bound in Great Britain by MPG Books Ltd, Bodmin

All rights reserved. No part of this book may be reprinted or reproduced or utilised in any form or by any electronic, mechanical, or other means, now known or hereafter invented, including photocopying and recording, or in any information storage or retrieval system, without permission in writing from the publishers.

British Library Cataloguing in Publication Data
A catalogue record for this book is available from the British Library

Library of Congress Cataloging in Publication Data
A catalog record for this book has been requested

ISBN 0-415-25862-6 (hbk)
ISBN 0-415-25863-4 (pbk)

FOR
BEN GLASER (1908–96)
AND FOR
EMILIE CONSTANCE (1999–)
– THEIR OWN PERSONS

'I am not a man, I am dynamite'
                                (Friedrich Nietzsche, *Ecce Homo*)

'You think me the child of my circumstances: I make my circumstance. Let any thought or motive of mine be different from what they are, the difference will transform my condition and economy. I – this world which is called I – is the mould into which the world is poured like melted wax. The mould is invisible, but the world betrays the shape of the mould. You call it the power of circumstance, but it is the power of me.'
                            (Ralph Waldo Emerson, *The Transcendentalist*)

CONTENTS

List of figures	x
Foreword by Michael Jackson	xi
Acknowledgements	xv

PART I
Propositions 1

1   Preliminary statements   3
   The book's questions 3
   A metaphor of individuality 6
   A Nietzschean ethos 9
   The book's voices 11
   A tactical humanism 16
   The book's course 20

2   The life of power: an existential framework   22
   Individuality: consciousness, world-view, narrative, life-project and interaction 22
   Individuality and ironic displacement 42
   Displacement and 'in order to' motives 50
   'In order to' motives and prior conditions 55
   The conditions of political power and existential power 74

CONTENTS

PART II
Illustrations   91

3   Friedrich Nietzsche and the wilfulness of power-quanta   93
    1 93
    2 96
    3 98
    4 101
    5 Will to Power 101
    6 Truth 105
    7 Interpretation 108
    8 The Apollonian and the Dionysian 111
    9 Tragic art 115
    10 Overcoming 117
    11 Overman 120
    12 Individuality 122
    13 Writing 126
    14 127

4   Ben Glaser and the composing of 'Cosmos 1' and
    'Cosmos 2'   131
    From Poland to Wales 132
    Ben and personal relations 135
    A private life 143
    A life of self-intensity and control 149
    Envoi 150

5   Rachel Silberstein and the relentless road to personal
    completion   153
    Development town 154
    Rachel and Giacomo 156
    Individuality and mental illness 161
    Judaism and morality and identity 163
    Pottery-making in Mitzpe 166
    A political animal who touches the earth 172
    A dialectics of personal growth 175

6   Stanley Spencer and the visionary metaphysic of love   179
    A brief biography 181
    An artful autobiography 184
    The Resurrection with the Raising of Jairus' Daughter 196

CONTENTS

The church-house 204
Fulfilment or compensation? 206

PART III
Discussions   213

7   **The power of any body-in-its-environment**   215
    The body in anthropology 216
    The science of bodies-plus-environments 220
    The extended body and its self 224
    The bodies in question 226
    The body in practice 235

8   **Total institutions and the violence of society: the death of power?** 240
    The Shoah 241
    Primo Levi, the Lager, *and the reprieve of writing 242*
    'Democratic' as against 'nihilistic' violence 250
    A personal view of the morality of self/other relations 253
    Enshrining 'in order to' 259

Bibliography   261
Index   275

FIGURES

1 Ben Glaser, *Sketched Self-portrait* — 151
2 Photograph of Mitzpe Ramon from the desert — 154
3 Stanley Spencer, *The Fairy on the Waterlily Leaf* — 180
    © Estate of Stanley Spencer 2002. All rights reserved (Dacs).
    Stanley Spencer Gallery, Cookham, Berkshire, UK / Bridgeman Art Gallery
4 Stanley Spencer, *The Resurrection with the Raising of Jairus' Daughter* — 199
    © Estate of Stanley Spencer 2002. All rights reserved (Dacs).
    Southampton Art Gallery, Southampton, UK / Bridgeman Art Gallery

FOREWORD

By and large, most anthropological accounts of the individual are, in Goethe's sense of the word, *allegorical*, since the 'particular serves only as an instance or example of the general'. By contrast, *poetry* expresses the particular without any thought of, or reference to, the general, though 'whoever grasps the particular in all its vitality also grasps the general, without being aware of it, or only becoming aware of it at a late stage'. Goethe's tireless search for significance in the appearance of particular things inspired the work of Walter Benjamin (who cites these lines from Goethe in *The Origin of German Tragic Drama*), and while, as Hannah Arendt remarked, Benjamin was not a poet, he *thought poetically*, fascinated less by the generality of ideas than by the quididdity of things, and filled with wonderment at the ways things appear to our consciousness.

It is this same fascination with the presence and power of the individual, this same profound interest in the phenomenon of uniqueness in a plural world, that has informed Nigel Rapport's writing for many years now – writing that reflects his philosophical concerns, literary sensibilities, and ethnographic fieldwork in diverse places (an English village, an Israeli settlement in the Negev, the Canadian city of St John's, a hospital in Scotland), and offers us new perspectives on a staggering array of subjects, including the novels of E. M. Forster, English rural life, the meaning of home, narrative, individuality, community, and violence. His latest work is not only a brilliant summation of his arguments for bringing the individual closer to the centre of our anthropological concerns; it is a subtle and arresting critique of contemporary social science.

Nigel Rapport is perhaps alone among contemporary anthropologists in his intractable attitude towards any form of reductionism, in his steadfast refusal to explain individuals in terms of those limiting conditions of history, ethnicity, culture and biology, whose traces may be felt or divined in our various lives. What characterizes his writing, and makes it so different from other recent anthropological essays in life-history (Michael Herzfeld's 'ethnographic biography' of Andreas Nenedakis springs to mind), is the absence of any desire to strike a balance between a view of the world based on 'uncompromising personal vision' and a view based on socio-cultural determinants.

Like the individuals whose life stories figure as 'illustrations' in this book, Nigel Rapport cultivates what he calls an ironic relation to the world. Reminding us constantly of the *décalage* between consciousness and the objects on which it fastens, between private and public realms, and between experience and episteme (an argument, incidentally, against a common tendency to conflate the universal *empirical* sense of selfhood and individuality with the historically specific, modernist cult of individualism), Nigel Rapport sets his sights on the multifarious ways in which individuals transcend – in their capacity for action, imagination and fabrication – the situations imposed upon them by happenstance and history. Although the question may be asked to what extent his chosen subjects actually *experience* their lives in the terms with which they rationalise, narrate or fantasise them, the point is well taken that lifeworlds are never reducible to world-views, whether these are products of social history or personal ingenuity. Moreover, it is useful to remind ourselves that, as psychoanalytical anthropology has shown, delving deep into an individual life does not occlude the social; rather it discloses 'countless worlds in every dust-mote' as Mahayana Buddhism puts it, and confirms, as Montaigne observed, that 'there is as much difference found betweene us and our selves, as there is betweene our selves and other'.

What is truly impressive in Nigel Rapport's work is not only this commitment to the psychic unity of humankind, but his insistence that social and cultural macrocosms have no reality except through the energy, creativity and will that individuals impart to them. Though this appears at first sight to dismiss a central assumption of social science – that our realities are socially constructed if not socially determined – Nigel Rapport's method is phenomenological. It simply brackets out such considerations *in order to* (a phrase he makes his own in this book) explore the world *as if* (another key phrase) from the standpoint of the individual. Reductive this is not, since as he points out time and time again, unless we are to fall into the pathetic fallacy of assigning to abstractions like history and society the will, consciousness and determining power of persons, we must accept that vitality exists nowhere but in individual lives, and that it is through the ways individuals decide and construe their destinies that all forms of collective life are possible. To be sure, the tradition of all the dead generations weighs like a nightmare on the mind of the living, as Marx famously put it, and antecedent circumstances – historical, genetic, social or cultural – foreshadow and shape our lives, but the individual is where life is actually lived, endured, decided, denied, suffered, imagined and reimagined. And it is individuals – not society or history or circumstance – who make and unmake the world. Nigel Rapport calls this projective and creative faculty 'existential power', and cites Nietzsche's view that 'the individual is something quite new which creates new things' – a capacity which Hannah Arendt calls 'natality' – our power to bring new life into the world, whether through childbirth, revolutionary action, regenerative ritual, or acts of reconciliation and redemption.

FOREWORD

So what may seem at first sight a repudiation of social reality is, in Nigel Rapport's hands, a new way of approaching the social. For it must be stressed that his emphasis on the individual is motivated less by a desire to build an epistemology around the person than by a kind of tactical humanism that has aesthetic and ethical aspects. The aesthetic reflects, as I have remarked, the value he places on the significance to be found in phenomenal rather than ideal or intellectual realities – in the particular, fugitive, and everyday actions, thoughts, moods, decisions, resolutions and gestures that all too often we are inclined to overlook or trivialize as banal and inconsequential, yet which delineate allegories of human existence – Stanley Spencer's painstaking and transfiguring depictions of Cookham; Rachel Silberstein's love of her dogs; Ben Glaser's unflagging fascination for the physical world; Friedrich Nietzsche's struggle with loneliness and illness. The *ethical* argument for making the individual central to our concern is a pragmatist one. Nigel Rapport invites us to consider the worldly consequences of working with the view of the individual that he espouses – of acting *as if* it were valid.

The argument here is that the defence of individuality is best made neither on ontological grounds (proving that individuals really do exist) or epistemological grounds (arguing that the notion of individuality is conducive to truer knowledge of human reality than any other viewpoint), but on the grounds that such a notion carries us into a more fruitful relation with other human beings, and serves us best in securing and defending human rights. Grounding human rights in communitarian ideals – the group, the nation, the folk, the culture – is, as fascism has repeatedly shown, fraught with danger. Thus questions as to whether or not individuality is a universal fact, a necessary experience, or a truth, are set aside in order to explore the ways in which the very image of individuality helps lend fulfilment, dignity and satisfaction to human beings, both within themselves and in their relations with others.

Objections may be raised that this view does not work in cultures far removed from our own. In the Truth and Reconciliation Commision hearings in South Africa, for example, arguments were often made for the notion of we, against the notion of I – the priority of the nation over the individuals and ethnicities within it. Yet it was individuals who suffered under apartheid, as it was individuals who suffered under Nazism, and to invoke notions of mass suffering, to analyse cruelty in general terms, to fuss about statistics, or argue over the categorical differences between various historical instances of man's inhumanity to man, is to perpetuate the alienating forms of language and thought that laid the groundwork for the possibility of such injustices in the first place. It is therefore ethically imperative that we do not lose sight of the individual person who suffers, who succumbs, or who survives. And whether we look towards the past or turn towards the future, it is inescapably the individual upon whom the existence of the world, even a world of we, depends. As William James once noted, 'the fons et origo of all reality, whether from the absolute or the practical point of view, is thus subjective, is ourselves'. And, he concludes, 'our own reality, that sense of our own life which we at every moment possess, is the ultimate of ultimates for our belief'. In the final analysis, invoking the social as explanation, pretext, or excuse is to act in bad faith. The impersonal is not the real. Only we live our lives. We alone are responsible for our world. Only we can redeem ourselves.

Michael Jackson
Institute of Anthropology
University of Copenhagen

ACKNOWLEDGEMENTS

Two events of personal significance compass the drafting of this book: the death, in 1996, of my stepfather, Ben Glaser (an emigré from Nazi Europe), and my visit to Auschwitz-Birkenau in 2001.

In between I also visited the Holocaust Museum in Washington DC, where I came across the following prescription from Chief British Prosecutor Shawcross at the Nuremberg trials:

> [T]he individual must transcend the state. The state and the law are made for man; that through them he may achieve a higher purpose, a greater dignity.

At the very end of his book *Moments of Reprieve*, where, some thirty years after penning his classic testament to life in the Nazi concentration camp (*If This is a Man*), Primo Levi returned to recount the stories of the few individuals who found the strength to achieve some kind of reprieve for themselves from the fate that had been institutionally assigned them, Levi writes against our nevertheless forgetting that: 'all of us are in the ghetto, that the ghetto is fenced in, that beyond the fence stand the lords of death, and not far away the train is waiting' (1994: 172). (A year after publishing this, Levi committed suicide.)

Individual over against institution, and the hope of achieving transcendence over against the inexorability of cultures of ghettoization – these also provide the terms within which this book plots its course. Levi and Shawcross in a way reiterate Ralph Waldo Emerson's contrast: the 'power of circumstance' over against the 'power of me'.

A number of people were kind enough to provide me with generous commentaries on my project, in particular Michael Jackson; also Anthony Cohen, Paul Stoller, Jeanette Edwards and Ian James; also Vered Amit, Jonathan Skinner, Mils Hills, Susan Lewis, Andrew Dawson, David Parkin,

ACKNOWLEDGEMENTS

Roger Goodman, Shirley Ardener, Marcus Banks, Huon Wardle, Mark Harris, Joanna Overing, Claudia Gross, Mario Aguilar and Phillip Mallett.

At Routledge I benefited greatly from the editorial acumen and friendly support of Julene Knox, and also Polly Osborne.

Using Ben Glaser's death partly to frame the book makes me further indebted to a family of significant others: Anita Glaser, Danny Glaser and Shan Henshall, Anthony and Jola Glaser, Karen and Stephen Glaser, Leo and Chaya Glaser; also Anthony and Claude Rapport, Frances Maggs-Rapport and Christopher Maggs.

At home, Elizabeth was always there for me, as was Callum; Emilie arrived in the middle.

NJR
St Andrews, 2003

Part I

PROPOSITIONS

1
PRELIMINARY STATEMENTS

The book's questions

- This is a book about power, but not power as conventionally understood and represented in social science. Rather than an appreciation of the structural power of what is institutional, collective, impersonal and not-individual to create and/or curb what is individual, this is a book about the existential power of individuals to create personally meaningful and viable environments and to traverse these in the pursuit of their own life-projects.

- Individuality has been the main focus of my work to date (e.g. Rapport 1987; 1993; 1997a). I have emphasized the diversity, multiplicity and creativity of individual consciousness; also the way that, due to the ambiguity of social-symbolic forms of exchange, this individuality need not be expressed or communicated on the surface of social life. Society and community, I have concluded, are represented and constituted by a public commonality and a private diversity. The chief criticism levelled against this work has been that the *real-politik* of power relations in which individual lives are lived escapes the attention. Social structures, it is averred, are more than mere forms for free individual expression; they are mouldings and constraints – if not the very origins of expression. Moreover, individual consciousness (even where it can be said to exist in a socio-cultural milieu) is a far remove from individual control; far from a manifestation of uniqueness, a means of transcendence, consciousness may be understood to be an emanation of certain systems of structural-institutional control.

- The relationship between consciousness and self control is the issue which this book set outs specifically to examine: between consciousness of an idea of self-in-the-world, and control over one's life in the world. Inasmuch as individuals are conscious of their environments (consciously create meaningful environments in which they live) and plot certain courses through those environments which they then endeavour to put into effect, can they be seen to be in control of their lives? To what extent does self-consciousness equate with self control, with freedom from the conditions of external circumstance beyond the self? Inasmuch as individuals lead their lives in terms of objectives and criteria of evaluation which are largely of their own making and choosing – so that their lives are actualizations of their 'life-projects' – can they be said to escape the sway of exterior forces – social structures and institutions, ideologies, discourses, systems of signification?

- I explore these questions through a biographical examination of the lives of four individuals in particular. *Friedrich Nietzsche*, the philosopher, constructed an original philosophical edifice both perspicacious and idiosyncratic; *Ben Glaser*, refugee engineer-cum-amateur astrophysicist, led a life of intellectual recreation of great complexity, and productiveness, in a new land; *Rachel Silberstein* (a pseudonym), an immigrant ceramicist-cum-political activist, construed a road to personal 'completion' that committed her to a life of brave and continual transition; and *Stanley Spencer*, the painter, engendered a visionary pictorial and also scriptural oeuvre, both engaging and eccentric. Each of these individuals, I argue, led lives of self-intensity and single-mindedness – singularly focused on a certain life-work of their own, directing their energies towards the accomplishment of a project or end or design which belongs within them – and thereby achieved a remarkable order in, and control over, their conscious lives. Each succeeded in placing themselves in the middle of an abundantly meaningful life-narrative, in the centre of a significantly unfolding world of relations. It is not that Nietzsche, Glaser, Silberstein and Spencer subordinated their lives to their 'art', to an abstraction, but that their lives became works of art: they lived their lives as their 'art', as extensions and manifestations of their creative visions. Nor is it that Nietzsche, Glaser, Silberstein and Spencer lived lives of isolation, of ostracism or solipsism beyond the relational; rather that their relations were construed in their own image, guided by a logic and a negotiation which reflected their confidence or *Machtgefuhl* (feeling of power) in their own life-courses and projects.

- I do not say that their life-projects necessarily afforded these individuals happiness (never mind bringing happiness to their contemporaries or consociates). In the concluding discussions (Chapters 7 and 8) I do come to argue that consciously leading one's life in terms of a life-project can afford that life a certain dignity, and can give onto an equitability and tolerance towards others', but happiness as such is not my focus (I am reminded, however, of an argument made by George Kateb, to the effect that 'democratic individuality' makes for a life of 'ecstasies' more than of 'happiness' and of 'pleasures' rather than 'herd contentments' [1991b: 206]). To reiterate my question: however happy or unhappy these individuals were – however 'unhappily' (nihilistically, chaotically, unpredictably, pessimistically, deterministically, whatever) they might be said to have construed the worlds in which they saw themselves as acting – did the very nature of their self-conscious and directed construals afford them a control over the parameters of their lives and relationships, and a determination over their fate?

- In specifying the approach to power taken in this book, 'control' appears to be a key term (cf. Hendry 1996: 155). I want to elucidate an existential power that individuals possess over and against an impersonal, social-structural or institutional power that I feel schools of social science have had a tendency almost exclusively to focus upon. This leads me to consider who or what determines the lives individuals lead: both the courses of action they adopt and the meanings they accord to those actions. Where, ultimately do individuals' actions and interpretations come from? The hypothesis offered in this book is that individuals who see their lives in terms of the pursuit of a certain life-project, who see the meaning of their lives significantly in terms of the achievement of a particular goal or goals, can succeed in giving their actions a certain robustness, power and independence such that they escape the influence of external forces and of other individuals who might have wished to have directed them in other ways.

'Control', I understand, then, as extending both to the 'objectivity' of actions and the 'subjectivity' of meanings or interpretations. Ultimately, I would understand both of these as pertaining to the subjective realm, since the meaning or effect of action is a subjective interpretation; but then the social-scientific apprehension of another's subjectivity is an objective act – at least, that of an exterior subjectivity – and the testing of my hypothesis will rest upon my biographical and autobiographical accounts of others' autobiographies.

- The complexities of 'control' within individuals' lives thus ramify. Richard Fardon suggests that there is an inevitability and an interminability to the question of control because it is in the very nature of power to play host to a 'fundamental equivocation' (Marilyn Strathern): never directly visible, only metaphorically (Fardon 1987: 7–8). Suffice it to say that I am exploring 'existential power' by way of an examination of the extent to which individuals can be said to be responsible for determining the interpretations they make and the actions they take. These might include succeeding in feeling out of control, or in putting oneself in positions of helplessness; one might be in control of one's beliefs that one is under the control of others, and as social-scientific observer and analyst I reserve the right for myself to distinguish between a personal rhetoric of powerlessness and a powerlessness determined by others.

Of course the latter distinction does not give rise to necessarily watertight compartments. Insisting on one's powerlessness, putting oneself in positions of helplessness, might reach a point when one is unable to change tack, whatever one's present determination. Hence the existential or developmental dimension of the hypothesis; perhaps construing oneself to be in control of one's life itself figures as a source of one's being able to continue considering oneself in control – itself figures as a source of one's actions being self-determined;

'[c]onsciousness of our powers augments them', as the Marquis de Vauvenargues once put it (1997). Hence the thesis: The very possession of a life-project, the conception, intention and practice of seeing one's life in terms of a certain directionality, velocity and destination, serves as a source of self-control, the possession being instrumental in one's continuing capability to be responsible for interpretations made, relations entered into and actions taken.

• Clifford Geertz has called social and cultural anthropologists 'the miniaturists of the social sciences' (1971: 4); in attempting to answer 'grand questions', anthropologists paint 'delicate strokes on lilliputian canvases'. They are 'always inclined to turn towards…the microscopic' in order to ascertain the truth about 'humanity' (1971: 4). In my estimation this is so because it is in the individual – in individual energy, creativity, will – that the force of the social and cultural lies. Scale does not give onto a supra-individual reality, and the same mechanisms of individual consciousness – of our human being-in-the-world courtesy of interpretive mechanisms which give onto a distinct sense of self and other – operate within large-scale, institutional or grand-historical situations of interaction as in more personal or private ones.

Another way of putting this is that no subject is intrinsically small-scale or large-scale; it depends rather on how they are approached. For, every subject is ultimately the same subject: the construction and interaction of individual world-views; individual interpretations of social situations and cultural practices (cf. Rapport 1997a: 12–29; also Samuel 1975: xix). In this book, four individual lives are put under a microscope as a route to elucidating the nature of human social life and the potentialities of Everyperson. 'Thick description', as William Blake might have counselled, is to 'see a World in a Grain of Sand' (1975: 585).

A metaphor of individuality

Genius, according to Nietzsche (1994: 162–3), resides in the single-mindedness with which individuals approach an activity, and the continuity and complexity of the concentration they impart to their practices. To consider genius is to imagine individuals

> whose thinking is active in one particular direction; who use everything to that end; who always observe eagerly their inner life and that of other people; who see models, stimulation everywhere; who do not tire of rearranging their material.
>
> (1994: 162)

Moreover, genius is a craft rather than an innate gift or talent, Nietzsche insists. One 'becomes' a genius and one acquires its greatness not by virtue of something miraculous but via a certain seriousness and industry, energy and endurance which is potentially within the grasp of every one.

In identifying the project of this book, to myself and others, I settled upon a metaphor which had the benefit of providing a visual framework, while hopefully not too simplistic a one. (I am reminded of Robin Horton's [1967] description of the analogical relationship between theoretical and non-theoretical knowledge; an immediate sense of the theory of atoms, say, may be gained by analogy with the movement of balls on a pool-table so long as one remembers the only partial connectability of the two: that atoms, for instance, are not variously coloured). In approaching the theory of this book, then, I offer an avowedly impressionistic, but immediate, image.

Consider a self-propelled projectile careering through space. Its energy and momentum carry it along a certain trajectory, and it is deflected from this path only to the extent that it comes under the gravitational sway of another body, or is actually hit by another body. Even if this were to happen, the displacement caused to its original trajectory would depend upon its own force relative to that of the other body: its mass and its speed in a certain direction. If it is forceful enough it carries on its way.

Now think of that projectile as an individual human being 'thrown' into life (as the Existentialists put it), and the career which his or her life-course represents. And think of the other bodies met in space as other individuals, or as the so-called social systems, institutional structures and cultural discourses which are often seen as constituting the environments in which individual lives are led. Would not the extent to which an individual's path through life is affected, even controlled, by these outside bodies and forces be dependent upon the forcefulness with which that life was prosecuted? In other words, should not the control which a social-cum-institutional-cum-cultural gravity can be expected to exert upon an individual life, and the displacement caused, depend upon the intrinsic single-mindedness, the self-intensity, with which that person attends to the effecting his or her own life-course?

Returning to Nietzsche's commentary on genius once more, so many and varied are the impulses that living creatures are home to, so distinct are their constitutions and senses of consciousness, Nietzsche feels (1968: 46), that he would advise against any simple conceptual use of the term 'will'. Notwithstanding, there is a sense in which 'strong will' and 'weak will' resonate with experience; 'weak will', he suggests, translates as those occasions in which a 'lack of gravity' causes an oscillation and absence of systematic ordering between a multitude of 'disgregated' impulses; while 'strong will' translates as those occasions when the multitude of impulses are given precise and clear direction, coordinated, perhaps, under a single impulse which predominates. To be strong, then, is to acquire 'the orientation of a straight line' as against 'wavelike vacillation' (1994: 270). In Nietzsche's sense, the individual-as-projectile has the strong will to harness his or her impulses in one direction, producing a force which protects them against lesser wills.

The metaphor of a projectile might just be taken one step further. Besides rockets and missiles careering through space are also to be found bodies in more fixed trajectories, fields of influence or orbits: molecules and meteors, moons and planets, stars, solar systems and galaxies. All, however, are composed of the same physical matter (there is only one kind); indeed, the matter that comprises their individual identities at any one time will be broken down and recombined into other identities at other times. Finally, all the bodies are subject to the same physical laws, of momentum, velocity, mass and gravity. Their trajectories derive from the constellation of relations which comprise their own force relative to others' in the one physical universe.

Again, think of the individual human being on his or her life-course. For some this involves more habitual or fixed behaviours than others. Likewise, there may be more or less alignment with the lives and routines of others; the individual human being is not an isolate, and for some, life might consist of remaining within the ambit of particular others or 'orbiting' jointly with them. That is, besides the force to continue on one's own path, there is also the force to remain within others' domain or to organize joint trajectories. These latter can amount to aggregations, communities, societies of individuals, all of whose lives are to an extent aligned. The extent varies, the longevity and impersonality and institutionality of the arrangement vary, and the size of the aggregation varies. But the principle is the same. Individual trajectories through life come to be aligned one with another so that instead of their momentum taking them apart, it keeps them together, moving, for a while, more or less in tandem. Finally, however, the aggregations, the societies of individuals, are not greater than their sum; there is nothing beyond the matter that (temporarily) constitutes the identity of the individual, and nothing beyond the force which that individual life gives onto and, in collaboration with others, adds up to. In combination, in institutionalization, individuals may be more forceful than apart (to the extent that they can orchestrate their individual momentums in harmony), but the institution and the society has no life or life-force of its own.

The analogy has been taken far enough – without, I hope, seeming forced. Listen, now, to how Stanley Spencer is introduced by his first biographer, Maurice Collis (1962: 15, my italics):

> He stands a giant (though physically he was a very small man) *who was never deflected from his main concern*, which was to express himself. His story is bound up with three women in particular, and also a fourth. He was influenced by them for a time, *but remained unchanged in essentials*. They people his art from 1927 till his death and are the recurring subject of his writings. But he was a recluse at heart, a paradox of which [his posthumous] papers leave no doubt.

A second biographer attributed Spencer's behaviour to the 'self-intense nature of his genius' (Pople 1991: 209). What I mean to posit is this: do not individuals have the power to decide whether and how to align the energy and momentum of their lives with those of others? To the extent that individuals conduct their lives in the actualization of projects which they themselves author and to which they continually attend – single-mindedly, with self-intensity – are they not in a position to eschew or deflect the gravitational pull, the power and influence, of others, and to exert control over the trajectories of their lives?

A Nietzschean ethos

A Nietzschean commentary can be seen to underlie not only ideas on the 'genius of single-mindedness', but the book as a whole. In ethos it might be described as a Nietzschean 'fiction':

> I am not a man I am dynamite. – And with all that there is nothing in me of a founder of a religion – religions are affairs of the rabble, I have need of washing my hands after contact with religious people...I do not *want* 'believers'...I do not want to be a saint, rather even a buffoon...Perhaps I am a buffoon...– But my truth is *dreadful*: for hitherto the *lie* has been called truth. – *Revaluation of all values*: this is my formula for an act of supreme coming-to-oneself on the part of mankind which in me has become flesh and genius....I was the first to *discover* the truth, in that I was the first to sense – *smell* – the lie as lie....My genius is in my nostrils...I contradict as has never been contradicted and am nonetheless the opposite of a negative spirit. I am a *bringer of good tidings* such as there never has been.
> (1979b: 126)

Superlatives often accompany Nietzschean commentary (not least in his own writings), and seldom without hyperbole. Friedrich Nietzsche, we variously read, was, during his lifetime (1844–1900), philosophically speaking, 'almost wholly neglected' (Tanner 1994: 1); since his death, however, his writings have 'never ceased to disturb, provoke and inspire' (Ansell-Pearson 1994: 1). Almost no major cultural or artistic figure, it seems (certainly in Germany), has failed to acknowledge his influence; from Sigmund Freud: '[Nietzsche] had a more penetrating knowledge of himself than any other man who ever lived or was likely to live' (cited in Jones 1955: 385); to Thomas Mann: '[Nietzsche] is a personality of phenomenal cultural plenitude and complexity, summing up all that is essentially European' (1947: 3); to Martin Heidegger: 'it is in Nietzsche's light and shadow that everyone thinks who thinks today' (1981). Further afield, too, we hear: 'Nietzsche is our Bible' (Rupert Brooke); 'What we get from Nietzsche...is the greatest of all gifts that a writer can give us – namely, a heightening of our dramatic interest in life' (John Cowper Powys); and 'Brer Nietzsche' (George Bernard Shaw) (cited in Bridgwater 1978: 221–5).

Nonetheless, let me presume to add a further superlative: Nietzsche offers the most subtle insights into the complexities and contrarieties of the individual experience of socio-cultural milieux. Nietzsche's aphorism, 'I mistrust all systematizers and avoid them. The will to a system is a lack of integrity' (1979c: 25), taken as a rule of thumb, encapsulates a prejudice which offers the best chance of appreciating the integrity of the human condition.

Of Darwin's theory of natural selection, Richard Dawkins has remarked that '[n]ever were so many facts explained by so few assumptions; here is more economy, elegance and poetry than in any of the world's origin myths' (1996: 1–2). Nietzsche's achievement might be described as treating Darwinian insights – his notions of process, individuation, competition and change – as themselves an origin myth, and further adapting them as guides for strategic self-placement in a world of human interaction. Nietzsche, it seems to me, was inspired by the Darwinian revolution in biology, and by its philosophical implications, but he was also possessed of a sophistication which caused him to interpret and apply Darwin on a human social and cultural stage in a way far different to any vulgar sociobiology. Nietzsche wrote a kind of social and cultural anthropology out of Darwin's biological anthropology, but in a way which took account of human diversities: its phylogenetic and ontogenetic development, sensory manifoldness, multiplicity of drives, depth of consciousness, cognitive contradictoriness, rationality and irrationality, self-awareness and irony.

That Nietzsche achieved this subtlety of psycho-socio-cultural insight was due, perhaps (as Freud suggests), to his self-knowledge. Oscar Wilde once advised that, 'If you wish to understand others you must intensify your own individualism' (1913: 156), and Nietzsche's name is often associated with Wilde's. Thomas Mann, for instance, depicted Nietzsche and Wilde as fundamentally alike in regarding human life as an artistic production, and in exploring, in their lives, the limits of 'artistic power' in the construction of orderly human worlds; both were 'rebels in the name of beauty' (cited in Donadio 1978: 60–1). I certainly feel that Wilde's claim for individual understanding is very appropriate in Nietzsche's case; Nietzsche's appreciation of psycho-socio-cultural complexity was via his own personal complexity and contrariety: the radically spiritual figure who denied God; the homeless, restless, lonely, shy and ascetic figure who sought companionship through philosophical and stylistic individuation and excess (cf. Heller 1988: 11).

Nietzsche died in 1900 (went insane in 1889). What it is about such long-dead philosophers that makes them continue to be interesting and relevant, Hilary and Ruth Anna Putnam have suggested (1996: 14), is that the questions to which they sought answers are questions that concern us still: 'How should one live?', 'What is life anyway?', 'How does one presume to know?'. These are Nietzsche's questions and they are also those of the existential-cum-humanistic, the reflexive-cum-literary, social science I should like to advance in this book. By looking inside himself for a first-hand appreciation of the complexity of the human condition, Nietzsche both provided an argument and an epistemology by which the relativity and contingency of the social and cultural may be underwritten in terms of the eternity and transcendence of individual embodiment, and the individual's eternally shifting 'will-to-power'. It is for this reason that besides being the focus of one chapter in particular, a Nietzschean ethos imbues the book as a whole.

Nietzsche was well aware of the irony of his attempting to write convincingly about the inherently perspectival nature of human reality: wishing his readership at once to accept his conclusion as 'correct' and thenceforth to question all 'correctness'. He explained that his view on an eternal will-to-power was but a mental image – a fancy, a fiction – and yet the best conception he had come across by which to live his life. The image was personal to him, and yet others might hopefully profit from it too, as means to transport themselves forward to a view on their own lives which was of most pragmatic value (of most 'truth') to themselves. It is with equal irony that I measure the other chief protagonists in this book, Ben Glaser, Rachel Silberstein and Stanley Spencer, against Nietzsche and his thought. He poses the questions I would address to their different lives alike, while I would hope an appreciation of these latter to lead to answers to Nietzschean questions which are distinctly individual in each case.

An irony of which Nietzsche was perhaps less aware concerns the way his oeuvre was to be plundered, and by partial quotation (beginning with the Nazified transcriptions of his sister, Elisabeth Foerster-Nietzsche) made to speak against itself. (As I transcribe 'I am not a man I am dynamite', I write in the shadow of the terrorist attacks of 11 September 2001 on New York, of suicide bombings in Israel, Afghanistan and Pakistan, and the global 'war on terror'.) In having a Nietzschean ethos imbue this book, I shall try to do justice to his writings in two ways: exhibit his words in context so that they might themselves refute charges of anti-liberalism (masculinist, racist, social-exclusivist); and show how his words elucidate an abiding human condition.

The book's voices

How people arrive at their convictions, and they come to change them, seem to me immensely difficult questions – and largely unanswered ones. I am not convinced that all the talk of social-structural cause-and-effect in social science is more than 'half-baked' and 'wrong-headed' (Wittgenstein 1980: 62e); I am persuaded by Nietzsche, who wrote that our convictions are 'directed and compelled into definite channels by [our] instincts...in plainer terms physiological demands for the preservation of a certain species of life'

(1979a: 3). Our convictions become 'fantasies' or 'fictions': assurances derived from particular, individually embodied perspectives.

Questions of conviction are not the topic of the present work, however, at least not directly. As I say, I am convinced by Nietzsche – as by Ralph Waldo Emerson (the early American Existentialist), someone in whose work Nietzsche confessed 'never [to have] felt so much at home', 'so much in my own house' (cited in Donadio 1978: 41), and whose words provide the epigraph for this book. I take individuality to be ontological, and I believe that self-conscious life-projects afford individuals a certain dignity; I draw from Nietzsche's depiction of genius as single-mindedness, and from the metaphor that the ambition and achievement of a life-project makes the individual into a kind of projectile. Writing out of my convictions I produce a text which is as prescriptive as it is descriptive, which advances a particular Existential stance.

But I am aware, too, that all of the above can seem thoroughly unconvincing – naive, simplistic, partial, and so on – and that among the superlatives associated with Nietzsche's name are also ones of extreme excoriation. What I would ask, however, is that whatever may be the reader's convictions – whether or not an admirer of the individual, of Nietzsche; of determinism, of social-structural cause and effect – he or she initially bracket those convictions off and treat this book as an exercise in ideal types and 'as if'. What would be the implications – for living and for accounting for human life – if individual life-projects and existential power were true? This is the voice which animates the following, foundational chapter of the book ('The life of power: an existential framework'), mediating also the biographical illustrations Part II. In the concluding, discussive part of the book (Chapter 7, 'The power of any body-in-its-environment' and Chapter 8, 'Total institutions and the violence of society: the death of power?'), other kinds of conviction concerning what is 'really real' find their voice. I ask an indulgence of the reader, then: *to entertain the possible truth, the viability of the version of the world, which sees the individual as gaining control over his or her life through the composing and living-out of a certain life-project.* However distant from deeply held convictions of the reader it might seem, how might the world look to social science if it were theorized as a matter of the power and practice of individual convictions?

I do not do this merely as an 'academic' exercise or one in self-indulgence; it is not simply to take pleasure in my own writing, my rhetorical or moral conceits, that I request the reader's forbearance. A 'philosophy of "as if"' was developed by Hans Vaihinger (1924) as an elaboration of Kantian and Nietzschean ideas (and was adopted enthusiastically by Edmund Leach [1954] amongst others). Vaihinger described convictions, in Nietzschean vein, as pragmatically justified fictions ultimately deriving from sensation and the experience of emotion. What is important for human life is that acting *as if* their convictions were true, individuals assure themselves of hypotheses of the world which are useful – suggestive and consequential, beautiful perhaps,

PRELIMINARY STATEMENTS

powerful and satisfying – however much they might at the same time know them to have been made up. More recently Richard Rorty (1979) has advanced a version of pragmatism (of which 'the philosophy of "as if" ' can be considered a variant), which claims that one need never approach the question of truth *per se* (never 'unbracket' the notion of what is really real) and can merely concentrate on the place of human attitudes and beliefs in creating and satisfying human needs. (Leach claimed '[t]here are no "laws" of historical process; there are no "laws" of sociological probability' [1961: 51–2], while the 'cultural differences' of ethnographic analysis are 'temporary fictions' [1989: 137]; anthropological convictions perforce derive from 'a kind of harmonic projection of the observer's own personality' [1984: 22], the only 'ego' known 'at first hand' [1989: 137].)

This book is, in part then, an exercise in 'as-if social philosophy'. It asks: What would the social world look like if it were a matter of individuals' existential power? What would anthropology look like if it accounted for social life in these terms? What are the consequences, analytical and moral, for individual lives and for anthropology of such 'as-if constructions'? But my hope is also that, notwithstanding its pragmatism and fictionalism, the ideal-typicality of such as-if philosophy might ultimately serve as heuristic and tell us something about the kinds and extent of human knowledge *per se* – and not only regarding the capacity and disposition for construing as-if worlds.

Nietzsche dealt with the Kantian conundrum of 'phenomena' versus 'noumena' (of 'appearances' versus 'things-in-themselves') by claiming that an aspiration towards both the non-scientific and the scientific was necessary for human well-being – while also recognizing that the distinct 'forms of life' that each represented might necessarily keep them apart. The image he chose to depict this was of human beings as if possessed of 'a double brain': a brain with two chambers lying next to one another, separable and self-contained, aspiring to different things without confusion (1994: 251). Non-scientific knowledge was inspiring, Nietzsche argued, a source of human fortitude, but science was the source of truth; while non-science gave rise to those illusions, errors, norms and passions by which human life was heated, scientific knowledge served to protect from the pernicious consequences of overheating. If not for non-science, scientific truths would eventually seem commonplace and everyday, and lose their charm; if not for science and the continuing search for truth, the excesses of non-science would not be regulated, causing 'higher culture' to 'relapse into barbarism' (1994: 251).

Most importantly, Nietzsche felt that 'for moments at least', human beings could be released from the phenomenal, perspectival world of non-scientific appearances, be 'lifted above' the whole process of fantasy or 'as if', and through 'the steady and arduous progress of science' 'come to the true essence of the world and knowledge of it' (1994: 16, 29). Two discrete voices appear in the text to follow, then: that of Nietzschean fiction – rather declarative, prescriptive, impassioned and self-assured – and that of more measured and critical regulation. For those who do not feel as strongly as I about the ontology of individuality and the implications, analytic and moral, of this, I ask them to withhold judgement against the non-scientific passions of as-if, and to bracket-off questions of the really real at least until it is seen how viable a case for existential power can be made, and what its ramifications might be for exploring the relationship between individual self-consciousness and self-control.

As the book proceeds, the voice moves from the more declarative to the more discriminating, then, from 'conjecture' to 'critique' (as Karl Popper identified the processual acquisition of scientific knowledge [1997: 91–5]). But this is not the only kind of vocal movement in the book. For – as will have already become apparent – I move liberally between my own words and citations of others'; in the pages of my text thus far, the authority of some thirty other writers has been called in evidence. Is this more than plagiarism? Two further citations come to mind even as I write this. The first is from Roland Barthes, anti-humanistic in tenor, to the effect that the narratives which individuals write in and of their lives inevitably represent a 'tissue of quotations' drawn from cultural repertoires which in fact 'narrate them' – serving literally to hem in what may be narrated (1982: 293). The second, from Harold Bloom, is that it is by 'wrestling' with their precursors' writings, individuals can 'appropriate for themselves': as 'strong poets' – actors of 'capable imagination' – they can clear an imaginative-narrative space which is their own (1975: 5). Just as I ask my readers initially to situate themselves between a notion of power as it is conventionally, social-structurally apprehended in social science and a more existential appreciation, so readers might find themselves between Barthes and Bloom: between plagiarism as the inevitable consequence of socialization and community membership, and plagiarism as 'will to figuration', as the inexorable construction of novel, individual meanings housed in inherited, collective forms.

Not only do I construct my text from the texts of others, moreover, conscripting what I see as the truth, or otherwise, of their words to serve my own ends, I also conscript the lives of others, of four individuals in particular, to argue my own case. In a book which argues that construing and pursuing one's life as an individual project is a route to a dignified and accomplished life – and calling for a social-scientific appreciation of individual consciousness and agency – I proceed by ventriloquizing the voices of four significant others, immersing myself in their biographies and their wisdom, and vaunting the benefits of personal relations with them. Is this hypocritical? By way of a number of final citations, I would argue not. When we construct our life-worlds, it is often from other worlds, from the worlds of others, that we take our matter, Nelson Goodman has enunciated (1978: 6). One must be wary of thereby concluding, however, that these worlds are alike or even necessarily commensurable. Commonalities of form belie diversities of meaningful use: it is of individual interpretations that the life-worlds of individuals significantly comprise (cf. Rapport 1993). I borrow from other people's lives and life-projects, then, in order to compose and empower my own. All composition may be termed autobiographical in this way, all of it passing through the signifying prism of the interpreting self (Spengemann 1980: 168); while all biography is ultimately fictional, since one inexorably interprets the forms in which others' lives and experience are embodied and expressed in one's own way (Berger 1988: 126). Here, then, is a book centred on the individual life-projects of Friedrich Nietzsche, Stanley Spencer, Rachel Silberstein and Ben Glaser, by which I intend to persuade of a project and a construal of my own.

The four individuals are known to me in different ways. Friedrich Nietzsche is a philosopher in whose books I have found talismanic qualities for some twenty-five years now. Stanley Spencer is a painter whose oeuvre I have come to esteem fully, through books and exhibitions, only during the past ten years or so. Rachel Silberstein was someone I met whilst undertaking anthropological fieldwork in the Israeli development town of Mitzpe Ramon some fifteen years ago; I have not met her since then, but the time we spent together, as fellow new-immigrants, was one of heightened experiential intensity. Ben Glaser, finally, was my mother's second husband – the father of a close childhood friend, and then my stepfather – for over thirty years, until his death in 1996 at the age of eighty-eight. But all four represent, for me, 'strong poets' (in Harold Bloom's sense), figures of 'capable imagination'.

My conceiving of this book was significantly prompted by Ben Glaser's death (as I mentioned in the Acknowledgements). Indeed, I can connect together all four protagonists through Ben – whose mother-tongue was German, and could thus help me with my reading of Nietzsche; who painted and sketched, like Stanley Spencer, from life; who took a close interest in my anthropological research, as well as having a deep love of Israel, and visited me in the desert redoubt I shared with Rachel Silberstein. But I am not sure this is more than a convenient rationalization. In ethos the book was inspired by Nietzschean commentary, as I have said; it is likely that the project coalesced at the time of Ben's death because my impression was that here was an individual who had created space for 'leading his own life', 'being his own person', in Nietzschean vein. My text, with the addition of two more characters (Spencer and Silberstein), would be an exploration (and celebration) of what exactly 'leading one's own life' meant, and how it was brought about.

Not only do I move 'inwards' in my text, however, from biographies of these four individuals to my own autobiographical conclusions, but I also hope to move 'outwards' from these particular individuals to possibly general conclusions concerning human capabilities: I intend these individuals to stand for Everyperson. The consciousness, the creativity and the agency which I attribute to them I would wish to understand as part of the capacity of everyone, and as something which might manifest itself in any number of forms. I draw upon these four particular lives because in my estimation they manifest certain human qualities in an especially striking form.

But what of the fact that, of the four protagonists, three are men – adult, 'white' and deceased? Is this symptomatic of the book, the reach of its argument, its thesis and politics: another book about 'dead white males'? Besides saying that this is precisely the kind of categorial thinking that I would wish to hold in abeyance in this book, I might assert that in the details of individual lives – any particular lives – is to be found that data with which to overcome the reductive essentialisms of gender, class, nationality, race, ethnicity, religion, age, epoch, locality and so on, regarded as imperative statuses. (Does the inclusion of Rachel Silberstein demand her 'manliness'? The formulation is insulting.) The protagonists in my ethnographic work to date – Doris Harvey and Sid Askrig in Wanet, Dina Schwartz, Jerome Tirk and Laura Dumont in St John's, David and Mirium Feinberg in Mitzpe Ramon, Bob Hume in Easterneuk – whatever their categorial identities, I have presented first and foremost as individuals. This is how I would also wish my current protagonists to be treated. It obscures far more than it reveals to say that they exhibit an essential partiality because three are white adult males – Glaser, the Jew, and refugee from Nazi Germany; Spencer, the physically diminutive, home-loving artist, drawn to women who overwhelmed him; Silberstein, the new immigrant, pursuing a path of 'alternative energy' in a Near-Eastern desert; Nietzsche, the marginal poet-philosopher, who resigned his job at thirty-five due to ill health and thereafter eked out an existence on a pension. Even in terms of sociological profile, there is enough that categorially differentiates and particularizes the social positions of these four individuals for the case I shall make about their common genius for single-mindedness, for self-intensity, to be a strong one and striking.

But then an essentializing discourse in categorial thinking (along the lines of gender, class or whatever) is perhaps best refuted not by lengthily engaging with it. For this is to dignify it and, as the structuralists have explicated at length, can lead to infinite regress – the hegemony of the discourse seemingly to be demonstrated through the synthesizing of its binary opposite. (I feel I have already borrowed more than enough of this kind of discourse in my counter-characterizations of my four protagonists, above.) Rather, an essentializing discourse is best refuted by ignoring it: writing as if it did not exist. Hence, I have chosen to focus on the four people I have because their life-stories instantiate, for me, a kind of thesis concerning life-projects and existential power which I was interested in elaborating. Through their biographies I will hope to show common capacities existing alongside individual differences; also, to identify individual differences great enough for me to claim that their capacities can stand for the potentialities of Everyperson.

A tactical humanism

If an appreciation of the entailments of human individuality – an appreciation of the power of the individual to effect meaningful worlds – and the moral entitlements consequent upon this has a history and a politics, then that might be given the name 'humanism'. 'Existentialism is a Humanism', Sartre saw fit to boast (1975), and I would claim no less for this anthropology: the book is an exercise in humanism.

'Humanism', we know, is a nineteenth-century term, pertaining to the ostensible values, practices and ideals of the European Renaissance of the fourteenth-to-sixteenth centuries, and its rediscovery of the texts of classical Greece and Rome. The Renaissance appreciation of the latter, the so-called *studia humanitatis*, came to represent a radical break with the predominant medieval (religiously imbued) perspectives on the nature of life: a new faith in the power of learning and a desire freely to enlarge its bounds; a scepticism concerning the absoluteness of existing knowledge; a belief in the potentialities for rationality, creativeness, wilfulness, pleasure and growth of the individual human being; an interest in ascertaining the place of humankind in nature, of discovering the laws of nature, so that life on earth might be placed more within human control, and humankind could become what it willed. The success of this programme, over the centuries that have culminated in our own, then saw the humanism of the Renaissance give onto the rise of science, with its 'enlightened' belief in experimentation and critique (as against revelation) as adequate sources of human knowledge; also onto liberalism, and a belief in the inherent dignity of individuals and their right to freedom and self-determination; and also onto social science, and its belief in the possibility and the duty of applying knowledge about human affairs and individual relations to an improvement of the socio-cultural conditions of human life.

On one view, anthropology has a humanistic heritage, deriving from an image of humankind, and a belief in its capacity scientifically to know itself, with Renaissance roots; possessed of a history of rationality, liberalism and advocacy which may legitimately (and necessarily) be continued today (cf. Gellner 1993; Berger 1963). On other views, the case is less clear, and the relationship between anthropology and humanism one which might be subjected to more or less stringent criticism. Certainly, the humanistic tag is one that can be associated more explicitly with some names in anthropology than others, while some have positively decried it, linking it, historico-culturally, to Western acts of imperialism (over nature and otherness) and exclusivism (regarding who is 'human').

When Eric Wolf wrote that anthropology, as a discipline, was to be understood as: 'the most scientific of the humanities and the most humanistic of the sciences' (1974), it was clearly a more particular connotation of 'humanism' that he was dealing with, one to do with openness and pluralism. In order to deal with the 'vast intricacies' (Bateson 1959: 296) of socio-cultural milieux, to do representational and analytical justice to the complexities and diversities of human life, it was necessary to be open methodologically in one's approach, simultaneously to entertain a plurality of versions of the truth, and sceptical concerning the closure of fixed and absolute notions of what was or could be known. (The 'delimitation of the disciplines' in the West, since the Renaissance, Bateson decried as a 'tragic error' (1959: 296).) But then, such an emphasis on openness and pluralism of approach, on 'methodological eclecticism' (Rapport 1997c), may be said to be precisely the heritage of the *studia humanitatis*. Moreover, an emphasis on a diversity of ways in which humankind can come better to know itself is also a means, I would say, to encompass a large body of anthropological practitioners in a polythetic but still humanistic vision; here is a category of anthropological work which is linked together by overlapping commonalities of humanistic intent, even if not by common denomination.

A problem remains, however, for the humanist-anthropologist regarding the status of culture. Are human beings the same *inasmuch as* they all inhabit different cultural worlds, or *over and against* their inhabiting such worlds? Do they become human within culture or does their humanity transcend cultural particularities? Geertz has called this anthropology's 'recurrent dilemma' (1973: 22): how to square generic human rationality and the biological unity of humankind with the great natural variation of cultural forms. George Stocking concludes that the entire 'history of anthropology may...be viewed as a continuing (and complex) dialectic between the universalism of "anthropos" and the diversitarianism of "ethnos"' (1992: 347). Anthropological humanists may be both cultural relativists and Existentialists, capable, in short, of describing human consciousness as essentially individual and free, or as collective and culturally given.

Cultural relativism, indeed, can be taken far further, and turn into a thoroughgoing anti-humanistic critique. This has recently transpired under the monikers of 'structuralism' and 'poststructuralism'. If consciousness, its form and content, is not separate from the symbolic discourses and social practices in which it is culturally embedded, then not only may identity – human, individual, whatever – be seen as subordinate to cultural matrices (which may remain unconscious), but the whole idea of humankind, humanism, human dignity, and so on, may be deemed an historically contingent cultural product: ethnocentric, mythical, teleological. 'Man', as Foucault put it, 'is only a recent invention, a figure not yet two centuries old' (1972: 115).

However seriously one takes Foucault's historical claim, the implication is clear: humankind and humanism are concepts to deconstruct and overcome. Far from being transcendent, humanistic values, methods, truths are part of specific discourses which have created the world in a certain image so as to serve certain interests and ends. 'Humankind' – 'the subject' or 'subject-effect', better – is ever, inevitably and inextricably enculturated: hence multiply and partially constructed, conditioned, elicited, motivated and gendered. Even the existential certainties of the Western humanist – whereby, in H. D. Lewis' words (1982: 55), '[m]y distinctness, my being me, is quite unmistakeable to me, there can be nothing of which I am more certain' – amounts to a culturally derived (and rather unusual) 'metaphysics of presence'.

PRELIMINARY STATEMENTS

There are a number of possible responses to this structuralist-cum-post-structuralist critique. One is to reassert an Existentialist and rationalist position and say that cultural relativism and deconstruction – treating 'ethnos' as an absolute – is just plain wrong. Science, medicine, history, literature, diplomacy, the market and travel prove the existence of an universal humanity, and the inherent individuality of consciousness and experience through which it is embodied (cf. Rapport 1997a). However, this proof cannot force itself on those who would see otherwise. Hence the significant number of anthropological practitioners who will yet be found signed up to an anti-humanistic programme proclaiming the 'death of "man"', of the 'centred subject' and the agential voice (cf. Stoller 1997: 29–30). Hence, too, the number of times the word 'belief' appears even in a humanistic (agnostic) exposition of the fundamental capacities and characteristics of humankind (rational, creative, wilful, dignified, and so on). Nevertheless, it may be countered that humanistic beliefs are subjected to the most critical attention and are accessible to all who approach with an open mind (cf. Popper 1980).

Another response, as adumbrated philosophically by Rorty (1992), is to admit to the historico-cultural specificity of the humanist perspective but to claim, notwithstanding, that as a way of knowing the world it offers the best prospectus for a diversity of cultural world-views being able to live peaceably alongside and through one another. In what she calls a 'tactical humanism', Lila Abu-Lughod would seem to arrive anthropologically at a similar position (1991: 138). Humanism, she begins, may be a local discourse (despite its erstwhile claims) but it still has more global reach than any other: it carries most moral force as a language of equality. Of course, the discourse has suffered from being misapplied and abused. In the past, celebrating the example of heroic individuals has co-occurred with an ignoring of others' systematic oppression; positing individuals' autonomy has co-occurred with a masking of the inequalities of social-structural positioning; placing humankind at the centre of the world has co-occurred with a justifying of an exploitation of nature; and respecting a universality of human dignity and individual integrity has co-occurred with a denying of humanity to specified 'others' (women, children, natives, slaves, Jews). However, this abuse notwithstanding (and what discourse, finally, can protect itself from abuse?), humanism offers anthropology the best hope for describing both the universality and the universal particularities of human experience, and for speaking truth both to the social-structurally powerful and the powerless.

In particular, humanism offers anthropology an escape from imprisoning essentialisms such as 'culture', 'society', 'community', 'ethnicity', 'gender' and 'race', and the 'identity-politics' they engender (Amit and Rapport 2002). These concepts have operated as means of making and maintaining alterity: creating differences between people, and implying separations which have translated into hierarchy and inequality; creating samenesses, categorizing and stereotyping, so as to portray homogeneity, coherence, and determinism. To write 'against culture' (and other such generalizing, fundamentalist-essentialist conceptualizations) is, in Abu-Lughod's phrasing (1991: 157), to produce humanistic 'ethnographies of the particular': precise narratives of the existence of particular individuals in particular times and places. It is to eschew regarding others as 'typical examples of a [cultural] genus' (Watson 1992: 139).

The particularity of human lives manifests itself as something they have in common over and against their so-called cultural (*et al.*) differences. Humanistic narratives thus portray efforts to make meaning – describe the flux, movement and contradiction, the strategies, contests and interests, the practices, choices and improvisations, the disappointment and success – in the lives of Everyperson, and of the existential power whereby such meaning is effected. Through the stories of particular lives, of individuals amid the histories of their own particularities, an 'authenticity, voice and authority' can hope to be manifested (Stoller 1989: 29).

My stance in this book is a pragmatic one. I want to have included in the humanistic approach both those would define individuality as a transcendent form of subjective consciousness (cf. Rapport and Overing 2000: 185–95), and those for whom 'subjectivity and individuality may be understood as aspects, moments, modalities, and products of social interaction, to be placed on a par with notions of "objectivity" and "collectivity"' (Michael Jackson 2000, personal communication). Proponents of both of these positions can come together in a defence and celebration of individuality on pragmatic grounds: that the consequences of adopting individuality as a perspective are that it best provides for human fulfilment, dignity and satisfaction – the realizing of individual capacities for life – both as regards individuals in themselves, and in their relationships with others.

The book's course

The plan of the book is as follows. Chapter 2, 'The life of power: an existential framework', next, has five sections: (i) 'Individuality: consciousness, world-view, narrative, life-project, and interaction'; (ii) 'Individuality and ironic displacement'; (iii) 'Displacement and "in order to" motives'; (iv) ' "In order to" motives and prior conditions'; and (v) 'The conditions of political power and existential power'. In these sections, I conduct an examination of individuality, social structure and power as they are conventionally accommodated in much social-scientific literature, and as I would have these conventions emended. The different sections are woven around certain key terms or themes to which I return, signalled by the section titles but also including: body and mind, cognition, agency, imagination, creativity, freedom, determinism and will. Through its different sections and key terms, Chapter 2 is intended as the foundation of an argument concerning individual consciousness and control.

In Part II come the illustrative chapters of the volume (Chapters 3–6). My argument is substantiated by way of four very different lives, four 'ethnographies of the particular'; first, that of Friedrich Nietzsche, then Ben Glaser, then Rachel Silberstein, and last, Stanley Spencer. In each case I ask the question: 'To what extent can the self-conscious life-projects of these people be seen as increasing their control over their life-courses?'.

In Part III, 'Discussions', the above case-studies are contextualized in two analytical essays concerning, respectively, embodiment and environment, and institutionalism and violence. Chapter 7, 'The power of any body-in-its-environment', looks beyond culture as an explanatory matrix so as to seek out the body-in-its-environment as a possible originator of experience. Here, life-projects translate into how individuals attend to and interact with what is around them, thereby giving rise to a kind of environmental architecture: to adaptational, homeostatic conditions which extend beyond the skin. Here are life-projects as an individual and subjective ecology.

Chapter 8, 'Total institutions and the violence of society: the death of power?', draws on some of the autobiographical details of the life of Primo Levi – notably his experiences in the Nazi concentration camp, Auschwitz, during the Second World War – in order to place the architecture of the self within the apparently extreme environment of a most 'total' institution. In testing the thesis of existential power, of consciousness and control, against this limiting case, I would avoid the criticism of idealism: that the individual lives on which I primarily focus are 'successful' due to privilege, and that the institutionalism of social-structural circumstance which they encounter is less overweening than might be expected or imagined.

2
THE LIFE OF POWER
An existential framework

Individuality: consciousness, world-view, narrative, life-project and interaction

A metaphorization of individual as projectile is open to easy caricature. Alfred Whitehead (1925) was sufficiently scathing when he wrote:

> [T]he misconception that has haunted philosophical literature throughout the centuries is the notion of 'independent existence'. There is no such mode of existence; every entity is to be understood in terms of the way it is interwoven with the rest of the universe.

Understood – 'misunderstood', I should say – within the context of structuralist and poststructuralist social science, this has translated into a common refrain against conceptualizations of the autonomous, free-floating and free-thinking, sovereign, individual actor. There is an insistence that individuals only become individuals (to the extent that they do) within a socio-cultural milieu, as a result of socialization and enculturation, and as part-and-parcel of the ways in which processes of structuration engender a reproduction of other socio-cultural institutions – languages, modes of production and practice, systems of exchange, cosmologies, environments.

A short riposte to this is to say that the above caricature and critique conflates 'individuality' with 'individualism': confuses a particular socio-cultural ideology of personhood with the universal, biological nature of selfhood (Rapport and Overing 2001: 178–95). The individual-as-projectile is an attempt to pinpoint the distinctiveness that pertains universally to an individual's unique position *vis-à-vis* the rest of the world, and perception of that world, due to sense-making mechanisms of body and brain – of 'consciousness' or 'mind' – which are contingent and particular to that individual. Individuals accede to unique perspectives upon the world and become unique centres of intention and action – of 'agency' – within it because they know and they act by way of individual bodies and biologies which are 'at once the centre and circumference of knowledge' (Shelley 1954: 293).

Shelley, in the above phrasing, was actually referring to poetry. Writing in secular terms, Shelley chose to refer still to poetry's 'divinity' because of the way in which it both 'comprehends all science and [is] that to which all science must be referred' (1954: 293). 'Poetry', understood broadly as the creation and imaginative deployment of symbolic forms by which the world comes to be orderly, knowable and known, was a term by which Shelley hoped to capture the originality of all human knowledge – its original bodily source – and the foundation which this original knowledge afforded human life. Our poetry, our creative ordering of the world, really did provide us with both the figure and the ground (both the signifiers and signifieds) of our human experience. (In Weber's poetic image, it was by way of his creative imagination that man was able to suspend himself, above the void, in webs of significance of his own spinning.) Finally, Shelley looked back to Milton for his appreciation that this 'divine knowledge' had its origins in the individual human 'mind': a place that was unique both in its lineaments and in its power: 'The Mind is its own place, and in itself Can make a Heaven of Hell, a Hell of Heaven'.

It is an elaboration of these and corresponding ideas, concerning the entailments of individuality, that I shall hope to effect in the paragraphs of this section.

The grounds of our individual consciousness are a mystery to us – always with us but always elusive too. For consciousness cannot know itself: awareness cannot be approached as a separate thing-in-itself, nor as a Durkheimian social fact. Some theorists of consciousness posit that humanity can never know even abstractly the laws whereby a material thing – a human body – can accede to consciousness (cf. Cohen and Rapport 1995: 4–6). We know as human beings that we possess consciousness, but perhaps a scientific understanding of just what and how that is represents our Archimedean point. David Lewis puts this very well (1973: 35):

> We cannot tie down or place the organizing centre of experience in that way and make it just another object among the things we apprehend. It is not known as things are known but as a condition of knowing.

And regarding the experience of the individual:

> [If I am asked] what is this 'I' that has these thoughts and this pain, how is it in turn to be described over and above describing the thoughts and the pain...I am wholly nonplussed. There is nothing I can begin to say in reply, not because it is exceptionally difficult to give a correct description, but just because there is no description that can be offered. My distinctness, my being me, is quite unmistakeable to me, there can be nothing of which I am more certain, but

it is also unique and ultimate, not unique like a rare vase or painting where we can indicate the properties that make it unique, but unique in a final sense of just being itself.

(Lewis 1982: 55)

Kant called this elusive presence the 'noumenal self'; it is something without discernible character or tangible reality – an 'imaginary focus' – and yet it provides the grounds of our being.

What can be described more certainly is how it is through the prism of the self, and via the mechanisms of an individual, physiological and developmental consciousness, that the world and our knowledge of it come to be refracted. Kant sought to take this into account by differentiating between 'noumena', the reality of things, and 'phenomena', things as they appear in our apprehensions of them.

Furthermore, since consciousness is the condition of our knowing, Kant went on to argue, since we know what we know courtesy of our consciousness, we can never with certainty know things as they really are, 'in themselves'. In Gregory Bateson's phrasing: in the world of human being, '[a]ll "phenomena" are literally "appearances"' (1973: 429). All that we think we know, all that we think, is conditioned by the *a priori* nature of the knowing consciousness; any concept of 'knowledge' is dependent upon the latter and upon the situation of that consciousness in the world. There is no discernible subject/object dualism, therefore, and, *à la* Whitehead, no 'independent existence', only the knowing consciousness of the individual, of the individual body, in engagement with the world; there is no way humanly to access the noumena of the world except through consciousness – there *is* no human world without consciousness – and yet, as we have heard, there *could be no* consciousness without noumena representing the real ground of our embodied being.

If the humanly perceived world is always the proaction and reaction to the world by a self – hence, 'a refracted world' (Wagner 1991: 45) – any study of the world must begin with, and ultimately depend upon, an appreciation of situated human consciousness, of body-plus-environment. What this appreciation can or should amount to is open to question. For Kant, despite the fact that the ground of the 'subject' is the ground of being and therefore cannot be known in and of itself, still a form of systematic introspection and rational-subjective analysis is possible which might give onto a useful phenomenological anthropology. (In Otto Neurath's image, like sailors who perhaps never get their ships to dry dock to build or rebuild them from scratch, it is still possible to acquire an awareness of their position and to effect running repairs on the open sea.) For Nietzsche, contrastively, too gung-ho a treatment of introspection must be cautioned against, since the complexity of the self, its multiplicity, inconsistency and diversity, mean one may barely say for sure, 'this is the real me'.

What can be enjoined, to repeat, is an appreciation of subjective consciousness – a perspective on the world rooted in the individual's unique (embodied) interpretive processes – as implicated in all knowing: a substratum on which all else in the human world is predicated. Husserl referred to this as the 'brute subject' beneath our 'brute human being'; while Sartre spoke of the way that there is 'being' which always precedes the 'essences' which human beings make in and of their lives.

Emerson phrased it more lyrically: since we do not see directly, only mediately, and since we have no means to correct the colouring and distorting lenses that we are, thus

> every...thing is a shadow which we cast....Thus inevitably does the universe wear our colour, and every object fall successively into the subject itself....As I am, so I see....[We have a] constitutional necessity of seeing things under private aspects, or saturated with our humours.
> (1981: 284–7)

What introspection suggested to Kant was that a whole universe can be said to be destroyed each time a human being dies. Individuals are irreplaceable: this is what makes them different to machines, and other inorganic forms of life. This is also, for Kant, what ought to make individual human beings seen to be 'ends in themselves', and not treated as someone's or something's means to something else. Capable of consciousness – of awareness of self, world and other, of enjoyment, suffering and facing death – human beings universally construct universes of experience which are particular to themselves.

To unpack this somewhat, if subjective consciousness is taken as a fundamental implication of human being then it could be said that human existence is, initially and ultimately, an experience of inwardness – including inward awareness of what is outward. Again, in Emerson's poetic imagery (1981: 95), the world is 'a procession of facts [which] flows perpetually outward from a centre in the individual self'; all things can be said to possess an existence relative to their point of subjective perception.

In less poetic vein, the work of Gerald Edelman (1992) has posited neurophysiologically the ways in which consciousness (and the behaviours with which it corresponds) can be described as a phenomenon occurring separately, and distinctively, for each individual; it is a developmental process which turns on a unique engagement with the (noumenal) universe as effected by the cognition of a situated individual actor and his or her partial and changing perceptions. This is why, returning to Emerson, '[e]very new mind is a new classification'; moreover, being 'new in nature', it is impossible to know in advance what each mind will make of the noumenal universe until it has been achieved (1981: 158).

What this means sociologically, is that, inasmuch as the behaviour of individuals is intentioned, it is an epiphenomenon of their consciousness – of their ongoing perception and cognition of self, world and other. Furthermore, analysis which ignores individuals' consciousness is vacuous. Inward, subjective experience must be represented at the beginning and at the end of sociology, of generalizations and abstractions about human society and culture. Individuals' selves and their subjective experiences can be seen to be primary to sociological analysis, since social institutions and cultural forms are not only originally of individual (possibly collaborative) construction – however routinized and seemingly self-serving and self-sufficient they might become – but also ongoingly of individual (collaborative) operation and animation: '[t]here is no community, no constraint, no power, when individuals do not build them and maintain them' (Douglas 1977: xiv). To the extent that social institutions and cultural forms continue, they are imbued with subjective meanings and are made to serve the interests of individual perceptions.

In short, a social milieu can barely be comprehended apart from the individuals who compose it at any one time, nor a cultural symbology appreciated apart from the individuals who continue to find it meaningful. Meanwhile, we might expect the 'societies' and 'cultures' which individuals do ongoingly construct and inhabit to be (after Nietzsche) as complex, multiple, inconsistent and diverse as any other aspects of consciousness.

Where sociological analysis of society and culture might profitably begin is with individuals' '*world-views*' (Rapport 1993). Where 'a primary, if not the primary, project in life seems to be the insatiable need to discover meaning in order to make life work' (Kotarba 1984: 231), world-view (*Weltanschauung*) appears an apposite term for capturing the perspective of the individual and the meanings he or she construes. By virtue of their consciousness, individuals create meaningful worlds for themselves, thus coming to 'live in a web of ideas, a fabric of [their] own making' (Langer 1964: 126).

The key to an appreciation of world-views, of the worlds of meaning in which individuals live, is the imagination. Imagination is 'at the centre of human experience' (Langer 1964: 128) because it is imagination which makes worlds. Imagination is an act of consciousness, and a major human power. In fact, imagination likely represents the greatest force acting within the individual to give rise to his or her sense of reality. Imagination is thus at work before knowledge and before expression, providing the frames by which these are supported and guided; in Suzanne Langer's words again, 'the measure of [an individual's world] is the reach of his steady and coherent imagination' (1964: 125).

In a sense, imagination is also at work before 'reality'. For, inasmuch as human beings live in worlds of (Kantian) phenomena (or Humean impressions) rather than noumena, they can be said to possess 'self-creating consciousnesses' (Sartre) which structure, manipulate, animate and 'give reality' to the universe after their own developing natures and their perceptions of environmental relations. Imagination gives rise to 'sensible' reality by projecting structure and process, sameness and difference, agency and inertia, beyond individual consciousness. Sartre speaks of the workings and products of the imagination as 'spontaneous creations *ab nihilo*', emanations from individuals' subjective resources which negate the real world, transcend its objective existence, and surpass, distance and nullify actual facts in the creation of possible meanings (1972: 273ff.). Phrased differently, the meanings in whose terms individuals imagine their circumstances also become those by which they experience and act. By virtue of their imaginings, human beings 'put nature in its place' (Kelly 1969: 11); in Bateson's words, '[m]an lives by those propositions whose validity is a function of his belief in them' (1951: 212).

At the least, we can say that in the life of human beings, any so-called opposition between the real and the imaginary is actually ineffable because the events we live by, and their coherency, are always imagined; human beings are ever confronting themselves with events of their own creation. In Emerson's poetic summation: 'The Imagination may be defined to be the use which the Reason makes of the material world'; 'it is the eye which makes the horizon' (1981: 35, 285; cf. Berger 1988: 279). This imaginational use, moreover, is never-ending in an individual's life. The imagination ceaselessly enriches consciousness with new images, new possible structures and events; 'I believe I experience creativity at every moment of my life', Bergson asserted (1975: 398; cf. Maslow 1968; Rapport 2001a).

Notwithstanding, it is important at any one time for the individual to achieve a sense of closure, for the meanings which accrue to him or her through their imagination to amount to a schema or model (or number of these), and this is what is conveyed by the term 'world-view'. To the same end, George Kelly (1969) talks of a 'system of personal constructs', and Ulric Neisser (1976) of 'schemata'; what is implied, Kelly explains, is that, at any one time, 'each man devises his own construction system and plots events within it' (1969: 28). By virtue of this systematization, individuals construe not only events, anticipations of events and alternatives of events, but also construe criteria to classify and choose between events. An individual's system of personal constructs amounts to a personal philosophy.

Systems of world-views or personal constructs do not form a static whole, however. Since the individual imagination is always throwing up new possibilities, new ways of construing, world-views represent a system in continual revision. It is usual, nonetheless, for the existing system to represent the toothing-stone from which new worlds are built, the constructional norm against which the potential excess of the imagination is weighed and balanced; evolution in human cognition represents a more normal practice than revolution.

Whether evolutionary or revolutionary, it is important to recognize that the only limits on individuals' constructions of their worlds, as Kelly put it (1969: 125), are the limits of their imagination. What is devised is neither dictated by events nor a property extracted from them; this would be to reverse the originary sequence. The process of the imagination is one of externalization: of projecting images upon the world and of behaving in relation to them. In Emerson's words (1981: 138): 'the inmost in due time becomes the outmost'.

It is especially important to remember this in the sociological context of analysing the individual acting alongside other individuals, in a 'social' or 'cultural' milieu. Here, too, inward subjective experience and the meaningful worlds of the individual imagination are primary. Kelly puts the argument succinctly (1969: 230): 'regardless of the words he uses, each person does his own construing'; the conscious experience and the making of meaning precede the cultural symbology in which these come to be publicly expressed (and also follow these). Always open to imaginative newness, and operating from a subjective perspective on the world, individuals make meanings which are not overdetermined, far less constrained, by the symbolic forms presently in use in public exchange. Complicity with these forms should not be seen to entail individuals having lost their self-consciousness, subordinated or effaced the latter, or having passed up their will to self-direction. Far from it; individuals remain active and creative, protagonists in the centre of their world-views, making decisions on how to present themselves within the context of socio-cultural currencies of exchange – or working to change these. Currencies of exchange should better be seen as means by which individuals construct the terms of their socio-cultural membership (the forms of their social dwelling), while expressing the meanings of their selfhoods and their worlds, and having these fulfil themselves.

In sum, far from being over-determined or epiphenomenal, it is the individual imagination which gives ongoing reality to society and culture ('societies and cultures', better). Even while individual experience might be seen to be situated in particular socio-cultural milieux, it is still true to say that society and culture 'proceed out of the imagination' (Preston 1991: 102). To appreciate this is to apprehend individuals as 'self-motivated rather than socially-driven' (Cohen 1994: 136); in Nietzsche's phrasing, possessed of a 'will to power'. This will is the core of consciousness, of cognition and imagination, of feeling and perception; it represents humans' innermost being. Its power is such that it moulds reality – whether 'natural', or 'socio-cultural' – in its own image. It must be recognized, sociologically, as asserting its existence over other seeming hegemonies: that of noumena, of socio-cultural forms (language, tradition, convention, morality, social structure, symbolic classification, law), of history, of collectivities, of the unconscious (cf. Kotarba and Fontana 1984).

THE LIFE OF POWER: AN EXISTENTIAL FRAMEWORK

Each individual makes himself or herself what he or she is, as Sartre uncompromisingly concluded, and each is 'nothing else but that which he makes of himself' (cited in Golomb 1995: 24). Inasmuch as individuals' 'existence precedes their essence', moreover, individuals can go on making themselves and their world-views, the present essences which they construe not determining their future ones.

If Sartre stressed the freedom and spontaneity of the subjective imagination to create its own meaningful worlds, he also recognized the absurdity and the nausea which might ensue from an awareness of the contingency and gratuitousness of such meaning. The systemic nature of world-views is one cognitive response to this, I suggest. Individuals resort to cognitive closure, however transitory, in order to enjoy a sense of the habitual and aspire to the absolute. Another response can be found in the form in which individuals habitually recount the created order of their meaningful lives, self and world to themselves: *narrative*.

Narrative may be described as the form of human consciousness; it is the medium through which we make sense of ourselves, come to know ourselves, in the world. As Kerby puts it: 'narratives are a primary embodiment of our understanding of the world....[Narrative is] the privileged medium for understanding human experience...[and it] is in and through various forms of narrative emplotment that our lives –...our very selves – attain meaning' (1991: 3–9). Narrative entails sequence: the placing of data, of details of perception and cognition, in a particular order such that connexions are seen between them and an accumulative momentum is gained. Narratives can be said to embody stories. There are numerous forms that these stories can take, and limitless informational details that they can concern themselves with; what is common to them is the sequential narrational form, and the particular kind of understanding that this form gives onto. Narrative articulates isolated details, unifies them, and thus gives rise to a framing context or history which provides consistency of meaning across expanses of time and space. Placing experiences in a sequential, possibly developmental, context of other experiences allows meanings to be grasped (of accumulative, dialectical, recursive kinds) between moments of awareness that might otherwise seem fragmentary (cf. Bateson 1980: 141).

Another way of saying this is that we are temporal beings: our senses of self and world are embedded in an ongoing sequence or history which we 'write' and recount to ourselves (Archetti 1994). Indeed, not only do we live in narrative understandings, not only is narrative the form of our everyday consciousness, but narrative can be appreciated as the form in which we come to consciousness. The conscious self can be said to emerge, initially, by way of narrational acts, and to continue to develop by way of signifying practices; the individual self is a reflexive being which comes to itself and maintains its own sense of significance and reality through acts of self-narration. The self becomes a character, even a leading character, in stories of its own composing and recounting. Each individual, as Leach puts it (1969: 88), is a writer of stories with a specialism in his or her own private language of self:

> Every one of us is an artist with words. We create brand new sentences, we don't just imitate old ones. And, as you speak, you generate consciousness; what you create is yourself.

Narratives can be said to effect two kinds of vital order. First, navigational: constructing and recounting a narrative is 'a navigational act that fixes position' in a cognized world (Bruner and Weisser 1991: 133). It at once locates, relates and individuates, encompassing a model of the world and the individual's ongoing place within it. Second, is precisely its ongoing, sequential nature: narrative offers a sequence without end. It may take any number of shapes, comprise any degree of involution, but so long as the narrational acts making up human consciousness continue, so the story of self and world continues. Self and world can then be described as 'unfinished projects': informations that individuals continually rewrite, change and develop in a process of 'never-ending interpretation and reinterpretation' (Bruner and Weisser 1991: 136). This, to return to Sartre, means that individuals come to be free even from their own pasts; for, in the ongoing history of interpretive self-narrating, the remembrance of the past, and its meaning, are in no way fixed. What does remain fixed is the form: world-views expressed as, and lives known as, narratives.

'"[L]ives"', in Bruner and Weisser's slightly different terminology, 'are texts: texts that are subject to revision, exegesis, reinterpretation, and so on' (1991: 133). Cognition turns life into text, whether implicit or explicit – whether 'written' in the memory or materially inscribed, recounted by the individual in silence or aloud, in expurgated, encoded or openly evident form – and it is by way of this textualization that individuals come to know themselves and their worlds: to know what their lives are and have been about – and to give this knowledge a certain sequentiality and continuity. Human bodies become, in short, 'sites of narration' where stories give content to, delineate and embody, individual selves.

This does not mean that the stories in which individuals write themselves are necessarily happy or fulfilling or neat, or even specially coherent. Meanings and understandings are likely to be multiple and diverse, and, at least in part, problematic, uncertain or contradictory (cf. Rapport 1993; 1997b). That is, the closure of world-views and the sequentiality of narratives do not necessarily translate into singularity or consistency regarding the order that is constructed and conveyed either within or between such forms. 'Private paradoxes' in narrative and world-view may, in Kelly's words, be 'allowed to stand [by the individual] indefinitely' (1970: 12).

Such cognitive diversity may be conceived of in a number of ways. John Mair talks of a 'community of selves' of which an individual may be said to consist (1977: 130). Virginia Woolf similarly suggests that in the individual body a multitude of different identities may be seen residing, each of which possesses different attachments, rights and sympathies, and each makes different contributions (1980). Each identity may also make different terms regulating its appearance, Woolf continues; one appears only when it rains, perhaps, another only in a room with green curtains, another when 'Mrs Jones' is not there, another with a promise of a glass of wine. In some people there may be a 'captain self' who works to oversee the behaviour and interrelations of the rest, while in other people, the community of selves is more egalitarian or spontaneous and relations appear more free, even centrifugal (Woolf 1980: 192–6).

Amelia Rorty images individual cognition by way of analogy with kinds of city or city-state (1986). The phenomena of internal contradiction and self-deception, say, might suggest individuals operating in and as medieval cities; here is a loose confederation of autonomous neighbourhoods of different kinds, each with its distinctive internal organization, its own perspective on external relations, and its own ideas of confederacy with others. The phenomena of 'self-captaincy' and rational control, on the other hand, might suggest individuals in and as modern cities, with executive, legislative and judicial branches of the self in a central square, operating with one set of clear rules, and with broad avenues radiating out from there to sets of suburbs and outskirts.

Whether their community or confederation of selves is loosely organized or made more unified, conceiving of individual cognitions as encompassing diversity – of habits of thought and perception and motivation and action, of habits of rationality and irrationality, employed in the service of different ends – can be seen as further expression of the freedom and spontaneity of the subjective imagination. A diversity of selves is part of the complexity of changing environments which individuals image as contexts for their actions.

Regarding the inconsistency and multiplicity of individual interpretations, Douglas writes (1977: xv):

> Everyone knows immediately that he is a mass of complex, conflicting, momentarily changing feelings, and that is where he lives, where his dreams, plans and works begin and toward which they are directed.

It is important, however, not to equate the diversity of individuals' worldviews, and the contradictoriness of their narratives of self and other, with a lack of self-awareness or an inability to come to some true knowledge of self. For this is merely to accede, by another route, to a notion of individuals as externally driven rather than self-directed. Against the likes of structuralist positings of 'deep enculturation', poststructuralist positings of '*habitus*' and 'hegemony', or psychoanalytic positings of 'the unconscious', it must be argued that neither the inner organization of individuals' possibly multiple identities nor their content is removed from their own manipulation and control.

This seems something of which some anthropologists, at least, have long been aware. Thus, for Robert Redfield (1952: 30): 'in every society all men are conscious of self. Self is the axis of worldview'; while for Irving Hallowell (1974: 75): self-awareness is 'a generic human trait', 'a psychological constant, one basic facet of human nature and of human personality'. Again, for Victor Turner (cited in Ashley 1990: xix): 'We human beings are all and always sophisticated, conscious'; while for Roy Wagner (1991: 39): '[N]othing could possibly be more clear, distinct, concrete, certain, or real than the self's perception of perception, its own sensing of sense'. What is important, notwithstanding, is for anthropologists continually to take this seriously in their attempts to apprehend socio-cultural milieux. The consequences of self-awareness and individual self-knowledge must be followed up and comprehended.

For Wagner, for instance, it is the certainty, importance and extent of this subjectivity that acts as 'the very archetype, the inspiration, of everything we have ever imagined for the objective' (1991: 39). For Ong, meanwhile, the individual's 'I' – the most insistently accessible, open and transparent of all things in the world to him or her – is responsible for our conceiving of the possibility of unity, system, oneness and indivisibility, amid multiplicity and diversity (1977: 336–8). Individual self-knowledge, in short, is where an appreciation of extensive socio-cultural domains begin.

The knowledge individuals hold about themselves, the theories they formulate concerning their diverse identities and behaviours, are not of a different order or kind from other cognitions which they construct. As mentioned, there is no way for individuals to escape the 'mystery' of their own consciousness and accede to an Archimedean vantage-point, or meta-perspective, any more than they can hope for this with regard to worldly noumena or to others. The individual's self-awareness is grounded in the bodily consciousness from which derives all other awareness (which was why Nietzsche found introspection of little avail). Lewis pithily phrases the tautology to which this gives rise:

> We know ourselves...in the way each one finds himself to be the unique irreducible being he finds himself to be and having the thoughts, feelings, sensations, etc. he actually does have at any particular time.
>
> (1973: 82)

Nevertheless, what is important to recognize is that individuals do lay claims to self-knowledge, do reflect and theorize on their own identities; and these exercises in self-awareness and the knowledge they produce then importantly influence these individuals' ongoing behaviours, their narratives and world-views. Indeed, it has been argued (Bruner and Weisser 1991: 145–7) that the way individuals know themselves, the particular way they conceptualize their identities and their interrelations, amounts to those individuals' most fundamental theories about the world; not only are their perspectives on the world, their construction of the world, always subjective, but that subjectivity is shaped through the ongoing process of theorizing upon the self. 'Mind', in Bruner and Weisser's terminology (1991: 145), forms itself largely through the prolonged and repetitive acts of self-definition and the inventing of a world for itself. The process of reflexivity is thus foundational of human consciousness, and of the particularities of individual consciousness: how one is in the habit of conceiving of oneself is instrumental to shaping 'how' one is.

This emphasis on reflexivity and self-awareness, it should be made clear, does not imply disengagement from the world – as in Coleridge's definition of the solipsist: he or she 'impelled as by an instinct to propose their own nature as a problem, and who devote their attempts to its solution' (cited in Greenberg 1986: 36). It is important to recognize that the claim that self-knowledge is the source of, and route to, self, world and other, is not the same as claiming that individuals are naturally or necessarily solitary or self-contained. This is certainly an option but it does not equate necessarily with the kind of theorizing upon the self that is being discussed here. A 'Hamlet vocation', to use Greenberg's (1986) tag for a life of inwardness which becomes a preoccupation and which drains the energy and urge to act, represents, perhaps, one end of a range of reflexive practices, but there are other positionings. Even if individuals do choose to 'suspend their concern with things in the outside world' (Ortega y Gasset 1956: 166), this need not become 'vocational' so much as discretional, or a merely rhetorical preference (Yeats would speak of 'entering into the abyss of himself', Baudelaire preferring to live '[a]nywhere, so it were out of the world!').

What one can say is that all individuals are in a position to theorize upon their own natures, that these theories play an important part in the formation and development of those cognitive natures as such, and that it is from these natures that those individuals' worlds and their lineaments derive.

If a life of inwardness represents one kind of reflexivity, a kind giving onto outward inefficacy or stasis, then having a 'plan of life' may be described as a kind of theorizing upon the self which can give rise to a great degree of self-propulsion or movement. 'Plan of life' is a phrase of Josiah Royce's that John Rawls (1971) uses to compass the purposes and aims which he sees as pertaining to all human beings as conscious, moral persons. I intend a somewhat more particular or selective focus at this point, and therefore prefer the term 'life-project'. While not necessarily unified or rectilinear, singular in essence or unchanging, and while possibly coming into clear focus only gradually (even slipping in and out of focus), the life-project is a kind of self-theorizing and self-intensity that affords an individual life a directionality and a force. 'Life-project' conveys the sense in which an individual's world-views emphasize the single-minded achievement of certain goals above all else – the reaching of certain end-points, the overcoming of possible obstacles – ends and goals in whose terms present possibilities are judged. While not being always or necessarily an explicit plan or graduated design, still the life-project (aims, expectations, theories, visions) ensures a particular attention and a distinct colouration being given to different aspects of the individual's life. The individual exhibits 'active thinking in one direction', is Nietzsche's (1994: 162) neat summation of this kind of intentioning consciousness. Something is to be achieved, effected or accomplished in, with or through his or her life; this something takes precedence and directs action such that the individual attains a certain transcendence over any number of other things that his or her life might be or might become.

I have introduced 'life-projects' in deliberately vague terms because I wish to allow for as wide a range of individual conceptions of 'the projects of their lives' as possible. Some of this diversity will become apparent when the lives of Friedrich Nietzsche, Ben Glaser, Rachel Silberstein and Stanley Spencer, and what they made or make out of them, are juxtaposed. What I might add at this point is that conceptions of life-projects have a long philosophical history. If Rawls saw the life-project as part-and-parcel of conscious selfhood, then it was the Greek Stoic philosopher, Epictetus, who theorized how it was the intellectual quality of possessing a 'life-policy' (*proharus*) which caused people to be free, to have responsibility for their lives and to be in control of them. Through such life-policies individuals might free themselves from enslavement to externalities and devote their lives to a purpose which was inviolable. *Proharus*, for Epictetus, was an inner will which at once defined the person – the real and true self – and was something no extraneous, determining force could assail.

While suspicious of what he saw as Epictetus' polarizations between the proud life-policy of the Stoic and the 'passions' of the slave, Kierkegaard shared the conception of individuals possibly able to take conscious responsibility for themselves (against the vicissitudes of outside circumstance and contingency), and accepting that nothing in their nature was beyond their action or challenge. Individuals should identify themselves with the 'project' of attaining integrity and entirety in their lives, Kierkegaard adjured, and possessing a notion of who they were and what they should be, creating a purposive pattern. And like Epictetus, Kierkegaard postulated successful self-determination as deriving ultimately from a quality of individual will.

Will was something that Nietzsche, too, came to emphasize in his conception of the self-creation of individual life (as shall be portrayed in detail later). Nietzsche employed two images in particular in this connection: a biological one, in which life is like a plant fulfilling its seed's potential; and an aesthetic one, in which artists creatively form their lives like art-works. More often Nietzsche favoured the second image because it allowed of more spontaneity, and more of a free relationship between, as it were, genotype and phenotype: seed and plant. For what Nietzsche wished to convey, particularly in the phrase 'will to power', was that intrinsic to the person is the possibility, even the proclivity, of a self-becoming which amounted to a continuous self-overcoming. Rooted inside the individual was the power to create selves, and perspectives looking out from those selves upon the world, and to keep on recreating these. Against the appearance of having just one body, and against the notion that, with maturity, this body and self were fully and finally formed, Nietzsche (like Sartre after him) sought to portray an appreciation of individual lives as continually evolving, developing, growing: of the essence of identities changing even as the energy, the creativity and the will that was foundational of individual existence remained the same.

In place of physical maturity, then, Nietzsche formulated a conception of 'spiritual maturity'. This he defined as the unceasing will to overcome oneself, to create one's perspectives in a perpetual movement of self-overcoming; it was by continuing to jettison what had grown conventional in oneself that an individual attained 'authenticity'. Here, too (as with Rawls, Kierkegaard and Epictetus), is an appreciation of life-project as cognitive process: as an individual ethos of self-impulsion, rather than as adherence to any particular or consistent content. Treating one's life as a project, and making one's life into an art-work continually in the process of being fashioned, means that this individual enterprise shows itself in any number of different forms.

Not unrelated to Kierkegaardian 'projects' and Nietzschean 'will to power' are more commonplace, bourgeois conceptions of single-minded ambition – such as the nineteenth-century, German understanding of *Lebensentwurf* whereby any self-respecting person could be expected to work towards impressing their 'life-plan' '-design' or '-project' upon the world. In the twentieth and twenty-first centuries we have become equally accustomed to the self-help books of the 'me-generations' which encourage and extol the development of the self as route to fulfilment (happiness, health, wealth, communion, and so on) in longer, happier lives (cf. Heikkinen 1997). I make no apologies for the coming together of the philosophical and popular-cum-consumerist in this way: of narrated life-projects and narrative therapy; it is reminiscent of the way 'individuality' – a universal of the human condition – can encompass aspects of 'individualism' – a particular cultural form (cf. Rapport and Overing 2000: 178–95).

What I would say is that in a more technical or general understanding of 'life-project' I would see the bourgeois and the self-help versions to be partial manifestations only (just as Western individualism is a partial version of individuality); they are one instantiation of the way individuals' lives can become their projects – become, in Nietzsche's words, their 'works of art' – and their projects become their practices. But there are others – equally instantiatory of the individual's inherent imagining capacity. What is common to these different versions is an awareness of that existential power whereby a free-ranging, authorial intellect defines its own objectives, and projects these into and as the world, without being necessarily subject to the determinism of external circumstance.

The power of the individual to engender his or her own becoming, to create a continuing array of selves and for each of these to develop in a spontaneous, transcendent fashion, has a number of significant consequences. The first is individuals' ability ever to conceive of otherness and to become other to themselves. With the imagination as their primary tool, individuals possess the reflective capacity always to reevaluate, reformulate, and so transcend the present. This autonomy also applies to themselves: individuals are free from their existing (and past) selves and can regard them as other – something to be evaluated just as other objects are evaluated. Individuals have a supreme intellectual capacity to envision alternatives, to conceive of other ways of being, acting, striving and relating, and so to call into question the value and justification of the identities they presently hold and the practices in which they are implicated. It is this constant describing and evaluating of individuals by 'themselves', their conscious regarding of their own consciousness, and constant re-fashioning of self and world, which is distinctively human (cf. Edelman 1992: 112). As Virginia Woolf promised her diary: 'I will go on adventuring, changing, opening my mind and my eyes, refusing to be stamped and stereotyped' (1934). One can prescribe no necessary relationship to, or experiencing of, an individual's selves even by that individual.

A second consequence of the ability thus to reflect on their own past and present, on their selves' thoughts, feelings and actions, is individuals' proclivity of solving problems through trial-and-error. Karl Popper once described the process of experimentation and problem-solving as foundational to the process of life: 'all organisms', he suggested, 'are constantly, day and night, *engaged in problem-solving*', propounding trial solutions, subjecting these to criticism, and intending thus to eliminate error (1975: 242). In human beings this initially takes the form of individuals experimenting with their selves, testing certain thoughts and behaviours, and then looking at these askance from the vantage-point of other identities. The more general (Popperian) phenomenon is the way human beings experiment with and re-make their worlds, at one and the same time participating and observing themselves participating, towards the end of construing meaning. We might call it auto-anthropology or ethno-methodology: '[i]n the existential world we are all simultaneously ethnographers and subjects of ethnography' (Lyman 1984: viii).

A third significant consequence of individuals' ability to engender their own multiple becoming is their proclivity to hold conversations with themselves. Self talks to self, silently and out loud, in word or sentence-fragments and in articulated scripts, an internal conversation that proceeds even amid (in particular amid) external exchanges. It is not to be underestimated, George Steiner stressed (1978), the quantity and importance of such internal conversation. If one could measure 'the total distribution of discourse', indeed, then Steiner would contend that 'internal speech-acts' represent the denser, and statistically more extensive, portion:

> [T]he major portion of all 'locutionary motions', this is to say of all intentionalities of verbalization, whether audible or not, is *internalized*.
>
> (1978: 62)

In terms of its significance, Steiner would suggest that individuals holding conversations with themselves enact primary and essential functions of their forming and re-forming of identity; they test and verify their 'being there', and maintain the private spaces of their selves. Virginia Woolf would concur, going so far as to suggest that when individuals talk aloud it is because their different identities or selves are conscious of disseverment and are needing to communicate amongst themselves; when communication is established, individuals again fall silent (1980: 192–6).

Why should the axiom remain unchallenged, Steiner continues (1978: 62–5), that the origins of language lie in trans-individual communication: that the evolution of human speech is concomitant with, generated by, or creative primarily of, socio-cultural milieux and societal behaviour? For it is entirely possible to envisage an evolutionary scenario where the dynamics of survival entail the early development of inner-directed and intra-individual address as something preceding external vocalization, or at least correlative with it. Moreover, even if it is argued that naming, symbolization and denotation call for at least two organisms, a namer and a hearer (so that '[d]enotation is an exercise in intersubjectivity' and 'I think' only made possible by the prior mutuality, 'We name' [Percy 1958: 636]), still the complex individual self can be said to contain this called-for duality (if not manifoldness) and mutuality within itself.

Whatever the merits of such phylogenetic hypothesizing, Steiner's point is that notions of the ontogenetic primacy of internal conversation – of the extent and significance of the conversing which individuals undertake with and within 'themselves' – are surely crucial for an understanding of the nature of trans-individual conversation in the everyday. For the latter kind of interaction and exchange is as much to do with an enunciation of individual meanings and 'communication' by individuals with themselves, as it is with a communication of meanings between individual interlocutors; maybe first-and-foremost interaction involves this kind of intra-individual activity. The conscious activity of conversing always involves the individuals' selves, I would argue, and, talking 'with themselves' before, during and after a conversational encounter with another, this intra-individual communication may be the only comprehensive kind taking place (Rapport 1986). In short, communication by individuals with others – an exchange of world-views and a sharing of narratives – and any collective behaviour which might ensue, ought to be regarded as a possible outcome of inter-individual conversation rather than as something even necessary or likely. Inter-individual communication is far from a mechanical occurrence, it might even be regarded as something of an unlikelihood, and a triumph against the odds. For, as individuals talk from within their own meaningful constructions of the world, within the contexts of their developing world-views and in the process of extending their own life-narratives, it is common that they will talk past the selves of others (Rapport 2001b).

When it comes to an appreciation of individuals in socio-cultural milieux, then, the key-note is of aggregation. Socio-cultural milieux entail individuals engaging in multitudinous actions and activities on the basis of the meanings of worlds (objects and relations) which they construe around them; here is a 'traffic in meanings' (Hannerz 1980: 11). However, these meanings 'belong' to their perpetrators, initially at least, and are likely to be (and remain) distinctive. True, these individual actions and activities are carried out simultaneous to, and within the ambit of, those of multitudinous others, and in terms of common symbolic forms; nevertheless, such socio-cultural milieux are best approached as neither systems nor equilibria but as spaces in which a vast number of behaviours jointly occur, each pursued on behalf of individuals' own and distinctive purposes and interests.

Communicating with themselves, individuals test, experiment with and indicate meanings to themselves, dealing with what they note, and moulding individual lines of action. Linkage between these individual behaviours is highly variable and a matter of ongoing negotiation. Hence, group action and social structure can be understood as an interlinkage of separate individual acts, an articulation or collaboration which needs to be formed anew in each instance (cf. Blumer 1969). Moreover, even if most instantiations are repetitions of past ones, still such habit, institution or routine entails new acts of individual interpretation and new work of trans-individual articulation on each occasion. The habits, institutions or routines continue to be worked by conscious and intentioning individual participants, whose meeting is for the furtherance of a diversity of ongoing and changing life-narratives.

The structuration of socio-cultural milieux can be seen as an ongoing process of mutual individual interpretation. Testing inferences of one another, individuals gradually identify other people as objects which behave (which can be made to interact with them) according to certain principles. Trans-individual interaction thereby becomes 'mutual typification' (Dreitzel 1970: xi). From this mutual 'negotiation' of perspectives, habits of action may come to be aligned, and 'social structure' to emerge (cf. Wallace 1964). What can be said to be taking place in these mutual negotiations is an adopting by individuals of common cultural forms (behaviours and words, primarily) by which is mediated the distance between and diversity among individuals' discrete narratives and world-views. Words and behaviours are adopted which derive from a multiplicity of individual sources, and continue to be invested with a multiplicity of individual meanings, but which conveniently serve as synthesizing media by which distance and diversity are disguised.

Any resulting social structure is precarious, however, precisely because of the diversity of interpretations and motivations involved. It is always liable to collapse. For the norms of interaction do not cause common meanings; the common cultural forms which come to be exchanged are inert symbolic matter which individuals animate by employing them for their purposes and investing them with public, expressive life; forms have no power to determine what individuals will use them to do and mean. Hence, common norms and forms are guidelines for inter-individual meetings only so long as they are mutually felt to be meaningful. At best, social structure is subject to ongoing revision – not least as individual participants with their own ideas and reasons for doing things, and their own things to do, come and go (are born and die, become friends and strangers).

Social-structural norms of interaction, in short, are nothing without their continuing actualization or substantiation, their 'personalization' (Rapport 1997a), in the lives and life-projects of purposive individuals. The negotiated forms grant some commonality to public socio-cultural space, but individuals continue to live their private lives within them. As Wittgenstein put it (1978: 241): '[people] agree in the language they use: this is agreement in form of life not opinions'. Or in Anthony Cohen's terms: 'society is constituted by self consciousness and substantiated by the meanings which conscious selves impute to [common] forms' (1994: 146).

Wittgenstein, moreover, has important advice for the analyst hoping to access such socio-cultural milieux:

> You must not let yourself be seduced by the terminology in common currency. Don't take comparability, but rather incomparability, as a matter of course.
>
> (1980: 74)

Ongoing negotiation between individuals may result in a covering, a clothing, by which events, people and things come to appear alike in a particular milieu – a cultural symbology exchanged in the context of habitual social structures – but beneath or within this is a continuing prodigious diversity of life-worlds. In short, 'things which look the same are really different' (Wittgenstein, cited in Drury 1981: 171).

If aggregation is one key-note of socio-cultural milieux, then 'duality' is another: the distance and differentiation between the consciousness of one individual and that of another. Belied by the ambiguous synthesizing media that are common forms of behaviour and expression – cultural symbologies – there is, as R. D.

Laing terms it, the ongoing 'mystery' whereby individuals can witness one another's bodily expressions but not their experiences. Between different individuals' experience there is no contiguity, since '[m]y experience of you is always mediated through your behaviour' (Laing 1968: 22); and 'if two people do the same thing it is not the same thing' (Devereux 1978: 125).

In Sartre's terms (1956), there is a psychic cleavage or 'nothingness' (*décalage*) between consciousness and the objects of its attention, such that human beings are never one with the matter around them and must always signify it in their own way. Human consciousness, in other words, is never fully realized in a public world of symbolic exchange, and there is always the duality of conscious meaning versus symbolic form: of the usage of symbolic form by one individual (and the imparting to it of individual meaning) as against that of another.

A philosophical dualism, Lewis points out (1973: 13ff.), has been the touchstone of some of the most notable commentators – Plato, Augustine, Descartes, Kant – variously positing an essential difference between the nature of minds and of bodies. Such a separation of mind and body has been much criticized of late, both from the sense that mind and body are inevitably and inextricably intertwined – so that any mental understanding must be also an embodied one, and any bodily sensation must be also a cognized one – and from the sense that individual mind and body are always implicated in a broader (constructed) environing world. However, this critique should not be allowed to obscure continuing dualistic truths of human being. It is a relatively simple matter, as Lewis argues (1973: 19–20), to correct Descartes's notion of *res cogitans*, 'a thinking thing', by talking about 'a thing that has experience'. Then one might include in the category 'mental activities' such sensory phenomena as perceptual awareness of the environing world, emotional reactions and aspirations, discernments of worth in morals and the arts, loves and hates and other personal concerns, moral choice, and 'physical sensations' like pain and somatic sensations like touch and smell. The *res cogitans* comes to entail the full 'sensorium' (Fernandez 1992: 135) of 'mind, body and feeling' (Kohn 1995: 51): that panoply of sensory experience long admitted in artistic discourse (Sontag vaunts the 'erotics of art' [1967]) and increasingly so in social-scientific discourse (cf. Feld 1982; Stoller 1989; 1997; Csordas 1994). Paul Stoller is mindful that it was part of the original Enlightenment project for the 'scientist' to employ all of the senses in an exploration of the world; it was this which rendered the account a 'reasoned' one (1989: 7–9).

It remains an abiding dualistic truth, moreover, that 'the experiencing subject' knows its experiences and knows itself differently to how it knows others and how others know it. Only the experiencing subject has access to its sensorial states at the time and in the way that they occur. This 'privileged picture' (Humphrey 1983: 53), moreover, is not merely a matter of a different interior attitude to the same exterior facts but of the 'constellation of facts, of which [the individual] is the centre, [being] different' (Berger 1975: 94). 'All feelings...are internal creations of the subject's mind', based on his or her 'perception of and belief in' certain elements of the real world (Humphrey 1983: 73).

Furthermore, there is no way beyond this dualism, no way to overcome the distinction between private and public knowledge and perception. Experience remains significantly subjective, identity or 'selfhood rest[ing] on the essential privacy of meaning' (Cohen 1994: 142). It is misleading, then, to talk of 'intersubjectivity' as involving entering the subjectivity of another; the 'I' that individuals speak may be the most insistently accessible of all things in their world, the ground and border of all their waking experience and dreams, but each is also closed in on itself, self-possessed from within, and sealed off from others; we know what no-one else experiences when they say 'I'. As Walter Ong puts it, 'every bit of any other person's sense of "I" is totally different from mine'; even though it might seem 'like' when I say 'I' in some ways, '[t]he "I" that I utter is open only to me and closed to all outside me', and the converse (1977: 336). Compared with the openness and transparency of the individual's 'I' to himself or herself, all else is other and opaque.

This has two ontogenetic implications. We lead, as Ortega y Gasset describes it (1956: 168), an increasingly intense inner life through life, but we might at the same time be struck with an increasing 'wakefulness' or insomnia born out of an increasing awareness that the ongoing conversation in our heads does not necessarily give onto anything beyond itself, while our continuous becoming and self-othering does not necessarily give rise to a meeting with what is not-us to begin with.

It is for this reason that Wagner describes the reflex of subjectivity as doubt: doubt deriving from individuals' ultimate inability to share the self-perceptions of others or communicate their own. What is awesome, he suggests, about the subjective, 'the self-sensed self', is that it

> continually challenges human beings with the contingency, and ofttimes the utter hopelessness, of communicating, eliciting, or in any way doing justice to internal self-perception with external means.
> (1991: 39)

While possessing a rich and varied inner life, we are at the same time possessed of a sense of isolation, that 'unavoidable residuum of loneliness that dwells in every man' (Wallace 1961: 131).

Having begun this exposition on individuality with reference to the paradoxical mystery of consciousness, and the potential transcendence of the poetic, I end it in similar vein. Poetry, suggests Bachelard (1994), manifests the creativity and originality of the individual, imagining consciousness. It is something which eludes causality, whether of public culture or of existing private perceptions, since it bespeaks an imagination which is free, transcendent. There is a paradoxical purity to the poetic which both removes it from the world as is, and grants it a sublime awareness of itself as is.

Poetry is also a manifestation in miniature of a vital impulse which characterizes the human condition as such, Bachelard continues; here is a transformatory ability to take worlds to pieces and recreate them: an immensity within the self, a transcendental inventiveness free from normative or ideological constraints, a potentially limitless, expansion of being. This, in part, is what Nietzsche referred to as conceiving of the world as 'a work of art that gives birth to itself' (1968: 796). The existence of the individual imagination precedes the essences it creates of and by itself, and in revaluating its values, paradoxically, it transcends its own present and past.

To put it another way, the essence of any definition of 'imagination' and 'creativity' must lie in a giving birth to otherness, in 'going meta' and transcending what is (Rapport 1997a: 30–42); '[t]hrough every human being, unique space, intimate space, opens up to the world' (Rilke, cited in Bachelard 1994: 202). When it comes to an anthropological appreciation of the individual, then, should he or she not be seen in vital aspects as an autonomous phenomenon, independent of social-structural determination, their self-identities compassable by no singular or predictive portrayal, their world-views enjoying 'an original relation to the universe' (Emerson 1981: 7)?

Individuality and ironic displacement

The individual who 'goes meta' concerning the essence of what 'is', standing over and against the limits of the social-structural, might be described as exercising a capacity for *irony*. He or she transcends the absolutist claims of contemporary discourses. This, I shall argue, should be seen as a vital component in the individual cognitive treasury – a demonstration of what I would call existential power – and as highly significant for appreciating the potential relationship between self-consciousness, the imagining of a life-project, and control over that life's direction and force.

A definition

Besides its literary meaning, of certain figures of speech where there is an inconsistency or contradiction between what is said and what is meant or apparent, irony can be understood as compassing a certain cognitive detachment or displacement. It characterizes the potential for scepticism, for casting doubt on the necessity and truthfulness of the structure and substance of conventional thought and practice; Hayden White refers to irony as 'trans-ideological' (1973: 38). It also compasses the agency necessary for the 'revaluation of values' whereby, according to Nietzsche, humankind 'comes-to-itself'. If a state of mind and a quality of action could be accorded a supreme value, then this should rest with the ironic, Nietzsche felt, for here is a royal road to self-knowledge via self-reflexive displacement, to practising revaluation in potentially infinite regress.

Irony entails being at home 'in a world without guarantees' – without an Archimedean point of reference or transcendental truth – and being prepared to explore 'the tense truth of ambiguity' (Chambers 1994: 98). Its definition may be said to include an ontological premise that human beings are never cognitively imprisoned by pre-ordained and pre-determining schemata of cultural classification and social structuration. They can everywhere appreciate the malleability and the mutability of social rules and realities, and the contingency and ambiguity of cultural truths. Hence, people always practise a certain detachment from the world as is, for the purpose of imagining alternatives.

In unmasking the world of symbolic forms and phenomena as an ambiguous fiction, irony plays with the possibility of limitless alterity. Here is an ability and a practice, enduring and ubiquitous, by which individuals displace themselves: loose themselves from the security of what is or appears to be for the creative exploration of what might be. Here is a process by which human beings render even the most cherished of their values, beliefs and desires open to question, parody and replacement. It is, in Overing's phrasing (1987: 70), a 'dadaist methodology', whereby, in centring upon 'the creative process of translation', human beings refuse to take conceptual absolutes too seriously; however momentary the impulse, irony represents an endemic reaction against 'final vocabularies' (Rorty 1992: 88), a celebration of the fictive nature of all such human inheritances and the construing of other worlds.

The context of irony

Such a universal understanding may be disputed, and arguments have been made for the ironical stance or attitude being historically and culturally specific (cf. Fernandez and Huber 2001). Ortega y Gasset (1956), for instance, suggests that the ability to become detached from the immediacy of the world and treat it ironically is manifestation of a technological revolution in human civilization. Oppenheimer (1989) attaches an ironic consciousness to the provenance of certain literary forms: Socratic dialogue, the poetics of classical Rome, and an ironic renaissance with the rise of the sonnet and silent reading in the Rome of the twelfth century. Giddens (1990) describes irony as part-and-parcel of the process of 'reflexive structuration' by which modernity has come to reproduce and know itself; we moderns, specifically, examine and reform our practices in the light of incoming information about those practices, continuously altering their character and constitution amid our practice. Appadurai (1991) sees irony as part of the 'cultural economy' of processes of globalization; the balance between habituality and improvisation shifts, such that fantasy, projection and imagination become social practices in even the meanest of lives, and conventional cultural reproduction succeeds only by conscious design and political will.

Notwithstanding the above, I would maintain the position that the cognitive displacement of irony is a universal human capacity and cognitive resort. In Justin Stagl's words (2000), there is a human 'world-openness' which manifests itself in a recurrent practice, even need, of 'satisfying oneself about one's position' in the 'whole of the world', above and beyond 'a locally and temporally restricted point of view'. One achieves this by transposing oneself, cognitively, to a position outside where one currently is, and looking to 'attain superhuman goals', insights, powers, of transcendence, development and betterment (Stagl 2000: 35). The ironic may manifest itself in different idioms – religion, art, science – but it is a capacity and a proclivity which is a constant. As Victor Turner stressed:

> [T]here were never any innocent, unconscious savages, living in a time of unreflective and instinctive harmony. We human beings are all and always sophisticated, conscious, capable of laughter at our own institutions.
>
> (cited in Ashley 1990: xix)

Intellectually to distance oneself from existing conceptual universes and look at them askance is part of our 'human nature' (Stagl 2000).

Irony as 'alter-cultural action'

A profound exemplification of irony in practice is provided by Handler and Segal (1990), in their analysis of the 'ethnographic' novels of Jane Austen. Writing in and of a time and society (early nineteenth-century England) where irony might seem a far cry from a conventionally stable, unambiguous, axiomatic and homogeneous way of life, Austen, we are informed, shows no ironic 'reticence'. Readily ironizing any claims of a seemingly integrated and bounded socio-cultural system to give onto a singular or unitary truth, Austen insists upon her readers recognizing the normative, the institutional and the principled in culture – here, the implicit cultural principles of a genteel English society of marriage, courtship, rank and gender – as symbolic forms which are ever subject to, and needful of, creative interpretation: to independent manipulation and individual re-rendering.

That is, the schemata of nineteenth-century English cultural classification and social structuration, being arbitrary, and being recognized to be arbitrary, less regulate conduct or ensure the unconscious reproduction of an established order than give individuals communicative resource. In the process of individual constructions of situational socio-cultural order, conventional etiquette and propriety become matters for metacommunicative comment and analysis.

THE LIFE OF POWER: AN EXISTENTIAL FRAMEWORK

Handler and Segal term this 'alter-cultural action'; Austen and her characters display alike an 'alter-disciplinary' proclivity with regard to the cultural conventions of propriety and distinction. Rather than norms which are taken literally, conventions are transcended and displaced – part-and-parcel of the perduring human disposition to render the socio-cultural ultimately contingent.

What is true in Jane Austen's literary works is true for language as such, I would contend. Language is 'of its very nature, an ironic mode' (Martin 1983: 415), imbued with the intrinsic ironies of there being no certain or necessary accordance between the linguistic meanings of different individual users, or between those and the way the world is. The rules, norms, codes, social structures, that are symbolically-linguistically mediated in a socio-cultural milieu do not govern behaviour – as reified causes of human action. Rather they are interpretive devices, general, abstract, ideal-typical maps, used by individuals in specific and particular instances to account for behaviour, constitute rules, and create anew (cf. Irwin 2002).

Moreover, the ethnographic record is increasingly rich with accounts of individuals' alter-cultural meaning-making: from Marjorie Shostak's celebrated description of !Nisa, to the latter's equally 'playful' !Kung consociates, Jimmy (creator of a repertoire for thumb piano), N!ukha (a pioneer in a new women's drum dance) and Hwan//a (an innovative bead-weaver) (1993: 54–69); from Barbara Babcock's account of Helen Cordero (responsible for engendering a revolution in Cochiti Pueblo ceramics) (1993: 70–99), to James Fernandez's description of migrant village wit, versifier and sculptor Ceferino Suarez (1993: 11–29), to Leopold Pospisil's account of Ijaaj Awitigaaj, a Kapauku headman who amended the local laws concerning moieties and incest so as to further his marital ambitions (1971: 284). My own ethnographic experience furnishes me with appreciations of Doris Harvey and Sid Askrig, and their like, realizing a multitude of personae and world-views in the English village of Wanet (1993); of Sgt Ron Hibbs, barmaid Shirley Blanchard and physiotherapist Laura Dumont conversationally manoeuvring their ways around the 'violence' of the Canadian city of St John's (1987); of David Feinstein, producing social space adequate to his intentions as a new immigrant in an Israeli desert town (1998); and of Bob Hulme, hospital porter in the Scottish city of Easterneuk, obviating the hierarchies of a workaday institution through recreational bodybuilding (2001c). These ethnographic accounts (together with a growing number of autobiographical ones [Gatheru 1965; Boswell 1973; Lame Deer 1980]), evincing 'an ironic, transcending play of mind' (Fernandez 1993: 12), evidence individuals who have 'bent culture in the direction of their own capacities' (Benedict 1932: 26). What is true for Jane Austen's fiction, in short, may be demonstrated as being true for the individual fashioning of lives in other times, milieux and symbologies.

Linda Hutcheon notes (1994: 9) that the historical claim to be an 'age of irony' is a repeated one; however, equally or more true, perhaps, is its denial.

For, the social milieux in which the cognitive freedom (scepticism, imagination, idiosyncrasy) which irony flags – the will and the practice to complexify, multiply and call into question socio-cultural singularities and finalities – is welcomed, are at least balanced by dogmatic cultural fundamentalism and social absolutism where the reproduction of inherited verities alone is validated. Whether it is celebrated or reviled as a matter of public convention, however, the point to be made is the existence of irony as cognitive capacity and disposition. (Individuality, more broadly, may be described as a human perceptual and cognitive norm whether or not a discourse of individualism makes public self-distinguishment a matter of valued, normative practice.)

The non-ironic

Not all cognitive movements and displacements need be identified as ironic, nevertheless. Irony amounts to cognitive movement as a valued mode of being *per se*; it represents, as I say, something of a royal road to an ongoing revaluation of values. Certain other cognitions may partake of aspects of this movement, but not the valuing and vaunting of its habituation. It might be worth briefly referring to these other modes, however, so as further to isolate the ironic.

Conversion can be said to entail a cognitive shift or move such that one looks back at a position from which one has now become displaced – from which one has displaced oneself – due to an original sense of 'meaning-deficit' in one's life and a need for revitalization (Fernandez 1995: 22). This would seem to apply to Kierkegaard's understanding of religiosity *per se*. As he explains (1958), religious identity derives from believing something deeply offensive to reasoning, for it is the very difficulty of belief which provides its reward: the convert feels alive and singularly inspired in ways which believing something currently plausible could not achieve. The essence of religious belief, for Kierkegaard, is not being persuaded by the truth of a doctrine but becoming committed to a position which is inherently absurd, which 'gives offence' to those criteria of truth which existed prior to the conversion.

Then again, the apprehending of meaning-deficit applies to various theorizations which depict *self-consciousness* as such, the coming to a consciousness of oneself, as something akin to a conversion experience. These theorizations may also possess a Freudian character ('self-consciousness begins in frustration') in positing selfhood as deriving from that point in the maturation process when the individual achieves satisfaction only by repressing what he or she knows to be true. For Joseph Brodsky (1988), then, the origin of consciousness is to be found in childhood lying. Giving deliberately false self-reports, distancing themselves from what they know to be the truth, children first appreciate their power to change the world; they become themselves through becoming the source of its misperceptions, brokering a gap between themselves and how they are perceived (cf. James 1995: 63). From Ortega y Gasset (1961) we hear something similar; '[m]an is a sort of novelist of himself', he writes, who conceives the fanciful figure of a personage with unreal occupations and then occupies himself converting these fictions and unrealities into a believed-in world. By making themselves into their fancies, human beings consciously juggle with their senses of what is real.

Lastly, a conscious embracing of 'untruth' and 'irrationality' accompanies Gellner's understanding of *ethnic-cum-community belonging*. As he provocatively asserts (1995: 6), a cultural grouping is a collectivity united in a belief: '[m]ore particularly, a collectivity united in a false belief is a culture'. For while truths are universal and available to all, errors are culture-specific and define a community of faith and its believers. Hence, non-facts, absurdities, the unproven or unprovable, are what become badges of community and of loyalty to it; '[a]ssent to an absurdity identifies an intellectual *rite de passage*, a gateway to the community defined by that commitment to that conviction' (Gellner 1995: 6).

In short, irony is not the only cognitive practice that might be seen to entail a characteristic movement and displacement; conversion, consciousness and community identity, it has been argued, might equally be founded on these. But it is nevertheless possible, and appropriate, to distinguish the ironic. For these latter descriptions do not entail movement and displacement being seen as ongoing cognitive resorts, as habitual ways of being; they do not lead to an appreciation of *being* as, in its very nature, an endemic becoming, an *overcoming*, and they do not claim endless revaluation, as distinct from replication, as being itself the major value. And yet this seems to be essential to irony. It is a living with displacement, a living in cognitive movement: life, and one's reflections upon it, in fusion (Williksen-Bakker 1994: 298; cf. Simpson 1998: 223). It is a refusing to take any value as absolute, as free from revaluation – except for the value of revaluation *per se*.

Irony and determination

Irony's distinctiveness is worth pursuing a little further, in particular with regard to the question of when precisely an ironic mode comes to be instigated and by whom. If, as I have argued, irony is a cognitive resort, disposition and capacity open to all, then why might it seem to be practised by some people and at some times more than others? A place to start is perhaps provided by Kenelm Burridge, and the nice differentiation he draws between 'individuals' and 'persons' (1979). 'Persons', Burridge suggests, are those whose practices replicate certain traditional and prescribed categories of thought and behaviour, those whose lives realize given orders. 'Individuals', on the other hand are those who create anew, refusing conventional orderings and conceptualizations, existing conditions and intellectualizations; they live in spite of these prescriptions, disdaining to abide by things as they are. If the person is a social 'someone', then, according to Burridge, the individual is a 'no-one': one who has stepped beyond the pale of social normativity – at best, an 'eccentric' – eschewing self-realization through the mere fulfilment of normative social relations, and become invisible. Clearly, the 'individual', as depicted above, is one who is operating in terms of an ironic mode: one who holds in abeyance conventional verities, and refuses the security of fixity and stasis. Indeed, Burridge explicitly refers to individuals as 'people of movement' (1979: 184), those who focus their energies and attention on the dialectic 'between what is and what might be' (1979: 76).

Most people, Burridge continues, are both 'individuals' and 'persons' in different respects and at different times. All, nevertheless, have the capacity to 'practise individuality', to transcend the truth of established moralities. This they do by way of cognizances which arise not from present conditions but from the perceiving, intuiting and deducing of alternative truths; it is the capacity for *'metanoia'*: to 'change one's mind' (1979: 215). Moreover, all have the opportunity to practise individuality in this way, Burridge insists. Expressions of individuality may be diverse, as one might expect – indeed, a formulaic individuality would be a contradiction in terms – but it is to be found alike among hunters-and-gatherers, pastoralists, subsistence agriculturalists, peasants and industrialists, among village people, townsfolk and city-dwellers. It is true also that socio-cultural milieux differ in the extents to which they recognize, validate or discriminate against individuality – institutionalizing conditions intended to encourage or inhibit its expression – but the capacity and disposition towards ironizing cognitions and individual interpretations remain the same. Over and against socio-cultural circumstance, one might say, people retain the creativity whereby they produce the conditions which allow them their individualizing opportunity: hence, !Kung 'story-tellers', Aboriginal 'men of high degree', Cuna 'shamans', Nuer 'prophets', Hindu 'sanyasi', American 'hippies', and so on (!Nisa, Ijaaj Awitigaaj, Doris Harvey).

While some people will exercise their capacity and opportunity to be individuals more vigorously than others, notwithstanding, individuality may be described as a 'thematic fact of culture' *per se*, Burridge concludes (1979: 116), as constitutive and expressive of our very human being. Paradoxically, practising an ironic state of social non-existence – taking time-out to reflect on what is, in the light of what might be – represents the universal instrument behind the diversity, adaptation and renewal of socio-cultural institutionalism. Explicit recognition of this in cultural discourses – of the way their symbolic-categorial constructions rest upon and derive from ironic deconstructions – will vary, but it is individuality which represents the actual source of socio-cultural vitality, and its real presence in different socio-cultural milieux should never be doubted.

Burridge may not directly answer the question of why some exercise their individuality more vigorously than others, then, but he does provide significant insights – which address at the same time the disposition to ironize. He posits individuality as a universal capacity, opportunity and practice, distinct from socio-cultural conditions, and, indeed, invisible to them, deconstructive of them. Individuality at once undercuts and undergirds the socio-cultural. Ultimately it is a question of determination: the determination of some to live more of their lives as 'singletons' and eschew the habitude of established rationalizations and discriminations. The irony is that the universal capacity for individuality, for ironic detachment and revaluation, may take shape only as an 'absence' on the social scene, an invisibility – a gratuitous, 'violent' act (cf. Leach 1977; Rapport 2000) – whose truth may go unremarked.

Irony and life-project

'Determination' is a useful word in this context because of the way it combines the idea of decision with that of will. Individuality, the assuming of an ironic stance with regard to given verities, is a particular kind of an act of will. This also returns us to the Nietzschean notion of 'will to power' whereby the individual has the proclivity to overcome originary and routine socio-cultural conditions in acts of ongoing self-creation. In the individual, Nietzsche suggests (1994: 286), lies a nature which provides a unique source of experience and an original ladder to knowledge:

> I believe that each person must have his own opinion about everything about which it is possible to have an opinion, because he himself is a special, unique thing that holds a new, previously nonexistent view about all other things.

Through acts of will individuals are able to achieve the 'spiritual freedom' to 'become what they are'. If this is not practised by everyone then, for Nietzsche, this is because 'laziness' is often 'at the bottom of the active person's soul' (1994: 286). Having, on the other hand, the 'toughness, endurance and energy' to maintain an individual life-project – the ironic quest for continued individual being in the world – can amount to the work of 'genius' (1994: 263).

Notions of determination, decision and acts of will, of energy, toughness and endeavour, seem to me more appropriate for reaching an understanding of irony as an individual cognitive resort than seeking correspondence with particular times or socio-cultural conditions or categories. The individual ironist is self-made – becoming himself or herself, indeed, through ongoing ironicizations – and not conditioned. The ironist is his or her own person.

Likewise the individual pursuing his or her own life-project: here, too, I shall argue, is involved the genius, the 'uncommon energy' (Nietzsche 1994: 230), consciously to plot a course that can take one beyond the conventional or given. Entering upon a life-project is neither an emanation of particular times, socio-cultural conditions or categories, nor a representation of these. In their life-projects individuals propel themselves along a life-course determined by their own consciousness, imagination and will.

Inasmuch as individual consciousness of this kind is seen to afford someone control over their life, finally, irony can be found to play a vital part. Emerson argued on behalf of that 'self-reliance' which he felt a continual distancing or displacing of self from oneself afforded. 'Self-examination' and 'self-recovery', he claimed (1981: 138–64), were ingredients in the strength by which individuals could withstand the descriptions others made of them, and thus go on thinking their own thought. For a self-examined self was set at a distance from the immediacies of present experience and thus kept itself safe from presentist critique. It distanced itself from the seeming sacredness of extant traditions and engaged with what was ultimately 'sacred': its own integrity. Living from within, with self-intensity, and dependent on no particular time or place, individuals were their own centre; their nature, their mind, provided their own measure: '[e]very true man is a cause, a country, an age.... Where he is, there is nature' (Emerson 1981: 148, 147).

While Emerson's epical imagery may appear dated (in need of being taken ironically), this should not detract from its truth. Irony is part-and-parcel of this individual force which 'insists on itself' and proceeds continually to create and to live its own truth. Moreover, this is a continuous process because every truth reached is recognized to be contingent and perspectival, and bound to be left behind in a progression of meaning which, potentially, is without limit. Holding an ironic attitude towards one's deepest convictions, one's 'final vocabulary', as it currently seems, is tantamount to appreciating how the world is (at least) as full of final vocabularies as it is of people. 'Ironic' recognition of this kind is a resource which takes an individual not only beyond any one final vocabulary but beyond such conceptual-cum-grammatical limits *per se*.

If the individual resists the temptation to cherish particular values, beliefs and desires over and above their continuing revaluation, then, as the Existentialists have it, the individual is 'free'. In the individual capacity to transcend present ontologies and epistemologies, to create *ab initio*, to insist on the integrity of an individual's own being and becoming, is to be found not only a royal road to appreciating infinite cognitive regress (or progress) but also individual 'authenticity' (Golomb 1995). To hold on to an inner truth over against outward conditions, to exchange an attachment to the currently conventional for the pathos of individual becoming, can be to partake of a life-project authentic and free.

Displacement and 'in order to' motives

Irony, I have argued, gives onto transcendence, and irony is mediated by detachment and displacement – concepts which are closely intertwined with movement. Displacement, in particular, entails 'a measure of difference between an initial and a subsequent position': 'the shifting or removing or ousting of something or someone from an erstwhile proper, usual, official or dignified position or place' (*Shorter Oxford Dictionary*). Etymologically, the term derives from Old French: a negation of place. A 'displaced person' is consequently 'stateless or a refugee, someone removed from his or her country as a prisoner or slave' (*Chambers' Twentieth Century Dictionary*). It is in and through 'movements and displacements', according to Bourdieu (1977: 90), that the deconstruction and reconstruction of individuals by habitual social practices and spaces takes place.

But a negation of place or state can also be a positive move, and displacement a conscious and creative act by which individuals shift and remove and oust themselves (and perhaps others) as a route to growth. Displacement enables the individual to measure the difference between an initial identity and a subsequent one. Becoming a refugee or exile from a social milieu or relationship or world-view, becoming someone else, individuals assure themselves of a distance by which to look askance and consciously create anew. ('Power', according to Emerson, 'resides in the moment of transition from a past to a new state, in the shooting of the gulf, the darting to an aim'; and it 'ceases in the instant of repose' (1981: 152)). In displacement lies a route to personal empowerment.

This view is encouraged by George Kateb. To stay in one place (intellectually or emotionally) is to put at risk one's experience and creativity, Kateb suggests (1991a). Indeed, even to come to know oneself, it might be argued (following Ortega y Gasset, and Brodsky, above), it is necessary to become alienated or estranged to some degree, and thus to see oneself as from a distance. One explores and become oneself. Reminiscent of Emerson's 'self-reliance', Kateb calls the process one of 'self-recovery': arriving 'home' to live 'in one's own place' (1991a: 135; cf. Rapport and Dawson 1998). Periodically examining oneself, one finds one is not the self-same person as the non-displaced one; thinking through one's thoughts, one finds one's displaced self constructed from its own materials, not unconsidered or merely socially answerable questions. With an appreciation of the particular movement and course of his or her own life – recounting to themselves the narrative of their movement – the displaced and self-examined person might accede to a self-knowledge, and a confidence in that knowledge, secure from the external judgements of others.

Displacement as alienation

Emerson's statement concerning the power of movement and progression, alluded to above, ends as follows: 'This one fact the world hates; that the soul *becomes*; for that forever degrades the past, turns all riches to poverty, all reputation to a shame' (1981: 152–3). And this does seem true; when it comes to that cluster of concepts which have been identified as surrounding the ironic mode, particularly displacement, analysts, from Freud, through Marx and Durkheim, to Heidegger and Homi Bhabha, degrade the notion by identifying it with alienation, anomie, homelessness and *depaysment*: with individual powerlessness and lack or loss of control. Analysts fight shy of celebrating the displacement to which 'the becoming soul' is party (at best, displacement is treated with suspicion).

Modernization, for instance, Berger and Kellner explain (1973: 138), amounts to a 'spreading condition of homelessness' which is the inevitable price to be paid for individual liberation from the controls of family and community; the 'homeless mind', uprooted from an original social milieu and forever now migrating between a plurality of divergent life-worlds, finds itself displaced socially and metaphysically, alienated from society, self and the universe. Displacement, seen as a phenomenon of modern social relations, as socially driven, is something which increasingly happens to people – something done to them; it is not something self-motivated which an individual might be consciously and creatively responsible for determining and effecting. In Schuetz's phrasing (1972), causal or 'because' motives easily predominate in analyses of displacement over intentional or 'in order to' motives.

To my mind this also accords with a general social-scientific tendency to regard the individual actor as put upon rather than 'putting on'. I find much here in the critique of displacement which accords with social-scientific analyses of individual behaviour in socio-cultural milieux *per se*: 'because' motives are widely inferred while 'in order to' motives barely figure. Questions such as how individuals deal with life, how they make meaning in the midst of everyday life and change, suffering and good fortune, become questions largely of social determination. In Michael Jackson's designation, in the rush to depict the 'political power' of techniques of influence and oppression, a recognition of the 'existential power' to act and constitute identity is lost (1996: 22); a focus on 'institutional processes of governance' eschews a broader conceptualization of 'the power to do, the capacity to achieve things or projects' (Eves 1998: 20–1). Plainly put, individual agency is seen to be overwritten, more or less vulgarly, by social structure and institutionalism, hierarchy and history, *habitus* and hegemony.

I would wish to turn this around, however, and, as with the according of a positive characterization to displacement (regarded as a source of personal power), locate forces of behavioural determination, of the instituting of meaningful worlds, in the individual as such. I would go so far as to say that (in Schuetzian terms) there are only 'in order to' motives, exercised by wilful individuals; 'because motives' are what we formulate out of bad faith in order to claim that something or someone other than ourselves is responsible for what we feel, think, say, or do.

Existential power and bad faith

'Bad faith' is a Sartrean notion (1956; 1972) and it is the Existentialists who have perhaps put the case I should like to argue for most forcefully (cf. Amit and Rapport 2002: 128–38). Individual consciousness creates the meaning of the world and the objects in it, Existentialism insists, rather than such consciousness being the immanent manifestation of another, extraneous force – such as Society, the Unconscious or God. We have an awesome freedom to imagine and shape our own individual destinies. Indeed, we have little choice in the matter. Inasmuch as the world is in itself meaningless, we are, in Sartre's wording (1975: 352), 'condemned' to be free. Awareness of this, moreover, can cause anguish; we are fearful and unconfident concerning the consequences of our action or our inaction, and our responsibility concerning the choices and decisions of our lives. Hence our flight from an absurd world into 'inauthentic living' and self-deception; confronting our authentic selves in their freedom and power is frightening and so we shirk the responsibility, in bad faith, and say our choices, our lives, are determined: by our religions, our personal and social pasts, our cultural traditions. We shift the responsibility for our survival and security, for the directions our lives take, good and bad, onto something other, something stronger, hopefully wiser, perhaps benign. Our awesome freedom, in a meaningless universe, we exchange for orderly systems, theoretical schemata and determinate structures. We choose to relinquish choice; we erect objective and impersonal phenomenal idioms as defences against experience, and so make the world an impersonal, other-then-individual, place (cf. Rapport 1997a: 12–29).

This is both a trick which we play on ourselves and which others would play on us; it is a means of oppression. Impersonal and extraneous 'because' motives serve the interests of those who would exercise power over others. To maintain its rule, Pareto once explained (1966), a governing class, individual or elite must employ either force or guile, or a combination of the two. The currency of an impersonal idiom of extraneous determination both speaks to a supra-individual *force* arrayed against the individual actor, and also seeks *guilefully* to convince the latter that the active, interpretive, constitutive power of human subjectivity is superseded by powerful, objective social functions. To borrow Whitehead's phrase, impersonal idioms of determination usher in a 'fallacy of misplaced concreteness' concerning the order to the world and its source; the impersonal is taken and mistaken for the real.

At one point in Shakespeare's *Henry IV (Part 1)* (Act V, Scene IV, lines 88–92), having just fought and slain the rebel (with kingly ambitions), Harry Percy, the Prince of Wales, remarks:

> Ill-weav'd ambition, how much art thou shrunk!
> When that this body did contain a spirit,
> A kingdom for it was too small a bound;

> But now, two paces of the vilest earth
> Is room enough ...
> (*The Oxford Shakespeare: Complete Works*, London: Oxford University Press, 436)

This is the same contrast — between the circumscribed, seemingly insignificant human body and the boundless individual ambition and spirit that might emanate from it — that John Berger flags in order to suggest an origin for metaphysics. All religious systems, he argues (1969: 111), begin with the contradiction between the extension and the diversity, the possible displacements, of the human imagination on the one hand, and the limited specificity of the individual human body on the other. The need metaphysically to explain both suffering and death, for instance, can be seen to come down to finding the imagination a better home: one more permanent and worthy, one more transparent of and responsive to the images and imaginings which the body appears to transport but which in reality transport it. Surely, the power of imagination has another source than the earth-bound, mortal human body.

This contrast (limited body versus limitless, ambitious imagination), it strikes me, also underlies the opposing analytical positions introduced above concerning 'in order to' and 'because' motives, and their relation to the individual. The case for 'because' motives contends that the finite and mortal individual body functions within the causal sway of extraneous (bureaucratic, environmental, supernatural) forces: is historically, socially, culturally conditioned. The case for 'in order to' motives asserts that individuals' infinite and ever-vital imaginations exist on their own terms, beyond the sway of the intentions of others: responsible, indeed, for the shapes that the otherness of the environing world assumes.

It is my assertion, the assertion of this book, that, to repeat, there are, in truth, no 'because' motives, only 'in order to' ones; and that wilful individuals promote the former conceptualization out of bad faith. I side with those, then, who would reconcile the contrast between earth-bound human bodies and ethereal imaginations with reference to the creativity, the seemingly 'divine' poeticism (Shelley), even the mystery, of the transcendent individual. The aim of this book is to try to make that position convincing.

I am aware that an Existentialist stance can appear negatory of certain imaginatory-metaphysical constructions, also insensitive and unhelpful to the plight of those seemingly enmired under the oppressive sway of political systems; it can seem 'improper', to borrow a phrasing from Ian James, 'to speak Existential truths to the powerless' for whom the ambitions of a self may appear a luxury (2002, personal communication).

Notwithstanding, I would claim that an imaginative self is not a luxury but an ontology, an inevitable aspect of our embodiment (our 'condemned' state [Sartre]). And it is a celebration, a moral safeguarding, of the powers of human embodiment that Existentialism promotes. In the course of this book, it is an insistence upon the potential (and 'mysterious') movement between body and imagination, between authenticity and bad faith, between displacement as 'put upon' and 'putting on' – between power as political and existential – that provide my terms of reference.

'In order to' motives and prior conditions

Our convictions are 'directed by our instincts', by 'physiological demands', Nietzsche propounded (1979a: 3), our theories are allegories of our lives, and our philosophies are inadvertent memoirs: 'species of involuntary and unconscious autobiography' (1979a: 6). (What Everyperson 'apprehends as truth', he or she first 'acts as life', Emerson concurred [1981: 8]).

If our theoretical convictions are versions of the way we experience and lead our lives, then rational argument will not necessarily be a route to overcoming differences between, say, those who stress 'in order to' motives and those who stress 'because'. In both cases there is, perhaps, a founding intuition, grounded in individual embodiments which then ramify into an overall outlook, becoming too implicated then to be vulnerable to counter-reasoning. This is how Abrams argues in his examination of the history of philosophical debate (1995); only a 'conversion experience' dislodges opponents from contrasting intuitions, he contends, something which at the same time entails them conducting themselves physically or bodily by way of different orientations. To change one's mind is to have changed one's body. (Even the cognitive movement of ironic displacement would then be grounded in an embodied intuition: that there is a bodily capacity and proclivity to rewrite self and world. One experiences irony as an embodied state.)

Nor does this line of argument (tracing back contrasting theoretical convictions concerning individual motivation and power to contrasting individual experiences of body) seem so anthropologically alien. Leach (2001) remarked upon the way that poetry and novelty, the capacity to look askance at what is and imagine anew, were 'products of individual human brains'; they both betokened our individual freedom, and our delimitation 'by the biochemical machinery of which we are made up' – our inventiveness a matter of the way individual bodily machinery 'is designed'. More elaborately, trope theory, à la Fernandez (1971; 1977; 1982), may be seen as an illumination of the way we project what are initially psycho-somatic experiences of body and mind out into the world. 'Our experience is anchored in our body', Fernandez writes (1977: 478), and the elemental vectors of human existence are the way individual bodily projections ramify out into world, via cultural symbologies, in social milieux, as strategies of identity, distinction and progression. This may also account for the way movement is so much part-and-parcel of our conscious experiential growth; since our bodies are imbued with 'endless internal motilities', part of a constant organismic movement, so our minds become 'endowed with a primordial appreciation of the need for [such movement]' (Fernandez 1977: 478).

Such theorizing, finally, also makes room for the self-deception or bad faith which we play on ourselves: our refusal imaginatively to come to terms with our bodily experiences. For instance, accepting that our bodies amount to the organ through which our conscious perception and interpretation of an outer world is inexorably mediated, threatens us with solipsism and loneliness. Our identities threaten to remain forever closed off from others and the outside, formally 'problematic and not precisely defined', in a word 'inchoate' (Fernandez 1982: 544). Our codifications of individual experience as cultural trope thus can be understood as continuing attempts to communicate: to posit a more fixed identity and understanding for ourselves before others. Moreover, we not only externalize and project ourselves in cultural codes, we also look to these symbologies for exogenous meaning. That is, not only do we employ metaphor and other common linguistic tropes (metonym, simile, synecdoche), and build these tropes into recounted narratives, in an attempt to compare our compositions of our experiences with others', we also trick ourselves into believing we can learn something from the codes *per se*.

In short, we use cultural symbologies as means by which to attempt to make more concrete, comprehensible and resolvable what is awesome and fluid in our lives. In so doing we may deceive ourselves into forgetting that the symbols are mere containers, empty of anything bar what we have chosen to place there; we forget that the symbologies are inert artefacts, dependent upon our energy to animate them and our contextual recognition to grant them identity and meaning. Bad faith represents itself as a belief that the inchoate nature of our bodies and experiences is, was or will be known by another – God, discourse, society – an other no doubt responsible for our bodies and experiences in the first place.

'In order to' versus 'because' as social-scientific conviction

The opposition between those who would emphasize 'because' motives and those who would emphasize 'in order to' is so great that, again in Abrams' depiction (1995: 33), to proponents of one position the argumentation of the other can seem like that of 'aliens', whose world is unrecognizable and whose use of language is at odds with ordinary reality. Certainly, the opposition seems to be of enormous, continuing significance in sociological analysis, as well as of great longevity; the history of social science, according to Brian Morris (1997: 323), may be characterized as an ongoing dispute between the two ontologies: divided as to whether it is social structure or individual agency which is the fundamental reality (and which epiphenomenal).

The opposition has taken a lively, recent form in debates between 'humanistic' and structuralist (or poststructuralist) commentators over the nature of symbolic meaning. As summed up by William Ray (1989: 2), for the former humanists, meaning is primarily a function of the intention of an individual who uses a symbolic form (whether as speaker or hearer, writer or reader). It is also a specific, historically bounded act, so that no two meanings are likely to be imparted to a symbolic form in exactly the same way, even by the same individual at different times, and no one interpretation is exactly 'correct'. Meaning is something invested in an act of interpretation as a result of individual decision, and symbolic forms mean nothing in particular until someone chooses to mean something by them. Certainly, the act of making meaning can transcend and hence wilfully alter or subvert any existing limits or conventions surrounding the language or system of which the symbolic forms are part. Meaning, in short, is part-and-parcel of the effects which derive from individuals' imaginative constructions and 'in order to' motives.

For the structuralists (and poststructuralists), by contrast, a symbol has meaning by virtue of its orthographic structure and the lexical spectrum it surveys. Meaning is a collective, structural, social fact which transcends the volition of any particular user and which is apprehensible by any individual possessed of the language. 'What the symbol means' can be found in a dictionary or phrase-book, or by specifying its surrounding context to its habitual users. Meaning derives, in short, from culturally determined codes and socially sanctioned practices; it is not a personal possession or right and no single individual interpretation accedes to an independent authority. Individuals mean 'because' they (are motivated to) speak the language.

Tension between these opposing notions has taken the form of a mutual othering, according to Ray (1989). A structuralist reading, say humanists, is overweening, totalitarian, dehumanizing – subversive of all that is valuable in our use of symbolic languages (poiesis, movement and mystery). A humanist reading, say structuralists, amounts to idealism and solipsism: to 'privacy theories' which maintain an overindulgent attitude to the illusions of subjectivity, and remain indifferent to the socio-historical determinants of experience. Humanists cling onto an exploded mythology, whether because of timidity, self-interest or nostalgia; their commitment to the sovereign individual is a root cause of social ills (materialism, consumerism, societal fragmentation), while also masking economic, gender and ethnic repressions. But then, the humanists counter, what are such inequities and oppressions but infringements of human dignities and rights, which humanism remains responsible for identifying and advocating.

Sometimes calls are made for an overcoming of the humanist/structuralist opposition – collapsing the distinction – and a plague on both extremes (cf. Jenkins 1983: 9). A polarization of symbolic usage into either the denotative or the connotative, it is said, in neither case succeeds in apprehending the phenomenon, while reifying either the autonomous individual or the environing structures of his or her life succeeds no better in doing justice to the complexity of social life. Equal emphasis, in short, could and should be placed on appreciating individual practice and on the institutional *habitus*, and on apprehending the inextricable reciprocity between the two.

I am not persuaded, nevertheless, that any such elision between these theoretical positions is, in practice, possible. The longevity of the debate, the virulence of the exchanges, the mistrust and miscomprehension between the protagonists, and the variety of tropes by which what are variations on the same disagreement manifests itself – not just connotation versus denotation, then, or individual versus collectivity, or transcendence versus determinism, or 'in order to' motives versus 'because', but also atomism versus holism, subjectivism versus objectivism, process versus structure, action versus system, event versus matrix, performance versus competence – all go to convince me that the division is not so simply overcome.

Ray concludes that the opposition is perhaps unresolvable, and that it is a matter less of reciprocal or dialectical than of parallel universes (1989: 3). Akin to the conundrum surrounding consciousness (the question of just how a material being – without a spirit, a discrete *res cogitans* or a soul – gets to be conscious), perhaps we shall never be in that Archimedean position to know except corporeally, inwardly, just how the individual relates to the environmental (including the socio-cultural), and it must be sufficient for us to know that an inexorable relationship does exist. We might then concentrate our efforts on one side of the phenomenal divide or the other, respect the disciplinary efforts of others, but not seek mistakenly either to elide the two or to suppress consciousness of the division. The two dimensions of human reality co-exist in an indeterminate relationship and require the deployment of different but complementary models of interpretation: the humanists here, the structuralists there, a kind of methodological pluralism. The issue then becomes less an ontological than an epistemological one. As Michael Jackson puts it (2000, personal communication), rather than ask what is true – whether in reality or according to discursive logic – engage in a practical inquiry into the consequences and implications of creating and adopting a 'sociocentric' as against a 'self-centred' world-view: what is to be gained from privileging one or other perspective? (Ask, as James put it, whether it is 'proper' to speak Existentialism and agency to the impoverished and oppressed.)

But – to speak out of my conviction – I do not find such conciliation satisfying either. And again it comes down to experience. I am not happy to let live a disciplinary division of labour – say, humanistic versus structuralist social science – which cuts across my knowledge of my own life or that of others. I am not happy to see myself and my life, nor those of others with whom I have sought to empathize, represented in sociological models and theories which have little real room or respect for subjectivity, autonomy, agency, poiesis and transcendence. I am not happy even with granting notions of reciprocity to a relationship between the individual and the socio-cultural: because it suggests a relationship between equal things, between things that are equally things.

But the socio-cultural is not a thing; baldly put, the socio-cultural is a concept, existing nowhere but in the minds (the habits of mind and body) of individuals. It does not even exist between individuals. Between individuals are only symbolic forms (words, artefacts, habitual actions) which are inert and empty when not filled with individual meanings, and which are synthesizing processes by which individuals can come together and live together only to the extent that each agrees to go on recognizing their existence, and each remembers how it has been negotiated that they will be routinely exchanged. The socio-cultural has no life of its own, no agency and no momentum. At best it has an inertia; the phenomenon of past practice leaving physical remains (dictionaries, roads and edifices) which can have emotional value to individuals when faced with doubts over an entropic future. The socio-cultural has no interests, no needs, no functions; at best, certain habitual symbolic exchanges serve the interests, the needs and functions of some individuals – usually of some more than others – and it becomes a strategic practice, for some, rhetorically to dress personal interests in impersonal terms.

This is not an argument for solipsism or for socio-cultural milieux to be seen as idealistic manifestations of individual desires. Violence, exploitation, institutionalization, enslavement, imprisonment are real enough (as the concluding part of this book bears witness) but it is crucial that one does not misconstrue the nature of the *interaction between individuals* which makes for socio-cultural milieux.

Interaction by way of symbolic forms gives rise to socio-cultural milieux, continually and routinely, but not as things-in-themselves (Collins 2002); social milieux remain aggregations of individuals-as-projectiles – their members traversing individual trajectories or 'pathways' (Amit-Talai 1994: 202). Cultural symbologies may formally synthesize 'individuals' into 'members', but living *in alignment* with others does not translate as living through or by virtue of others (cf. Rapport and Overing 2000: 195–206). I would give no quarter, therefore, to those who would treat the socio-cultural as in any way *sui generis*: whether through some kind of reciprocal relationship with the individual, or in ontological isolation.

In anthropology and sociology, of course, such treatments of the socio-cultural have been legion, and they tend to have nineteenth-century progenitors. According to Popper's critique of totalitarianism, *The Open Society and its Enemies* (1980), Plato was the first major figure to claim a priority for the social realm and to prescribe a form of closure, political and theoretical, whereby cultural institutions were seen to afford the grounds and conditions of individuals' lives (their constraints and their freedoms alike). Moreover, while the debate has never really ceased – Plato's position itself amounting to a critique of those of Pythagoras, Heraclitus and Socrates – major developments came about in the nineteenth century, Popper suggests, when, in the aftermath both of the philosophy of Hegel and of large-scale and widespread changes in the nature of social life such as industrialization and urbanization, there came the institutionalization of a 'science of society'. Popper subtitled volume II of *The Open Society*, 'The high tide of prophecy: Hegel, Marx and the aftermath' (volume I had been 'The spell of Plato'). But other nineteenth-century figures besides these two were also influential in this societal 'scientizing': Saint-Simon, Spencer, Engels, Pareto, Weber, Simmel, Durkheim, and Comte ('[a society is] no more decomposable into *individuals* than a geometric surface is into lines, or a line into points' [1951: 181]). In no wise did these figures speak with one voice concerning the paradigm of a social science or its precepts. Nevertheless, while something of this diversity has come to be reflected in the different traditions of twentieth-century anthropology and sociology, and their being influenced variously by (say) Weber, Simmel, or Marx, the influence of Durkheim has been ubiquitous, and his collectivist, totalizing orientation towards the social as a separate holistic realm, an autonomous datum, with its own universal laws.

To Durkheim, '[t]he individual is a product of society rather than its cause', and 'individualism is a social product like all moralities and all religions' (1915). Human beings may be regarded as *homo duplex*, comprised of two parts: the biological individual with its bodily, material consciousness, sensations, impressions and appetites – egoistic and anti-social – as opposed to the conscientious individual, with a socialized mind or soul, moral and altruistic, conceptually and intellectually aware. Individuals can thus be said to lead 'a double existence…the one purely individual and rooted in [their] organisms, the other social and nothing but an extension of society' (1915). Through socialization within the collective, the individual's 'soul' is allowed to rise above his or her mean and petty, animal physicality so as to attain to a higher consciousness: *the conscience collective*.

It is true that a tension permanently remains, for Durkheim, within an individual's 'dual nature', between natural appetites and social demands; indeed, as civilization has advanced, so the tension has increased. Nevertheless, in a properly functioning society, individuals are seen as being obedient and obeisant to the *conscience collective* as they worship in the society's churches to society's gods; their 'sacred immortal souls' are tantamount to their social consciences. Their intellection, meanwhile, is tantamount to social classification; for it is from the collectivity – its self-identity, its social organization, its territoriality, its institutional cycles and its force – that individuals derive the understanding and use of categories of consciousness: self, class, space, time and cause. Or rather, individuals' consciousness is made up of those social facts which their place in the social structure call for them to know in order to fulfil the obligations of their role. It is for this reason that: '[s]ocial life should be explained not by notions of those who participate in it but by more profound causes which are unperceived by consciousness…mainly in the manner in which the associated individuals are grouped' (Durkheim 1915). Individual selfhood reflects social identity; in short, the cultural and moral centrality of the individual under the aegis of 'individualism' reflects, for instance, a complexification in the rise of the societal division of labour and a culmination of a certain social-religious history (Protestant Christianity). Individuals with rights and sacred souls are merely conditioned actors with sacred and rightful individual relations to the social structure.

To reprise a sample of prominent anthropological-cum-sociological summations which accept or paraphrase this Durkheimian lead — from the social fact of a *conscience collective* to those of social structure, language, *habitus* and discourse — might be to recall the following:

Marcel Mauss Our conceptions of ourselves, of our physical and psychological persons, are not natural or self-evident or universal. Rather, they are socio-cultural in origin and derive from the way the social group submerges the biological individual within itself. The collectivity exerts its force directly on the physiological individual by way of collective representations which condition the mind, and collectively determined habitual behaviours which condition the body. These collective representations and behaviours operate as a kind of rhythm, a collectively transmitted and received impulse, which manifests itself directly in the action of the individual, transforming the specific into the routine. Thus englobed in the collectivity, individual members, their behaviour and their morality, can be said to embody 'the direct union of the sociological and the physiological' (1979: 22).

The precise nature of this conditioning rhythm is intimately linked to the forms of social organization of the group in question, and these, in turn, can be historicized and classified. Thus, bounded tribal societies and their clan organizations gave onto individual members who were *personages*: enactors of a limited number of names and roles who exercise certain rights and duties but possess no inner conscience. Meanwhile, the Classical *polis* and republic produced *personae*: individual enactors who were conscious, independent, free, responsible and autonomous legal persons and state citizens, but still possessing no inner life or conscience. Next, the rise of Christianity produced *personnes*: individual enactors who were metaphysical persons in possession of indivisible sacred consciences, also rationality, and able to partake in universalistic institutional practices. Finally, modern Western society has produced the *moi*: members with a sense of individual consciousness and agency, who make plans for their lives (life-projects), and hold values by means of which different courses of action can be judged and choices made.

Finally, Mauss could conclude, since these notions of the individual enactors of collective rhythms are historically, socially and culturally specific (since the individual as *moi* is unique to Western thought and morally and experientially absent elsewhere) there is no saying how the conceptual category of collective membership will evolve in the future.

Michel Foucault 'The researches of psychoanalysis, of linguistics, of anthropology have "decentred" the subject in relation to the laws of its desire, the forms of its language, the rules of its actions, or the play of its mythical and imaginative discourses' (1972: 22); '[m]an', 'the subject', has been found to be 'only a recent invention, a figure not yet two centuries old, a simple fold in our knowledge' (1972: 115). More precisely, the modern 'individual' can be shown to be an artificially constructed unity or individuation, part-and-parcel of a particular provenance of morality and law, of certain notions of sexuality, rights, rationality, responsibility, sanity, sovereignty, medicine and time. The individual is formed from institutional norms: of discipline, therapy, confinement, treatment and rehabilitation; the seemingly autonomous, rational self is sustained by social dealings with unreason, madness, perversity and the criminal. These socio-cultural forms and dealings subjugate human bodies, gestures and behaviours so that certain individual subjects are constituted. Far from an elemental nucleus, a primitive atom, the individual subject is, hence, 'a variable and complex function of discourse', of certain socially sanctioned and culturally constructed ways of speaking, thinking, knowing and interacting: a body 'totally imprinted by history', subject to forces beyond its control (1991a). Far from being an originator, individuals are the bearers of a history which ideology and social structure produce through them. They are not their own subjects, and cannot be the subject of historical, social or cultural activity. Ultimately, for Foucault, ideology, discourse and social structure are themselves effects, manifestations of the forms and circulation of 'power' – a kind of metaphysical, impersonal given, 'not an institution, and not a structure', which has a totalizing nature, ever-present in interaction (1981: 93).

In short, the Foucauldian individual is an effect of power. Far from power being 'a certain strength [individuals] are endowed with' (1981: 93), it is 'one of the prime effects of power that certain bodies, certain gestures, certain discourses, certain desires, come to be identified and constituted as individuals....The individual which power has constituted is at the same time its vehicle' (1980: 97–8).

John Law Power is a set of precarious relational and transformational effects, in networks comprising technologies and techniques. 'As agents, as stores of power, as discretionary centres of calculation, [individuals] are only possible in the first place because [they are] constituted in and caught up by a heterogeneous socio-technical network' (1991: 186). An individual may be pictured as a node in sets of relations, between certain social objects: 'people', 'materials', 'techniques', 'effects'. Individuals have the 'power to' do something, gain 'power over' other things, only inasmuch as they are members of a social organization which places them within certain networks of inegalitarian and exploitative relations. As agents, individuals amount to 'structured set[s] of relations with a series of (power) effects' (1991: 173).

Pierre Bourdieu One must reject the subjectivist vocabularies of 'knowing subjects', and locate the generative forces of social life outside the immediate lived reality of an individual's lifeworld. Even if one might be wary of a wholly mechanistic modelling of society as unconsciously self-reproducing, this is not to refute objectivist conditions *per se* or to reduce the significance of the actions of individuals to their conscious and deliberate authorial intentions. Rather, individual actions reproduce social structure because individuals are socialized to act in terms of a set of learnt dispositions or '*habitus*' (1977). To be a member of a social group is to know how to act and speak in a certain conventionally meaningful and appropriate way, to act in accordance with a cultural *habitus*. The *habitus* can be conceived in impersonal terms as an 'intentionless convention'; it is a 'structuring structure' of both regulated and improvised individual acts; it constitutes an objective basis of society and gives rise to a coherent, institutionalized cultural world.

The *habitus* achieves its end because it manifests itself as a set of social practices which are embodied in individual members, and effected through their actions; it amounts to a system of durable, transposable cognitive and behavioural dispositions – 'a common set of previously assimilated master patterns' – which functions as the generative basis of homogeneous social conventionality. Moreover, individuals are not conscious of the ultimate consequences of their actions because of 'misrecognition': a symbolic-cum-cognitive process by which a proper, objective perception of social relations (inevitably ones of inequality and the skewed distribution of power) is replaced by an ideology which grants the extant legitimacy and thus makes way for its unconscious reproduction.

Harvey Sacks Cultural norms govern individuals' actions not only as exterior sanctions but also as perceptual constraints. They provide expectations for what individuals perceive, and are explanations and guarantees of order, sequentiality, cause and identity. '[T]he fine power of a culture [is such that it] does not, so to speak, merely fill brains in roughly the same way, it fills them so that they are alike in fine detail' (1974: 218).

Claude Lévi-Strauss An unconscious structure of rules, behavioural and linguistic, are the key to explaining the individual-within-the-social. The Cartesian notion of an individual actively and consciously endowing the world with meaning is to be vehemently rejected as an illusion. Individuals' seemingly rational means-to-ends choices can thus be seen to operate at a deeper and unconscious level of social structure as a set of pre-determined moves which the individuals themselves do not control and of which they are not even aware; their 'rationality' is engendered by an underlying social system. 'Men do not act as members of a group in accordance with what each feels as an individual; each man feels as a function of the way in which he is permitted or obliged to act' (1962: 114).

For instance, it is not that 'men think in myths, but [that] myths think in men, unbeknownst to them' (1975: 20). Or, more generally: 'human beings speak, but they are themselves also symbolic elements in a communication system' (1963: 61); their symbolico-mythic expressions become more properly seen as moves within an impersonal matrix which calls for the repetition of certain patterns of exchange. This being the case, 'the goal of the human sciences is not to constitute man but to dissolve him' (1966: 326): dissolve the individual human self so that its Cartesian functions are taken up by a variety of interpersonal and finally impersonal institutions ('constitutive conventions') that operate through it.

Roland Barthes   '[T]he subject is no more than an effect of language....It is language which speaks, not the author; to write is, through a prerequisite impersonality...to reach a point where only language acts, "performs", and not "me" '(1968).

Peter Berger   Individuals are socialized into a pre-structured life-world where they find their meanings and their interpretive rules, typifications of reality and recipes for social interaction. In particular, social structure and language determine individual knowledge and identity: 'the self exists by virtue of society' (1970: 375). This is the basis even of an individual's imaginative explorations. Hence: '[s]ociety not only defines but creates psychological reality. The individual realizes himself in society – that is, he recognizes his identities in socially defined terms and these definitions become reality as he lives in society' (1970: 375).

The key to this understanding is an appreciation of social structure and language as institutional social facts. They are external to an individual and there whether he or she wants them to be or not; they are historical, both pre-dating and most likely post-dating the individual; they are objective, and exist not by virtue of individual perceptions or idiosyncratic preferences; they are coercive, with the power to sanction an individual who resists or ignores them, who does not come to terms with them as they are collectively understood and enacted; and they are morally authoritative, with their own legitimations. As social facts, in short, language and social structure coerce the individual within the conceptual modalities which they provide; individuals conform and cannot see themselves apart from these institutions.

Erving Goffman   Individual selves are products of normative social scenes of interaction, and not their cause; they derive from the public performance of certain rule- and role-bound behaviours. Far from individuals owning or creating their selves, it is simply the 'dramatic effect' of certain properly staged performances which leads an audience of social peers to impute a certain self-identity to the individual performer (1978: 245). In this way, society allots a variety of identities to individuals and demands their acceptance. The only freedom an individual might have is in swapping one role in one social system for another; roles imply social determinism. The individual's body provides 'the peg on which something of a collaborative manufacture will be hung for a time' (1978: 245), while their individual 'owners' enact a 'bundle of obligatory activity' (1972: 76).

In short, from Durkheimian sociology (Mauss, Berger, Goffman, Sacks) through *Structuralisme* (Lévi-Strauss, Barthes) to poststructuralism (Foucault, Law, Bourdieu), one finds the same presumption, the same conclusion: 'individual experience is made possible by the symbolic systems of collectivities, whether these systems be social ideologies, languages [deep sets of cultural norms and semiotic conventions], or structures of the unconscious' (Culler 1981: 26). To understand individual phenomena is to reconstruct the collective system of which they are manifestations. These systems are responsible for and constitute the individual self, depriving it of any erstwhile status as sovereign 'source and master of meaning' (Culler 1981: 33); meaning can thus be explained in terms of sign systems which the individual does not control. Social life as such can be imaged as the playing out of unconscious systems of signification: 'anonymous, depersonalized networking of images', 'games of transmitted signs' where one finds individuals 'being spoken' by unconscious, preconditioned linguistic codes and knowledge-practices (Kearney 1988: 13–14).

One can go further afield, moreover – Marx, Freud, Lorenz, Skinner, Steward, Radcliffe-Brown – and find a similar thing: individuals and their behaviour caused by something extraneous to their conscious control – ideologies, unconscious forces, instincts, ecologies, or socialized values and norms. Whatever the theory, it seems, these variants of social analysis with their nineteenth-century, systemic origins are happiest when able to posit the individual as determined (knowingly or not, unconsciously or not) by 'because' motives. Above all, as Kapferer urges, one resists the 'descent into psychologism' (1988). Hence, as soon as one form of determinism becomes untenable – Marxism, say, or *Structuralisme* – another is ready to take its place – Foucauldian discourse analysis, Bourdieuian 'habituation', the Lacanian unconscious.

Because I came to read John Stuart Mill before I read Durkheim – thereafter considering myself more experienced – it seemed to me, once, that there was a fullness and a breadth of vision to Durkheim (and social structuration) which Mill (and liberal individuation) lacked. Mill gave an arresting portrayal of individual freedoms ('All good things which exist are the fruits of originality'; 'The worth of a State, in the long run, is the worth of the individuals composing it' [1972: 123, 170]), but was he not, perhaps, naive? Did not Durkheim undercut Mill in his insistence on contextualizing individuals, their freedoms and worth, their interests and originality, within social frames? Surely the process of contextualization – seeing the figure always in terms of an explanatory ground, which circumscribes and conditions the nature of that figure's being (cf. Dilley 1999) – is always promissory of a more considered, inclusive and fundamental analysis (whether that context is provided by history, society, language, class, culture or the unconscious)?

Well, perhaps not. Perhaps, to adapt the title of a well known anthropological essay, understanding 'context' in this way 'is a con' (Hobart 1985). Perhaps generalizing individual findings, and abstracting causes to socio-cultural collectivities, is, as Edmund Ions (1977) lampoons all such 'behavioural science', simply our modern-day astrology, and just as tautological. Do not structuralist attempts to expunge the subjective from analytic discourse simply accede to obscure tautologies: 'social structures produce cultures which generate practices which reproduce structures' (cf. Crews 1995: 48)? Do not poststructuralist attempts to eschew the possibility of secure knowledge while simultaneously advancing foundational propositions, treated as givens – 'power-knowledge', 'discourse', 'habit-memory', 'subject-effects' – amount to metaphysical tautologies (cf. Jenkins 1992: 175–6)? In their functionings, moreover, are not these contextualizing and collectivizing frameworks as objectivist, deterministic and totalizing as any astrological predication? In its doctrinaire insistence on individuals being seen simply as socialized and respondent effects, without independent agency or consciousness, there is, indeed, the tendency of this modelling to become totalitarian; the social is the moral, in Durkheim's reduction, and it is proper for individual actors to be determined by the objectivities of social facts and collective representations (cf. Louch 1966: 239).

If it is a question of maturity of approach, then, it seems to me now that efforts at social-structural containment, reducing phenomena to contextualizing (and collectivizing) frameworks, have a fearfulness and inflexibility about them: a shying away from the original, the random, the limitless, the individual, and from taking creative responsibility for these (Rapport 2001a). Individuals remain the only 'anthropological concrete' (Augé 1995: 20); 'society itself is neither a substance nor a power nor an acting being. Only individuals act' (von Mises 1949). Moreover, 'every argument for the death of the subject is', as Michael Jackson reminds us (1996: 22), 'authored by a human subject'; the determinings of reified abstractions – society, culture, discourse, *habitus* – might appear credible but they are not real. And Jackson goes on:

> [b]y dismissing the subject, [the likes of] Bourdieu and Foucault would deprive us of the very site where life is lived, meanings are made, will is exercised, reflection takes place, consciousness finds expression, determinations take effect, and habits are formed or broken.
>
> (1996: 22)

It now seems to me that Nietzsche strikes the truest note when he says: 'I fear we are not getting rid of God because we still believe in grammar'

(1979c: 38). And Nietzsche goes on to ask whether humankind can 'meet the awful challenge of becoming adult and godless?'; an Existentialist approach, I feel, *can* offer a chance of apprehending the complexity and subtlety, the individuality, of the relationship between phenomena and environment, between individuals' 'in order to' motivations and the circumstances in which they might find themselves.

The experiencing of prior conditions

Sartre's aphorism, 'being precedes essence', is, for this reason, such an important prescription. For, it contains a recognition that human consciousness and activity are never reducible to that which is supposed to determine the precedent conditions of their possibility; they will always go beyond the essence of what is or has been.

Sartre's thinking moved between more Existentialist and more Marxian formulations, but notionally, to a Marxian thesis – 'Men make their own history but they do not make it just as they please; they do not make it under circumstances chosen by themselves but under circumstances directly encountered, given and transmitted from the past' – Sartre responds (1956) that while individuals make their history on the foundation of prior conditions, it is they and not inhuman forces who do the making. Moreover, individuals do so in terms of their own relations with, and interpretations of, those conditions, such that they and the conditions take present and future form in an individual, undetermined and indeterminate fashion.

Lived experience is characterized by a dialectical irreducibility, Sartre continues. Individuals are not determined by prior or extraneous conditions but are always in active relationship with them: the experiencing of these conditions is neither preconditioned nor passive. Indeed, the dialectic is such that the conditions and the experience achieve a certain form and meaning at one and the same time: the conditions are only what they are experienced to be, while the individual self emerges out of the act of experiencing the world. Ego and environing world are involved in a mutual becoming: 'Without the world there is no self-ness, no person; without self-ness, without the person, there is no world' (Sartre 1956: 104). The individual amounts to a perennially unique interplay of the given and the experienced: a unique synthetic unity of experienced environment.

This gives human life a characteristic form; Existentialism emphasizes human beings as something emerging (not something fixed and static), something surpassing rather than conserving given conditions: not a blind recapitulation of givenness but a 'going beyond'. As Rollo May puts it (1958: 60):

> World is never something static, something merely given which the person then 'accepts' or 'adjusts to' or 'fights'. It is rather a dynamic

pattern which, so long as I possess self-consciousness, I am in the process of forming and designing.

The interplay between the given and the interpreted thus has two paramount features: an openness at one time, and an openness over time. Since there is an indeterminate relationship between conditions and their being experienced, there is no saying how the individual interpretation will progress. Meaning is produced in the phenomenal context of particular lives, while the interpretation of context is itself individual in provenance; contextualization amounts to a 'personalization' of the world, an externalization of personal imaginings (Rapport 1999). Moreover, the phenomenal context of individuals' particular lives is also in constant flux. Individuals are in possession of a diversity of world-views, find themselves acting in a shifting mosaic of realities, and produce interpretations of environing conditions which are multiple and transitory. This makes both self and world something never finished or brought to a close; self and world are always in the making.

The emerging self of the individual will thus go beyond the prior self, might find itself, indeed, in conflict with it as it interprets the world in a contrasting fashion (Rapport 1997b). Just as there is no externally predetermined selfhood, so there is no necessary internal consistency regarding future selfhood; there is, instead, a comprehensive and radical freedom to choose selfhood over and again.

One corollary of this is that any fixity, habit or routine in the world is something which has been achieved, and which must continue to be worked at so as to be maintained. Even when the routine takes the form of sociocultural institutions, there is no stability in the latter beyond their ongoing recognition and continuing employment by individual interpreters. A second corollary, however, is that even where socio-cultural institutions are aspects of environment that are maintained by mutual acts of interpretation of different individuals, there is no saying that the meanings each draws from the experience of those institutions, at one time or over time, will show any consistency or commonality. There remains, as Jackson phrases it (1989: 33), an 'ambiguity at the heart of all social existence: the indeterminate relationship between the eventfulness and flux of one's own life and the seemingly frozen forms of ongoing cultural tradition' – forms, norms, habits, routines, that different individual lives will animate differently (cf. Rapport 1993: 163–70).

In short, in the making of their circumstances people imagine, interpret, negotiate with, protest against, and endure prior conditions in complex and individual ways. And while part of their world-making and sense-making involves the use by individuals of given and conventional cultural forms – languages, behaviours, institutions – still, these are properly viewed as 'instrumentalities, not finalities' (Jackson 1989: 1): means towards individuals' diverse, progressing ends. Hence the structuralist, collectivist notion that common cultural symbologies determine common individual experience and belonging (Geertz 1973: 44–52) is a simplistic reduction. For, an active participation in the maintenance and development of such symbologies, shaping and manipulating them as resources for the fulfilment of individual needs and desires, means that the self which emerges is neither learned nor a reflection of what might appear to be socio-culturally 'provided' for it, instituted and given. Individuals determine how and when to employ cultural forms towards the realization of their own world-views; their usage is almost always diverse, momentary, distinctive; and where it is not, it is the result of something having been deliberately (patiently and painstakingly) or coincidentally produced rather than of a mindless conformity. This makes of socio-cultural milieux sites of their own dialectics, where the common forms of the past are taken up and animated as means of expressing individual meanings in present and future; givenness is transformed into design. The objectivity of common conventional forms is mediated and maintained by ongoing subjective energies: by purposefulness, practical activity, and strategic and projective imagination. Indeed, to be 'condemned to be free' is also to know that without such subjective animation, existence would be meaningless.

To sample a selection, in turn, a growing anthropological-cum-sociological appreciation of such Existentialist insights might be to recall the following:

> *Anthony Cohen* So-called self-less cultures are better seen as mistakes in anthropological translation and imagination. Individuals are everywhere conscious of their differences from one another, and of their distinctive identities, however these are masked by socio-cultural forms: stereotypes, classes, and other categorial orthodoxies and generalizations. Individuals may use collective forms to assert their identities, but this is not the same as uniformities of identity, for forms are actualized, motivated, and given function by individuals in idiosyncratic ways. There is a vital difference between what people intend and what they appear to intend, and selfhood resides in the former, not the latter. Taking forms which are in the public domain – tropes, languages, rituals, dogmas, facts, names – individuals make private meanings (meanings which remain private until and unless individuals negotiate their disclosure). Individuals use cultural forms as 'vehicles' of conceptions and expressions – *à la* Geertz – but the forms do not cause individuals to think in specifiable or common ways. Rather, it is cultural forms which are made meaningful and substantial by individuals' interpretations – and hence given life. '[T]he self [remains] the essential dynamo of social process' (Cohen 1994: 50). 'Culture', in short, may be understood as the ongoing meaningful product of thinking, feeling and sensing selves; and 'society' as that which is constituted by an aggregation of self-conscious individuals. It is individual selves which have primacy, in a word, their behaviour being initiated by their consciousness, and their perceptions of their relationships to the worlds around them, social and other.
>
> It is the case that through the media of social institutions and cultural conventions, some societal members and officers endeavour to subvert others'

capacities for self-direction, to intrude upon others' personalities, identities and allegiances, even to dominate others' selves. However, while such socio-cultural functionaries may have an exaggerated faith in their ability to oppress, to cause 'selves' and 'roles' to be synonymous, individual complicity in others' games, rituals and institutions does not translate as them having lost their self-consciousness or their will. For individuals may assimilate socio-cultural conventions without being effaced by them or reconciled to them; they read collective forms through their own experiences. In usual practice, as orchestrators of social relations, individuals adapt conventions and commitments to their own circumstances, identities and interests. These adaptations are active (and pro-active) and ongoing; they are the outcome of negotiation carried out by creative and authorial psyches which are responsible for defining their own presentation and participation, managing their own obligations and objectives, and contriving their own alternative institutional orders.

In sum, individuals are responsible for making their own worlds through acts of perception and interpretation. This means that social milieux cannot be understood apart from the (perceptions of) individuals who compose them – both alone and in relationship. It also means that collective behaviour is a triumph of ongoing symbolic mediation and negotiation, and not something mechanical or deterministic. Via common sets of symbols, individuals come to express their common membership of groups without, in the process, negating their individuality.

James Fernandez Individuals are to be found engaged in a lively, insightful, resourceful and ironic search for, and assertion of, a social identity which is adequate to the senses of self which they derive from their psycho-sensory experiences. Finding the socio-cultural categories surrounding them disinterested, frustrating and constricting, they evidence a 'play of mind…that transcends the materials out of which it arises' (1993: 12).

Kenelm Burridge Most people are, at different times, both 'individuals' and 'persons'. One asserts one's individuality through autonomous action, being prepared to play with those criteria which measure what is right and proper (moralities of rules, statuses and roles). It is then the latencies, the relationship between what is and what might be, which become evident in individuals' behaviour:

An individual is one who has experienced and been experienced by that event – physical, psychic, intellectual, or spiritual – which reveals the current cultural categories – and so the person – as false, illusory, not in conformity with the real truth of things. Attempting to articulate the experience indicates a movement from the person to the individual, a movement from apprehension to comprehension.

(Burridge 1979: 74)

To be 'individual' is to transcend the normative values of thought and world of the 'person'.

Such movement or transcendence, *metanoia*, can lead to alienation from all that presently is, and to a sense of anomie. But it can also lead to life within a new order, a new set of givens. Individuals are moral innovators, formulating and articulating new rationalizations which offer to change or restructure the moral environment of social relations and persons. No new actual conditions might result, however, or not the ones the individual has articulated, because other people must be convinced; and others' interests and perceptions (both as individuals and as persons) might make them unprepared to accept a new morality. Moreover, established moralities have official guardians who see new ideas as a dangerous, destabilizing influence, and hence 'evil'. They will seek to have the non-conforming labelled as deviant and eccentric. Nevertheless, there seems to be a human impulse to discover the truth in events, and to seek out the well-springs of power. Experience is weighed against the burden of socio-cultural representations and expectations and if the latter are found wanting a new truth is sought. New moralities arise in this way – and new conceptions of conventional persons are the outcome. In other words, 'successful' or socio-culturally recognized individuality ends in personhood; for, as soon as an individual persuades others of a new morality, his or her individuality dissolves into a social identity. But then the ideology of the new order is challenged by further drives to individuality, and so the cycle continues.

Morality and individuality are thus inextricably linked in an ongoing dialectic of order and renewal which is constitutive of human being. Moreover, individuality affords too those displacements which make the social analysis and cultural critique of sociology and anthropology possible. Is it not an abiding irony, then, that so much of social-scientific theory and analysis is intent upon transforming the individually inspired cycles and vicissitudes of life into impersonal systems of structural reproduction – and inscribing individuals merely as persons?

Michael Carrithers Anthropology's default position seems to be a notion of culture as an impersonal, shared, moral and cognitive system which is compelling both to local subjects as sources of their behaviour and to anthropological analysis as an explanation of behaviour. Here are Geertz's 'cultural forces' weighing on subjects, penetrating them and making them act as they do without choice (the effect is stronger than coercion because culture offers no choice, no way of understanding a choice). Here is Mauss' 'category of the person' as historically and culturally conditioned; here is Dumont's definition of modern Western individualism as peculiarly distinct from the norms of personhood found elsewhere in time and space – sociocentric, constrained, dependent.

But this notion of culture as a determining system – forceful, hegemonic, pervading action and consciousness – provides a picture of social life as mere role-playing, in a closed and static universe. No opening is offered into the realities and fruits of choice, experience or mutability. Such a picture is only possible by denying empirical reality, particularity, idiosyncrasy, and an apprehending of the non-systematic. Empirical reality rejects any West/Rest distinction and everywhere bears witness to strong senses of individuality, and the desire to express this in both public and private life, whatever the normative social ethos.

Indeed, human beings are ever open 'to experience and change beyond their established moral conceptual language or ideology' (Carrithers 2000: 373). Culture, morality, ideology, are not agencies in their own right, not things imposing themselves impersonally with ineluctable force; culture is not an organized whole which excludes alternatives. Neither systematic nor irresistible, culture is a collection of variegated and partly contradictory conventions, ideas and values – received and newly created – that people use as quotations, as landmarks, rhetorically and strategically. Culture is a crust beneath which social life flows.

An open picture recognizes social life to be 'a sort of Brownian motion of interpretations and relationships' (Carrithers 2000: 375), where identity or personhood are contingent upon individual responses to setting. But these responses, again, are not the effusions of ideologies or conceptual apparatuses or social groupings, but of a consciousness which develops out of an accumulation of 'interactive experience' (2000: 369). Consciousness and action, history and change, grow from an interpretation of experience which is fundamentally and everywhere idiosyncratic and individual.

Michael Jackson   There is a dialectical irreducibility between concepts and lived experience, amounting to an 'ambiguity at the heart of all social existence: the indeterminate relationship between the eventfulness and flux of one's own life and the seemingly frozen forms of the ongoing cultural tradition' (1989: 33). Conceptual classifications and generalizations do not represent inherent orderliness in the world, then; theorizing in terms of 'society' or 'culture', 'structure', '*habitus*' or 'history', may give us momentary satisfactions – a sense of order and control over nature and others, even mastery and authorship – but far from being accurate or privileged isomorphs of the world, they are forms of wishful thinking, defences against impotence, or consoling illusions: quasi-magical attempts to conjure up categorical truths in the face of the complexity, contradictoriness, situationality, flux and instability of everyday life. Rather than attempting to subjugate lived experience to abstractions, anthropology should be dialectical: trace out the play between social structures and the actual experience of individuals in the everyday, illuminate the experiences which lie behind the masks and facades of conceptual order.

Grounding anthropological discourse in the sentient life of individuals will show human practice always surpassing rather than merely conserving the givenness from which it arises (even if the reproduction of convention is an outcome, this is a consequence not of mindless conformity but of self-conscious fabrication). Culture, gender, ethnicity may amount to particular contexts in which individuals live out their humanity, but they do not speak to the essence of identity. Individual lives cannot be 'reduced to cultural determinants' (Jackson 1989: 26), indeed, for experience is an open-ended matter deriving from interpretation; human life is in active relationship with circumstance.

The place to begin a phenomenologically informed anthropology – avoiding 'the pathology of [burying] the experience of the individual subject in the categories of totalizing explanation' (Jackson 1989: 89) – is with narrative and life-story. Since experience of otherness proceeds from within experience of the self, an informed subjectivity provides the royal road to any authentic objectivity.

Nancy Chodorow Anthropologists have traditionally acted as though there were no psychological life of any interest beyond the publicly shared, linguistically labelled cultural categories that describe life. *Après* Durkheim, they have refused to see psychological meanings over and against cultural realities, as the force by which culture is created and shaped: 'people (individually and in interaction) create and recreate cultural meanings' (1994: 3). Anthropologists have relativized the psyche but treated culture as a given. Instead, there should be an appreciation of the psychological as irreducible, and as a powerful force constituting human life and society.

No generalization about shared meaning will be sufficient, moreover, for there will be as many individual interpretations of cultural categories and practices as there are people. 'Meaning...is always psychologically particular to the individual' (Chodorow 1994: 7). Nor is there any time in the life of the individual when this has not been and will not be the case. Cultural realities are individually created anew not just once-and-for-all, but each time an individual experiences them with personal psychological force, and this process is life-long: 'we create projective and introjective meanings from birth and throughout life' (1994: 8).

One of the ways this occurs is by making the world into a personal fantasy or fiction. The fantasizing process would seem to be an innate potentiality and capacity whereby we make the world subjectively meaningful by endowing it with emotion-laden narrativity.

People personally animate and tint, emotionally and through fantasy, the culture, linguistic, interpersonal, cognitive and embodied worlds [they] experience, creating and interpreting the external world in ways that resonate with their internal world, preoccupations, fantasies and sense of self and other.

(Chodorow 1994: 4)

> Such infusing of experience is found in the earliest moments of perception and meaning-creation in children; even before language develops, people, interactions, selves, feelings and things are emotionally and fantasy-toned.
>
> Contrary to the (Lacanian) behaviourists, primacy need not be accorded to cultural or linguistic reality, therefore, because the latter derives from the infant's personal creation of self-experience; reality is constructed by the individual as she separates-out self from world. Ego and reality (self and environment) are therefore constructed simultaneously, from the subject's point of view, rather than the individual being inscribed into and accommodating to something pre-given. Psychological meanings, then, continue to interact with, animate and interpret cultural categories, images and language. Experiencing the latter in an ongoing fashion, and in particular contexts, individuals continually create new meanings by way of their unique biographies and personal histories of intrapsychic strategies and practices.
>
> Only an anthropology which remains centred on the emergent, *sui generis* psychological reality, which emphasizes the pan-human universality of these processes and capacities, can do justice to the individual in both its particular and general aspects (Chodorow 1999: 218).

'Every man's condition', Emerson wrote, 'is a solution in hieroglyphic to those inquiries he would put' (1981: 8; cf. Auden 1951: 83). The form taken by 'prior' conditions, in other words, is inextricably tied to their appreciation and use at the moment of their individual interpretation. While appearing to emerge from prior conditions, individuals, through their own activities in the world — acting on the basis of 'in order to' motives — are responsible for creating and recreating the conditions, the circumstances, in which they act as an ongoing part of the process by which they create and fulfil their senses of identity. Here is the individual as 'a centre of orientation of the objective universe' and 'an origin of actions' (Laing 1968: 20) whose power turns the circumstantial into 'the direction of [his or her] own capacities' (Benedict 1932: 26).

The conditions of political power and existential power

A central issue here is the nature of power and its relations to social life. Indeed, it is as a rejoinder to certain conventional, structural or institutional conceptualizations of power — an appreciation of the 'existential' over and against the 'political', as Jackson put it, or the 'personal' over and against the 'corporate' (Peters 1990) — that this book can broadly be conceived. In the same way that I would specify 'in order to' motives alongside 'because' motives and call into question the provenance of the latter, I would approach the topic of power by way of existential foundations, questioning the extent to which the political should be understood as a separate, impersonal domain, a thing-in-itself, whose structures determine action.

Existential power

Power can be conceived of existentially as an inherent attribute of individuals as active beings, beings who, through their ongoing activity-in-the-world, create and recreate meaningful environments in which they live. Emerson and Nietzsche refer in this connection to individuals' native 'force', John Dewey to their 'impulse', Max Weber to their 'will' (cf. Beteille 1977: 49). Residing within individuals, and lent to the relations and groupings to which they lend their allegiance, 'existential power' compasses the force, the will, the energy, in a word the agency, whereby individuals produce effects in their worlds – effect worlds, in fact (cf. Rapport and Overing 2000: 1–9).

Such existential power is at once something metabolic, something pertaining to individuals as embodied physical organisms, and something intelligent, pertaining to the capacity to sense and make sense. It is a drive and an assimilation; it makes individuals discrete centres of energy (Bateson spoke of individuals as 'energy sources' [1973: 126]). While individuals' bodily boundaries are permeable, then, and while they are dependent on energy-transfers across these borders, inasmuch as they exist, individuals have an inescapable physical and experiential separateness which differentiates and distinguishes them from the rest of the world.

As discrete centres of energy, individuals begin, from before birth, to become distinctly themselves: to accrete identities and personalities. This takes place through activity-in-the-world, through movement and through assessment of what the senses relay to be the results of that movement. Bateson referred in this connection to the individual 'organism-plus-environment' and 'organism-in-its-environment' (1973: 423, 426), and Fernandez to a human 'phenomenological subjectivity' (1992: 127, 134–5); what develops is a personal, environing 'sensorium' in which individual minds dwell. Two things are further to be stressed: not only does the energy behind this activity-in-the-world remain individually based, it is also individually directed. From the moment the individual energy source begins moving in its environment and becoming itself (its selves), a unique history of embodiment, of worldly engagement, unfolds and grows which compasses its own logics, its own habits, its own ways of doing and being, and its own purposes.

Of course, the individual organism-plus-environment is not alone in the world. It is discrete but not alone. It has embarked upon its distinct voyage of activity-in-the-world (-in-*its*-world) and sense-making, but it is surrounded by a plurality of other things-in-the-world, inorganic and organic, some engaged in comparable voyages to its own. On this view, social science might be broadly described as the study of the effects energetic things-in-the-world have upon one another. This is a far from singular or easily generalizable matter (which is why a respect for the individual case goes to the very heart of social science as a project). Since each individual centre-of-energy is driven by its own metabolism, within its own embodiment, along its own historical course of activity-in-the-world, how each will react to other things is not determinable; more specifically, it is difficult, if not impossible, to predict how one human being will affect another human being with whom it comes into contact. This is so for three reasons: first, to repeat, because each is set upon its own life-course, each is engaged in furthering a life-world whose direction and logic has been distinct from the moment 'it' began; second, because each engages with others from the position of outsider: each is dependent on bodily sense-making apparatuses which are discrete and distinctive to itself, which imbue it with its own perspective on the world and no other; and third, because the sense-making procedures of each is characterized by a creativity – a 'randomness' even (Rapport 2001a) – which makes their generation of perspectives unpredictable even to themselves.

An appropriate way to conceive of human social life, Emerson suggests, is as a proportionate meeting between individuals' 'native force' and social conventions: '[l]ife itself is a mixture of power and form' (1981: 280). Simmel spoke similarly of the 'reciprocal influence' between social form and individuals' vital 'impulse' (1971: 24). Even as they deal with and employ conventional social forms as means and modes of expression and communication, it is individuals' native force which drives them to accrue and maintain senses of themselves and their worlds. A 'prosperous' social life, Emerson concludes, depends on how 'sweetly' individuals are able to effect the meeting between their intrinsic force and the surface conventions which act as both buffers and points of contact between themselves and others: '[w]e live amid surfaces, and the true art of life is to skate well on them' (1981: 280).

Existential power and the structural

The above introduces a very different concept of power to that often presumed in social science, where it is conventionally regarded as something residing in and deriving from abstract and impersonal entities and forces such as 'social structures', 'languages', 'discourses', 'unconscious drives', 'habituated practices', 'institutions', and categorial designations such as 'class', 'gender', 'ethnicity', 'nationality'. These abstractions are seen to be somehow responsible for their own effects, and as controlling those individual functionaries said to be living within their compass, whether or not the latter are aware of their so being controlled. Indeed, poststructuralists would argue, as we have heard, that such impersonal forces are responsible for giving rise to the consciousness of their human functionaries *tout court* – responsible for our conceiving of the possibility of there being something called 'personal' experience and 'individual' power – thus collapsing any distinction between social structure and agent, cultural form and will. In current dispensations, the impersonal becomes an 'anthropomorphized agent', assuming many shapes – 'vector, instrument, technology, technique, discourse' (Kurtz 2001: 29) – but always eluding the control of human agents.

THE LIFE OF POWER: AN EXISTENTIAL FRAMEWORK

Nor is this conclusion so far removed, in outcome, from more traditional functionalist and structuralist theorizations which saw 'social order' as emanating from a system of 'social control' (a set of external sanctions or a system of interiorized morality), and where the power of one individual over another derived from the institutional contexts and practical routines by which they found themselves encapsulated. 'Interactional', 'organizational' and 'structural' 'modalities' condition the settings and contexts in which individuals exercise their 'potency [and] capability', Eric Wolf recently concluded (1999: 5); while Timothy Earle (1998: 951) speaks even more plainly: 'four sources of power exist: social, military, ideological, and economic', and maintaining a social position 'depends on using one or more of these power sources' – of which 'the economic is primary'. At best, a hierarchy of kinds of power is admitted in social science in which existential 'modalities' tend to be thoroughly overwritten (cf. Blau 1967; Jacobson 1978).

The place I would begin, however, in theorizing upon such seemingly impersonal, structural or institutional facets of power, is with the vital distinction between the forms of social reality and the force, the will, behind them; the significance, the meaning, they carry. There is no way that such experiential dualities (form and force, form and meaning) can properly be elided or eschewed; they are, Simmel insisted (1971), 'co-present dualisms', and form should never be seen as overwriting content. There are, in other words, both political or institutional and existential or personal manifestations of power – an experientially authentic distinction, a distinction clearly instantiated in the different ways individual incumbents of the same political office, functionaries of the same institution, fulfil (define, maintain, extend, subvert, personalize, anonymize) their role. But the relationship between the institutional and the existential is not a mutual one; I would not be happy, to repeat, to intimate that here is a relationship between equal things, between things that are equally things. Rather, I would wish to argue that there is a fundamental sense in which the institutional must be understood as conditional upon the existential.

The structuralist (and poststructuralist) argument regarding the power of the institutional is often framed, as we heard from Ray (above), in terms of language; the power of language over its individual speaker-hearers – individuals as 'inhabitants', willy-nilly, if not prisoners, of discourses, language-games or symbolic codes – is often taken to be paradigmatic of the institutional or structural as such. By contrast, an Existentialist appreciation might begin with a description of language as an institution whose 'very nature', to repeat Martin's phrasing (1983: 415), is to function in 'ironic mode': dependent on and determined by its being continually animated by individual speaker-hearers, who use it for construing personal meanings and furthering possibly private purposes (cf. Rapport and Overing 2000: 117–26).

Of course, one can read significant give-and-take between the two positions. Without the institution of language individuals would not have the medium through which to express and possibly communicate their meanings, to metacommunicate notions of register and code; perhaps they would not have the means even to formulate such meaning, certainly not with the same facility. Notwithstanding, there is something ontologically and qualitatively distinct in the agency with which each individual is responsible for imbuing language with meaningfulness, relevance and validity, through their continued, intentioned use of it – without which the institution would simply remain inert cultural matter – and so maintaining language's role as a synthesizing process in social life. To claim for the institutional something akin to its own animating force and function is an hypostatization.

George Steiner (1975) offers an apposite formulation (echoing Simmel) when he describes language as exhibiting a 'dual phenomenology'. Here, he says, is a common surface of speech-forms and notations, of grammar and phonology – the conventions of collective public exchange – resting upon a base of originally private meanings and associations, meanings which derive from the 'irreducible singularity' of personal consciousness, from the specificity of an individual's ongoing, articulate somatic and psychological identity (Steiner 1975: 170–3). Speaking a language does not translate into that language possessing agency or achieving hegemony, then, determining or causing meaning, or eliminating the interpretive work of individual speaker-hearers. Linguistic norms and routines may institutionalize (also hierarchicalize) certain conventional avenues of expression but they in no way determine what is meant as individuals partake of the language from within the personalizing contexts of their world-views (cf. Rapport 1993: 161–77).

Linguistic usage, moreover, is never unmediated by a creative individual improvisation of its conventions. Individuals at once partake of language's rules and routines (take part in the continuing constitution of socio-cultural milieux to which linguistic interaction gives rise), and make these into instruments of their own ongoing, changing understanding and use. Whatever the order and sense – the power – purportedly instantiated by the institutional logic of the language as such, the individual speaker-hearers partaking of its rules and routines animate them according to their own mental and bodily, verbal and behavioural, presence in those routines, and so are able (are 'condemned') to go on making their own sense. (For this reason, there can be worlds of difference between shared grammatic-cum-paradigmatic competency – shared institutional membership – on the one hand and shared cognition or mutual comprehension on the other.) Individuals in interaction can thus be seen to be both assisting in a continuing collective performance – in the performance of an institution – and, at the same time, creating, extending and fulfilling ongoing agendas, identities, world-views, life-projects, of their own.

More broadly, I would contend that the existential power – the energy, will and force – which underlies the work of interpretation in linguistic usage equally underlies the extent to which *institutions as such* gain animation in public life, and continue to be a manifestation of power – the power of normativization, of hierarchicalization, of exclusion, and so on. There is a dialectic between the existential and the institutional, as between individuals and others (a theme dealt with more fully in Part III), but the existence of a dialectical relationship should not interfere with our recognition of the ontological priority of the existential, also its qualitative distinctiveness. The existential possesses an instrumental priority, too, inasmuch as the power of the institutional is dependent on the animating work of individual functionaries (individuals who are active in the world, *inter alia* as institutional role-players). To begin to understand the 'power' of institutions is to see their being worked, and resisted, and negated, in all manner of ways, for all manner of purposes and in every moment, by wilful individuals; one needs to have a conception of existential power as a 'real quality', a 'concrete thing', prior to and independent of anything else (Helms 1993: 9).

The individual role-player is never to be seen as subsumed within the logic of the institutional, moreover – the 'individual' collapsed into the 'person', in Burridge's terminology, 'content' by 'form', in Simmel's. For the individual always possesses the power – the existential awareness, the ironic capacity and proclivity – to say: 'Here I am partaking of an institution, playing a particular language-game'. Sometimes individuals play the game better than at other times, and sometimes the playing is more trying, intrusive, than at other times, but there is no moment at which individuals do not possess the capacity – and experience the mixed emotions – to recognize both where the logic of the institution (as personalized by fellow-players) would take them, and the distinctive, individual place they stand – emotionally, cognitively – in relation to it. It may not always be an easy matter determining how to reconcile these positions – how to act, what to say, how to seem – both as institutional players and as themselves, but it is never difficult for individuals to see themselves both present and detached: conscious players in the game – however reluctant, however conventionally disempowered – but never played unconsciously, willy-nilly, by it.

Power as relational

A recognition, within social science, of the relational qualities of the exercise of power is widely evinced. Leach (1977: 17) spoke of power as transactional, something pertaining to that liminal interface or contact zone between human beings; while Benedict Anderson (1972) described power in terms of those interactions where someone obeys someone else's wishes thus effecting a causal link between the behaviours of both. Power as a relationship, in fact, is basic to the way many theorists have traditionally sought to define power as such. From Max Weber (1947):

> Power is the probability that one actor within a social relationship will be in a position to carry out his own will despite the resistance of other participants.

to Richard Tawney (1931):

> Power may be defined as the capacity of an individual or group of individuals to modify the conduct of other individuals or groups in a manner which he desires, and to prevent his own conduct being modified in a manner which he does not.

to F. Hunter (1970):

> [Power describes] the acts of men going about the business of moving other men to act in relation to themselves or in relation to organic or inorganic things.

to R. N. Adams (1977):

> [Power refers to] the ability of a person or social unit to influence the conduct and decision-making of another through the control over energetic forms in the latter's environment.

What is perhaps missing from these writings is an (existential) appreciation that, analogous to the way language as inner-directed and intra-individual may be seen to precede external vocalization (Steiner 1978), perhaps the first and paradigmatic relationship in the exercise of power concerns individuals' relations with themselves. Before changing relations with other 'organic and inorganic things' – 'influencing or modifying the decision-making or conduct of other individuals or groups in a social relationship' – an exercising of power effects changes by individuals within themselves: an interpretation of the world, or an ironic displacement (cf. Rapport 1997a: 30–42). Emanating from within themselves, 'power' might then be said paradigmatically to describe relations between two or more distinct states of consciousness or embodiment – a before and an after, a potentiality and a consummation – within the individual.

On this view, the individual body becomes the original site of that 'liminal interface or contact zone' (Leach) between two states of being, also that 'overcoming of resistance' to change (Weber), and the 'causation' of a 'modification' to awareness and behaviour (Anderson/Tawney). Here is the first 'moving' of individual selves – relative to themselves; the imposing of will – upon themselves; the coordinating of effort (Hunter). Here is that 'controlling' of 'energies' whereby the exercising of power leads individuals to having an effect on others (Adams). In other words, fundamental to our understanding of power might be an appreciation of those processes of drive and assimilation, of progression, whereby individuals effect a change to themselves: to their conscious senses of self and world, to their activity-in-the-world, to the personal sensorium that is themselves.

Putting this another way, the exercise of power may well engender a relationship, but this relationship is of two, possibly very different, kinds: with individuals' own selves and with others. The former, I would argue, is paradigmatic: it may proceed without the latter but not the other way around (an individual may concentrate wholly upon self-control, and impact upon others not at all or only indirectly). To engage with others, indeed, and seek to wield power over them is epiphenomenal upon that prior relationship an individual has with himself or herself; only as a self, active in the world in an ongoing accruing of meaning and identity, does an individual construe otherness and relate, consciously and intentionally, to other things-in-the-world.

Rather than the simple proposition, then, that power entails a relationship between individuals, a number of continua suggest themselves: between those who seek to use others as a way of exercising their power, and those who only use themselves; between those who would use others in such a way that it would become impossible for these others to use themselves, and those who would use others in such tangential or accidental ways that it neither assisted nor even affected their use of themselves; between those who used others in ways these others can understand, and those whose use of others is, even must be, incomprehensible or unknown to the latter; between those whose would-be use of others is modelled upon their use of themselves, and those whose use bears no relation or is diametrically opposed; and so on. In short, individuals may wield power over themselves – in the advance of their ideas, or their sensibilities, or their strength – quite autonomously: with effects quite distinct and in manners quite different from attempts to advance their contemporary reputation, say, or their economic wealth or that of their retinue, by wielding power over others. Indeed, the relationship between individuals' effecting of power over themselves – directing themselves – and their affecting of others cannot be easily specified or determined, as I have suggested. There is no logic intrinsic to the effects energetic things-in-the-world have upon one another: their relationship takes no *necessary* form, and its significance is a matter of interpretation.

For this reason, too, it is necessary, phenomenally and analytically, to treat the power of the individual on the one hand, and the relationships to which that power gives rise on the other – both within the individual body and without – as distinct (cf. Helms 1993). The power of existence precedes the relations in the world to which it gives rise. In structuralist or poststructuralist theorizing, as we have seen, these distinctions – between power, agents and relationships – are dissolved; individuals, 'dividuals', role-players and persons, as culture-members, are who and what they are, possess the intrinsic natures and inhabit the life-courses they do, due to the characteristics elicited in them through their relationships: they are the sum of their social relations. In an Existentialist construal, individual power is ontologically prior to its effects, distinct from the 'essences' of identity, relationship and change it creates.

This is not to take issue with Batesonian dicta (1973) that, 'things are appearances', and 'things are epiphenomena of the relations between them'; rather it is to insist (as does Bateson) that it is the 'energy sources' of individual physical organisms which possess the intrinsic power responsible for construing relationships and perceiving things in the first place. The things and relationships which are constructed in this way will be many and varied, and will be ongoing – things and relationships will come and go – but the exercise of individual power that goes into their making will keep existing. In Sartrean terms again, being and power remain constant even as the 'becoming' of things, and their relations, change. For this reason too, as with forms and their contents, things and relations should never be confused or conflated with the energy (the force, the will) behind them, with the power that speaks through them. Through particular forms of things and relationships, individuals have the power to express and effect any number of states of affairs – to make any kind of sense – and to cause ongoing changes in these.

Power as constant and fluid

Power, we have heard from Emerson (1981: 152), pertains to movement and transition: from a past to a new state, from a potentiality to a consummation. And power, I have just now concluded, is an attribute of individual being – an energy, a drive – which is constant even as the outward forms of things and relations to which it gives rise change. There is at once, then, a constancy to power *and* a diversity and fluidity concerning its effects.

These contrasts – between the 'being' of power and the 'becomings' of identities and relations it gives onto – resonate with Leach's counsel concerning the complexity of human behaviour (1954: 13). Rather than seek to conceptualize behaviour in terms of discrete types, he advised – 'ritualistic' as against 'political' as against 'familistic', and so on – regard it at once as a living complex, a polythetic whole (cf. Wolf 2001: 384). Individuals approach this whole (whether as protagonists or observers) differently at different moments, interpreting, classifying and weighing according to their diverse interests and will. Experientially, something becomes 'ritual behaviour', or 'political behaviour' and so on, when it is accorded this formal appellation for the purpose of characterizing a certain behavioural expression, a certain context of social exchange, towards certain ends (cf. Epstein 1968: 53; Cohen 1974: 33–4). Analytically, however, one might say that all behaviour is one: embodiment of an existential drive to make sense and maintain individual-plus-environment.

'Power', equally, might be seen less as a particular kind of behaviour than as an aspect of all behaviour. Power is present in all self-expression and all social interaction because power, as Nietzsche would have put it, is a manifestation of that life-force – the 'will-to-power' (1968) – which all individual beings possess, driving them towards construction of a livable environment and towards self-determination within it. The circumstantial characterization ('ritual power', 'economic power', and so on) changes in accordance with the individual definition of context, but power ultimately expresses an underlying energy by which individuals effect a relation between different moments of being.

An emphasis on the constancy of power and the fluidity of its effects on identity and relationships has other social-scientific implications. First, the distinction between 'power' and 'authority' remains intrinsically ambiguous, a matter never likely to be free from contestation. 'Authority' may be defined as power which is exercised, first, in a politico-legal context, and second, in a manner interpreted to be legitimate (Weber 1946). But so much here is contingent that Geertz, for one, would eschew the term 'authority' completely: 'all politics is quarrel', he concludes, 'and power is the ordering such quarrel sorts out' (Geertz 1995: 39; cf. Moore 1958: 9). Maurice Bloch imagines (1997: 80–1) a gradational relationship between power and authority, and something set in train for strategic purposes; by institutionalizing power and 'ritualizing' communication in an 'alternative code' of role and rank, as if the expression of a functionary, the reality of power's particularizing and partializing function is obfuscated, impersonalized and safeguarded. (Recognition of these contingencies avoids the definitional tautologies in which Beteille (1965), for example, becomes caught, where power is said to be consequent upon a structure of institutional office-holding, while authority is power wielded legitimately within an institutional framework.)

Second, the relationship between power-cum-authority and social structures, whether hierarchical or equalitarian, can be expected to be complex and variable; there is, to repeat, no neat homology between power relations on the one hand and formal or institutional relations on the other, no way to collapse the distinction or elide the two. Power is a kind of existential content whose relationship with conventional cultural forms is variable, unpredictable, and not a matter of logic. A stable social structure does not evince a necessarily stable structure of relations of power-cum-authority, then, nor a single social structure necessarily become homologous with a single fount of social or political power. A surface of institutional routine may disguise a fluidity of lived effects: ongoing contestation, negotiation, accommodation, between any number of exercisings of power, both within individuals and between them (cf. Bachrach and Baratz 1968; Cheater 1999: 2–6).

In short, nothing categorical can be assumed about socio-political power in any particular structure of social relations; the distribution of power need not be a permanent feature of social relations nor reflected in social-structural forms (cf. Polsby 1968; Marx 1990: 6–7). The fluidity of power and its relationship to the conventional-cum-institutional is such that at different moments and in different contexts of interpretation, its effects according to the individuals who compose the society are unpredictable. Affixing power to institutional form is 'an erratic process', in Abner Cohen's phrasing (1974: 31), and a contingent one. All that can be presumed is power's existential constancy.

Power as experiential

In phenomenological vein, Dewey argued against reducing lived experiences to causal principles of which the subject was not aware; 'things are what they are experienced to be', he counselled, and the truth consists in 'the meaning that is experienced'. Nor is there any justification in looking behind experienced phenomena for, as Goethe put it, in human life '[phenomena] themselves are the truth' (cited in Dewey 1981–90). This seems to me as possibly true for the effects of power as for anything else. Power is a matter of personal experience: the experience whereby individuals achieve their aims through the exercise of their will; and the experience whereby individuals feel hindered from doing what they intend, or coerced into doing what they did not intend, due to the will of others. On this view, while, existentially speaking, power may be a constant, the fluidity of its effects translates into something only phenomenally apprised in the eye of the experiencer.

Contrariwise, as we have seen, social science has tended to posit power, its enabling and disabling effects, as intrinsically impersonal, structural. Power is something deriving from, and residing beyond, the conscious individual, belonging to a separate domain of social facts, cultural traditions, discursive practices, epistemic possibilities, unconscious urges, and so on. The life of power, as a reified force, even *sui generis*, follows its own rules and logic, while individual actors serve as conduits, pawns in its unfolding drama.

But there is no such impersonality to power, to my mind, and there are no human experiences which are not personal experiences; what appears as impersonal is simply the personal at a distance – whether physical distance or social (cf. Rapport 1997a: 12–29). Analytically to posit power and control as matters of impersonal forces and institutions, in short, is to obfuscate: to misconstrue power's individual face and inherently personal nature, and to mystify. There are, to repeat, always individuals responsible for the ongoing animation, the working of institutions. In the same way that institutions as such have a social existence only insofar as they continue to be personalized by individuals who use them towards the ends of their own sense-making, within their own world-views, so 'institutional' or 'socio-political' power is the formal logic of the institution put to work and experienced within the context of particular ongoing, momentary, individual lives.

Even when, due to the power of others, individuals feel hindered from doing what they wish or coerced into doing what they do not wish, the experience is a matter of personal interpretation, of 'in order to' not 'because'. Individuals interpret their own oppression, just as they do their freedom. This is the case so long as those who interact with them do not possess murderous or otherwise wholly debilitating intents (a matter returned to in Part III). That is, insofar as one is not limited or coerced by others to the point where no space remains for interpretive work – due to psychological trauma or incapacity, physical injury or death – one is responsible for one's own interpreting.

THE LIFE OF POWER: AN EXISTENTIAL FRAMEWORK

Insofar as one interacts with others in a 'viable' manner, a manner that might feasibly become routine and long-term, then one's experience can be described as self-authored – however seemingly oppressive.

If experience is self-authored – including that of the effects of power – then Fred Bailey goes so far as to argue that all routine relationships between individuals and others should be deemed 'consensual' (1971: 15); the operation of power in a social milieu is always a matter of consent. Even where this translates into a situation of seeming exploitation and 'coercion', the individual remains ultimately in control of his or her actions and reactions, and hence gives their consent to the systemic inequalities which may ensue. For people can be ruled only to the extent that they are willing to accept the exercise of power of others: to follow certain rules of interaction and to perform obeisance to the authoritative patterns of relations and statuses these might bespeak. By granting others obedience, people create, licence (and outwit) their own tyrants.

An oppressive system collapses, meanwhile, when respect for the rules and obeisance to hierarchical relations are systematically refused. What is required to negate others' power-cum-authority, in Richard Tawney's words (1931: 229), is 'to be indifferent to its threats and to prefer other goods to those which it promises'. Excepting those limiting cases where individuals' 'indifference to threat' eventuates in their incapacity any longer to author their own experience (through psychological or physical injury), even authoritarian regimes rest on individual members' consent or cooperation, or at least apathy. Over and against the 'naked power' of the institutional is the 'people's power' not to authorize compliance (Skalnik 1999); over and against the 'material power' of oppression is the 'normative power' of experience and interpretation (Rubinstein 1998: 990).

This line of argument begs the question why people, individually and collectively, should abide by an exercising of power by others which they experience as having deleterious consequences for themselves – which inhibits their own will. Certain classical sociological formulations may be looked to for insight: such as Vilfredo Pareto's (1966) thesis on how people may be induced to do others' bidding 'bureaucratically', *by force* (a 'conservative' means employed by 'rentiers'), or else 'commercially', *by guile* (a 'radical' means employed by 'speculators'); or Talcott Parsons' (1937) argument that people are controlled by way of 'inducements' or 'deterrence', the first representing the positive power of rewards, the second the negative power of sanctions. Combining the two, people may be induced into doing what does not appear to be in their interests by being either forced or tricked into seeing that a chosen course of action chosen by another *is* in their interests; balancing their options, they see this course of action to be the least deleterious and self-abnegatory, the most rewarding, available. The two sociological formulations meet, then, in the phenomenological insight that to analyse the exercising of power by some individuals over others is to have an appreciation for the management of meaning, of people's convictions concerning what is best and true. The issue of the effects of power, of being empowered or disempowered, turns on the nature of conscious experience (cf. Cohen and Rapport 1995). To talk of some individuals achieving their ends seemingly at the expense of others, and to talk of the latter appearing consciously and consensually to maintain their own inferiority in a relationship ('doing what does not appear in their interests'), is to focus attention once more on the relationship between control over individual life and consciousness within it.

A particular interest in this question has been taken by 'ideology' theorists, from Marx (1887), to Gramsci (1971), Althusser (1977) and Bourdieu (1977). Among these writings (and echoing Pareto, above) is the prevalent notion that coercive control – rule by force – which is inexorably exercised by the ruling elite within a socio-political milieu over the rest of the population, is complemented and completed by a cognitive control over subjects' beliefs, opinions, attitudes, values and world-views (cf. Turton 1986: 39–40; Smith 1999). Burdened with a mystifying 'false consciousness', a 'misrecognition', which comes to be instituted by socializing apparatuses such as the family, the school, the worksite, religion and ritual, individuals' attention comes to be diverted from the essential 'infrastructural' mechanisms and features of power and exploitation to inessential 'superstructural' aspects of life which seem natural and inevitable and which may seem, paradoxically, to establish proof of their own power. True insights into power and domination are never gained, because a 'doxic' field of taken-for-granted assumptions and counter-assumptions delimits what can be thought, practised and opposed. The ideology acquires 'hegemony', extending redundantly, indeed, beyond the political sphere to all aspects of life, such that its totalizing effect is likely to be inescapable. It is ideology, in short, that causes the exercise of power by some over others to be taken-for-granted, even colluded with, or else to become invisible (cf. Williams 1963; Eley 1994).

But ideology theory does not stand up to empirical scrutiny. The ethnographic record is rich with case-studies wherein those apparently immersed in oppressive, hegemonic regimes reflect upon, discuss, confront, resist and undermine predominant inequalities, and inscribe their own 'transcripts' of understanding and resistance (Scott 1990: 215). The existence of so-called 'weapons of the weak', of a critical consciousness and ironizing practices, puts paid to notions of self-reproducing social systems (Scott 1985; cf. Vincent 1990: 403–4). Even an institutional milieu as apparently hegemonic and totalizing as, say, the army (Irwin 2002) – an apparently reified social structure, extraneous and autonomous, of arbitrary rules and orders, coercive codes of conduct and systems of value – is something that exists only in and through the generative practices of its individual participants, something worked up in their ongoing encounters. Military reality comes to be 'constituted as a bounded world through interaction in particular situated moments' (Irwin 2002: 77), where seemingly objective conditions – of buildings, uniforms, texts, ranks, titles, forms of speech, bodily activities and movements – are interpreted and negotiated, subjected possibly to a great deal of manipulation. As with institutional reality more generally, it is participating individuals who 'constitute structures, then orient themselves to them as if they had an objective existence prior to and independent of their discourse' (Watson 1991: 75); what appears as constraining may more nearly be understood as an interpretive device.

It is ideology theorists, ironically, who have assumed a hegemonic, elitist perspective in their analyses and failed to appreciate the multiplicities of power, or the shaping of power relations 'from below' (Gledhill (2000: 144). Viewing the seeming exercise of power over the consciousness of another with less partiality and mystification, then (without resorting to the impersonalism of a 'false consciousness'), can an argument be made in terms of 'in order to' motives instead of 'because'? Perhaps by recalling that the personal interpretations of self and world in whose terms individuals act are likely to be shifting and multiple; one should not expect individual consciousness to be singular or consistent or especially coherent even under the 'best' of conditions (cf. Rapport 1993; 1997b). Consequently, there is no saying that all that an individual wants for himself or herself and acts towards achieving, at one particular time or over time, will be consistent or non-contradictory – or obviously 'self-serving'. What seems false consciousness under external ideological sway, may more nearly be understood as the internal effects of a transcendent, self-overcoming imagination – its 'random' effusions (Rapport 2001a) – and an ongoing will-to-power. (If one ought to expect 'self-interest' – the progression of an individual point of view – even in acts of seemingly outright altruism, as Nietzsche urges (1968: 777, 785), then one might expect a version of self-interest in acts of seeming disinterest, even self-denial.)

It is inordinately difficult, in short, to identify what is in someone else's 'best interests' to do, or what they might have done or otherwise intended to do, were it not for the seeming overwriting of a coercive ideology; 'ambiguity', in Bailey's phrasing, 'occurs all the way up and down' political exchange (2001: 13). It would be impossible for the ideology-theorist to assert, from among the contradictory array of interests, intentions and desires of which an individual may hold possession, how that individual would, 'under the best possible conditions', organize a coherent ranking or sequencing of intents, how he or she would act upon this ranking, and how this ranking and acting would come to differ under conditions of ideological hegemony and false consciousness.

All one may say is that people act in terms of their own conceptualizations of the world and their own interpretations of their interests and goals within it. Which brings us back to Dewey: 'things are what they are experienced to be', and power equally so: the so-called hegemonic effects of ideology are in the mind of the interpreter. If the individual does not conceive of them then they do not exist; if the individual does conceive of them then they exist in the way that, and to the extent that, he or she interprets them as existing and takes account of them in his or her life and actions. Even if it can be argued that this 'conceiving and taking account of' is, sequentially speaking, 'consequent upon' the interested actions of others, then, in terms of its significance, the consequence is still of the individual's own making; there is no direct causal or logical link between the two, because there is no saying how the exercise of power of the one will be interpreted and acted upon by the (exercise of power of the) other, no 'necessary' way in which this should occur. Power differentials are 'ironic conditions' rather than 'definitive' ones, inasmuch as their interpretation is indeterminate and never fixed (Torres 1997: 137–8); ideology is never hegemonic because there is always 'an actual plurality' of interpretation (Wolf 1998). This is the case even where it appears that whole societies or groups experience a collective trauma or suffer power differentials, violation or oppression 'together' (Werbner 1991; Tonkin 1992). A plurality of interpretations, a diversity of meanings, come together under the convenient rubric of a common cultural form – in order to fulfil any number of individual motivations (a phenomenon George Devereux called 'ego-syntonism' [1978: 126–9; cf. Rapport 1994b]).

'[T]he capacity to manage meaning', Anthony Cohen and John Comaroff have concluded, 'is perhaps the most valued and valuable resource structuring political life' (1976: 103), and they go on to describe the politics of social life as a contest between individuals publicly to express and propagate their own interpretations of reality (cf. Yelvington 1996: 329). But then to express is not necessarily to propagate, and to formulate is not necessarily to express; and if the management of meaning gives rise to the structure of sociopolitical relations, then such sense-making and managing is initially (mainly?) a matter of individual and private interpretation. Expression of meaning is preceded ontologically by the capacity and proclivity to make meaning, that is, the public life of political exchange being underwritten, sourced, by the private life of interpretation. It is 'the very act of interpretation', as Roy Dilley puts it (1999: 35), which is the 'act of power', and I would continue to lodge power as an existential constant in the personal and private domain, something employed in the constant managing of individual relations in the world.

A key value embodied in a public life of social relations, I shall go on to argue in Part III, involves a securing of that (cognitive) space within which individuals can continue to make sense, and do not suffer the 'nihilistic violence' of having their interpretive capacities nullified (Rapport 2000). Free from the effects or threat of physical force, of physical-cum-psychological incapacity, individuals live out their own meanings.

To the extent that individuals remain focused upon their own life-projects, keeping faith with their own interpretive narratives and world-views, it can be the case that instances of their experiencing the power of others as debilitating, and of themselves as oppressed, are displaced or eschewed. This is the story of Part II.

THE LIFE OF POWER: AN EXISTENTIAL FRAMEWORK

Envoi

Existential power, I have described as a constant energy or force that individuals possess which yet manifests itself in a fluidity of forms and effects. It derives from the individual self and yet is also responsible for that individual's self-overcoming. It creates relationships, yet relationships which are first and foremost between different versions or instantiations of an individual's own self. It is something personally experienced, yet also admits of the possible influence of others. In Part I of this book I have offered an Existential framework compassing individuality, consciousness, world-view, 'in order to' motives, and the life-projects of individual organisms-in-their-environments. Part I has also comprised an 'as-if philosophy', of personal convictions, where individuals are seen to embody subjective phenomenologies, are capable of ironic revaluations, even transcendence, and are responsible for transforming the given nature of the worlds into which they are born into their own imagined and interpreted versions of identity, self and other – even to the extent that the relations they construe are seemingly oppressive.

To what extent does the above as-if portrayal achieve its heuristic potential: point to a convincing account of the driving force behind the complexity, fullness, ambiguity and diversity of the human? Can it truthfully be said that, by way of self-conscious life-projects, individuals exercise an existential power sufficient for them to achieve a control over the sites and perspectives, the processes and passages, to which their lives amount?

In the next part of the book I provide four illustrations of existential power, through the medium of four individual lives: Friedrich Nietzsche's, Ben Glaser's, Rachel Silberstein's, and Stanley Spencer's. As 'ethnographies of the particular' (Abu-Lughod 1991), these biographical portrayals do not share one presentational style. The individuals on whom they focus are known to me in different ways, as I have said, and the details of their lives warrant a different treatment in each case. What I have sought to maintain throughout, however, is an extent of empathetic presence by which I engage with my protagonists. Each narrative aims to put the reader in the position of being able to judge the extent to which it might be true to say that the conscious pursuit of a life-project amounted to this individual acquiring a sense of control over his or her life.

In Part III the style is different again. If one were to accept the four biographies as fitting illustrations of the book's central thesis, then to what extent could these individual cases be treated as paradigmatic? Could Friedrich Nietzsche, Ben Glaser, Rachel Silberstein and Stanley Spencer be taken as Everyperson, acting in Everysituation? What, in particular, of the limits of existential freedom and power, of those situations where acting freely upon interpretations in anything but a severely delimited way risks the individual's physical demise? Where so restrictive a regimen is placed on the individual that their very freedom to interpret may be said to be under threat?

Part III begins with an account of the way individuals may be said to be responsible for the effecting of a personal ecology in which their lives take place. Existential power is an embodied attribute, an energy or force originating in and manifested through physical, individual bodies, and by its use individuals may be found pursuing a life-project in an environment that represents an extension of their sensoria, their subjective phenomenologies, beyond their apparent bodily integuments. Part III ends with these individual bodies-in-their-environments in the nihilistic setting of the concentration- or death-camp. What purchase does the life-project offer *in extremis*, when the existential power of accruing personal environments is threatened by physical negation, in a most total of institutional milieux?

Part II

ILLUSTRATIONS

3
FRIEDRICH NIETZSCHE AND THE WILFULNESS OF POWER-QUANTA

1

His will, however, rising mightily out of the dark abyss of the drives at a very early age, preached to him heroism against his emotional nature, even in regard to pity, and it always sovereignly dominated his world of knowledge, this mighty will of which he says:

'Yes, an uninjurable, unburiable force is in me, something that gallops over rocks: it is called *my Will*. Silently and unchangingly it strides though the years'.

(*Thus Spoke Zarathustra*, p. 135).

Disgust, Nietzsche's disgust with himself as a particular individual, arose again and again....He swallowed painfully. His features were completely contorted with emotion, until they then took on a stony calm. 'I have given him [God] up, I want to make something new, I will not and must not go back. I will perish from my passions, they will cast me back and forth; I am constantly falling apart, but I do not care.' These are his own words from the autumn of 1882!

These are extracts from accounts of Nietzsche by two acquaintances, Resa von Schirnhofer and Ida Overbeck, who recalled their meetings with him, in 1887 and 1883 respectively, during what have come to be known as Nietzsche's 'migrant years' (Gilman 1987: 144–5, 195). This is roughly the period 1870–88, after Nietzsche had reached the high status of Professor of Philology at the University of Basel (aged twenty-four) but almost at once had developed doubts over the possible status of a university as a site either of radical thought or of national ethical-scientific education; hence he had embarked on an increasingly peripatetic lifestyle, moving between university terms at Basel, health cures (from numerous ailments in a sickly constitution) in spa towns, and recreational journeys in the Alps and Italy. He stayed in lodging houses, journeyed and wrote.

More precisely, between 1870 and 1888 Nietzsche's life took the following form (cf. Hollingdale 1965; Stern 1981; Chamberlain 1997):

1870

Nominated full Ordinary Professor of Classical Philology; serves as volunteer medical orderly in Franco-Prussian War; collapses with dysentery and diphtheria after tending casualties at Erlangen for seventy-two hours without break.

1870–1

Applies unsuccessfully for Basel Chair of Philosophy; exhausted and on sick leave from university post; sojourns in Lugano, Naumburg and Leipzig.

1872

Publishes The Birth of Tragedy from the Spirit of Music; *delivers public lectures at Basel, 'On the Future of our Educational Institutes'.*

1873

Publishes Thoughts out of Season (part I); *migraines increase, eyesight worsens.*

1874

Publishes Thoughts out of Season (parts II and III).

1875

Sojourns in Steinabad as cure from migraines and vomiting; sister Elizabeth moves to Basel and sets up home for them both.

1876

Granted long period of sick-leave from university and sojourns in Klingenbrunn, Bex, Genoa, Naples, Sorrento and Ragaz; publishes Thoughts out of Season (part IV); *several old friends marry; his own attempted proposal of marriage fails.*

1877

Resumes teaching at Basel.

1878

Publishes Human, All-too-Human: A Book for Free Spirits, *which is disparaged by friends from whom he feels increasingly estranged; dissolves his Basel household.*

1879

Publishes Assorted Opinions and Maxims; *health deteriorates further with worse migraines and vomiting; resigns Basel Chair and is retired with a pension; sojourns in Schloss Bremgarten, Zurich, St Moritz and Naumburg.*

1880

Publishes The Wanderer and his Shadow; *sojourns in Riva, Naumburg, Bolzano, Venice, Marienbad, Frankfurt, Heidelberg, Locarno, Basel, Stresa, Genoa.*

1881

Publishes Daybreak: Thoughts on Moral Prejudices; *sojourns in Recoaro, Riva, St Moritz, Sils Maria and Genoa.*

1882

Publishes The Joyful Wisdom; *sojourns in Genoa, Messina, Rome, Tautenburg, Naumburg, Leipzig, Basel, Rapallo; falls in love with Lou Salome but is ultimately rejected; rejects other friends such as Paul Ree; plagued with headaches and exhaustion.*

1883

Publishes Thus Spoke Zarathustra: A Book for All and None (parts I and II); *decides to live neither in Germany nor with his mother and sister; sojourns in Genoa, Rome, Sils Maria, Naumburg, Nice.*

1884

Publishes Thus Spoke Zarathustra: A Book for All and None (part III).

1885

Privately publishes Thus Spoke Zarathustra: A Book for All and None (part IV); *sojourns in Venice, Sils Maria, Zurich and Nice; sister Elizabeth marries schoolteacher (and renowned anti-Semite) Bernhard Foerster and moves with him to New Germania (Paraguay) to found an Aryan colony.*

1886

Publishes Beyond Good and Evil; *buys back copyright of his books from his ineffectual publisher and rewrites introductions to most of them; sojourns in Naumburg, Leipzig, Sils Maria, Genoa and Nice.*

1887

Publishes Genealogy of Morals; *begins writing notes for a summation of his philosophy, under the possible title* The Will to Power*(the notes finally being published posthumously in 1914); sojourns in Sils Maria, Venice and Nice.*

1888

Publishes The Case of Wagner: A Musician's Problem; *writes* The Antichrist: A Curse upon Christianity, *also* The Dionysus Dithyrambs, *also* Twilight of the Idols, *also* Ecce Homo *(they remain unpublished at his mental collapse in 1889); sojourns in Nice, Genoa and Turin, Sils Maria; health worsens again; his sister accuses him of only being read by 'riff-raff' and 'smart Jews'; suffers physical breakdown (syphilitic paralysis) in Turin.*

1889

Causes public commotion in Turin (when embraces a beaten carthorse) and is escorted back to university clinic at Basel, thence to a university sanatorium at Jena, and thence to his mother's house at Naumburg.

2

Writing, according to J. P. Stern (1978: 65), was for Nietzsche an all-encompassing and dominating passion; it culminated in the above 'meteoric course' (Stern 1978: 74) of some dozen major works in some sixteen years, but writing was also a favourite practice of Nietzsche's, a pastime, an escape – a means to revalue past and present, to map the future – for most of his life, from his days of early, solitary boyhood on. It was also a grace and a deliverance from colic, migraine and stomach cramps.

Nietzsche's father, a Lutheran Pietist pastor (and, like his mother, from a long line of clergymen) died when Nietzsche was five. The cause of death was recorded as encephalomalacia, or 'softening of the brain', but it is unclear whether this was the result simply of disease or from a fall. Whatever the precise details, it meant Nietzsche was left without a father-figure (until he found, for a while, a surrogate in Richard Wagner; but that was when Nietzsche was already twenty-four, and was to last only some eight years).

By the time Nietzsche entered his teens, he had began to suffer himself from persistent headaches and eye-trouble. These were never to leave him;

they caused him to be absent from school and also from his peer group. But it was also around this time that Nietzsche took up writing in a concerted fashion. He wrote literature and poetry (including a laudation of Byron, of the poet as outlaw-hero), he composed music, and he started keeping a diary in which he reviewed his own scriptural progress.

Notwithstanding his bodily (congenital?) weaknesses, Nietzsche was said to have been a very physical man by nature, enjoying exertion and sport, keen to experiment with his body and diet, and ascertain the conditions of best performance (Chamberlain 1996). Food, sex, music, walking, and 'brainwork' were all tested similarly and the results recorded in diarian form. Moreover, the body's economy was that of the mind, Nietzsche felt, while the life of the body had spiritual consequences too. In this regard Nietzsche looked back to the poet-diplomat-scientist Johann von Goethe (as well as earlier Renaissance figures) and to the 'general economy of the whole' which Goethe endeavoured to practise in his life (the latter becoming, in Nietzsche's estimation, the well-nigh perfect example of a complete person).

But then, having begun, in 1865 (aged twenty-one), accompanying university friends to Leipzig brothels, Nietzsche contracted syphilis in 1867 – a wasting disease, at the time incurable. To this he added diphtheria and dysentery in 1870 during the Franco-Prussian War, as we have heard, and he spent the rest of his life both extremely focused on his bodily states and unable to allay a gradual deterioration. Finally he suffered a physical breakdown in Turin in late 1888, and a mental breakdown shortly thereafter from which he never recovered. He lived on another eleven years but remained incapable of coherent thought (his manner being gentle and childlike).

Completing the outward form of Nietzsche's life, his remaining dates are as follows:

1844

Born 15 October in Roecken, Saxony, and christened Friedrich Wilhelm after the King of Prussia.

1846

Sister (Elizabeth) born.

1848

Brother born.

1850

Brother dies; family (mother, grandmother, two maiden aunts, and the children) moves to Naumburg.

1852–64

Attends private (Protestant) preparatory and boarding schools, with an emphasis on the classics to which he avidly responds.

1864

Matriculates in classical philology and theology at the University of Bonn.

1865

Abandons theology and loses Christian faith; moves to University of Leipzig along with one of his professors.

1867

Publishes philological essays; begins military service as a cavalryman in Prussian artillery regiment; treated for syphilitic infection.

1868

Sustains chest injury (falling from horse) and returns to Leipzig.

1869

Nominated Extraordinary Professor of Classical Philology at the University of Basel; awarded doctorate by Leipzig without examination; applies successfully to be relieved of military duties (and thus to give up Prussian citizenship) but fails to acquire Swiss citizenship; remains stateless for the rest of his life.

1890–1900

After his collapse, nursed by his mother and sister (now returned from Paraguay after suicide of fraudster husband) at Naumburg and, after his mother's death (1897), at Weimar; his sister becomes owner of his copyright and appoints herself his editor and the founder of a 'Nietzsche Archive'.

1900

Dies 25 August, Weimar.

3

Loneliness and sickliness are perhaps the existential permanencies in Nietzsche's life, joined in adulthood by poverty and obscurity. Nevertheless, he possessed a quality of *Machtgefuhl*, as Lesley Chamberlain describes it (1997: 12ff.) – a sense of his own strength or power – coupled with a strong will concerning what he must do with his talents and his time. Moreover, through the effecting of this will there were also feelings of great intellectual joy, of triumph, and of affirmation of the world he made for himself.

Homelessness deepened this sense of self and of becoming. (It also, incidentally, engendered a respect for the non-nationalistic conditions of European Jewry, and the suffering the latter had incurred as a result of Gentile (particularly German) scapegoating: the latter's envy of Jewish 'genius' for 'money and patience, mind and spirituality', for 'extraordinary endurance, courage, subtlety and liberality' [1991: 205–6].) Homeless, jobless, companionless, godless, Nietzsche saw himself becoming the individual stranger-outsider *par excellence*.

Nietzsche's *Machtgefuhl* primarily expressed itself, throughout his life, in and as his writing. He wandered, thought, monitored his bodily and mental states, and wrote (about them). In this writing he sought to transform his experience of pain, to overcome himself: the lonely man transcended by the solitary, questing philosopher-poet. He wrote about the 'revaluation' or 'transvaluation' of all values as a philosophical-cum-poetic potentiality and as a socio-cultural value, and he imagined a transformation of his bodily experiences too. Writing in this way was both necessity and source of strength.

At times, by way of compensation, Nietzsche's writing became pugnacious, ferocious, overtly masculine, even contemptuous and malicious. It was as if his writing was the work of another person entirely: 'I am one thing, my writings are another' (Nietzsche 1979b: 69). In this mood, his heroes became men of battle, of discipline, concentration, purpose and might. At the same time, however, Nietzsche wanted his writing to embody the tensions he felt; so that it might be subtle and metaphoric, its meaning manifold, open-ended and unfixed: 'I am a nuance' (Nietzsche 1979b). Above all he wanted to capture in print both the complexity of his knowledge, and its rootedness in himself: in his life, his bodily experiences. Individual knowledge of the world not only emanated from bodily (including mental) states, Nietzsche believed, but was also contained by bodily states, and yet this was something that philosophical discursi traditionally ignored. All of Western philosophy to date (Christian philosophy, certainly) might be said to have instantiated a misunderstanding of the body and of the role of desire, of sentiment and will, in knowledge. Whereas, in fact, 'there are no philosophies, only philosophers', and every philosophical insight is infused with personal value judgements: philosophical insight is desire made abstract.

Certainly, in the oeuvre he created – even the 'genre' (Chamberlain 1997: 177) – Nietzsche was determined to do justice to individual being-in-the-world. What he personally knew was wholly an emanation of his individual bodily becoming: a complex of emotion, will and spirit, all proceeding contemporaneously, sometimes in alignment with one another, sometimes in opposition, sometimes completely apart. But these were distinct bodily forces, none of which explained or caused another; his body was like a community or a state of struggling forces but only his name, Friedrich Wilhelm Nietzsche, gave the impression (maintained the illusion) of singularity, stasis or self-identity. The forces struggled with one another and with the world beyond the body, and all the time the body as an entity changed (ingested, grew, moved, became diseased, died), its mental and physical states changed, and its knowledge and identity changed.

At the same time as he wanted to do justice to the shifting and contingent nature of an individual's (his) bodily knowing – and give vent to his loneliness, his shyness, his ambition, his morbidity, his weaknesses, his strength of character, his feeling for melodrama, his sense of tragedy, his unworldliness, his insightfulness, his personableness, his impatience – Nietzsche wanted the doing justice to be a form of overcoming, of self-overcoming. To write of the shifting complex of bodily forces and experiences, in their becoming, was, he contended, to gain an overview and a narrative sense of process. In this way one could hope not only to see and know but also to control: to overcome the body, its sickness and needs, to see through the illusions of mental categories, of forms and names imposed on life (at least to see them as illusions), and hence to reevaluate, to 'transvalue', one's existence.

To overcome, transvalue and control one's life in this way Nietzsche set as life's goal. It was an art – *the* art of life – it seemed something extremely difficult for human beings to achieve, though a few had (Goethe *par excellence*), and it was something for which Nietzsche hoped, through his own writings, to pave the way more widely in future. The reason was that self-narration – and hence, self-management – gave onto that rich fullness possible in human life. Managing time, diet, body, desire and lifestyle, acquiring the strength of self-mastery, provided individuals not only with access to their full, embodied selves (to an integrity which Christian moralities had denied), but also access to a fullness of life which they were now in the best possible position (healthy and hungry) to join with.

Fullness, in style and in content, characterizes Nietzsche's scriptural output, to which it is almost time to turn. Neither simply philosophy nor psychology nor history nor poetry nor science, it is an attempt to represent the diversity of an individual's forms of life and the inextricable links between them; it is 'anthropology'.

It is, by turns, perspectival and generalizing, metaphoric and literal, aphoristic and verbose. Above all, it is narrational. It records the self and its experiences, poses questions to the self, offers provisional answers to those questions, and further questions the self to which this new knowledge of the self has given rise. No static resolutions are entertained, however much peace of mind may suffer as a consequence. To systematize and close off the diverse shifting, becoming of the self-in-the-world was merely being weak, and did not give onto real self-knowledge or self-control. Hence Nietzsche worries himself with questions, and examines what his bodily (and mental) states, at different times, stages and moments of his life, tell him about such existential notions as Will, Knowledge, Reality, Appearance, Order, Interpretation, Communication, Power, Objectivity, Singularity, Change and Truth.

4

Lesley Chamberlain, a recent biographer, describes Nietzsche as playing a 'fantastic' game with the world: 'Godless, jobless, wifeless, homeless', *et cetera*, but still feeling that he was in control (1997: 137). He focused very much on his own body and his own words, but he successfully imagined his greatness and consequence thereby, acquiring a powerful means with which to protect himself throughout the passage of his life. In the next nine sections of this chapter (5–13), the contents of Nietzsche's philosophico-poetic argument are examined in some detail – albeit that a sequential sectioning might lend to his oeuvre a surfeit of coherency – before the question of the control over Nietzsche's life which this form of self-consciousness afforded him is returned to in conclusion.

5 Will-to-power

'Will-to-power' represents what might be said to be the foundational concept in Nietzsche's mature philosophy (to the extent that something anti-systemic has one foundation). Here is an ultimate and all-inclusive principle; for Nietzsche, the whole of reality *is* will-to-power:

> Every living thing reaches out as far from itself with its force as it can, and overwhelms what is weaker: thus it takes pleasure in itself.
> (1968: 769)

Every living thing possesses a drive for free expression of itself: a desire to grow, expand and develop. Every 'specific body', as Nietzsche puts it, acts as a 'centre of force', in constant struggle with others, seeking to increase its power at others' expense. Hence the world can be said to consist of a vast aggregation of individual wills to power, a plurality of discrete and separate 'power-quanta', expanding or contracting depending on their overcoming or being overcome by other quanta. But each unit of 'will-to-power', each power quantum, has one existential tendency, one fundamental drive: to increase its power by dominating or assimilating others:

> The 'ego' subdues and kills: it operates like an organic cell: it is a robber and violent. It wants to regenerate itself – pregnancy. It wants to give birth to its god and see all mankind at his feet.
> (1968: 768)

What Nietzsche includes in his conception of 'living thing' or 'specific body' (even 'ego'), moreover, is 'everything' that the world contains, organic and inorganic. Everything is alive in the sense of being constituted out of the fundamental active drive to increase its power. Crystals encompass molecular particles in order to 'be'; liquids compass the energy of gases. Acids attack metals, assimilate their constituents and so 'grow'. Animals assimilate vegetable matter and one another; bacteria break down animal matter. Humans domesticate animals, and also one another; they employ scientific, poetic and moral knowledge in order to further their earthly interests.

The only real differentiation between things in the world is in the quality of their power: in things' ability to assimilate and overpower and control other things, other power-quanta; in the complexity and diversity of things' strategic approaches to dominating other things; in things' ability to make tactical confederacies and contingent alliances with other power-quanta so as to increase their own potential and strength. If inert and live things *are* different – organic as opposed to inorganic, animal as opposed to vegetable, human as opposed to animal (and Nietzsche devotes most of his attention to the organic and the human) – then it is merely in terms of the one and same criterion of the quality of their power – weaker as opposed to stronger.

As the world consists solely of competing power-quanta, so there is no room in this conception for fixed or permanent 'things'; there are no Kantian *noumena*, things-in-themselves, for Nietzsche. In a world of power-quanta, continually struggling with one another for ascendency, aligning and realigning to increase their chances, nothing remains the same between moments of struggle besides the mass of struggling power-quanta. There are no consistent cases, no self-identical objects, no stable facts, no overriding or underlying order; continual transition forbids one to speak of individual things for the 'number' of beings is itself in flux.

Rather than things-in-themselves, single substances or unities, the higher organisms in the world should be conceived of as federations of separate and ultimately antagonistic forces which temporarily exploit their mutual alliance. A human 'individual', for instance, far from being an homogeneous and unified entity, ought to be regarded as a power-constellation. He or she is composed of a plurality of opposed power-quanta, allied and organized in a particular arrangement or 'union' for a while, joining forces, pooling resources and engaging in a common drive for the purpose of a joint increase in power. In the individual human body resides an aggregation of different drives and instincts, affects and urges, orchestrated with more or less longevity and success by such forces as intellect, reason and conscience. These latter domineering forces or ruling passions – whether seeking sex, athletics, learning, drink, moral purity or a combination of these – cause the different power-quanta within the constellation to direct their energies efficaciously, and not against one another, thus keeping the personality and the body intact. Should fragmentation or disruption occur it might be termed 'neurosis' or 'disease', which could be short-lived, chronic or fatal. At the best of times we might describe human thought not as the activity of a 'unified mind' so much as the outcome of tensions and struggles between power-quanta comprising the individual body. However unified we might conventionally conceive of them to be, the human 'ego', 'will', 'thought', 'reason' and 'consciousness' are actually emanations of an aggregation of wills to power – turbulent, multiple, ephemeral – and an aggregation which is 'itself' non-conscious. We are no happily harmonious wholes, certainly; and, ultimately, breakdown is inevitable. The death of the individual occurs and the constellation 'returns' to component parts. The self-identity of the higher organism, in short, is of a tenuous and provisional kind: an issue of tensions between power-quanta, themselves comprising units of power at particular moments of evolution.

The picture of reality that Nietzsche construes is thus a chaotic one. With the will-to-power as the driving force of the world, the motive force of all phenomena, and with an immanent contrariety existing between different power-quanta, tension and antagonism give onto a grand and monumental worldly chaos, characterized by contradiction, ambiguity, paradox, mobility, activity and incessant change. Certainly, will-to-power denies inactivity, inconsequential action and stasis any place:

> [T]he total nature of the world is...to all eternity chaos...in that order, structure, form, beauty, wisdom, and whatever other aesthetic notions we may have, are lacking.
>
> (1960: 109)

Nietzsche's notion of the aesthetic, and the notions of worldly order which we human beings 'may have' (construct), we shall return to later. Suffice it to say for the moment that Nietzsche explains the currency of concepts such as 'order', 'structure', 'form', 'beauty', 'wisdom', also 'things-in-themselves' and static 'being', also 'qualitative' differences between things ('colours', for example, as against merely quantitative differences between light frequencies), as simply useful strategies by particular power-quanta for the further increase of their power. Thing-ness *et al.* may be described as the interpretation, the fiction, of a power-constellation which is in a relationship of competition and opposition with other power-quanta for the purpose of increasing its power. We keep with concepts because of their practical usefulness; we 'acquire knowledge' of the world (conceptualize order in the world in a particular way) as a means of furthering power (1979a). The world, however, remains nothing other than an aggregation of power-relationships.

The notion of a perduring 'I', for instance, of an individual human being having a fixed and substantial centre of intellectual and spiritual gravity, has been of considerable use to human development – playing a central role in the evolution of religious, legal, artistic and scientific discourses, and ramifying into such philosophical (Kantian) notions as there being an enduring substrate beneath the ever-changing 'appearances' of the phenomenal world which thus ensures the latter's continuity and predictability. From the perduring 'I' we also get the philosophies of individualism and socialism, forms of the will-to-power through which there is agitation against existing social order, and validation for escaping that order and replacing it with an alternative one (which makes possible the advancement of different power-quanta).

Likewise, from the perduring 'I' we get an ontology of object-ness and objectivity; if 'I' exist, then other things can be expected to as well with which I might engage. In short, the concept of an 'I' (also of its 'ego', 'mind' and 'consciousness') has been extremely efficacious in increasing human power; this interpretation of the world has successfully helped yoke together a number of disparate forces in human life. 'Individuality' has been indispensable as unifier of an individual's innate complexity, and giving the combined energies of the latter a common name and direction, and integrity has proved a good strategy for increasing the power of all the componential power-quanta involved.

In reality, however, Nietzsche is keen to stress, there are no such objects, only will-to-power. Whatever order we humans (and other power-quanta) see in the world is there by dint of our own projection – which derives from the will-to-power. Ultimately, there is no 'person', no 'I' who interprets; rather, interpreting is a form of the will-to-power which has personal-being-in-the-world as the effect of its interpretation: the human subject is not something given so much as something invented and projected behind what there is, the 'mind' is an aggregation of the activities of power-quanta and their relationships: it has no special ontological status.

All so-called objects, in short, whether material or immaterial, are aspects or manifestations of will-to-power. Will is the principle by which reality is afforded any sustained character. Which also means that for different power-quanta the world is a differently constructed ('interpreted') place, with different pleasures and pains, different orders of things; and as the 'same' power-quantum changes, increasing or decreasing its influence, so does the world it sees, the objects and subjects and qualities it constructs. If one power centre were strong enough, it could mould and structure ('know') the world entirely at its own liberty and against all resistance, constituting all worldly objects from within the domain of its own interpretive activity.

By putting forward the notion of 'will-to-power', finally, Nietzsche hopes to offer a more useful fiction by which now to take all of humankind forward. The old fixities and certainties have served a purpose, but may now be left behind for a more plastic and creative view of reality in which there is nothing behind or beyond the drives of power-quanta – their activities, actions and relations, their will to dominate others, their meeting with, overcoming, and falling prey to resistance.

6 Truth

Nietzsche rejected a correspondence theory of truth – that our language and concepts give us direct access to reality; that there is a correspondence between what we say, think and know and an external world of stable and self-same objects and verities which exist independently of the cognitive processes of their being perceived – in favour of a more Humean view that we impose categories on the world and thus make it intelligible. He also rejected a vulgar positivism – that we can access the world through sensory experience and empirical observation. Our concepts and categories ('cause', 'law', 'freedom', 'subject') he saw as merely convenient fictions, an 'army of metaphors' (1911: 180), for the purpose of communication rather than positivistic explanation; it is not that our *a priori* conceptual judgements are true, but that there is a human need to believe that they are; this increases our feeling of power in the world. Here are human beings furthering their mastery and control over the world, over reality, by employing as a basis for a scheme of behaviour the notion that things are comprehensibly calculable and constant.

At any one time there will exist such humanly comprehended truths, things that come to be taken for granted, but at different times, and at different levels of phylogenetic and ontogenetic development, human beings comprehend very different calculables and constants. Human knowledge develops and changes, in short, as a matter of will-to-power. When religions and philosophies talk about truth, what they are actually construing is the 'will to make being thinkable'. The logic of language and category ought, however, to be divorced from that of reality; for all judgements are interpretations, and all interpretations are made for the sole purpose of increasing power.

Power, as we have seen, plays as close a role to an ontological absolute in Nietzsche's philosophy as anything can. While he shares Hume's view that we are responsible for imposing ideational categories on the world (as does Kant), Nietzsche does not derive these, as does Kant, from an absolute truth. Rather, they derive from our will-to-power; the will-to-power is the condition by which we can formulate a notion of truth – whatever this is for us. Categorial systems, for Nietzsche, were a matter not of right and wrong, of true and false, then, but of authenticity: 'Is this system appropriate for this person, given his or her will-to-power?'. 'Is the belief in this system sanctioned by personal experiences (moral, intellectual, painful) necessary to see its truth?', hence: 'Is this system true or untrue in the person who uttered it?'.

Not only is the will-to-power the condition of a particular truth, but the nature of truth *per se* is a function of power: what is true is what invigorates us (stimulates our intellect) to behave more efficiently in our drive to increase power; what is false depresses us and lessens our capability to master our environments. Hence, each individual power-quantum sets its own standard for determining the truth: as a function of its will-to-power. What is true for different individuals or the same individual at different times is different; the same thing can be true and false in different situations, different circumstances of employment, without there being any real contradiction. Truth is not a property of statements but a function of an individual's activity. 'P' is true and 'q' not if 'p' works and 'q' does not for a particular power-quantum.

In short, since there is no abiding order in the world for our statements and systems and classifications of things to which to correspond, what we take as truths should be seen as creative possibilities: neither descriptions nor explanations of a 'real world' but propositions, illocutions, with instrumental value. Truth concerns the behavioural employment of a proposition; truth is that idea which carries one best between experiences, working securely and simply to provide intellectual and emotional links.

To this extent only, Nietzsche regards the notion of truth as having a human usefulness: the enhancement of power. Truth, even an instrumental or pragmatic version, may be seen to be an 'error', a fiction, an 'illusion' (1911: 180); but it serves its purpose to the extent that it makes human life more endurable. The trick, however, is to remember its fictional nature: that truth is something we do, not discover or possess; that to 'discover' self-identical instances and things is simply to find something which is implicit in our world-view to begin with; that new knowledge is the metaphorical linking, the tracing back, of something strange to something known in order to comprehend the former; and that, hence, 'facts' are to be seen as statements about how our linguistic metaphors relate one to another.

The process of language-formation Nietzsche envisions as a metaphorization of our original sense impressions into images in the brain, followed by a metaphorization of the latter images into words. Language therefore exists at a double remove from sense-data. It is for this reason that language can tell us little about the way things truly are in the world or about actual human experiences. Language is neither a description of reality nor a means of getting to reality. It is a mere system of signs, labels and names which does not correspond to objects in the real world. To label something 'dog', for instance, even to elaborate upon this analytically as 'carnivorous mammal', etc., tells us nothing about the 'true nature' of dogs and does not describe or explain dogs' inner nature. The process merely entails a substitution of metaphors. Thus does Nietzsche give short shrift to all questions of epistemological dualism, of the relationship, and correspondence between words and real world, and the problems that derive from this.

The tragedy, Nietzsche finds, is that we come to stand by the concepts of our language rather than the sense-experiences from which they originally derive. The pre-conceptual sense-experiences are the most real; words, at a double remove from these, are unable to render our thoughts and feelings without translation and transformation, and yet it is by words that we allow ourselves to become imprisoned. The traditional Western search for truth as something unchanging gives onto a mummification of the world: a wrenching of an experience from the ongoing change of the world so as to make facts and natural laws from linguistic-conceptual schemata.

Rules of grammar become equivalent to rules of nature for us. Worse, in fact; we would rather break a leg than break a word or a linguistic habit. Think of our attachment to such linguistic practices as our conceptualizations of: 'subjects' versus 'objects', 'appearance' versus 'reality', the 'will', an 'ego', 'cause' and 'effect', a 'thing'. Thus does linguistic and conceptual petrification transform erstwhile malleable metaphors into rigid and inflexible categorial schemata: human beings' so-called *categories of reason* (1968). Words are taken to represent consistent self-identical objects in the world, when the constantly changing stream of power-quanta actually make a statement referentially obsolete as soon as it is uttered; useful metaphors become crude pre-suppositions which represent obstacles to the creation of more useful, better fictions and interpretations.

In short, experiences are killed when they are made into abiding concepts, facts, truths and statistics. The latter become smug and comfortable parts of our existence, while experiences are robbed of their immediacy and vitality. We say 'fire burns', 'thunder crashes' and 'wind blows' when we should also see that there is no actual thing as fire, thunder or wind as distinct from their effects; these 'things' are the sum of their effects. Equally redundant, then, are the distinctions: subject/object, doer/deed, and thinker/thought. For without 'subjects' there could be no 'objects', and vice-versa; 'objectivity' is a subspecies of the concept 'subjectivity'. Similarly, we should recognize that 'I do' and 'I am' are purely grammatical constructions; we should see that human 'activity', 'essence' and 'existence' are identical – that thinker, thought and object of thought are identical – were it not for their linguistic differentiation (1979c).

While human language has an instrumental utility, then – is indeed part-and-parcel of the human condition – there are better and worse attitudes towards it; and an ironic, voluntaristic, critical or sceptical attitude which recognizes its contingency and constructed, fictional nature (and grants it truthfulness temporarily) is preferable. If the latter attitudinal 'trick' could be learned and recalled, then human language could ever be seen for what it is: an intensely dynamic and creative medium through which to shape and reshape the world which we live in and see. Language only retains its constant potential plasticity and creativity if its illusory nature is recalled.

The best example, to date, of an ironic attitude to truthfulness, Nietzsche feels, is to be found in Western science. Unlike religious metaphysics, science – at least in its non-positivistic guise – is motivated by a willingness fearlessly and impartially and continuously to offend existing pieties in the search for a 'better' (more useful) truth: a more sublime illusion with which to tolerate reality's chaos, a more enabling, empowering set of metaphors through which to construct mastery of a competitive environment. This science gaily accepts that language consists of metaphorical illusions – its own included. It refuses to descend to the tragedy (or farce) of (religious) dogma: to interpretation of the world according to schemata which we then refuse to throw over. To adopt a scientific attitude and method is to repossess ourselves of language as a creative tool, rather than being possessed by it as a static *Weltanschauung*.

In sum, Nietzsche felt that we must choose between a truth that knows itself to be fictional (a sceptical science or a stoic art) and one that masquerades as absolute truth. Truth is a contingent will-to-power, something actively determined, not discovered: we create contingent facts about the world, we are not passive spectators of eternal external verities. To be unjust to ourselves, moreover – to alienate ourselves from our own creation and creative potentials – is to 'disown' the world.

Finally, if it were objected that Nietzsche does indeed conceive of a truth independent of human desires and needs, of thoughts and language, a real order of things that human beings are not free finally to ignore – namely, the fact that 'the world' is transitory, competitive, cruel, contradictory, chaotic and ultimately meaningless, a matter of continuous will-to-power – then Nietzsche would riposte that even the notion of the world as will-to-power is not 'true' in the traditional sense. He offers it merely as a metaphor – another fiction or illusion – more flexible, it is to be hoped, than previous ones, more useful for action, but by no means the only possible 'truth' or the best for everyone. Nietzsche explains how, to be sure, he finds it the best philosophy for his own increase of power, his own fulfilment, but this is not to say that others will or should find it so too, since there is no absolute, unchanging standard for truth. Everything we say about the world is a fiction, even if Nietzsche finds himself saying this in a quasi-philosophical language which contains assumptions of absoluteness, and will probably lead to his words being misconstrued.

Only a philosophy, Nietzsche reiterates, which recognizes the perspectival nature of its own propositions ('there are no facts only interpretations' [1968] – 'and this too is, of course, only interpretation' [1979a]), a philosophy of conscious illusion, with an ironic, an 'aesthetic' view of the constructed nature of human truth, can find itself 'in agreement' with a chaotic reality which has no ultimate nature.

7 Interpretation

Traditional philosophical notions of truth are associated with a stable world order or reality about which true knowledge can be gained: 'facts'. For Nietzsche, as we have seen, the world possesses no underlying structure which is subject to laws and regularities, and nothing in the world has intrinsic features of its own. There are no facts without interpretations – themselves, changing perspectives on an ever-flowing, ever-changing chaotic 'reality'. Independent of interpretation, the world and its things possesses no character. Freed of all relationships with 'subjects', things cease to be 'objects';

if granted features, effects, relevance and conceptualization, the 'objectivity' of things increases. Facts and objects should be seen, in short, as idiosyncratic effects of perception, something 'each person must have his own opinion about' (1994: 286).

Nietzsche prefers to portray the world as if it were a sort of art-work or literary text. As with an artwork, he explains, the world requires reading and interpretation in order to be mastered, understood and made livable. It is interpretation which creates the meanings which might then be attributed to the world's 'text' (which make it a text as such). The world becomes a vast collection of read signs, each 'thing' in it being constituted as a sign through its relations of sameness and difference to other signs. Neither invented nor a thing-in-itself, the world, its character and constituents, is the joint product of exterior causes (power-quanta) and individual interpretation.

Furthermore, with the death of God (as hero and author) the world should no longer be viewed, philosophically, as subject to a single, overarching interpretation – God's will or intention. Rather, as with a literary text, the world can be said to be viably or workably interpreted in vastly different and deeply incompatible ways. There is certainly no singular or objective, absolute or holistic, truth about the world; if the world is made whole, systemic, then this is an interpretive act and choice.

Interpretation, however, is not necessarily or always conscious, deliberate or reflective; nor a simple armchair adventure or imaginative play. For interpretation constitutes engagement in life: a process in which all power-quanta partake. Simple organisms, then, 'interpret' when they divide the world up into edible versus inedible, determining in this way how they will see the world so as to increase their power. Higher organisms realize the world in more complex fashion, with less simple fictions; our various human modes of life and socio-cultural practices can be described in this way as interpretation of the texts of life.

Each perception and interpretation derives from a power-quantum or -quanta, as we have seen, which Nietzsche also refers to as a 'centre of force'. As the fundamental drive in life is the will-to-power, so each centre or unit of power engages in the practice of construing the rest of the world from its own viewpoint: measuring, feeling and forming the world according to its own wilfulness. Each power-quantum is a 'perspective-setting force' (1968), with a tendency to rearrange that which confronts it and to stamp its own impress on what it finds. The world is thus constituted of a mass of active centres of force, each creating different worlds for themselves through their interpretations – creating its own world from its own perspective.

It is for this reason that 'the world' is full of interpretations; 'no [divine] meaning [exists] behind it, but countless meanings' exist within it (1968: 481). Not only will each power-quantum possess its own interpretation (each giving onto a different way of arranging and mastering its relations with the world and hence increasing its power), but complex constellations of power (higher organisms such as human individuals) will contain within them any number of different perspectives, knowledges and truths, each interested in and useful for the increase of power of certain of its quanta, but each also competing with other quanta, and each developing its perceptions as a result of that competition. No reading of the text of life should be seen as final or as complete, therefore; existence represents a palimpsest of fictions which perception and imagination invents, a process of experiencing an endless multiplicity of meanings.

In this way, too, Nietzsche steers between a purely idealist and a materialist position on the human individual. To say, after Descartes, that 'because there are thoughts there must be an *a priori* thinker or subject' is, Nietzsche argues, merely a matter of our grammatical custom: a metaphysical postulate, and tautological to boot. The singularity of a philosophical notion of the subject is unnecessary; and neither thinkers nor thoughts (interpreters or interpreted) need be granted an epistemological absoluteness. Rather, we have thinkers-with-thoughts-in-situations (and similarly desirers-with-desires, rememberers-with-memories, beings-with-states, actors-with-dispositions and -drives).

Notwithstanding, it is the case that each situational thought-about-the-world can be traced back to a power centre, an agent. Why not, then, Nietzsche suggests, conceive of the human individual as a multiplicity of subjects whose interaction and struggle is the basis of our human thought and consciousness (consciousness as an outcome of the tension between power-quanta)? Here is the 'individual' subject as multiplicity, tension and flux – and yet still a site of independent agency. Furthermore, Nietzsche would place a value on this multiplicity. In the same way that he urges a preference for a philosophy which, in recognizing the perspectival, fictional, nature of its own propositions, finds itself 'in agreement' with a chaotic reality which has no ultimate nature, so he feels that embracing and affirming multiplicity might best serve the interests of our will-to-power. Since the world has no character, every view being only one among many, and each power-quantum being bound to see things from its own perspective (creating the world in its own image), so being open to as many as views as possible is the best adaptational strategy – as well as being prepared, in an open fashion, to move between and exchange these views. To remain free, Nietzsche concludes (1979a), is to resist 'enslavement' by a particular current view of the world – whether those of others or one's own.

To recap: the world is a vast uncreated void, whose meaning has been imposed upon it by power-quanta (crystals, acids, sea-anenomies, human individuals, societies) according to their particular interests and needs. There is no way of arriving at the truth of the world-in-itself, for the world is only accessible to perceptions as a 'relation-world' and hence differs (contradictorily, incongruently) according to the perspective of its knowing. 'There is *only* a perspective seeing, *only* a perspective "knowing"' (1973: 3.12), and, Nietzsche is keen to stress, finally, this is *all* there is; it is within this 'determining' perspectivism that life on earth is lived (1994: 'Preface' 6). The perceivers are implicated in their own perceptions, not mere spectators of them. If we compose texts of life as we 'read' (and hence come to 'know') the world, then our readings give onto the text that we read in the future: they have consequences. In this way the readers of the texts become some of its own parts, its own characters, continually engaged in the process of developing the text as they extend their own lives and selves through their reading. Thus, the various interpretations and modes of life contribute to the complexity and multifariousness of the indeterminate object that is 'the world'. Here, Nietzsche concludes, is 'the world as a work of art that gives birth to itself' (1968: 796).

8 The Apollonian and the Dionysian

As a function of the will-to-power, all organic life orders the world – in action, thought and imagination – until it has made of it something it can use, something it can reckon with. Different wills-to-power will reckon or interpret the world in different ways, as we have heard, for each interprets so as to facilitate a power-quantum in a manner most conducive to itself. However, all organic life posits some world-order and continuity as a survival strategy. By interpreting an environment in a particular way, simplifying, structuring and adapting, editing, arranging, generalizing and schematizing it to its needs, an organism, for instance, gains a measure of environmental control. Life, then, is an ongoing process of imposing a superficial, convenient order on a chaotic reality; while the ability to create (invent, form, imagine) is the fundamental capacity of the organic world. Maybe even the inorganic world shares this capacity, only differentiated in terms of the extent to which the capacity is exercised and the speed and flexibility with which impositions of world-order take place. *Homo sapiens* – the 'fantastic animal', the 'architectural genius' (1911: 182) – distinguishes itself, however, as do a number of other higher organisms, by the elaborateness of its creations; while humankind alone employs a particular medium – language – with such special elaboration.

Common to all organic orderings, nevertheless, is what Nietzsche describes as their 'Apollonian' character. Drawing on the mythology of the classical Greek sun-god, Apollo, the patron of poetry and music, Nietzsche implies that all such orderings are, essentially, appearances. By 'Apollonian', Nietzsche refers to the art of making beautiful representations, which includes skills of clarity, individuation, the drawing of sharp edges and boundaries between things, the separating of objects and persons, the distilling of lucid characterizations, and the formulating of neat aphoristic doctrines of truth. The Apollonian, in short, is appearance as distinct from 'reality': the represented, contingent and fictional as opposed to the absolute.

In human terms, by way of linguistic grammar and vocabulary, the ceaseless change and process, and the constant movement of the world, are simplified into subjects and objects; what is actually ever-changing (a complex assemblage of shifting power-aggregations and relations) is given an abiding, self-identical existence.

Two features of this human-linguistic ordering Nietzsche is particularly keen to emphasize: its originality and its necessity. We want a stable predictable world in which to operate for the best furtherance of our power and so we have created one. But this order derives from 'inside ourselves' and not an external source (1911: 183): the world and its objects are a spontaneous projection from within human selves outward. Knowledge is thus a 'poetic' process (from the Greek *poieein*, 'to make'), imposing forms upon a formless, ambiguous reality; the cognitive act is an act of free creation, thought being more a matter of artistry than of rationality. We are, however, inextricably implicated in our knowledge; rather than simply descriptive or explanatory, our knowledge is prescriptive and constructive, an instrument of our power against competing power-quanta and their knowledges. Knowledge can be said to give onto our environment and how we live within it.

The will-to-power is an inherently poetic force wherever it shows itself. Even for lower organisms there exists the creativity of ordering their world, practised even without there being a conscious artist, psychically aware or ego-centric. Whatever the organism, however, an ordering of the world is necessary for continued survival. We cannot avoid living within a framework of Apollonian appearances. This is due to the fact that organic beings with sense organs and conceptual apparatuses find an apprehension and knowledge of complete flux to be impossible; feelings, thoughts and language metaphorize life into *the appearance* of one experience as distinct from another. Appearances become interpretive fictions necessary for life; over against the shifting evanescent world of becoming, an environment of rounded-off being is set up which is foundational of the process of knowledge and acts in the furtherance of our power. Nietzsche counsels (1979a): we must recognize such Apollonian 'untruth as a condition of life'; 'lies [which] are necessary in order to live'. '[W]ithout a constant falsification of the world by means of numbers', humankind could not exist.

What is also necessary, indeed of the greatest importance, is that we human beings remain aware that that is what our orderings of the world are: fictions and appearances. Invented conceptions – 'causality', 'matter', 'reason', 'subjectivity', 'objectivity', 'morality' – have proved indispensable to humankind, but we should never be fooled concerning their universality or absolute factuality. Even religious and numinous presuppositions may be acted upon profitably in certain circumstances: by intelligent and responsible people in full realization of their fictionality. For here are varieties of lies which conceal an unpalatable void at the heart of existence and give faith in life. If and when meaning is needed, human beings can be great liars – and great artists. Just so long as they do not mistake their lies for absolute truth (or posit the possible or necessary existence of such truth); human beings should guard against being taken in by their own sophistry.

'Causality', for instance, is a useful means of interpreting new or unfamiliar experiences in terms of past ones: a reassuring route to controlling the environment, its present and future, by claiming that nothing is fortuitous or arbitrary. But it should at the same time be recalled that construing separate agents and activities entails falsifying the dynamic continua of life. To separate cause from effect by 'activity' and 'motion' and so compel fluid experience into distinguishable and manageable shape, is a fiction imposed on the world.

Or again, we live in a world composed of a dizzying multitude and maze of centres of force: particles vibrating at astronomical frequencies having no qualities we could possibly recognize. Notwithstanding, from this vague mass of swirling atoms and sub-atoms, continually organizing and reorganizing themselves into contingent power-quanta and constellations, we construe reassuringly solid 'objects' for our experience. We usefully model particles as billiard balls, if not as clouds of energy with statistically predictable points of charge; and these then give onto the 'tables' and 'chairs' of our everyday existence. We need unities and self-identical 'things' in order to reckon with our environment – modelling an idea of thinghood on our ego-concept, an ancient article of our faith. But, again: this is not to say that they exist:

> We set up a word at the point at which our ignorance begins, at which we can see no further, e.g., the word 'I', the word 'do', the word 'suffer': – these are perhaps the horizon of our knowledge, but not 'truths'.
>
> (1968: 482)

When ordering fictions are erroneously posited as absolutely real, indeed, Nietzsche felt them to be the cause of enormous harm in human life. For, to become convinced of absolute truth is to become less adventurous and creative; while to accept change, contradiction, contrast and danger in one's life, to remember always the fictional, apparent and contingent nature of one's foundational orderings of the world, is to afford oneself a constant stimulant to increased power and the enhancement of life: to attune oneself to the inherent flux of wills-to-power.

The ironic attitude of realizing that our human orderings of the world – that any orderings or interpretations – are but Apollonian fictions and appearances, Nietzsche calls a Dionysian attitude, after the classical Greek god of wine and intoxication (1967). Here, in the way that one 'lost one's senses' through being intoxicated with wine, Nietzsche envisaged an overcoming of the appearance of order, individuation and classification in the world, and an acceding to, a merging of oneself with, a deeper, formless, fluxional reality. In the Dionysian, Nietzsche provides an image of humankind momentarily confronting reality rather than constructing an appearance of beautiful (or at least orderly) things, and so recognizing that life was at base nothing but will-to-power, eternally destructive of any solid, individual thing-in-itself.

In classical Greece there was an appreciation that Dionysian reality must be entered into with maturity and self-respect by human beings if they were not to risk being destroyed by this reality – being made nihilistic if not mad. Hence the Greeks reserved doses of the Dionysian 'bacchanal' (*Bakchos* being the Greek form of the Latin Dionysus) for particular festive occasions. But they were adamant on the need to forge the Dionysian and the Apollonian together. And Nietzsche is too. In the juxtaposition of the gifts of Dionysus against those of Apollo is to be found the most fruitful way for human beings to live; far better than adopting one god alone. For while Apollo provided the beautiful illusion that life was meaningful, orderly, progressive and worth living, that there could be trust, love and rest for the individual, Dionysus offered the overpowering and intoxicating brew wherein the individual became a contingent part of the excessive whole. While Apollo presented life in a reliable way, Dionysus forced an awareness of the indiscriminate, anomic, eternally changing face of the will-to-power.

Nietzsche felt that it was the insistence in classical Greece on the Apollonian-plus-the-Dionysian, on a celebration of the provisional nature of human world-views and values, which created the classical environment of buoyant vitality and aesthetic sublimity. He felt that the Greek interpretation of life was the best so far conceived for enriching, strengthening and inspiring human life: the best fiction for enabling human survival and the increase of power. And it might be so again, in our present, post-Darwinian epoch.

By and large, however, Nietzsche finds the world today under the sway of inferior fictions – both scientific and supernatural – which fetishize conventional form over content, complexity and contradiction, and are ultimately sterile. They label and analyse the world but they do not seek to create anything original. They petrify the world, reducing its ambiguities and contradictions, its flux, and so removing from our appreciation a major stimulant to our cognitive growth. Indeed, when form, order and harmony come to be imposed on the turbulent, flexible creativity of the will-to-power, on the inherent chaos of the world, then Nietzsche can but describe it as a tragedy, something which threatens to rob us of our unlimited potential as a species and keeps us all-too-human. Only a weak will-to-power would demand that the world be stable and consistent and unambiguous: that the simple, reliable and predictable be 'true'.

In short, contemporary conceptions of the world, whether rational or religious, material or metaphysical, Nietzsche finds inferior to the classical because the desire to create a world of timeless truths is itself a sign of weakness. Ultimately, of course, it is not a question of truth value but of power value, and Nietzsche feels that a strong world interpretation should now lead humankind forward; to recognize complexity and contradiction, to interpret (and keep reinterpreting) these into manageable environments calls for strong will-to-power – and humankind should not measure itself in terms of the weak.

9 Tragic art

Nietzsche was intent upon a world-view which would take account of what he called 'the general economy of the whole', as we have heard. He sought an appreciation of the rich and awesome abundance of life on earth in which he includes pleasure, love, joy, happiness, suffering, cruelty, pain, violence and contradiction. There were a number of reasons behind this calling. First, Nietzsche felt that such an appreciation would put humankind more in touch with the ultimate nature of 'reality'. There was no final aim or purpose to history or the universe, no underlying meaning or plan, no overarching goodness or harmony, only eternal indifference; to deny or attempt to obviate this was somehow to devalue the wholeness of sensual, vital, life on earth, and also to deny and devalue oneself, as a creature of the earth, and the entirety of one's sensual experiences thereon.

What was important, Nietzsche felt, was a comprehension of the real variegated nature of the human sensorium, and the way in which all experience has a part to play in the furtherance of the will-to-power and the preservation of the species. Instead of denial and devaluation of the wholeness of earthly experience there should be an attempt at transformation, a continual 'transvaluation':

> [R]*emain true to the earth*, and do not believe those who speak to you of superterrestrial hopes!
>
> (1980: 42)

Life should entail transforming everything we seem – including suffering and pain – into 'light and flame'. There may be no escape from the predicament that is the human condition; it may be impossible to establish concord and justice on earth, politics may not ameliorate suffering, and knowledge may not penetrate being and improve or correct life. Nonetheless, if we appreciate that (due to the flux of will-to-power) everything on earth is connected and everything comes about 'in spite of' – 'all things are entangled, ensnared, enamoured' (1980) – then even the experience of pain may afford humankind the deepest insights. Coming to terms with the 'general economy of the whole' on earth may not make us better people, but it is sure to make us more profound ones, able to affirm whatever we might experience, affirm the world's woes as well as its joys.

The necessary attitude to adopt is one Nietzsche terms a 'tragic pessimism of strength': being prepared to view the indifference of the world, its merciless forces, aesthetically, as a spectacle. In the absence of God, a sense of the tragic can redeem the world, transmuting a fateful despair into the bliss of ultimate acceptance. Even in a cruel world devoid of final purposes, a pessimism of strength may lead to affirmation, not to say gratitude, energy, wisdom, courage – and transcendence.

The attitudes of his contemporaries, however, Nietzsche finds to be very different, doomed to fail. They inevitably produce nihilism, born out of alienation and anomy, out of a disjunction between experience of the world and the concepts at hand to interpret it. On the one hand, there is the (Christian) religious world-view which emasculates humanity by way of a sentimental flight from a serious appraisal of the earth and humankind's potential on it. It breeds small people with small virtues, disguising in a vaunted 'love of one's neighbour' a love for the cosily known, the present and oneself. On the other hand is scientific positivism which ascetically denies most of the affects of a sensual reality, which preposterously claims for itself a method applicable to all ambiguities; seriously devaluing the human capacity for irony, parody and play, positivism proposes a single, stagnant truth which disguises how its origins lie in a mythic world-view properly exultant of the free play of imagination and experimentation. When examined more closely, indeed, the Christian and the positivistic are hardly even alternatives: the will to singular truth of the latter is a mere derivative of the emphasis on confession in the former; while the privileging, in the former, of the real world of the soul over and against the apparent world of the body finds its continuation in the latter's hierarchical division between abstract explanations and complex phenomena (or true *noumena* and the Kantian categorical imperative).

What is called for, Nietzsche pronounces (1967), is a reawakening of that sense of tragedy which animated classical Greek civilization. Above all, humanity would benefit from the tragic *art* of the Greeks, wherein suffering and pain, terror and absurdity are recognized as inevitable, as earthly, and hence rendered intelligible, even welcome. Greek civilization had the intellectual honesty to recognize the economy of the whole, and to integrate the pain of the human condition into the edifice of society and morality; it brought together the Apollonian and the Dionysian, thus transcending 'good' and 'evil' rather than fetishizing a differentiation between them. In this way, Greek art represented a supplement to life of the greatest import, responsible for no less than life's transvaluation.

Tragic art was able to effect this transcendence by way of a number of characteristic effects. Most important, as has been discussed, it dealt with the wholeness of life; it did not hide ugliness, or explain it away (as would religion and morality), rather it portrayed the pathos, the sublimity of suffering (and of struggle, and failure), and the way it was possible to carry on living regardless. Also it provided a vantage point on life beyond that of the narrowly quotidian, particular or personal. It offered a wider order in the narrow chaos, a coherence which might be imbued with meaning and value. Furthermore, in the imposition of meaning and value on the things of the world, tragic art afforded a mastery over reality; by showing humankind to be part of that broader life – its dread and its beauty, a justification was provided for all of experience. Finally, tragic art transfigured the world, creating illusion and deception, so that our experience appeared to accord with our expectations and purpose, to accede to pattern and form. Deceived by art, we overcome a sense of powerlessness and fear in the face of the chaotic world; through its 'lying genius' we become invulnerable to the assaults of reality. Tragic art serves as the supreme means of making life possible: the great seduction into life:

> Truth is ugly. We possess *art* lest we *perish of the truth*.
> (1968: 822)

Tragic art thus nourishes a will in humankind more profound, more primeval, than any other – certainly stronger than the will-to-truth, to keep faith with what 'really' and 'truly' is – namely, the will-to-power, the will to keeping on living. Tragic art acts as the great stimulant of life, overcoming the debilitating effects of looking into the abyss of the human condition: its pain, its meaninglessness. Once it is appreciated that human beings cannot fix in time and make certain their ultimate insights, that human beings do not even share the same insights, knowledge, perspectives, or world-views, nor the same ability or desire to overcome these, then: 'it is only as an *aesthetic phenomenon* that existence and the world are eternally *justified*' (Nietzsche 1967: 5). Only art is powerful enough to construct an illusion which protects humankind from a truth which threatens to destroy its capacity for action.

Tragic art provides a paradigm for all human activity, in short: 'the highest task and the truly metaphysical activity of this life' (1967: 31–2). It is by becoming 'artists of life', 'artists of man', that Nietzsche feels that we human beings can redeem the whole world of experience and at the same time transcend our own positions within it.

10 Overcoming

The relationship between culture and suffering – historical and possible, weakening and empowering – is one of Nietzsche's perennial concerns. He sees suffering as omnipresent; the question is how a cultural morality can best come to terms with it: what table of values best accommodate human suffering within a general economy of human experience as a whole.

In inquiring into a 'genealogy of morals', Nietzsche's first observation concerns the multiplicity of contradictory ways in which different people have sought to cope with suffering. To deal with it in some way seems a human universal, and to do so by way of erecting a table of values, a moral world-view of achievement in the face of adversity, equally so:

> A table of values hangs over every people....Praiseworthy is whatever seems difficult to a people; whatever seems indispensable and difficult

is called good; and whatever liberates even out of the deepest need, the rarest, the most difficult – that they call holy.

(1980: 84)

In the face of suffering, there is a human need to create value in life, to 'esteem'; moreover, Nietzsche emphasizes the facts that values are humanly created, there being no inherent values in the world to discover or reveal. Indeed, evaluating or esteeming, Nietzsche finds to be the greatest thing:

To evaluate is to create.... Through evaluating alone is there value: and without evaluating the nut of existence would be hollow.

(1980: 85)

Human life depends upon a 'necessary vigilance of evaluation'.

If humankind has always done this – created, esteemed, valued – in the face of suffering, then it has not always known it is doing this. Indeed, it has more often than not explicitly denied that this is what it does, repressing awareness of its own creativity in the name of a tradition, a divinity, a nature, which is worshipped in its stead. What is now of the utmost importance, Nietzsche feels, is a bringing of human creativity to widespread consciousness:

We have to *learn to think differently* – in order at last, perhaps very late on, to attain even more: *to feel differently*.

(1991: 103)

Nietzsche hopes for a general cultural revolution in which humankind will transform its appreciation of language, truth and knowledge, without descending into nihilism (apathy, distrust, fatalism, despair) at the humanly constructed nature of language *et al.*, the latter's underlying contingency and constant change.

What is needed is an appreciation of the way in which humanity creates values, and in which values create the world, as part of a continuous process of contingent interpretations. If the fundamental reality of existence is will-to-power, then as this changes (expanded and contracted; constellated and fragmented) so do the values it propounds in order to comprehend and master the world. All values and ideals can thus be expected to undergo an evolution, beginning as 'lies', becoming 'convictions', ruling as sovereign 'virtues', and being overthrown as 'dogmas'. What is called for, Nietzsche concludes, is a cultural attitude, a morality, which is able to accommodate the nature of life, in its present (Apollonian) dispensation, as always something that will be and should be overcome. The only 'actual *immortality*' in the world is 'that of motion', the eternal return of change (1994: 208); a morality which values its own eternal overcoming will speak with the voice of the will-to-power.

Such an attitude to change might be described as 'greatness' or 'nobility':

> All great things bring about their own destruction through an act of self-overcoming.
>
> (1973)

Greatness entails cultivating oneself, taking risks and making experiments, so as to create something nobler beyond oneself. Instead of being 'the actor of one's own life', one works towards its overcoming – even though such becoming can aim at nothing presently known or esteemed, and can achieve nothing that is not equally mortal in its turn. Never granting oneself psychic security or rest, one constantly achieves new being, thus realizing the constant becoming of the world. Greatness entails the capacity to withstand, absorb and use suffering and pain; putting them to work rather than denying them.

To be great, moreover, is to stand 'beyond good and evil', beyond all the categorial certainties that have been allowed to determine the body of present thought, beyond the present morality of the crowd; to exceed the extant through a creative distrust and to create new norms and rules. As the world has no fixed, final, or necessary form, neither should the individual's own conceptions; one resists the self-tyrant of self-deception and remains critically detached from one's own cherished views. Such greatness, the 'law of self-overcoming', Nietzsche sees as necessary for human life to be lived to its greatest potential. If culture and politics can be said to have a purpose, a utility, then this is it: means to the end of the perpetual self-overcoming of humanity, self-subversion, and the achievement of nobility.

When Nietzsche turns to a consideration of what kind of polity might best be able to promote the cultivation of greatness in humankind, he finds more around him that is dispiriting than encouraging. 'Nations' only benefit royal and commercial dynasties and set false boundaries on the free wanderings of the 'homeless' cosmopolitan mind. 'States' merely cultivate the monstrous tyranny of the majority – public opinion – at the expense of individuality and creativity. ('Socialism' promises, in fact, to be even more despotic than other regimens, demanding more subservience of the citizen to the state, regarding the individual as a mere organ of the community and a luxury. To interfere in individuals' private lives so as to achieve their equality, to abolish private property – the private realm *per se* – involves the use of state power to perpetrate political violence to an unparalleled extent; it threatens individual liberty and its gains in an intolerable way.) Nevertheless, Nietzsche is hopeful. The modern democratic age is characterized by a secularization of political authority – a disappearance of unconditional authority and definitive belief – which spells the end of the tyranny of absolutism and autocracy. Secularization might initiate a period of tolerance, pluralism and wisdom. Thus Nietzsche speaks of the 'good Europeans' of the future (1994: 475), who might transcend nations, states and '-isms', and who, through '[t]rade and industry, books and letters, the way in which all higher culture is shared, the rapid change of house and scenery, the present nomadic life' might become 'entitled to call themselves homeless in a distinct and honourable sense' (1960: 377).

This will be a strong age in which a chasm – of beliefs, of values and interpretations, of selves, of wills to power – will be recognized between person and person. And not just recognized but itself valued as coming closest to an alignment with the underlying nature of eternally contingent reality. A 'pathos of distance' between people will allow the multiplicity of human types to stand out, enable different individuals to be themselves, to experiment with different tables of value; will enable, in short, the true expression of different wills-to-power. This is not to say that many actions labelled moral or immoral today will not be still followed or avoided then, rather that the reasons given for so doing or not doing will be radically different. For morality and value will no longer be based on the false premises of permanency, homogeneity or revelation. Above all, a 'pathos of distance' between people will promote an awareness of the constant potential of humanity, and hence encourage recognition of the possible distance between 'man' and 'overman'.

11 Overman

The eternal truth is that humankind has to live without truth. With the death of God, however, and with Darwin removing the sacredness of humanity, each person, Nietzsche fears, becomes his own enemy. However much people might wish to reform society and themselves (be good socialists or scientists), their deepest striving will nevertheless be informed by a panic-struck determination not to ask themselves the question: 'What is the meaning of our lives?'; as 'the questioning animal', *homo sapiens* cannot but seek such assurance.

While Enlightenment philosophies have thrown over theistic precepts, they have failed to replace the latters' theodicean foundations, either denying the validity of their need or else relying on their being answered by mere 'intuitions'. However, humankind cannot endure this doubt – at the same time hating itself and the world for not enduring it. Alongside any reform and helping of others, then, will likely be terrible nihilism, annihilation and war. Philosophical doctrines will devastate the world with their competing ideologies of non-theistic compensation.

What is needed is a new validating belief and a transfiguration of values:

> He who does not find greatness in God finds it nowhere. He must either deny it or create it.
>
> (1960: 125)

And Nietzsche is certain that humanity needs greatness: that without greatness life not only has no point but no means of inspiring that superlative tragic art through which experience can be mastered.

Hence the vital greatness of the concept of the 'overman'. The overman is what humanity might become if it were to cease taking itself for granted. For humankind to see itself as the meaning and the measure and the value of things is naive, Nietzsche feels. Rather, '[m]an is the animal whose nature has not yet been fixed', and 'man is something that should be overcome' (1979a: 62). Instead of a narrow focus (a 'weak' and presentist interpretation) which places the human condition at the centre of a viewing of the universe, imagine the overman.

In the overman, Nietzsche portrays he or she who will live the agonies of earthly existence and forever transmute them into the Dionysian rapture of tragic acceptance. And while for humankind Dionysian delight must remain a temporary intoxication, an episodic narcotic against disgust – whether in the form of tragic art, or music, or mysticism, or hero-worship, or fanaticism – the overman will be possessed of a new kind of psychic health which can accommodate at one and the same time a perfect self-knowledge *and* perfect self-transcendence. Through possessing the will-power eternally to overcome that which is, the overman will be 'Lord of the Earth'. Humankind, as is, must suffer for its (Apollonian) individuation of the world. The world of individual persons and things is a lonely, combative, 'evil' one of strife, and individual identity is a painful burden; while Dionysian oneness spells the death of sensible being. In the overman, however, can be imagined that which is strong enough to compel the Apollonian world of individuation into oneness by organizing the universe entirely around itself, making itself the entire world. The overman will make his or her arbitrary existence into a work of art which will encompass and give meaning to the entire world. So strong is the overman's imagination that he or she transcends all human limitations of presenthood (self, society, language, morality) and achieves a condition of real freedom. To 'recognize the lie as a lie', to accept unequivocally the 'death of God' (1980), is something which only an attitude of greatness might achieve, and this is the great capability of an overman.

Nietzsche regarded his notion (image and trope) of the overman as his special gift to humanity. It offers a purpose to life on earth – once it is universally recognized that God is dead and that the will-to-power is the cause of eternal earthly contingency and flux. '[M]an is a rope, tied between the animal and overman' and 'what may be loved in man is that he is a transition' (1980: 58–63). 'Man is the creature who must constantly overcome himself to live fully', and the overman can certainly be something 'bred, willed and attained' by humanity in future.

The route to the overman of the future is through present individuality. Humankind must work continually to produce 'great individual human beings'; this 'and nothing else' is its task (1997: 161). It is certainly a fundamental error to place the society or group over and above the single individual in value, or to conceive of the group as an individual in itself. Only individual agents, centres of force, possess that explosive energy, stored up inside them, which might be sent forth into the world and so subject the latter to their individual will.

Finally, if the overman represents a future goal, then Nietzsche feels, nonetheless, that in certain past figures (even recently past) humanity has been afforded important precedents. Johann von Goethe, Napoleon Bonaparte, Ludwig van Beethoven, Stendhal, Heinrich Heine, Arthur Schopenhauer: taking their lives in their own hands, these individuals freed themselves from overdetermining histories and conventions. They overcame their cultural and otherwise circumstantial specificities and achieved a self-definition independent of their time, nation, class, age, society, environment, *Zeitgeist*, whatever. If their lives had meaning, then here was meaning which they and they alone had granted those lives, a meaning, moreover, which was not relative but transcendent. Their existence became a result of their conscious, subjective will (not anonymous external forces); they displayed an individuality distinct from any predominant conventions regarding the individual. Coming to occupy the centre of their own world, they became the measure of themselves.

Only 'strong personalities' might thus 'endure history', pitting themselves against the 'blind power of the actual' (1957). The overriding value of such individuals, to their own age and to every human age, was their overcoming of their age, and hence their representation of human potential fully realized; they became truly human by instantiating values which transcended the present. These 'highest specimens' of humanity, conferring value and meaning on people and events around them which in themselves had none, made the meaning of the world a function of their own taste. Thus they pointed the way to images of future greatness.

12 Individuality

Nietzsche takes the case of the strong individual of the past – the 'Goethe' figure who increased his power by creating and projecting new values and environing conditions, thus making his existence bigger, richer and more sublime – as precedent not only for the overman but also for what any individual human being might presently set out to achieve in his or her life.

Nietzsche places great significance in, and store by, the 'single' creature. In part this is due to its contingency: the chance of its birth out of the temporary coming-together of any number of discrete power-quanta; and the uniqueness of its own power to perceive and marshall the world in a certain way:

> The individual is something quite new which creates new things, something absolute; all his acts are entirely his own.
>
> (1968: 767)

Individuals derive the value of their acts from themselves because they can but interpret in a quite individual way everything they perceive. This applies even to the conventional grammatical forms and words which human individuals inherit in their languages:

> [The individual's] interpretation of a formula at least is personal, even if he does not create a formula: as an interpreter he is still creative.
> (1968: 767)

Paradoxically, the contingency of individuality also instantiates an eternality. In individuality one witnesses an eternal return of the same on earth; eternally the world comprises power-quanta and their constellations making individual interpretations − constructions of the earth so as to further their particular wills-to-power. Hence individuals are precious because: 'every single creature constitutes the entire process [of the becoming of the world] in its entire course' (1968: 785).

Moreover, Nietzsche would have every human individual become aware of this, and set out to achieve something particular and special in their lives − as warrants the individuality of those lives. He would have people stand beyond any one cultural-cum-moral interpretive schema and, as cultural critics, as 'anthropologists' (Tanner 1994: 63), survey the whole human scene. Indeed, it is in terms of such 'individuality' that Nietzsche would index the extent to which a person may be said to be fully human, free and alive.

The project seems to Nietzsche a timely one, furthermore. With the death of God, there is the chance to broaden the realization of human potential and control of life on earth. Now that the will of God as external authority and source of order has failed, the inherent meaninglessness and instability of the world might inspire us as individuals continually to create and recreate more satisfactory, rational, scientific realities for ourselves. Through (albeit) supreme assertions of individual will − through 'your reason, your image, your will, your love' (1980) − the world can be rendered an intelligible phenomenon, a coherent order of things, centring on the individual alone. All that is needed, Nietzsche feels, is for people to cease 'taking themselves easily'.

The place to begin is with oneself: with one's attitude towards oneself, one's recognition of oneself, of one's contingency and one's potential power. More precisely, the place to begin is with an interior attitude, an ego focus, with an appreciation of interiority:

> Beneath thy thought and feelings there is a mighty Lord, an unknown sage; it is called the self; it dwells in your body.
> (1980)

Nietzsche gives this attitude a name: he calls it a 'master morality', and he describes it in terms of explicit contrast with a morality of 'slavishness' or weakness; where the master is 'authentic', the slave 'resents'. Masters exteriorize their world on the environment; the direction of their will-to-power is from inside to outside. Masters devise their own virtues and categorial imperatives; they possess their own measure of value and, without guilt, and they posit this value from the centre of themselves upon the outside world. Masters act as independent agents with a will to self-expression and self-responsibility. They affirm themselves in their own uniqueness, and the world which their uniqueness gives onto.

Whereas masters act upon a world, slavishness essentially entails reaction to a world created by others – a hostile world, therefore, since it is constructed in others' image and interests. It is for this reason that a slave morality bases itself on resentment: on first saying 'No' to what is outside and different to itself as a means latterly to say 'Yes' to itself. Slave morality needs external stimuli in order to act; it begins by looking outward instead of inward to itself. Turned in on themselves, slaves develop 'bad consciences' as replacements for their authentic, or 'true', potential selves; the selves they do develop are merely reactions to other'. There is slavishness, Nietzsche concludes, in Christian meekness and humility, and slavishness also in a Marxian and socialist fetishizing of class exploitation and the dialectic of history.

To become 'what one is', first, then, is to liberate oneself from resentment; true selfhood calls for self-affirmation not the negation of others. One must also liberate oneself from historical ties, recognizing one's potential dominion over time; a true master morality is grounded in a willingness to separate oneself from the past (one's own and that of others). Rather than honouring the past, the authentic individual practises an 'innocent semi-forgetfulness' in regard to the past, and balances this against historical knowledge so as to be fully creative. He or she strives heroically to resist both the flux of time and its habitual process, and thereby attain his or her own moment of eternity and imperishability; so that while the slave 'honours his parents' and their traditions, the master achieves individual excellence. In sum, masterful individuals redeem the past by reinterpreting all 'it was' into 'thus I willed it' (Nietzsche 1980). They affirm all time, as if it were the responsibility of their own individual acts of will, and so endow the whole with their own meaning.

To become 'what one is', furthermore, and to be in full (masterful) possession of oneself, is for individuals to become an orderly, 'stylish' world unto themselves:

> To give 'style' to one's character – a great and rare art! It is practised by those who survey all the strengths and weaknesses of their nature and then fit them into an artistic plan until every one of them appears as art and reason, and even weaknesses delight the eye.
> (1960: 290)

Style involves individuals becoming the artists of their own lives, transforming the givenness of what preceded them – time, culture, creativeness, abundance – into a dynamic figure. Through hard work and long practice, individuals transcend themselves, adding another nature and removing an earlier one; they subordinate their creatureness to their creativeness and consciousness; they free themselves from blind impulses; they obviate a chaos of potentiality through a creative giving of names to unnamed things; they hide ugliness in their lives or reinterpret it as sublimity, connecting up disparate, embarrassing or humiliating experiences into a larger schema, and focusing experiences which could lead to self-loathing or disintegration upon an exonerating circumstance; and they maintain a longsightedness with regard to themselves so that their lives can be viewed in terms of a distant horizon, beckoning them towards the immeasurable and the far:

> In the end, when the work is finished, it becomes evident how the constraint of a single taste governed and formed everything large and small.
>
> (1960: 290)

Nor is 'constraint' a merely rhetorical choice of Nietzsche's here; for, it is in opposition to oneself, above all, that one achieves a higher unity in style. One's intellect is strained by difficult, problematic, frightening and paradoxical thoughts, and one's affect by painful feelings; in all cases it is by acting 'in spite of', pushing beyond limits and overcoming resistance, that one becomes stronger and more developed, more stylish, characterful and free. Freedom (individuality), Nietzsche concludes, can be measured according to the resistance to one's individual expression (in oneself and in others) which one overcomes. Not to overcome obstacles to individual style is tantamount to arresting one's development, stopping looking for one's truth, and ultimately failing to realize one's potential to become more than one is.

To give individual style to one's character in this way – to become 'the poet of one's life' (1960), first of all in the smallest, most everyday and private matters and then in the biggest and most public – is, finally, to admit to oneself the constructed nature of the self, also its plurality and ambiguity. And from becoming an orderly world unto oneself, it is a feasible step to the individual making the rest of the world artistic and orderly in his or her image. Since the existence of things is a function of their perception, the creation of oneself as a work of art is also a means of creating an aesthetic world: as a reflection of one's own style and dynamic logic. As one has disciplined one's own individual fragments into an ideal formal whole, so might the world come to have beauty, unity and order. Thus do the artistry of the self and the world interweave – and continue to do so. Through the activity of self-artistry, self-mastery, individuals have a means for the continual assertion of their personality and mastery of experience; through maintaining the integrity of their individual identity, they possess the power to order a meaningless, formless, valueless and chaotic existence which otherwise, at every moment, threatens their individual obliteration.

In the 'Goethean' figure of the overman, ultimately, Nietzsche prescribes an ideal, individual-moral way of life. Organizing and mobilizing a diversity of impulses, interests and productions, redeeming each loathsome particular by uniting them into a dynamic whole which negates nothing, individuals can achieve integrity. Overcoming the mutual extraneousness of reason, sense, feeling and will, Goethe 'disciplined himself to a whole, he *created* himself' (1979c: 102). Imposing an ideal form on themselves, other individuals likewise can free themselves and thence the world.

13 Writing

Great philosophy Nietzsche describes as its author's self-confession or memoire: 'a heart's desire made abstract' (1979a), and 'an unconscious autobiography' (1979c). But this is not to devalue it. On the contrary, writing can in this way be regarded as perhaps the most important part of thinking; and since 'thinking is an action' (1968), the most important part of living. If the world is a work of art, both constructed and comprehended aesthetically, then writing is a most significant means of composing, evaluating and transcending one's earthly environment. Certainly, Nietzsche's books were his life, and it is through them that he both reinterprets the world and secures his own place within it.

But Nietzsche also intends this autonomy for his readers. The aim of his philosophy is the promotion of the sovereign individual: one, as he puts it, 'who has the possibility, who has earned the right, of making promises he can keep'. Hence Nietzsche challenges his readers not to believe something but to do something: to overcome what they have hitherto held to be their own, and human, limitations. Even if his readers dislike his philosophy, that dislike will possibly fuel them to create their own. Indeed, this would be for his philosophy to achieve its real aim; Nietzsche wishes his philosophy to represent that power-quantum in spite of which his readers might formulate their own new interpretations, and with which they might usefully and powerfully overcome their present:

> Now lose me and find yourselves; and only *when you have all denied me* will I return to you.
>
> (1979b: 36)

To achieve this, Nietzsche develops his own inimitable writing style. First, he uses a diversity of forms and voices, with the result that the reader might never get used to one authorial presence – never get habituated to Nietzsche's role as writer and narrator – and so remember that what is being read is

Nietzsche's view only. Nietzsche's interpretations announce themselves, as it were, and attempt thus to guard against their being taken as a positivistic account of reality. Second, he employs contrariety and paradox in his writing, rather than the logical conceptualizations and *termini* of much conventional philosophy and science, as means to signal his struggle with and contempt for such paradigms. In Nietzsche's writing, in short, readers find polysemic signs calling for their own interpretation, and so engendering their own increase in will-to-power. As with a person or an art-work, with Nietzsche's philosophy it is a matter of the ongoing development of a particular relationship.

Third, Nietzsche teases, even insults his readers so as to shock them out of the routine complacency of who and how they are. By subverting readers' assurances regarding existing conceptualizations of the world and their value, Nietzsche hopes to point the way towards a possibly enhanced sense of who and what we might be; also a realization that all interpretations of experience are just that – and there to be subverted and overcome.

Not only is his style a heuristic device, then, but a way for Nietzsche to write which better reflects the fluxional nature of the world as will-to-power. Since the world is dynamic and paradoxical, written language conceived of as a fixed and static medium of communication is useless if regarded as anything but a metaphorical indicator of a realm of meaning inaccessible to such fixity and stasis. By writing diversely, paradoxically, polysemically and teasingly, rupturing the structures of his own text, Nietzsche can hope to break through to another realm – of aesthetic worldly appreciation.

Finally, in his writing, Nietzsche is focused on the future, on all futures, on the eternity of futurity. 'My time has yet to come: some are born posthumously', he concludes in *Ecce Homo* (1979b: 69), his most autobiographical tract. But the paradoxical spirit of his philosophy is that Nietzsche's time will come inasmuch as it never comes – his time is always that which is to come, that which overcomes the present and those who slavishly cling to it. He wants to be read and be 'understood', then, but not just in any frame of mind:

> We, the new, the nameless, the hard-to-understand, we firstlings of a yet untried future – .
>
> (1960: 381)

14

Erich Heller (1988: 142) has suggested a differentiation between those philosophers whose work one either understands or one does not – for whom one knows what is there to be understood – and those for whom it is impossible truly to answer the question 'Do you know so-and-so's work?'. In the first category, Heller would place the writings of Descartes, Locke and Kant, and in the second those of Augustine, Kierkegaard and Wittgenstein – and Nietzsche. Approaching their work, Heller says, borrowing two of

Wittgenstein's tropes, is like reading the features on a human face, or exploring an ancient city. The engagement is a highly personal one; the details are too complex and too subtle for one ever to be sure one has read them in their entirety or read them aright, and, in a way, the details keep changing, evolving, so that one's past readings are not necessarily pertinent for the present.

Nietzsche, as we have seen, might rather have liked this evaluation, believing as he did in the necessary authenticity of what an individual takes to be true. To read his work, then, is not a matter of right and wrong but of appropriateness: 'Is this reading sanctioned by the personal experiences which would warrant the individual understanding its truth as such and such?'

In another sense, I think Lesley Chamberlain is correct when she says (1997: 141) that Nietzsche was not a philosophical writer, one who engaged in disinterested philosophical inquiry, at all. For his contributions to the modern philosophical canon were unintended, inasmuch as his writings were dealings with his bodily and mental states rather than with disciplinary schools of thought, or issues of debate. He engaged with Schopenhauer, with Charles Darwin and with Emerson, with the Ancient Greeks, with Blaise Pascal, with Jean-Jacques Rousseau and with Kant amongst others, but his engagement was coincidental to his purpose: which was to know himself, or to chart the course of his knowing self.

Another way of putting this is to say that (despite his seeming protestations) Nietzsche's writings and his life are not properly differentiable. Nietzsche was no lover of things-in-themselves (as we have also heard), and it would be wrong in any way to set his writings apart from or counterpoised with his living. He played with different voices and personae, some of which critically distanced him from what another part of him was thinking or feeling at the time of writing, but there was no sense in which he regarded his writing simply as an impersonal, a professional, a disciplinary or a scholarly venture. Nietzsche lived his writing. Moreover, he seems to have done so throughout his life, starting from an early age: the solitary child who both penned literary and musical compositions and then critically reviewed his progress in these in his diary.

We have heard Nietzsche philosophize about movement representing the only real 'immortality' in the world, and we have seen how itinerancy across Europe amounted to perhaps the major consistency of form in Nietzsche's life. To this homology should also be added the consistency and the continuity (the 'immortality') of Nietzsche's writing, and the movement which writing to him represented. In his writing Nietzsche continuously moved from voice to voice, position to position, persona to persona, mood to mood – power-quantum to power-quantum. The movement was the thing, the means to and manifestation of a constant revaluation and reinventing.

What then, finally, did this life of writing, this life-as-writing, achieve for Nietzsche in terms of control? Not undiluted happiness, or fulfilment in relations with others, it can be said; he grieved the early loss of his father, and also his failure to control the destination of his relationships with his mother and sister, and with the likes of Wagner, Lou Salome and Paul Ree. But his life-project of writing did enable Nietzsche, I should like to say, to choose the site of his major fight: his own body.

From his early years Nietzsche seems to have had a penchant for introspection; while recognizing that introspection, however scrupulously undertaken, did not remove the viewer from the prism of interpretation, nevertheless Nietzsche possessed a passion for exploring the paradoxes and testing the limits of an individual's capacity to know himself or herself. As an adult he came to feel that this was a proper and necessary exercise in which all aspiring and truthful people might engage, since it opened a way not only to self-control, self-overcoming and self-improvement, but also to moral improvement: to that future state of being a proto-overman in a Europe without destructive divisions between people, and where people knew themselves first and foremost, deeply if contingently, as 'individuals' (1986: 475). Feeling that university teaching kept him both from proclaiming this message and from further knowing himself, he resigned and lived on his pension, and spent his remaining sane years a stateless person, wandering with, and recording, the reactions of his body. His published writings become records of a life in progress, of a life being lived as it is recorded and also in its recordings.

Did Nietzsche win the fight of his body: make his body the central figure of a complex, changing, composed world? In a way, and for a time. As we have learnt, he was myopic and prone to debilitating migraine; he was possibly heir to a disease of the brain. He contracted diphtheria and dysentery and a syphilis which seems finally to have eventuated in his paralysis, collapse and insanity. And yet, Nietzsche succeeded in putting himself in a position, material and psychological, where he could compose a metaphysics of strength. His writing represented both an overcoming of bodily contingency and pain, and a groundedness in it.

In choosing the site of his existential struggle, his will-to-power, as being his own body, as I have put it, Nietzsche brings the question of this book into focus in a particularly significant way. 'Is the individual with a life-project better able consciously to steer his or her life in a direction, at a rate, and to a destination of their own choosing?', it is asked, and Nietzsche answers (in his life and writings) that it is a matter of the quality of wilfulness of the diverse and shifting power-quanta that go to make up the individual body. It is a matter of the 'single-minded' harnessing of those power-quanta whereby they can be seen to respond to an overriding will. Better put – respecting Nietzsche's pronouncements on the diversity of wills in the body and on there being no overarching ego that represents the will of wills – it is a matter of aligning power-quanta so that their energies come under the sway of a ruling passion, at least for a time: '[t]he formula of my happiness: a Yes, a No, a straight line, a goal' (1979c). Control yourself, know yourself, and you control the life-in-the-world, the art-work, you thereby come to fashion. Nietzsche took control of his body and brought it under the conscious sway of his writings until the centrifugal forces of constitutional weakness, disease – perhaps the very, energetic extents of the competing power-quanta of which he saw himself constituted (cf. Stern 1981: 33–4) – became too great: parts flew apart.

To end, here are some final words from Nietzsche, some six years into his eleven years of paralysis and madness, as recorded by his mother (cited in Gilman 1987: 235). He still converses with himself, perhaps, on the subject of his body, but seemingly having given up the fight to organize 'his' power-quanta into a conscious whole:

> Do I have a mouth for it? Should I eat that? my mouth I say, I want to eat, What is that? Nice milk I always liked. What do we want to eat now. Precisely the thing. Will that taste good? That is tasty. What else do we want to eat? Nice things. Who will eat this? eat it yourself. What does Frau Pastor have? beautiful eyes. What is that here? a spoon. What is his designation? Friedrich Nietzsche.

4

BEN GLASER AND THE COMPOSING OF 'COSMOS 1' AND 'COSMOS 2'

30/3/1996

A scientist asked me to give the reasons why I think that my theory is superior to others – like the Big Bang. I shall attempt this in the form of the experience during my life: how my theory started, developed and arrived [at] today.

About 1927–28 I got acquainted with the basics of the Special Relativity Theory. Physics was the subject that interested me then mostly. Why are things in the world made the way they are made?

Reading the little booklet (by Walter Becker) I asked why is such an important parameter of our cosmos, namely the speed of light – the information signal by which our cosmos works (electromagnetic propulsion) – why has it a unique value of just 300,000 kms per second? I knew then, of course, of Ole Roemer's explanation of its value through the delay of light arriving from the Jupiter moons via the diameter of the earth trajectory; also the experimental verification of Fizeau and Foucault was known to me. Yet, I asked myself, why should this be so? I had no answer to this, though I thought perhaps this may not be so under different cosmic conditions, or perhaps in another world. Much literature, mostly fiction, was then making the rounds describing mostly 'unfriendly' worlds; with today's hindsight, of course, all nonsense, [but] which a young mind at that time accepted uncritically.

I later learned that scientists of renown also had ideas (with some mathematicians) which I had, that 'c' [the speed of light] might not be a constant.

Thinking more about this, and appreciating the beauty and excitement of the General Theory of Relativity, I learned that this theory in some way is going beyond Special Relativity, in changing 'c' near large masses. This is very beautifully explained in a popular Einstein booklet which I received from the author at that time, when I asked in a letter some relevant questions about his new field theory on which he was working; that was 1929.

Hirsch Baruch Benjamin Glaser was born in Vienna, in 1908, and grew up there and in Cieszyn/Tesin – a town split by a river and divided between Poland and Czechoslovakia. He died in Cardiff, Wales, the city he had lived in for most of his adult life, in 1996. An engineer by profession, Ben was at the same time a *bricoleur*, using the materials he found to hand to shape a full and idiosyncratic life; he was a Goethean figure, as Nietzsche draws him, one who fitted into an individual frame an organization and mobilization of a diversity of impulses and productions.

Outside his professional labours, then, for his pleasure and recreation, Ben painted and sketched, learnt the craft of woodcarving (making his own violin and his own picture frames), travelled around Europe and communicated in many of its languages, followed keenly the fortunes of the state of Israel and gave generously to its charities. Above all, Ben was a voracious reader, particularly of the hard sciences. He would pick up and browse through any book (including anthropology) and his collection of art, travel and historical literature was extensive. Ben's great love, however, was astronomy (including astrophysics and mathematics). One of the first gifts Ben gave me was a telescope, and one of the first books a map of the night sky, and, as he aged, and especially after he retired, reading astrophysics and making his own mathematical calculations concerning the age of the universe and its characteristics became all-consuming.

There were a number of heroic names Ben looked to – Rembrandt van Rijn, Ludwig van Beethoven, David Ben-Gurion – but perhaps the greatest, for him, was Albert Einstein. As a young student Ben had once corresponded with Einstein, while throughout his life he painted and drew likenesses of Einstein from newspaper articles, photographs and posters (also pinning these latter to his study walls), and towards the end of his life his passion focused on a theoretical engagement with Einstein's theory of the speed of light. Learning basic word-processing skills, Ben spent parts of his last years composing two theoretical papers, 'Cosmos 1' and 'Cosmos 2', which set out to prove that the speed of light had not always been a constant: at the moment of the 'Big Bang' of the universe's birth, the speed of light must have been accelerating.

In this chapter I present Ben's story, setting the achievements of Ben's explorations in, enjoyments of and enquiries concerning, his physical environment (culminating in his neo-Einsteinian theory) in the context of an equally complex personal life. Ben's life-project, I shall argue, represented itself as a rich and efficient recreational intellectualism which afforded him fulfilment.

From Poland to Wales

Born in his grandmother's house in Vienna, Ben's early years were divided between there and Polish Cieszyn, where his parents ran a shop. Ben's mother had the business head, leaving his father ('Why sell something? If it's good enough for them to buy its good enough for us to keep!') primarily to study: Hebrew, and the Kabbala (traditional Jewish lore, metaphysical and magical). Ben's father also lectured on Zionism and raised funds for Jewish-national causes. Cieszyn/Tesin hosted a sizeable Jewish community (and people would cross the bridge to shop on either side), while in Vienna the Jewish community thrived. Vienna, indeed, housed a ferment of nationalisms (as the Austro-Hungarian empire drew to a close [cf. Gellner 1998: 11]); *inter alia*, Vienna was also home to the writings of Theodor Herzl, modern Zionism's founder, whose tract, *The Jewish State*, was published in 1896. During the First World War, Ben's father was conscripted into the Austrian army, and the family to'd and fro'd between Vienna and Cieszyn as food supplies varied.

Jewish life at the time was lived quite separately from the Gentile one. Ben's parents, for example, had married under Jewish law but not according to the statutes of the Polish state (German, meanwhile, was the language they spoke at home). When they went to register Ben's birth, the Gentile authorities claimed no knowledge of the legitimacy of their household as such. The official date of Ben's birth, according to Polish records, was to remain out of kilter – a few months later than his actual birthday as recognized by the Jewish community.

In his teens, following the end of the First World War, Ben's parents moved their family to Vienna again in search of more stability and income. Ben was the eldest child, but now there were three more: two girls, Josephine (born 1910) and Theresa (born 1916), and a baby boy, Leo (born 1920). After his schooling, Ben moved back to Czechoslovakia and entered Prague University, where he gained a degree in engineering; he intended to study physics (his great love) but the quota on Jewish students enrolling in this subject had already been filled. Money was always short – he gave private mathematics lessons to boys in Cieszyn to supplement what his family could forward him – and Ben determined to complete his degree in three years rather than the usual four (he was keen to begin earning properly). At one point this led him to ignore medical opinion, and tear up the doctor's letter advising him that he had a case of tuberculosis which needed immediate treatment. Shortly after completing his degree, then, Ben suffered a tuberculous breakdown, entering a sanatorium to have a lung collapsed for recuperation (and being left with a weakness in the chest and a proneness to infection). Nonetheless, it was not long after leaving university that Ben took up paid employment, working for a Jewish-owned manufactory pioneering a new product: zip fasteners; Ben began laying the foundations of his professional career.

With the progress of the 1930s, however, the situation for European Jewry deteriorated. With foresight, the owner of the company for whom Ben worked, Joachim Koppel, began transferring funds and stock to Britain. Koppel set up the London Metal and Refining Company (later Aero Zip) and put in train the processes of his own (and his family's) emigration. In

1938, Ben joined a number of Jews convinced by Koppel to leave the Continent, and was assisted by Koppel to gain an entry visa into Britain. Ben's job would be to purchase the equipment necessary to begin pilot-production of zips in a new factory Koppel was planning in south Wales; Ben would become the factory's Technical Manager. The effects of the economic depression of the 1930s on Western economies were felt particularly acutely in industrialized areas of intensive, semi-skilled labour such as south Wales, and there were financial incentives offered by the British government of the time to attract entrepreneurs from outside the area. A number of these came to be Continental Jews, prepared to bring capital and skills to the area, and hoping, at the same time, to gain a march on the Nazification of Europe (cf. Glaser 1993: 196–7).

The year 1938, then, saw Ben's arrival at Koppel's new Aero Zip factory in the Welsh capital, Cardiff, on the Treforest Industrial Estate in the city's suburbs. Ben was now thirty years old. Two years previously, he had seen his parents and younger brother (then aged sixteen) embark on a somewhat precarious overland journey to Palestine. They had arrived safely, however, and remained there safely during the Second World War, and the War of Independence following the formation of the state of Israel. Shortly after his own arrival in Britain, Ben managed to arrange a visa for his sister, Theresa, to join him (in 1939); she had been sheltering with an uncle in France. The older sister, Josephine, by now married, succeeded in remaining hidden from the Nazis, on the continent, during the war, but her husband was interned in Auschwitz. He survived – if barely – and after the war ended the two of them also came to Britain. They began a family – Josephine gave birth to a daughter – but her husband died shortly thereafter. Many other relatives of Ben's – uncles, aunts and cousins – failed to survive the Nazis, and he was left with only one cousin beyond his immediate family.

Ben remained with Koppel's Cardiff firm for some seven years, until 1945. Then he joined his brother-in-law, Felix Lowbury (married to his younger sister, Theresa) in a new venture. Felix was a refugee too (from Austria), and a Doctor of Law, but in 1939 he had set up a company, Lionite Chemical and Asphalt Products Shortly after Ben joined him, and with expansion in mind, the factory was moved from the Treforest Estate to the Cardiff Docks area. The venture was a financial success, and, in the early 1950s, they moved again to a larger site which they planned and built themselves, in the Canton district of Cardiff. By the end of the 1950s, their company employed some 200 people; now renamed Lionite Specialities, it produced metal electric-shaver cases for a number of major manufacturers, and jewel boxes for high street retailers.

In 1963 Ben and Felix parted company, less than amicably, however, and the firm was sold. With his share of the proceeds, Ben started up once again, returning to the Cardiff Docks area and buying another factory, Vicrem Engineering. Vicrem employed 120 people in the manufacture of components from plate metal and tubular steel: valves, filters, mirrors and other automobile parts, baby chairs, safes and luggage handles. Throughout the economic turbulences of the 1970s and 1980s, while resisting laying off staff (and causing their long-term unemployment), a number of other directions of production were experimented with; a factory in Bristol, Digicon Electronics, was bought and sold, and a further one in Cardiff, Burkem Electrics. Finally, in the mid-1980s, Ben sold Vicrem as a going concern and retired; he was nearly eighty years old. He had managed to maintain a workforce of seventy, to an extent to his own detriment, and largely withstood the recessionary policies of a Conservative government which had caused so many other small companies to perish.

The initial years of Ben's retirement were taken up with a protracted litigation against the buyers of Vicrem, entrepreneurial 'cowboys' (common at the time) intent on asset-stripping the business (rather than paying Ben the remainder of sums that had been agreed) and then claiming bankruptcy. The court case was eventually won, but, financially speaking, the victory was a hollow one; while Ben enjoyed a materially comfortable retirement, he did not succeed in recouping the full worth of his investment and labour.

Ben and personal relations

Later I learned of the famous four Planck equations, each containing the mysterious 'h' that Einstein himself used, to explain certain so-called ultraviolet paradox observations. Nature expresses itself in quanta 'h' at high energies. I eagerly grasped these equations at a technical library in Prague, where I studied engineering at the time.

Observing in these Planck equations the appearance of the 'h', applicable to the microworld of particle physics, it lingered with me for a long time, whether there could not be an equivalent in macro. This gave me no rest for a long time. But I did at that time not know how to get an answer to this.

The history of events in Europe, the dark days of Munich took over. That was 1938. Since I had obtained my degree, in 1934, my thoughts, of course, had been for survival. But a long period from then up to 1983–4 (about 50 years) also seems irrelevant to my physics problems, filled instead with earning a livelihood. Only after retirement (and a time-consuming court case) did I continue with my physics. These 50 years were, only at leisure time, used to keep somehow abreast with developments of Astronomy and Cosmology, but very little with Quantum Mechanics.

Ben's first wife was someone he met shortly after immigrating to Cardiff in 1938, a local woman from the south Wales valleys. The relationship did not flourish, but they had a son, Anthony (born in 1941). Ben's second wife,

Masha, was a Continental-Jewish emigrée like himself. She too had had an earlier marriage, and a child from it, Lily; Masha was now a widow, however (her husband having been another victim of the Nazis). In the mid-1950s, therefore, now nearing his late-forties, Ben set up house with Masha and Lily in a fashionable, middle-class (and Jewish) neighbourhood in Cardiff.

Small Jewish communities had existed in south Wales (Swansea, Merthyr Tydfil, Cardiff) since the late eighteenth century (cf. Henriques 1993). A larger Jewish influx occurred in the late nineteenth century and early twentieth century, as a result of pogroms in Eastern Europe, and the possibilities of providing services to the neo-urban Welsh communities which the Industrial Revolution had caused (in the nineteenth century Cardiff was the biggest coal-exporting port in the world). To this south-Walian Eastern European Jewish community had been added a Central European layer since the Holocaust of the Second World War.

The pre- and post-Second World War layers of Jewry in south Wales were distinguished by their different longevity in Britain and by differences in attitude which accompanied this. The first (nineteenth-century) layer had tended to be rural in origin, and had found a niche for itself in Britain in commercial activity, particularly wholesaling and pawnbroking. The second (mid-twentieth-century) layer tended to be more urban in origin, less religious, and more urbane and bourgeois in its accomplishments and aspirations. In Cardiff, the two layers still met in the same synagogues (Orthodox as well as Reform), were buried in the same Jewish cemeteries (one site originally donated by the [Catholic] Marquis of Bute), and gradually, over years of inter-marriage, they were to become relatively homogeneous. Ben's generation of Central-European Cardiff Jews remained, however, distinct.

It was distinguishable, for example, in terms of the accented English with which it spoke and wrote (German remained Ben's 'first' language, both when it came to mental arithmetic and to sounding like a native speaker). It was also distinguishable in its attitude towards feeling 'at home' in Britain – indeed, in any one place at all (outside, perhaps, Israel) – and in its desire for attainments in high culture and the arts. As a married couple, then, it was within a sub-community of more recent, Continental Jewish emigrés in Cardiff that Ben and Masha largely moved. In 1956, when Ben was forty-eight, they had a son together, Daniel ('Danny').

Ben's marriage to Masha also ended prematurely, however, in 1969. Shortly after their divorce, and my mother's divorce from her first husband, Anthony (my father), Ben and my mother married. It was 1970 and Ben was now sixty-one; my mother, Anita, was thirty-eight, and I was thirteen (my sister, Frances, nine). Having moved out of his and Masha's house, Ben was by now living in a flat in the nearby seaside town of Penarth, also near the private preparatory school in which his son, Danny, and I were then studying for our Common Entrance examination into 'public school'. At their marriage, my mother and Ben set up house once more in Cardiff, but in a less traditionally Jewish neighbourhood; what Jewish families there were around tended to be Central European (and relative newcomers to Cardiff).

Ben and my mother stayed married for twenty-seven years, until his death in 1996. Before I turn to a more detailed account of the way I was to come to know him, however, let me present the following brief genealogical table by way of recap:

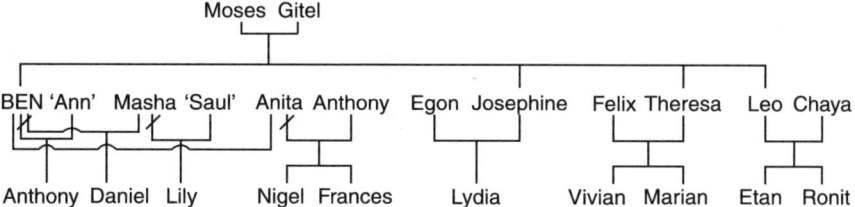

Ben and me

Ben's 'sentimental geography' is, by now (1970), very much divided between Cardiff and Israel. In Cardiff, he has his (new) wife, my mother, his two sons by previous marriages, Anthony and Danny, and his younger sister Theresa. When Anthony marries Jola (Polish, half-Jewish, and met on vacation *en route* to Israel) and gives Ben grandchildren, Karen and Stephen, the Cardiff connection obtains a further generational attachment. In Israel, meanwhile, there are Ben's parents' graves; his father had actually died in England, on a visit, but Ben had had his body returned to Tel Aviv for burial. Leo, Ben's brother, lives in Haifa, now with a wife (Chaya) and two children (Etan and Ronit); while Ben's older sister, the widowed Josephine, has emigrated (from London) to Jerusalem with her daughter Lydia. With his own peripatetic life – between Poland, Czechoslovakia, Austria and Britain – and the 'accident' of his final ending-up in Cardiff, with his international connections across Europe – and one niece (one of his sister Theresa's daughters), a concert musician, again living in Germany – and with the reasons for his having left the Continent in the first place (National Socialism) never being forgotten, Ben's family remained of central value and concern in his life. When his own parents died, indeed, Ben felt himself the responsible and loving family-head.

I first came to know Ben when I was about eight. He was the strange (foreign-sounding and -smelling) but friendly father of my best infant friend, Danny. I had known Danny since we had gone to the same, Jewish kindergarten together at the age of three (my parents were part of the older-established Eastern-European Jewish immigration to Cardiff); Danny was six months my senior. Then, at five, we had gone to the same local primary school, at seven to the same private, preparatory school (and were destined, at thirteen, to go to the same fee-paying public school in Bristol, Clifton College). Throughout this time, Ben had appeared as the generous adult, the lenient and adoring parent, who had provided Danny with an amazingly realistic electric-train set and then an extensive 'Scalextric' model-car motor-racing set. Ben was fifty-seven by the time Danny and I were nine, but I remember admiring the seriousness and good humour with which Ben would strip off his jacket and kick a football (erratically) with Danny in the back garden after work.

My house was just around the corner and I would often cycle to Danny's to play. The only time I can remember Ben being less than attentive to my arrival was when I found him chatting in his Rover car, on the street outside the house, with a strange man in the passenger's seat. That man was Anthony, Ben's elder son. He and Ben had kept somewhat apart, not seeing a lot of each other, for a number of years after his mother and Ben had divorced, but now, in adulthood, Anthony had approached Ben again. They were, indeed, to become very close, with Ben taking a keen interest in Anthony's university education, in his inaugural trip to Israel, and in his eventual employment as co-director of Vicrem Engineering.

I first became aware that Ben's marriage with Masha was going awry when I did not get to celebrate a birthday with Danny (his eleventh, probably), or to give him a present. My mother explained that it was nothing to do with me personally; relations were strained because Danny's mother was not getting on so well with his father, and my mother (and father) were more friendly with Ben than with her. I ought not to worry about it. It seemed very complicated to me, however, and it did seem to concern me very much. I loved Danny and had done for as long as I could remember – even though that affection had always been accompanied by a kind of self-sacrificing frisson. (A favourite pastime of mine, while walking home with Danny from the local train that took us from Cardiff to the preparatory school in Penarth and back, was to list, and ask Danny to list, in descending order, the people we most loved; Danny always appeared closer to the top of my list than I did to his.) Now, if I was to be deprived of Danny's company because of his parents' relations with each other, then it felt a strange and real loss. When my mother and Ben married, a few years later, the sudden return of Danny, now as step-kin, was one of the compensations (and potentialities) which made my parents' divorce more sanctionable.

When my mother and Ben were courting, my sister and I were occasionally taken along to visit Ben in his makeshift new bachelor pad in Penarth. I remember him frying up a large steak and serving it to us with chips; it was a new (and extravagant) experience, and I can still taste the cooking oil. His lounge was full of bookshelves and books, and musical instruments littered the floor. Upstairs, the floor of the room Danny occupied when he came to visit was completely given over to the Scalextric motor-racing set, designed into a most intricate circuitry. My mother told me that Ben wanted to buy me a gift of a book, so what would I like? I felt his generosity beginning to envelop me too.

My mother had told my sister and me about her impending divorce from our father in 1969; I was twelve and my sister eight, and we were both about to be sent away to boarding-schools in Bristol. My sister did not really understand the situation and was tearful. I was quite upbeat, and tried to explain it to her: we would not be losing our father so much as gaining Ben, another warm father-figure, prepared to be nice to us.

By the time I returned home to Cardiff from my first school term away, it was all settled. My mother had a new house (with woodland behind it) where she was going to live with Ben. There had been a plan for them to leave Cardiff and buy a house in Bristol, near to both my sister's boarding-school and Danny's and mine, and also to Ben's new electronics factory, Digicon; but then my mother's mother (resident in Cardiff) had suffered a stroke and it was thought best to stay put. In their new Cardiff house, I found large bedrooms for my sister and me, decorated according to our tastes, and a room for Danny, too, when he came to stay. Indeed, as Danny's mother sold her Cardiff property, moved to London and then to Australia, his presence in our house during the school vacations, and on holidays abroad, became a regular feature. The whole situation was so novel, unexpected and also strange, that I remember competing for Ben's attentions and affections with Danny on our first holidays together abroad; were we not now kind of brothers? Walking the warm promenades of Dubrovnik, and recounting the day's ski-ing exploits in Myerhoff, I would compete to be the one holding Ben's hand and receiving his commendations. I think now I would describe it as my first experience of culture-shock. Ben was an exotic other by whom I was romanced: his different sound and manner, and dress-sense, his somewhat ungainly body (with a less than neat scar on his back from the removal of a kidney) – my father had always been slim and athletic – the things he did not take seriously (cars), and his serious passions (there was a public pool-side dispute with a fellow-tourist in Faro about South African apartheid).

My only worry was whether Ben and my mother would have children of their own (I became very upset on first seeing my mother emerge, in the morning, from the bedroom she and Ben now shared). If my mother now loved Ben more than my father, I calculated, then would she not also love more any offspring she had with Ben than with my father? But my mother reassured me: she and Ben would not be having children together, and nothing could lessen her love for me.

After my initial 'honeymoon period' with Ben as an additional father-figure, our relations settled down. I grew to expect him to be there and to like, too, the way that I could play off one parental household against the other. My father remained unmarried (playing the field) for eleven years after the divorce, but he kept on the house he and my mother had lived in, and my sister and I would enjoy returning there. His girlfriends came and went with some regularity and I also came to enjoy, vicariously, his attractiveness. I remember asking my mother shortly after the divorce who was the physically stronger man, my father or Ben; she had answered, equitably, that my father was far younger and was fitter, but that Ben had a fiercer temper.

Throughout my teenage years, however, I would continue to make comparisons. My father was tall, a success with women, and obviously charming; he was trusted by his customers at work (in the family wholesaling firm) and he was a popular after-dinner speaker and raconteur, and office-holder (Treasurer of Canton High School Old Boys' Association, and the South Wales Art Society). He drove fast (Jaguar) cars (taught me to do so), took me to watch Wales play rugby, and played me at squash. Everyone in Cardiff seemed to know him (as he strolled its streets and gestured hello's) and it was truly his place. He seemed to be at home there in the way I wanted to feel at home myself (having been schooled away in Penarth and then Bristol). Ben's allegiances, meanwhile, seemed more distant and less personal to me. He claimed to be able to feel at home anywhere, and he suggested the same for me; but I balked. Cardiff, Wales and Britain were temporary loyalties for him, he explained, which could be left behind should the need arise; but I could not imagine the need. I wanted to be Welsh above all, while Ben, it seemed, insisted on remaining Jewish (beneath all), and loved and defended Israel with a passion which I found impolite, ungrateful and foreign. He always behaved so foreign too, and with a hearing ailment (from the hubbub of factory machinery) which gradually became minor deafness, his public persona was not one to pass unnoticed – to give confidence of the possibilities of Jewish assimilation. At work in the factory, people shied away from his intensity of engagement (staring intently, grabbing arms) and the brusque manner with which he would display his engineering knowledge and relay instructions; while at home it was peculiar the way he could amuse himself for hours with his music, art or odd-jobs, and rarely become engrossed in front of the television. Furthermore, he had no knowledge of how much superior Jaguar cars were to others, and would only buy sedate-looking Rover saloons. And he openly and frequently kissed Danny, which I found embarrassing and attractive in roughly equal measure (my father hugged but never kissed me).

In my early adulthood, things changed between us again. My sojourn on an Israeli kibbutz between school and university began a feeling of care, even of responsibility, for that country, not to mention joy and pride, which did not leave me; it brought me too to a closer appreciation of Ben's feelings. When I came to spend time in Israel with him, I saw how he effervesced in the heat and could spend the entire day walking and sketching, entranced by the ambience, and oblivious of time. As I also came to live for a time in Canada, before returning to a country whose best social characteristics Margaret Thatcher's Conservative governments were busy despoiling, I felt distanced from Britain (England, at least) in a way which again helped me to realize the value of

Ben's philosophy of depending on nothing but one's own 'head' for feeling at home, and 'belonging'.

As I furthered a university career in anthropology, Ben was always there, keen to read what I was reading and writing, to know what I was learning, and to argue (against me at the time) for the logical-positivistic and objectivist perspective on reality with which his traditional, hard-science education had provided him. His breadth of knowledge, his thirst for more, his ability to move from painting pictures to making music (and taking music lessons), to reading of calculus or history or anthropology, to odd-jobbing around the house, without wasting time on television or something that did not call for concentration – this impressed me, astonished me. It was also exhausting: Ben never seemed to relax into mindless pursuits. Whenever I returned home, he was keen to hear my news and thoughts, and told me how proud of me my mother was. And whenever I left again he came to the door and shook my hand, hugged me (even kissed me), and told me to: 'Mach es gut!' ('Do well!').

Ben and astronomers

Back to Physics in 1984. I had an idea: what if today the speed of light being constant may not always be so at other 'times' of cosmic history? This constancy of light (or not) was, of course, with me during the above 50 years. If I accept, so I thought, today's parameters in the Planck equations, what will be the result in macro if I reverse the problem and ask what 'h' will be? I found a consistent 'h' is approximately equal to 10 to the 95 g cm squared per second. I was frightened at first, but I probed further; (curiosity may kill the cat, I thought, but not me). Suppose this new 'h' value is a constant in macro as pl 'h' is in micro! I added now the notion 'at all different times', not just the present. Of course, the parameters of today could not then apply; it would not make sense. The parameters must then change, and of necessity the value of 'c'. As a consequence of existing (manipulated) equations, my old thoughts of a non-constant 'c' seemed to bear fruit.

This was then further developed by me and resulted in a complete, consistent, non-contradictory system, which is now presented in a paper called: 'A new interpretation of the history of the cosmos (The Big Bang unlocked)'.

If this now sounds simple, it is only a shortcut, over a period of 2–3 years, in which time doubts and lots of mistakes alternated from day to day. Around a dozen papers were the result, and when these were shown or cited to interested people, rejection was the result, most of the time. At best, I was told that it was beyond comprehension.

Towards the end of his life, well into his retirement, Ben became even more intense and concentrated. Sitting in the upstairs room which had once been my bedroom but was now his study – as distinct from his sketching and painting room in the attic, and his tool-workshop in the garage – he would pore over his physics and astronomy books. Danny bought him an old computer and he learnt the fundamentals of word-processing. Gradually, his readings and calculations gave onto an idea: that Einstein – genius though he was and world-creating though his theories of relativity had been – was wrong concerning the speed of light at the time of the universe's beginning, the Big Bang. After all, there were gaps in Einstein's knowledge, astrophysicists such as Stephen Hawking at Cambridge still worked on the Unified Theory of 'everything' which would unite particle theory and wave theory, and Ben would play his part in this. The idea became a passion and then a working paper: 'A new interpretation of the history of the cosmos (The Big Bang unlocked)', or 'Cosmos 1' for short. And whenever and wherever he could, Ben would talk about it to people, holding his interlocutors by the arm so that they could not escape his rapt exposition until complete. One did not know quite how seriously to take what he said – so esoteric in their provenance, so potentially far-reaching in their consequences. He was getting on in years, he seemed to have lost a sense of proportion as regards how much time and interest and knowledge other people had, and I, certainly, with only a basic understanding of physics and mathematics, had no way of knowing the likelihood of what he said being true (however often Ben explained the equations and graphs to me). I am not sure if anyone did. Ben eventually contracted the Professor of Astronomy at University College Cardiff, Mike Disney, as an interlocutor, and over the years they became friends; Ben acquired a special pass to allow him to park in the UCC grounds and attend Disney's lectures. When another astro-physicist whom Ben had avidly read, Chandra Wikramasingha, chanced to be met visiting our residential neighbourhood and looking for a house to buy, and Ben and my mother were considering moving somewhere smaller, Ben was keen to offer Wikramasingha favourable rates if only he would promise to take on Ben as a talking-partner (Wikramasingha did not quite know what to make of Ben's humour).

Ben also attended whatever astronomical colloquia were open to the public in Cardiff, bent the ears of any delegates he could, and worried them with correspondence afterwards (he succeeded in causing one visiting professor departing from a conference to miss his plane). But he never seemed to manage to procure a hearing which was more than polite. Perhaps it was his amateur status, or his age, accent and increasing deafness. Perhaps it was that he was wrong and could not be made to see this; perhaps it was that he was right and the people he engaged with could not entertain the possibility of this being the case.

Ben certainly believed he was right. For the first time there was a non-contradictory and concise theory, 'hypothesis' at least, by which all the parameters, relations and equations of our cosmos were linked, at all times, into one complete and unique system. The distinct values of these parameters might have been established separately (Roemer's observation of Jupiter's moons, Fizeau's measuring of the speed of light, Oetves' measuring of Newton's gravity constant, Einstein's establishing of the mass-energy relation, Hubble's telling us of the age [and radius] of the universe), but all fitted together nicely, like a jigsaw puzzle, in his one theory of the cosmos. Admittedly, the theory referred in its entirety to classical physics, but even so, there were indications of a link with quantum mechanics and thermodynamics for which more work was imaginable.

Ben explained himself with the excitement and conviction of a new prophet: at home, at cocktail parties, at dinner parties, in libraries; to family, friends and strangers. My mother grew to be embarrassed at this growing eccentricity – although he had always been one to take little account of British niceties of polite interaction (or even Israeli, for that matter); I avoided spending more time than I had to in his study, being repeatedly harangued about the theory's latest developments or versions. 'Cosmos 1' became 'Cosmos 2', with my mother helping to make Ben's Germanic English somewhat more readable (the passages of Ben's words quoted throughout this chapter come from the papers' preamble). But at the time of his death, neither paper had been published, and they have not been since. Which, in a way, makes the question I have to ask concerning Ben's life more encompassable: How might one characterize the relationship between the lifetime of intense, and to an extent private, passions which Ben composed for himself, culminating in 'Cosmos 2', with the everyday quality of that life?

A private life?

Is it correct, however, initially to characterize Ben's passions as private? I would argue so. Because although his music, his learning, his familial generosity, and especially his art, gave pleasure to others, I believe the impetus for his doing them was a strongly personal and 'self-centred' one. Ben was a very proud, confident and definite person. He knew what he knew was right and he had little patience for those – especially those close to him – who would waste their time on what he regarded as fripperies.

The one occasion on which I remember Ben becoming angry with Danny, was when Danny (then a teenager) played him a track from a new LP he had bought by the rock group, Hawkwind. Danny was impressed (and thought Ben might be interested) that on one track, 'Quark, strangeness and charm', the lyrics mentioned Einstein, albeit to the effect that his theory of relativity missed out on the way that the subtle power of male sexuality could enable 'heavenly bodies' to 'pull' a female. Ben showed his displeasure by telling Danny midway through that he was listening to rubbish, and abruptly leaving the room; Ben expected those he cared for to share his seriousness, and where possible, his point of view. He found it hard even to extend to an adolescent son respect for his individually chosen (musical) values if these were incompatible with his own (even diminishing his hero through silliness). He had little time, either, for my mother's great love, English literature, because it was something he found difficult to esteem seriously in comparison with the hardness of science and its technical power to get to grips with the ultimate questions of existence; for my mother's recreational interest in old Hollywood movies he had even less appreciation, and when forced to sit and watch them with her, would invariably fall asleep. Meanwhile, he accepted my mother always being there, in the house, to provide for his creature comforts, and he grew jealous if she were absent for too long a period. I do not remember ever seeing Ben cooking after he married my mother, or doing more domestic chores than making himself a lemon tea – and this, only when there was no one else there to make one for him.

Meanwhile, Ben devoted his time to his serious interests – and expected others to recognize their seriousness and value, not just to him but in the ultimate scheme of things. He played the violin and cello (performing in an ensemble of Jewish emigrés) even as he grew deaf, and when for others to hear him without complaining sometimes felt like an act of charity. He made thousands of sketches and hundreds of paintings, often framing them and offering them as gifts to family and friends. More often, however, they stayed with Ben, either accruing in his attic studio or jostling for every available inch of space, alongside the purchased art, on the house walls. Finally, his generosity and good-heartedness were directed towards those persons and that work which fulfilled his expectations of worthiness; he would show intense interest (at the expense of his own time) in the serious passions of those he esteemed.

Regarding that which was less worthy, Ben could show less patience; I remember numerous arguments with him (during my student years) concerning whether the plight of the British poor could be rectified by their own hard work and self-help: who precisely were worthy recipients of state hand-outs? Ben, in short, was not always the easiest person to live with or live up to, and his own polymathic achievements translated into high expectations for those he thought something of. He expected others to aspire to his set of values and achievements, and few half-measures were to be countenanced in anything.

The conservative-minded philosopher Michael Oakeshott once employed a nice phrase to convey that 'unrehearsed intellectual adventure of the imagination' which could succeed in linking minds across time: he called it the 'conversation of mankind' (1962); here was something which gave 'place and character' to all human activity and utterance, and which might be deemed perhaps the greatest of human accomplishments. Ben, I feel, would certainly have agreed with this summation; the life-project he set himself was to partake of this conversation at a fundamental level and take it forward.

Let me return to an early scenario in Ben's bachelor flat in Penarth. His second marriage (to Masha) has broken down, and he has left the family house, removing to a seaside suburb of Cardiff where Danny attends preparatory school. I first visit the flat with my mother and sister when my mother and Ben begin courting, and we find him in his new living-room. The walls are covered with book-cases (which he has made) and are filled with books, and musical instruments are laid across the floor. In comparison, the rest of the flat is quite bare; even Danny's room with the Scalextric has little beyond that to give it a lived-in feel. But Ben's 'living-room' is clearly where he does a lot of important living. It is part of a vital balance in Ben's life: transition, change, even upheaval in domestic arrangements and personal relationships…but order and fullness and variety in terms of personal interests and artistic passions. His wide choice of favourites among the latter – Rembrandt, van Gogh, Bach, Beethoven, Einstein, Born, Weizmann and Ben-Gurion – also provide him with a long-term perspective on life. These are world-historical figures, and by making them a part of his own life, Ben is able to view the latter in terms of the *longue durée*. What are domestic upheavals, what even are personal relations, when set against the lasting achievements of such great European masters who have become Ben's heritage? He might have moved between four countries at different stages of his life, his family might be spread across two continents, he might have begun in business half-a-dozen times, and he might have two sons from two broken marriages and be about to embark upon another such engagement, but by copying the art and music-making of world-historical figures, and reading in their science and their epoch-making achievements, he lifts his own sensibilities onto that world-historical stage too.

During his working life, it was this sort of balancing act that Ben practised. He set up and ran successful engineering and electronics firms, he acted as successful head for an increasingly large and dispersed family (both of orientation and of procreation), and he balanced this – transcended this – by artistic, scientific and musical passions which removed him from the merely here and now.

These passions, during his working life, were mostly imitative in execution and desire; they were acts of connection with the *longue durée* but not real extension (except in the act of relating them to his own life and time). Perhaps this gave onto the balance: the extension into the future of Ben's working and familial life juxtaposed against the connection to the past with time-honoured and proven masters. Hence, Ben's violin and cello playing was of classical repertory, his scientific and philosophical reading was largely historical (Euclid, Maimonides, Galileo, Spinoza, Newton, Darwin, Einstein, Hawking), and his sketching and painting in the style of Baroque, Dutch and Romantic periods. He would sketch family and friends and the house garden from his attic window, and on vacation he would sketch panoramas and strangers, charming and befriending his subjects as he did so (sketching the waiters who attended upon us one summer holiday in Portugal led to our table in the dining room being embarrassingly surrounded with attentive hands for the duration of our stay, while the remainder of the tables seemed badly neglected). But these fine-art products were notable more for their sensitivity and emotion, their subtleties of dark and light, their intensities of colour (Ben was part colour-blind), than the originality of their conception. Meanwhile, Ben also copied postcards and newspaper photographs that had appealed to him (his large series of Einstein representations came about this way), and filled the house walls with his copies of old masters: Raphael, Rubens, Rembrandt, Schiele, van Gogh. For all his self-confidence and certitude, there was modesty in this mimicking. He was amazed at what Rembrandt could achieve in a few pencil lines, gaining a wholeness of representation which his own fussy and over-full efforts still might not obtain. Likewise, his colours faded before van Gogh's, he admitted, his playing of Bach's violin concertos were never quite right, and his understanding of Hawking Radiation never quite complete.

But a change happened after he retired. He found it hard to let go of the reins of his company, Vicrem Engineering, and throughout the late 1970s and early 1980s (and through his late seventies), as I have described, he kept going. His son, Anthony, was mainly managing the company by then, but Ben still did not want to hand over control, or sell, until the business was a good going concern: worth at least part of what it was before the Thatcherism of monetarism and deregulation had succeeded in running down the British manufacturing base. Ben was not exactly bitter – as my mother was – concerning the policies of the governments they had voted in, and was never really exercised about so material a consideration as his savings and standard of living (although those of his wife and sons he did care for), but he wanted to part from the company he had made, over twenty-five years, properly.

When eventually Ben did sell, he initially found himself at a loose end. It was 1988 and he was eighty years of age, but his intellectual capacity and his curiosity were undimmed; even with his recreational interests, it was difficult being at home with so much time, and it was hard to accept that Vicrem Engineering no longer needed him at its helm. Gradually, however, a new passion flowered (or returned), and an innovative one: the improving of Einstein's theory of light.

I have said that of all the historic figures of heroic importance to Ben, Einstein was by far the greatest; any book by Einstein or on Einstein, in any language (Chinese included), Ben was pleased to acquire. Ever since their brief correspondence in his student days, Ben had measured his life against Einstein's, noting their similarities in trajectory (through various marriages and nationalities), even embroidering for the sake of a closer fit – Ben's recounting their adult successes as likewise based upon lacklustre diligence as students. In his retirement, this fixation was taken to new levels (the book Ben was reading and annotating at the time of his death was a new Einstein biography). It also gained a new orientation.

BEN GLASER'S 'COSMOS 1' AND '2'

One of the problems besetting post-Einsteinian astrophysics, and a stumbling block for those, like Hawking, now attempting a unified theory which would conjoin relativity theory with quantum mechanics, concerned the constancy of the speed of light. Ben had known of the problem, of course, from his readings over many years, but now, in his retirement, with all his time being devoted to his reading, a new confidence was born: mathematically he would offer a proof to demonstrate the inconstancy of the speed of light, and its accelerating qualities in those vital fractions of a second following the Big Bang. The idea behind what would become the academic papers 'Cosmos 1' and 'Cosmos 2' was formed. A non-contradictory structure of the cosmos could thus be theoretically arrived at without the well known drawbacks to which the Big Bang theory was prone (singularities and pre-set parameters).

For the final six or seven years of his life, the idea dominated his thoughts – often, as I have said, to an extent which others found disconcerting and embarrassing. Nothing mattered to Ben as much as this, and nothing was as interesting. Between Ben and his grandson Steven (Anthony's son) there had always been a warm relationship; now, with Steven as the most patient of listeners (and a science graduate), their talking-relations took on a new closeness. Correspondingly, I found it harder to be patient or attentive in our exchange, and some other members of the family did so too. But as before, the impetus for Ben's passions was a strongly personal one – 'self-centred' – and his caring about their consequences was too. Ben's fixations would follow their own headstrong course. When I would return home on a visit and Ben would launch into a detailed and urgent account of his latest calculations, with an insistence that I recognize the rectitude of their advance, I would repeat that he should try to have his work published – and have done with it. I could not gauge its accuracy (and I was embarrassed to be reminded of his mathematical knowledge, since he still sought to borrow anthropological books and data from me) and I felt that Ben was directing his efforts of persuasion at the wrong audience – was wasting his time among the scientifically non-literate. But while Ben did try, largely unsuccessfully, to have professional astronomers seriously engage with him, as mentioned, I do not think he ever tried having 'Cosmos 1' or 'Cosmos 2' (with its slightly more felicitous English) published.

But maybe I was missing the point. Whatever his advertisements, Ben did not want the judgement of others, professional or lay, concerning the final worth of his mathematical explorations. He was in fact continuing to beat out the individual path of his life. In the past this had meant balancing familial, financial, marital and personal (artistic, musical, astronomical, etc.) interests, and charting a geographical course across Europe and a business course across changing times, while keeping a sense of personal self and home alive in his head. Now, in retirement, financially secure, with a number of successful and loving families around him, he charts the individual course of the speed of light 'sub specie aeternatis', as Spinoza might have said, across time and space as such.

Because I was certain that I had found something of importance, there was only one path possible: to make the paper easier to follow. In this I only succeeded at about the start of this year (1996). Hence the above 'Interpretation of the history of the cosmos (The Big Bang unlocked)'.

In my humble opinion, this paper is only a beginning, and implications following have to be investigated, and mainly tested against the existing Big Bang theory. Both cannot exist side by side; only one can prove to be correct, or, better, nearer the truth (not to claim ultimate truth).

One more word. Since the second half of this century, it has often been mentioned by scientists that apart from the basic laws of non-contradiction and inconsistency, a theory should be simple and beautiful (perhaps also free of infinities, since mathematics abhors this in certain cases, as is well known). In contrast to this, we observe today in science the opposite. The science of Physics drags itself deeper and deeper into more and more complicated assumptions, that are further and further removed from simplicity; through a sort of mathematical acrobatics, and infinities, it ends up in higher and higher dimensions. This seems not to be what science requires.

I now state why the inconsistency of the Big Bang's theory loses out against this theory of mine; here is the conclusion of 'A new interpretation...':

My theory	The Big Bang theory
1. 'm' is constant, but activity varies from nothing to maximum and back to nothing.	'm' is invariably constant.
2. The definition of time is equivalent to duration.	–
3. All parameters are interdependent.	All parameters are cosmically independent, and derived from separate abbreviations or from calculation.
3a. In particular: E/C squared m(const), C/G constant.	–
4. There are no infinities.	The cosmos starts, suddenly (an act of God), with infinities.
5. All parameters can be extrapolated	All parameters are fixed (constant).
6. The horizon problem is solved	The horizon problem needs artificial boundary conditions.
7. The controversy of the steady state and the Big Bang finds a solution.	–
8. The micro and macro values indicate an affinity (? more work is needed)	–

A life of self-intensity and control

Is it possible to isolate the intense passions with which Ben adorned his life on the one hand, and the everyday details of that life on the other and to examine their relationship, or is the notion of such differentiation misguided? If Ben had not been designated Jewish he could have studied physics at university; if he had not been assisted to emigrate from Austria in 1938 he would likely have been killed by the Nazis (as members of his extended family were). If Ben and his first wife had not proved incompatible living-partners, then he might not have been deprived of witnessing the early years of Anthony's growing up. If Margaret Thatcher's Conservatives had not come to power in 1979, Ben might not have missed out on a fair return for his years of labour and investment in his factory, and retired with more time and money to enjoy. On one view these represent factors and events beyond Ben's personal control and yet with direct consequences for Ben's concerns. On this view too, Ben's personal passions, whatever their intensity and effectiveness in his own life, may be seen merely as reactive forces and devices, not a life-project of conscious planning and self-direction. To the extent that Ben was able to have resort to his passions, he could deflect the full psychological impact upon him of discrimination, of marital break-up, of Thatcherism, but he could not actively affect them.

But on another view, Ben's passions, Ben's individuality and personality *per se*, play a significant part in defining what these impinging factors and events *are*, to Ben, in the first place. Ben did not so much react to discrimination, to marital upheaval and to Thatcherism, then, as have them as part of the personal, cognitive and imaginative environment within which he plotted his life-course; 'discrimination' was part of his European environment when he decided to emigrate to Britain, 'Thatcherism' part of the British environment when he was plotting his retirement, and 'marital discord' part of the environment which accompanied his development of personal and intellectual destinations. Rather than reacting to these factors and events, Ben might be said to have continued his life-course, continued writing the individual narrative of his life with these as backdrop: as some of the publicly better known landmarks in relation to which his personal journey can nominally be charted. The nature of the landmarks depends on their apprehension, and while some of them are unavoidable, formally speaking, or only avoided by taking drastic or last-minute evasive action, still, how they affect the individual life depends on their interpretation, and the course which that life chooses to take before, during and after the encounter. To the extent that Ben was affected by discrimination, marital break-up and Thatcherism, he was so in his own way and as a result of decisions he made concerning his life-course before encountering them and through encountering them.

To take the analogy of landmarks and their individual apprehension one step further (and to return to my introductory metaphor of the individual as projectile), the gravitational pull which the landmarks are able to exert on the trajectories of the journeying individual within his or her environs depends on the velocity and the force which the individual possesses. (A speeding individual, headstrong, single-minded, determinedly fixed on a life-course, has less chance of having his or her direction changed.) Ben, it seems to me, had a sense of self, of the integrity of his identity, and a consciousness of a personal life-project, the force of which stayed with him and gave his life direction and shape – projection – almost irrespective of those seemingly world-historical or otherwise momentous, compulsive, extraneous factors and events in his broader environment. He composed his own world-historical life-content and -course, carrying on the name of Rembrandt, of Beethoven, of Ben-Gurion, and elaborating upon Einstein's.

Of course, it is a question of emphasis and of subtlety of appreciation. It is also the case, then, that in charting his own course Ben remained 'a Jew': not a believer but actively a member of Jewish communities, charities and synagogues, enjoying Jewish holidays and rites – conducting his own at home (in particular the annual *Kaddish* prayer, or *Jahrzeit*, to his parents' memory) – and maintaining Jewish contacts in Britain and abroad. He might have moved between countries, marriages and businesses but Jewishness stayed with him. And yet, it seems to me that while Ben did not eschew partaking of (making interpretations of) Jewish communitarianism, just as he did not escape making interpretations of Nazism, of marital discord and of Thatcherism, he was not motivated by these: he did not act 'because of' them. Equally, he did not act 'because of' Vicrem Engineering, or Danny, or my mother. He acted, rather, through his relationships with these. And the way he acted demonstrates a continuity and a continuousness, a 'purity' or integrity, also an idiosyncrasy, deriving from acting 'in order to' further certain (recreational) life-interests of his own. Ben was Ben over and above the particularities and conventionalities of his relationships of the present moment, while the relationships that were fundamental to his sense of self – the 'significant others' of his 'reference group' (Rembrandt, Beethoven, Ben-Gurion, Einstein), Jewish and other – were the imagined conceptualizations of his own world-view. The purity or integrity to Ben's self-sufficient identity made him forceful, independent and free.

Envoi

When Ben died suddenly in 1996, aged eighty-eight, of an infection following a successful operation for cancer of the colon at a Cardiff hospital, he was busy sketching the man in the bed opposite while introducing him to the intricacies of his astrophysical theory; after his death, the man said that Ben was one of the most marvellous people he had met. When I returned Ben's borrowed physics and mathematics books to Cardiff University Library, the lady behind the counter remembered Ben well and said how sorry she was; if I did not mind, she would like to inform the other librarians too, because they would all miss him. At the funeral, there was a goodly crowd, including my father (always on somewhat uneasy terms with Ben), having flown back from a vacation in France; and at the gravestone-setting ceremony, a year later, there was a large contingent of Ben's brother's family which had flown over from Israel.

Figure 1 Ben Glaser, *Sketched Self-portrait*, 1967
Source: private collection.

Ben was his own man, it seems to me. He made an environment in which to nurture the passions of his full life as he journeyed across countries, jobs, marriages and eras, and he made it in his own image.

About time

Do we really know what our brain perceives when imagining ordinary time? But we have to accept these pictures as real if no better alternative exists. It equally may also apply to matter. We experience time unidirectionally, unlike space. When asking 'why is this so?' there is much speculation but really no answer. But now we do receive a strange signal via our equations: 'Time has a dual meaning'. Firstly, there is the usual understanding of time as singly directional, explaining events in space past, present and future (though even here Einstein tells us to be a little more careful). Secondly, we get a new conception of duration. A double parameter seems to be built into the cosmos, similar to Newton's duration. The brain accepts this duality with suspicion, at least with some difficulty. One should investigate where this leads to, however, rather than rejecting it outright. If it leads to inconsistencies or contradictions, then abandon it. But if it results in a better description than existing interpretations such as the Big Bang theory, then this paper deserves to be seriously investigated.

5

RACHEL SILBERSTEIN AND THE RELENTLESS ROAD TO PERSONAL COMPLETION

> When I came here from the States folks said I must be either crazy or else idealistic. But it was a personal journey....I was brought up very morally and also as a Jew. And I thought putting the two together would make me complete; it was a road I had to go. But it has just led to more illusions being broken. Though I guess I still have a few, deep inside, about Judaism.

Rachel Silberstein would often use road and travel imagery, and not just to recount her *aliyah*, her immigration (literally, 'ascent'), to Israel from the United States. She described being 'a ceramist' in the US, but of having 'taken it as far as it [would] go': 'it [would] not go much further' for her; 'whatever others might do with it', she could see precisely where it would take her. Once arrived in Israel, however, Rachel came to find the very idea of engaging with the state's bureaucracy dispiriting: she told herself that she had gone this far so she may as well go the rest of the way, 'to see the heights at the end', but then she 'never seemed to get there'. At the start of her *aliyah* she had thought that the desert town of Mitzpe Ramon was the perfect place for her – 'a place to grow' – but soon she found she had 'gone past that'.

This chapter tells the story of the road to individual completion down which Rachel Silberstein relentlessly proceeded during the seven months that we knew each other, as fellow new-immigrants in Israel. It is an account of personal journeying: of seeking community, of coming to know oneself as a Jew, of questing after the moral life, and of tapping into those sources of 'alternative energy' which made a continuing journey in the face of obstacles which were both pathological and institutional – bureaucratic, communitarian, nationalistic, militaristic – possible. Rachel made a life-project out of her journey. She did not know where it would end up, how she would get there, nor what she would pass *en route*. But she knew what made her happy, she trusted her intuitions and her inquisitiveness, she believed in her right, even her duty, to tread a path to personal growth, and she possessed the self-assurance, the energy and the calling to know that individual completion was her proper goal – her right and her duty to herself.

ILLUSTRATIONS

Development town

I first met Rachel on the streets of Mitzpe Ramon, a development town deep in the Negev desert in southern Israel. The history and condition of these Israeli projects in new urbanization have been roundly recounted (Cohen 1970; Aronoff 1973; Efrat 1984). Initiated over a fifteen-year period after the disputatious founding of the state (in 1948), in peripheral and strategic parts of the country (the Galilee, the Negev), here were some thirty settlements deliberately set away from the heavy concentrations of population along the country's Mediterranean coast. Established by government decree rather than arising out of local demand, the towns were largely financed and planned by national development agencies. After their founding they were to become political footballs, kicked around by competing governments and their ministries more in accord with exterior partisan policies than local experience. Not surprisingly, many of the towns were to find great difficulty in maintaining a social core, attracting a rural hinterland or achieving economic take-off.

Mitzpe Ramon was founded in 1954, with the strong support of the Israeli Ministry of Defence, and soon acquired a complete infrastructure (shops, industrial zones, apartment blocks, schools, synagogues, clinic, local and national government offices); some 2,000 recently arrived Moroccan-Jewish immigrants were housed there as a citizenry, a step towards the initial planned population of some 6,000. However, with only army bases, long-established and self-contained *kibbutzim* (collective farms) and meagre Bedouin encampments for company, and lying one-third of the way between Beer Sheva (a town of 100,000 on the Negev desert's northern edge) and Eilat (a town of

Figure 2 Photograph of Mitzpe Ramon from the desert
Source: Nigel Rapport, 1989.

40,000 on the southern tip), Mitzpe Ramon was isolated. Moreover, when, in 1967, a new paved road between Beer Sheva and Eilat took a different route (via another new town), Mitzpe Ramon lost even the company of passing traffic – and its main source of income, aside from some light industry, and gypsum and clay mining – and people left in large numbers. The population total sank below 1,500. Distant from the main Israeli markets, entrepreneurs put no trust in the longevity of compensatory government subsidies for new businesses, and put little faith in the diligence or skill of the immigrant workforce. With empty, often vandalized factories and flats, the atmosphere in Mitzpe Ramon was generally found to be depressive. In majoritarian Israeli perspective, Mitzpe Ramon became akin to the 'Wild West' and a stigmatized place to live: 'a badly designed, thrown-up, concrete mass', in the words of one outsider-commentator.

Figure 2 shows a view of the town from the desert.

In the hope of attracting new settlers, the government advertised further 'development zone' dispensations, however (on income tax, on rental prices, on mortgage terms), and in the late 1980s the population again began to grow. For, notwithstanding its problems, perched high on the imposing panoramic brim of *Machtesh* Ramon (an enormous wind-gouged crater) and at 850 metres above sea-level, Mitzpe Ramon did possess an aesthetically very singular location. Artists were encouraged to colonize the empty apartment blocks, and asthmatics too; the local high school launched an art-focused programme for gifted teenagers who wished to board. Tourists began to be more professionally catered for, not only in a futuristic-looking visitors' centre but also in a youth hostel, restaurant and irrigated gardens. Following the

Palestinian *intifada* ('uprising') further north, hundreds of thousands of tourists have been known to flit through Mitzpe Ramon in one year; a new Ramon Crater Nature Park complex has been planned, which might cater for a million visitors. Finally, in the 1990s, when reformed Soviet-bloc states finally opened their borders to those who would emigrate, a large new influx of Soviet Jews to Israel filled Mitzpe Ramon to capacity.

Even before this, however, a small group of English-speaking Jews, mostly Americans, had become resident. It is the case that the notion of making *aliyah* to the Holy Land has not been central to American Zionism, which has more entailed political and economic support for the Jewish state, and since 1948 less than 1 per cent of American Jewry has become immigrants (cf. Isaacs 1966; Avruch 1981; Gitelman 1982). Of those who do come, some 75 per cent settle in established urban locations (or else in *kibbutzim* and *moshavim* (cooperative farms); only an estimated 7 per cent settle for development towns. Most American immigrants to Israel are found to be under thirty, moreover, to be single and religiously observant, and to have invested heavily in an ethnic Jewish identity whilst in the United States. They have also tended to be financially secure, and therefore neither in the position of being attracted to development towns by the carrot of government subventions nor prone to being bullied there by bureaucratic sticks. It is also the case, then, that those few American Jews who had chosen to move to Mitzpe Ramon were unusual among their (ethnic) number not only for immigrating to Israel and settling in a development town, but in terms of their sociological profiles too. For they were not so young, many were not single nor particularly religiously observant, more than a few were entering upon retirement, and, perhaps for all, there did seem to be a financial incentive: in Mitzpe Ramon they could buy a retirement villa or rent large apartments, and make do on an income or a pension in ways that would be precluded in the US or elsewhere.

Rachel and Giacomo

Out checking her mailbox at the Mitzpe Ramon post office, I first encountered Rachel Silberstein in the company of her dog, Giacomo, an Afghan Hound; and it is with details of Giacomo that an account of Rachel might appropriately begin.

'My dog is called Giacomo, after Puccini', Rachel explained to me when, unannounced, she came calling at my apartment two days later. 'Though I didn't know it at the time: I looked round for ages to "find" his name, you know? Then I discovered he and Puccini were born on the same day'. The deep attachment which Rachel had to Giacomo was readily apparent – it was no mere introductory affectation – and the respect too in which she held him. She had no scruples in buying him mincemeat, for instance, I was to learn, even though she herself professed a staunch vegetarianism (and expected all right-thinking humans to do so too). Rachel felt it a duty to do right by Giacomo's personal identity and his needs.

Rachel was forty-nine, tall, straight-backed and sturdy, with dark (though greying) hair. She grew up in Boston, Massachusetts, where she also went to university (majoring in political science) and married. From the age of twenty-four she supported herself financially through the sale of ceramics which she herself cast and fired. She developed a name for herself – and for her brand, Slithery Snake – on the American east coast; and despite emigrating she still maintained a US agent who marketed and distributed her produce, and (even with the added shipping costs) informed her of the continuing demand for her work.

When she was twenty-eight, Rachel and her husband separated. But it was only some twenty years later that they formally divorced, and it was the monetary sum her ex-husband settled on her which became Rachel's means finally to 'make the break' and emigrate to Israel. Over the years she had made a number of shorter trips to *Ha'Aretz* ('The Land'), her first couple being through an organization called Volunteers for Israel, which involved Rachel roughing it in army barracks for three weeks – not to mention sleeping with Israeli soldiers! Her second trip with Volunteers for Israel Rachel recalled as being less successful than the first – she encountered too many closed, 'Type A' personalities – but it still had not put her off, and finally she had decided to make *aliyah*.

For the first seven months of her immigration Rachel had lived in a government absorption centre in Upper Nazareth, with other new Jewish arrivals. Meanwhile she also sought out and visited artist centres, villages and workshops – En Hod, Kibbutz Nachshon – in order to initiate a network of relations with like-minded people. Finally, she struck out on her own and moved south to Beer Sheva, a city she hoped would connect her experientially to the Negev desert – an environment she found thrilling. On one trip into the desert she visited a field school in the small town of Mitzpe Ramon (some 50 kilometres away) and agreed to serve as a volunteer pottery teacher to those teenagers who attended the school, as part of their educational trip to the famous crater Machtesh Ramon; she would match her skills to their needs. Indeed, she liked the town so much, and she found the utopian vision of the old man who ran the field school, Uri Hazan, so beguiling that after only a month in Beer Sheva – where, sadly, she was 'experiencing nothing' – she moved to Mitzpe; it was still close enough to her then boyfriend who lived in the coastal town of Ashkelon, for them to stay in touch. She did not know at first that Mitzpe Ramon was within a special zone of state subvention: that in order to encourage immigration and new business the government subsidized 95 per cent of a person's rent for the first five years, and levied only minimal taxes. In a kind of catch-22 situation, however, you were meant to have procured employment for yourself in the town *before* you sought permission from the government housing agency to move in. In

Rachel's case, nevertheless, Uri's influence led to the local bureaucrats 'inventing' a job for her, and finding her an empty apartment in a block convenient for the field school and sheltered from the desert wind. As she explained to me that first evening in my apartment:

Rachel: I thought Mitzpe would be a great place for alternative energy.
Nigel: Oh, right…wind power, solar energy, and that.
Rachel: No. I meant mental energy.
(embarrassed at the misunderstanding, we avoid each other's eyes for some moments)
But there are so few people here, I don't know.…Before I left for my trip to the States I spoke with people who are spread throughout Israel but looking for a base; this'd be a great place to caucus. Yoga, meditation, that kinda thing.

When I first met Rachel she had spent a total of five months living in Mitzpe, but she had also just returned from an eight-month trip to the United States. The reason she had gone was that a dog of hers – Giacomo's father – was dying and she had wanted him to have the best care up to the final moments. When he had finally died, aged thirteen – she had a photo of him which had been taken on the very day he died – she had arranged to come back here.

The sad thing now was that Giacomo himself was not so well; and over the first weeks and months of our meeting Rachel would keep me informed of his changing condition. Mitzpe was a fine place for Giacomo, Rachel felt, and there were no dangers here, but, maybe because she had returned him to a tinned-food diet which had more salt – causing his body to retain water – in coming back to Mitzpe, Giacomo's water-on-the-lung had returned too. He was twelve and a half now, and so a fair age, but Rachel felt assured that he was not yet ready to die; all she needed was to give him pills to stop him hurting.

After Rachel had taken Giacomo to the vet in the local clinic, however, she complained to me:

this Russian guy couldn't understand my concern. 'Yes, its gonna die', he says, 'and I'm gonna die and you're gonna die. So what?'. I explained how I wanted the longest and the healthiest life for him that was possible, and also to know exactly when he was gonna go. 'Oh, you Americans!…', he says.

Rachel did not take Giacomo to the vet's again but he did improve temporarily when a new boyfriend of hers, Zvi (a gardener in Mitzpe Ramon, a Hungarian Holocaust-survivor with four children, whose wife had recently left him), gave the dog a pill to open his heart valves (and enable him to rid himself of some of the liquid on his lungs). Giacomo was soon bad again, however, and some five weeks after the trip to the vet he died. It was to be a date etched in Rachel's mind:

Rachel: I last saw you around the 30th of March, Nigel. I remember cos it was my birthday.
Nigel: Happy Birthday!
Rachel: It was also the day Giacomo died.
Nigel: Oh no.
Rachel: Yeah. It had been an extra bad two weeks; I knew he was dying, so I took him to the doctor here, Leo. I didn't want to take him to the vet again, *and* get caught up in an expensive racket. (Anyway, I did that in the States and had all the tests run on him.) The doctor said I was in more pain than Giacomo was! And you could just see how he was still 'into' what went on around him.
Nigel: Right.
Rachel: But then I found him dead on the carpet when I came back from shopping in Beer Sheva. His eyes were closed, so I hope it happened in his sleep....I buried him beneath a tree in the park. And I realized it was an Israeli grave as I ended up throwing pebbles on top of it. Then I painted his details on a piece of marble from the field school workshop, and Zvi planted some flowers that like shade him.
Nigel: Sounds like a nice ceremony.
Rachel: I go there sometimes to be near him.

It was 'a natural human desire to look after something', Rachel supposed. Even before Giacomo died, then, Rachel had also taken to looking after stray dogs from around town in her apartment. At one point she was catering to (feeding and bathing) four: a puppy from upstairs whose owner was a girl stationed in Mitzpe as part of her military training and who was often away on duty, and three dogs from off the streets which town officials were trying to kill by putting down strychnine-laced sardines. Having lost a dog to poison once herself (while a Volunteer for Israel at the army camp), Rachel found the deliberate practice 'horrible, and a terrible way to go'. She looked up an old copy of the *Encyclopedia Britannica* which she had brought to Israel in the hope of finding some information concerning the length of time strychnine might remain potent, but without any luck; she realized she was lost without a pharmacologist. But she thought three days would be a good guess; in any event, she was determined to offset the bad and irresponsible treatment meted out to dogs by many people in Mitzpe, even if it meant a gaggle of strays always following her around town and barking outside her apartment:

My neighbour keeps saying he's gonna get someone to take them away...I hate him. I spat in his face once, you know, Nigel. Actually spat. Whenever he sees the German shepherd he yells 'Hitler'. He's about seventy. Its understandable, but its sad. And yesterday, a policeman who lives in the building told me off too.

In short, Giacomo might have gone but she still had 'those other guys as company', Rachel explained. Moreover, unlike spoilt pups, the strays were grateful for every little attention.

In criss-crossing the Atlantic with (and, to an extent, for reason of) her dogs, in her spending time with them and expending energy insuring their comfort and security – even at the expense of securing easy relations with new human neighbours – Rachel demonstrated her continuing commitment to certain values she held dear. Bringing her dogs with her to Israel, continuing to visit Giacomo's grave to be near him, refusing to accept local practices regarding the poisoning of strays – finding them irresponsible – were ways too of embodying a continuity with a past life.

In a new immigrant such behaviour might be considered predictable: Rachel's dogs were transitional objects to which she adhered as she crossed between cultural milieux and social routines. But the behaviour also instantiated something more deeply and particularly Rachel's, I feel. Her love of her dogs seemed to be for its own sake, not merely symbolic of something else. I found no sense of affectation or facade in the way she spoke or acted in their regard; I could detect no calculation or cynicism in her enunciation of certain values through her dealings with them. Her dogs, her values, her behaviour, were just how Rachel found they had to be, and she had the sense of right, of self-righteousness too, stubbornly to maintain them, irrespective of consequence.

But then Rachel was well aware of their consequence. It became apparent that she deliberately related to local people, and the local milieux in Israel as such, by mediation of her relations with her dogs. She set up an opposition between herself and her dogs on one side and Israelis and their practices on the other, seemingly as a deliberate challenge, even provocation. Not only, I suggest, did Rachel maintain by this means a sense of self, of who she was in the US and should continue to be in Israel, but she also gained a sense of moral superiority. Her opposition (dogs versus Israelis) allowed her to test one thing against another, to represent options to herself, and to see which way she should go.

For Rachel was on a personal journey, as I have said. She might not know where it would lead her, nor in what company. Indeed, since she believed that 'individuals' were inherently 'incomparable', you could never know where someone else's path might lead, and you could not expect to secure specific human companions for yourself. What you took with you were certain values, and setting these in the context of where you happened to be at a particular time – testing how you and others would react to them – you discovered the way to proceed. Rachel's life-project, I have proposed, was to find and live her own life: to prosecute a personal journey to completion. Not to live one's own individual life, indeed, not to grow into one's life by one's journeying through it, Rachel believed to be not merely a waste but a sign of pathology, both social and mental. As we shall see, it was a pathology that gave onto immoral consequences.

Individuality and mental illness

Rachel knew that I was British (the name 'Nigel' was strange to her at first, and she had trouble remembering it), but she could not help admitting that she did not admire Britain; nationalism, imperialism and colonialism she found to be such backward manifestations of the human mind. Nevertheless, it had to be said of Britain that it was the home of the Industrial Revolution: that which had been responsible for 'tearing people away from traditional community life and giving them their individuality', as she put it, which in turn led to democracy. Britain was thus also responsible for developing the best form of constitutional government, and we, as individuals with individual minds, were better off as a result.

The contrasts involved were painfully obvious in Israel. For here, Rachel discovered many people who were 'literally crazy':

> There is lots of mental illness, Nigel; cos people come from repressive traditional societies – the Orientals – where individuality is not allowed and is repressed, and people's real eccentricities don't come out....All these young people you meet here: they know they're searching for something, but they don't know what. They're really keen to ask you all about the West, America and that – like, someone who actually came here, from there, by choice! Cos, I mean, here they are, school, army, 'Look after your Brother!', and all the time there's something individual inside wanting to come out. So they rush here and rush there – all this energy, and aggression – and they dunno for what...I take it you're not on the Right, Nigel!? [I shake my head and grin] Cos I don't think they're very good at playing countries here; they seem to pretend the rest of the world does not exist or is on a different plane....At least as more world government comes into force what happens here is not so important. That's one good thing. But you know what I think? I think a democracy here, that was not a Jewish state, would not be a bad thing. I mean, there are still enough Jewish institutions here now to carry on the same.

Over the months of our meeting – on the streets of Mitzpe, in my apartment or hers, in Hebrew class or the shops – Rachel returned to this theme repeatedly. She had been reading Edward Said, the Palestinian apologist, she revealed to me on one occasion, and been impressed by his claim that the ancient Israelites had only controlled the Land of Israel for about sixty years. So maybe, she continued:

> this great love that the Jews in Babylon and the Diaspora claimed for *Ha'Aretz*, and their boasts about how splendid it was and the rest, was, like, a psychological displacement for a real feeling that 'We blew it' which they couldn't admit to themselves. 'We had our chance in *Ha'Aretz* and we blew it'. I think we're seeing the great mental illness that's been lurking beneath Jewish culture for 2,000 years of Diaspora; it's finally come to the surface in Israel.

I asked her to explain what she meant by 'mental illness':

> I don't mean certifiable 'madness', necessarily, just that you can tell in their words and their actions that something is not quite right. Like, people do things that make a lot of pain in their lives and others' lives....I'd tie it in with the repression of individuality in primitive cultures; tribalism means closed minds and irrational antagonisms. Or here, they're torn between traditional culture and Western permissiveness. So their individuality comes out in other ways....And the young are often worse than the old. Like on the West Bank: do you know how much the Israelis are hated on the West Bank, Nigel? [I nod and grimace] All over. I mean its not surprising but its a real shame for the future. And its the young Israelis too, who haven't been anywhere else and don't have a broad experience. Plus, if they're kids of Holocaust survivors they get worse hang-overs from the older generation; they're very right-wing. They just wanna revolt against the whole situation – the country, their history – so they hit out at anyone; all they see is a mass of Arabs, not individuals....But they just don't get it: they don't see what's happening. The place is like a psychic cesspool! Don't you feel that, Nigel?

Sadly for her, Rachel came increasingly to find that she could put her discussions with many (if not most) Israelis to music; she knew exactly where she and they were going to converge and diverge, and it was always the same. It was a terrible thing to say – and she never thought she would say it – but she even found herself steering clear of certain topics of conversation – Israeli blindspots – just to avoid the repetition and aggravation. She was about to make it up with her Ashkelon boyfriend, for instance, when she happened to be holding a newspaper photograph of an Arab boy in the *intifada* holding up a V-sign. Suddenly her boyfriend exploded: an enormous emotional outburst. It wasn't directed at her either, exactly, it was just that she happened to be holding the newspaper. But it was so vehement that she feared that if he had not loved her he could have killed her! What was so depressing, Rachel concluded, was that the Israelis could not put the energy generated by their blindspot about the Palestinians to better use, to achieving something constructive.

What Rachel found she kept coming back to was the issue of education. Even in the West, she knew, education could be responsible for a lot of brainwashing of the individual. Whereas at best, one should not try to prescribe personal processes of development at all. Nonetheless, she did find it a shame that there was not more higher education in Israel; the real issue that had to be addressed was the large gap between the educated and the non-educated. Certainly, if more people thought like her there would be no wars:

> I had hoped nationalism was a thing of the past and gradually decreasing – though I was maybe being optimistic, cos that's what I wanted to happen. But Israel is so backward in this respect....The US, Russia, these other places are overcoming their nationalism and here's this tiny place, Israel, which by historical accident – World War Two, and the power of the Jews in the Diaspora – is able to set itself up and do nasty nationalistic things, *and* see it in Biblical terms! Like these Bible nuts who say the Bible foretold it all! Its all so different from the relativistic picture you get in Western democracies: 'You may not like everything beyond yourself but you've still no right to destroy it'....No: Israel is an experiment. Definitely. That's the only way to see it.

Judaism and morality and identity

The reflexivity, the introspection, the criticism and even dislike of her fellow Jews which Rachel demonstrated above could be interpreted as the self-consciousness and self-questioning to be expected of the new immigrant. It might be seen, also, as characteristically Israeli: a nation which the novelist Amos Oz pithily depicts as a 'screaming assembly of some five million prophets and prime ministers', all involved in a 'fiery collection of arguments' amongst themselves and about themselves (1992). And Rachel alerts us to this kind of interpretation when admitting to me, with a shake of her head and a wry smile, that: 'only a Jew could come here and understand the place – all the mental illness around. A non-Jew would not know what was going on'. Even: 'I get to feel a little mentally ill here myself!'. It is as if Rachel domesticates the mental illness she infers, and its accompanying effects, as something of an intra-family trait, something Jews can know about themselves, discuss among themselves, but not expect to overcome. Treated as 'a Jewish issue', mental illness becomes something in Rachel's life to which she grows acculturated, something that – like her attachment to her dogs – just is; something which Rachel expects to represent a certain fixity in her life, and which she might accept as such.

Equally, however, Rachel does not expect what 'just is' to be *a single thing*, alone and uncontested. Her relationship with her dogs was something, I suggested, which Rachel construed simply had to be. But then she also construed this relationship as existing alongside other essential things in her life: her personal journey across the globe, to where her values regarding dogs were contested by her new neighbours and their contrastive experience of dogs during the Second World War. In the epigraph to this chapter, likewise, we find Rachel talking about her upbringing in the US as both 'very moral and also Jewish'; here too there appears to be a fundamental contrast, a duality, and an ambivalence which Rachel possessed in regard to that duality. She was Jewish, but not necessarily in terms of her moral foundations, nor in terms of how morality and ethnicity might be squared. In Israel now again, Rachel admitted to her Jewishness but reserved the right to differentiate herself from the 'mental illness' it seemed finally to have spawned. Or again, Rachel admitted to her potential Israeli citizenship but at the same time distanced herself from Israeli 'backwardness': blindspots, chauvinism, under-education and institutions of state.

In other words, Rachel recognized the ontological nature of certain things – their 'is-ness' – but only as part of a deliberate agonistic or dialectic, cognitive process; certain things just were, but in their 'is-ness' they also thereby contrasted fundamentally with other things. Her recognizing ontological contrasts, contests and oppositions, I shall say, was an epistemological and developmental strategy by which Rachel would ascertain who she was at a particular time and place, and could discern how next to proceed. It was a life-policy.

Questions of Jewishness, not surprisingly, arose quite frequently in our exchanges over the months in Mitzpe. Part of the reason Rachel had come to Israel was, after all, out of a desire to understand her Jewishness better. And even though the two years since her *aliyah* had disillusioned her, in a way, there was still a deep sense of her own Jewishness to which she held true. And yet, 'what is this Jewishness?', she asked me one day, before answering her own question:

> It's something in me, Nigel. Like I lived in Yeruham [another Negev development town] for a while and suddenly, at a bus-stop, I chatted to a sixty-year-old Moroccan; and we liked each other. It wasn't sexual, but there was this immediate understanding. So what is that? Are we genetically alike, or do we have the same circuiting in the head, which causes similar behaviour and reactions? Cos we have something similar to all the different types in Israel, don't we?

Or again, she would ponder what it was that made being Jewish something special, before answering her own question in Jungian vein: there was perhaps something 'immortal, a divine spark, witnessed on Mount Sinai', which continued to descend the generations and engender ethnic characteristics.

On the other hand, Rachel would also admit that she had only really known religious Judaism before 'as a sentence', not formed it 'as a reality living beside her'. Furthermore, now that she had:

> I don't feel Jewish any more: I feel 'human', you know, Nigel? [I nod agreement] It was like, in the States I was deprived of Jewishness before I was ready. It was a bit like losing a father: you keep moping after him – even though working for him all his life may not in fact have been better! You know? [We laugh] But now I've worked Jewishness out of my system; if I went home now, I would take this experience with me.

I found it significant in the above interaction that Rachel spoke so openly of having worked through her Jewishness and of going 'home' to the US. It was, after all, only some days previously that Rachel had assured me that 'home' was something she carried round in her head. Now, however, she was above all 'pleased to be American':

> Looking back I like the blanket spread lightly over a very diverse society. I like America.... When I first came here I liked the family feel about the place, you know. But not now: people expecting you, as a stranger, to answer personal questions all the time, and them expecting to have the right to keep asking them.

In the US she found she was 'left alone' in all sorts of ways that made her testy here.

This vacillation or restlessness is something we might have come to associate with Rachel by now. What is perhaps distinctive in the above utterances was the way Rachel veered between what might be called the mystical and the practical, or between the mythopoetic and the empirical, poles of meaning. She both imagined an alchemical mystery of Jewish archetypes with divine origins, and she recognized a psychological rationale for the hold Jewishness had over her and the difficulties of actually living a myth; and she also admitted the gulf separating the two kinds of reasoning.

In describing Rachel's reaction to the 'mental illness' she found in Israel, I proposed that she had come to accept it as something of a 'familial' trait: something she could understand, even assume and find in herself, however sad the occurrence. Likewise, the 'is-ness' of her Jewishness was, I would say, something Rachel construed in familial terms. Jewish Israel was like one big family, one she grew to find suffocating. More than this, Jewishness itself was 'like a father': a genetic inheritance which engendered you – and was inescapable – but which you might not consciously know as a form of life.

But at the same time Rachel maintained a notion of her own individual identity. Her personal journey through life was not one that she expected to be overdetermined by her ethnic origins or necessarily similar to those who began where she did. There was more to her than her Jewishness, than her family beginnings and relations, however others might seek to apply such mystical or mythopoetic collective archetypes in her regard. Thus I was interested on one occasion to hear Rachel reasoning as follows:

> I was beaten up as a girl, you know. Cos I was more sensitive and apt to cry; and cos I was more intelligent than the blockheads around me. And my dad would blame it on anti-Semitism and get very passionate about it. But I knew it wasn't that at all; I didn't tell him though cos I didn't have the vocabulary. And he was so passionate about it he wouldn't have heard me even if I'd tried! But I also learned a psychological lesson: that when I finally hit back and beat the bully to a pulp – it took me a few years to build up to that level of violence – the bully immediately wanted to be best friends.

In other words, Jewishness understood as an inherited archetype – something genetic or neurophysiological, something as inescapable as one's family origins and as mystical as a divine spark – was something that Rachel could recognize in others' behaviours; it was even something that she could be drawn towards herself. But she still reserved the right, on her personal journey through life, to claim an individual intentionality which was practical, empirical and selective. She set up familial Jewishness against merely human Americanness, tested the experience of one against the other, and – at least while in Israel – chose to be more at home in the latter. However Jewish she might continue to feel, it was by no means all she was, or what she essentially was, and she resented it if others assumed the latter to be the case.

Pottery-making in Mitzpe

The individuality of her pathway through life was often enunciated by Rachel in terms of her ceramics: the means by which she had supported herself financially throughout her adult years. This was also true when speaking of others; she did not want to teach ceramics to children in Mitzpe, Rachel explained, because she would not want to 'get into their heads and spoil their development processes'. Pottery-making was a form of artistic expression, as well as an idiom for discussing the latter, which made manifest the individuality of a person's position in, and experience of, the world.

The meaningfulness to be accorded to ceramics became most clear in Rachel's considerations concerning the extent to which she could make Mitzpe Ramon her home. When Rachel emigrated to Israel, as we have heard, she thought she had possibly left ceramics behind her; it had taken her as far as it could and, holding no more surprises, was unlikely to be the route to the growth she next sought. Nevertheless, the men she found herself gravitating towards in Israel tended to be artistic (a painter in En Hod, a geologist in Yeruham), and it was as a pottery teacher at the field school that they had 'invented' a job so that she might legitimately settle in Mitzpe. In practice, the pottery-teaching had not amounted to much and she was soon drawing an unemployment dole from the government agency in town, while she sought out casual employment and considered her options. She cleaned rooms at the field school and at the youth hostel for free food – at least, until they began taking her for granted and trying to work her too hard. She did some piecework at the pottery factory in Yeruham, until they objected to her turning up and leaving according to her own schedules. On beginning a relationship with Zvi, the Hungarian, she took to working with him on the town gardens.

Gradually, however, Rachel realized how inspiring she still found the desert, how it kept drawing her in. Furthermore, it felt as if there were a large void in her life which could be filled only by her setting up a potter's wheel and kiln again, and creating her own ceramics. All along, Rachel admitted to me, collecting her unemployment cheque had made her

> feel a bit hypocritical. I hoped they wouldn't check their computer [and status as a new immigrant in Mitzpe] and see I had a business, and a kiln, and ask me how come I was unemployed. And I'd have to explain how the kiln wasn't set up yet and I hadn't really begun the business.

Once she had made her decision, however, she was energized. She bought and had delivered some tonnes of bricks which were being disposed of by a glass factory in Yeruham – despite the way the factory-owner's eyes lit up at the thought of her giving him shekels for what was his refuse – and she had a kiln constructed on an empty factory site owned by the field school in the town's run-down industrial zone. She fetched her container of personal effects, shipped from the US to the port of Haifa – despite the authoritarian manner with which the harbour official demanded a $700 deposit from her to ensure she did not sell, within the period of a year, any of the *materiel* she was bringing into the country tax-free – and she used the plywood packing-case to make a flywheel for a potter's wheel. Lastly, she ordered a kiln kit – the metal parts, the bearings and so on – from the US, and imagined one day owning a new fibreglass one which she heard they had developed from the Apollo space programme and could now be procured in Tel Aviv. Once her wheel was up she began to feel more like herself again.

Rachel had first moved to Mitzpe Ramon from Beer Sheva, I have said, because she was beguiled by the artistic vision which Uri Hazan had for the place – not to mention the nominal rent. She also found Mitzpe beautiful, especially compared to other development towns, and the youth hostel she first stayed in was run on a casual and familial basis which gave off 'good vibes'. In a word, she felt spiritually connected to the place; she could imagine Mitzpe as a centre for those like herself seeking an inspirational source of mental energy. It was not long after she and I met, moreover, that she told me that one of Uri Hazan's projects was for pots to be made at the field school clayery which might then be sold to tourists in the gift shop at the new Ramon Crater visitors' centre. And Rachel could now imagine making and selling something herself:

> Something that captured the *machtesh* [crater] somehow; I'm not sure how yet. Not glazed on the outside, definitely not. Possibly on the inside.

Making pottery in and of the desert would be a way of manifesting and signalling her newly fashioned, individual relationship to the desert town.

Another of Rachel's new ideas was for 'an energy centre'. In the US, she recounted to me, she and her husband and friends had opened 'a kinda cafe', a coffee shop, for poetry readings, plays and the like. Everyone had contributed $100:

> well, me and my husband put in $500, and the rest put in $100. Do you want to do the same thing here? Everyone chips in, lets say, 100 shekels and then they get in for free – for performances and refreshments and the rest. And in the end, like in the States, we get our investment repaid. Hopefully! [She laughs] It would have to be in some central place where people would see it and just drop in, like a store front. And with Americans and Brits and…Russians coming, it would be a cultural centre. For poetry and art, and gatherings, and getting energy.

At a public meeting of the Mitzpe branch of the immigrant organization for 'Anglo Saxons', Americans And Canadians in Israel (AACI), to which she and I both belonged, Rachel had mooted the plan; but she was met with, at best, a polite indifference from the audience of largely elderly townsfolk. She was thoroughly saddened and disappointed.

Her disappointment, moreover, was to become symptomatic of a change in attitude Rachel soon found herself experiencing with regard to Mitzpe as a place to live as such. It would be okay, she confided in me, 'if the place took off'; she could even imagine buying one of the scores of empty *cottagim* ('villas') for sale at ridiculously low prices if that were to happen. As it was, the place felt deserted and she did not find any community of interests between her and her heterogeneous neighbours. More particularly:

> I'm not surprised more artists don't want to move here.…I guess few people will have the mental energy to live in a place like this. (And

in a country of five million people, there aren't gonna be the numbers; they'll wanna be by everyone else.)

In her disillusionment, the place she had once regarded as potential source of alternative energy now seemed a drain on the very energy individuals possessed when they arrived.

Soon, indeed, I was to find Rachel's disappointment in Mitzpe turning to despair, especially when she returned from a visit with friends in Jerusalem or Tel Aviv:

Rachel: Don't you feel a sort of 'hud'
(she drops her shoulders and makes a noise of weary resignation)
coming back here to Mitzpe, Nigel? Have I missed anything?
(I shrug, and shake my head)
What would I do if I didn't have you to talk to?....I've been very depressed.
Nigel: Yeah, you haven't seemed your usual self.
Rachel: Oh! Did it show? I'm still depressed; but less so....I'm a bit schizo about being here. Are you as well, Nigel?

By 'here', it became clear before long, Rachel was including Israel as well as just Mitzpe:

Living anywhere in Israel leaves you with a 'hud' after a while.

But then I could also recall how disillusionment had been a recurring theme in Rachel's conversation from the beginning. It had not been long after we had met, after all, that she had confided in me how 'weird' her decision to come to Israel already seemed. She was, she explained, prepared to:

give the place one-and-a-half years, till my fiftieth birthday. A year seems like a natural, organic period of time to see if its right for me.

When they had divorced and her husband had given her alimony, she explained, one part of her was thinking that maybe she should use the sum to set up a business in the US; she knew the ropes there, after all. *Now* she could see that this was precisely what she should have done. But she could also see that she was already 'in a ditch' in Israel. If the extent of her 'experiment' here was her ex-husband's $3,000, then she will have spent some $1,000 on procuring a kiln and a further $1,000 assembling it, hardly leaving her enough to 'get home'. When she first came to Mitzpe, she now miserably recalled, Uri Hazan had introduced her to two artists, painters:

a Russian who was just leaving, and a woman, both of whom said 'Don't come'…you know, Nigel? The woman said they are so small-minded here; if they see you wandering round aimlessly, looking for a good artistic sight, they phone your husband cos they think you're after a man!

It was not long, then, before Rachel was telling me that she had decided to move away from Mitzpe altogether; I seemed to be the only person she had to speak to and she was simply not happy without more of a community of soulmates around her. She was going to find an apartment in Jerusalem; there she had already met up with a group of radical women affiliated to the Peace Now group, and to civil rights groups and the International Peace Brigade, who liaised with Palestinian counterparts on the West Bank.

But soon there was another new development:

Rachel: I'm in love, Nigel; for the first time since my husband and I split twenty years ago.
Nigel: Zvi? The gardener?
Rachel: Yeah, Zvi. You'll have to meet him.
Nigel: That's great!
Rachel: I mean I've had relationships, but not with anyone I could see no faults in. And if I get a flat in Jerusalem, Zvi also said he'd visit.

Leaving my apartment she rushed home to dye her hair, disguising the grey in his honour.

But then, as her relationship developed with Zvi, so did the confidence with which Rachel espoused the continuing contradictoriness of her feelings. On the one hand, she was still 'bored shitless' in Mitzpe and looking forward to going to Jerusalem, if only to 'check it out' for a few days. On the other hand, she found she was

> still learning here [in Mitzpe]; so I'm not ready to leave. You know, I find more of the kind of experiences here that are not clear-cut, they're not one thing or another: they're good and bad at the same time.

She also started to see – in particular after renting her room in Jerusalem – that there tended to be far more people on Mitzpe's streets than when she first arrived. In one light, the town was certainly improving – 'or something: changing at least!'. If all the Jewish religious settlers currently living in the West Bank were to come to Mitzpe Ramon instead too, then Rachel could really imagine there being 'something to the town'! This last was said somewhat tongue-in-cheek (Rachel having no love for the Religious Right), but it was also indicative of something specific Rachel felt she had learned:

> I was surprised to find that my feelings about Israel are shared by people who have been living here a while too. They still have reservations about the mentality and are not all taken in by the place.... Like this old Rumanian I got speaking to in Beer Sheva who said its okay here for the kids – cos they know no better – but not for the rest of us.

Meanwhile, she opened her copy of *Other Israel*, an 'alternative-minded' national newspaper, to learn that not even all the North African immigrants were amazingly jingoistic in attitude. Zvi had revealed to her, moreover, that the violent tactics being elicited from the Israelis on the West Bank reminded *him* of nothing so much as the early days of Nazism, and, also in *Other Israel*, she read a long lecture by a Tel Aviv politics professor, as well as an interview with Amos Oz, which came to similar conclusions. In short, Rachel began to find, in Mitzpe as well as beyond, people with whom she felt she shared 'similar vibes'; as she felt she did with me:

> Hey, Nigel: it's so nice having someone else here who isn't so sure about the place!.... We'll have to keep in touch, over the years, see who leaves first. But my life is full at the moment. I mean I'm pleased I went to Jerusalem; I couldn't have hacked it here much longer. But now I can get into both places. Like, my pottery is coming together here now; I made a big wall piece and the hotel said they'd like it. I wanted something that had come out of 'the individual-in-the-desert'. So its this huge wall-ceramic, with pockets – like, organic protuberances where you can put flower pots. And it would be easy to do again – it had no plan, it was just organic – and I could do it anytime, relaxed.

While the uncertainties Rachel seemed to feel about her prior decisions to come to Israel and to Mitzpe Ramon might be regarded as expectable fare from a new immigrant, then, what was distinctive to her – had by now become characteristic – was the vacillation between two opposed poles. Rachel divided up her experience of Mitzpe into 'desert' and 'deserted'; she found herself attracted by the beauty and spiritual potential of the place and, in seeming equal measure, put off by the narrowness and lack of focus of its emigre population. Having created the distinction, she knew more where she stood and where she was going. Life became full again, a learning curve, by way of new experiences which were grounded in, and consequent upon, this agonistic dialectic.

Rachel seemed to settle herself into Mitzpe, and into Israel more generally, by accruing experiences which were 'schizo' – neither absolutely one thing nor another – and between whose poles she might cognitively and emotionally journey.

ILLUSTRATIONS

A political animal who touches the earth

In America, as Rachel phrased it, there was both morality in her life and there was Judaism; putting the two together – the 'thesis' and the 'antithesis', one might say – had provided her with the logic and the impetus with which to seek a completion – or 'synthesis' – in Israel, and to pursue the next part of her personal life-journey. Out of this erstwhile synthesis a new dialectic was then born, in Mitzpe Ramon, between beautiful desert town and deserted development town: between the energy and the void. By the time I first met Rachel, a little over a year since she had first settled in Mitzpe (and after five months of actual habitation), this dialectical division within her experience of the town had, in its turn, given onto another vista: Mitzpe *vis-à-vis* Jerusalem. Here was a division between desert and metropolis, also between a new lover and a radical-feminist coterie, and between organic ceramics and a lively round of alternative politics. The final part of the story of Rachel as I would tell it – for I did indeed leave Israel before her – concerns her consolidation of these new-found dialectics.

At the same time as she and I attended Hebrew classes together in Mitzpe town hall, Rachel decided she would like to learn Arabic – if only to 'get a few words'. She was disappointed that no-one else in *kita* ('class') was taken by her suggestion, but for Rachel, it soon became apparent that this was part of a more general attraction:

Rachel: I had a great conversation with an Arab from Gaza who worked in that brick factory in Yeruham, Nigel. As a rule I think I have better conversations with Arabs than with Jews!
Nigel: Were you speaking in Hebrew?
(she nods)
That's impressive!
Rachel: Yeah; it helped that it was a second language for the both of us....But don't you find that? That with people who have similar views, whose head-space is similar to yours, you can communicate without words, or despite words, better than you can with people in the same language? I do.

Next, Rachel was telling me that she preferred Palestinians to Israelis: 'They're so normal. You can have normal relations with them – with words or without them'. When she first came to Israel, she remembered, she had had certain 'flash insights', one of which was that she would be happier living on the West Bank, with Arabs. She should have followed up her insights at that period, she now recognized; as you got more settled, something like that became harder to do.

At the same time, it was clear that the flowering of her relationship with Zvi and his children was finally giving Rachel a sense of belonging in Mitzpe. She took care decorating her apartment with her ceramics, and she built book-cases and furniture with the wooden packaging from her shipment that was left over from the making of her potter's wheel. She took an interest in local municipal elections and let herself be wooed by the town's political hopefuls (voting in the end for 'the only man for the job': an economics graduate with a cute face, and the only candidate who was 'not a political appointment'). Indeed, Rachel became cognizant of Israeli politics more broadly, noting that a few 'Anglos' (Jews of 'Anglo-Saxon' or English-speaking origin) who, like her, would in the past have simply retreated from a political culture they distrusted, were now putting themselves forward as electoral candidates around the country (not on any particular political platform, simply 'to get the bureaucracy cleaned up'). She also decided to join with other members of the Mitzpe AACI to lobby against the Israeli exit tax (a sum levied whenever a resident left the country for a trip), not so much for the money involved as for the 'nasty image' of the country which it compounded – part of a 'general repression'.

Rachel found the bureaucratic inefficiency endemic in Israel extremely disappointing. She laid the blame on the 'clerk' system of administration that had been set up, whereby money filtered down to functionaries from top officials which the clerks then used largely to maintain their own positions. It meant that all kinds of obstacles were put in the path of ordinary people's everyday life: because the clerks wanted them to keep them within their administrative orbit – not let them become independent actors, or distinctive or successful. Each time that Rachel had a bureaucratic appointment she had to gear herself up for the encounter long beforehand. But she still went through with it; so long as she was resident in Israel she recognized that she had to get to grips with the bureaucracy if she was to 'sort out some sort of a life' for herself.

One of the first things Rachel did, then, as she settled into her relationship with Zvi in Mitzpe, was to enrol at an Arabic course at the Buber Center in Jerusalem. It ran on Monday and Wednesday nights, and she would stay over in the city for that period. She became very excited at the prospect – and duly 'loved' the experience. She also kept up her Hebrew, with Zvi giving her simple reading and vocabulary exercises. What she appreciated perhaps most of all, she realized, was the 'learning situation' *per se*. Whenever she had a spare moment in Beer Sheva, for instance (while *en route*, by bus, north or south), she would spend time in the university library, reading all sorts of journals on all sorts of subjects – from numismatics to anthropology – just like she used to do in Boston. She could imagine herself having become an academic, indeed, enjoying the perennial flow and exchange of ideas.

In fact, Rachel now realized she had missed out on academia too long and it was time for a major change. She would enrol in grad school at the Hebrew University in Jerusalem, and study political science. 'What does it take to make the democratic personality?', she wanted to know; 'What is it in someone's upbringing and family history that leads them to respect democracy?'; 'How do you develop empathy in an economic system?', and 'Why are some people better able to empathize than others?'. She accepted that books were not the same as life, but she would like to acquire the research tools to try to answer these kinds of question.

Robert, a friend of hers, had just completed a postgraduate course at the Hebrew University, and he warned her how hard the language issue was going to be for her. But: 'Isn't grad school fun?', she sought my assurance, because:

> I would like to look at how people could be made to use democracy better, to appreciate it. Cos that's what its all about, isn't it, Nigel? Curbing evil men. Stopping evil men getting to positions of power. [I nod] Anyway, I've decided I'm gonna sign up for a pol. sci. course – and then procrastinate over when to start. Cos my Hebrew is not good enough yet for the background reading; a lot of it is in Hebrew.

In the meantime, Rachel would become more involved in the cause of alternative politics and non-violent protest in Israel. In company with her radical-feminist friends from Jerusalem, she attended demonstrations at prisons where the army was holding Palestinian 'troublemakers', and she helped set up 'tent cities' outside the prison walls. She visited villages in Israel where Jews and Arabs lived in harmony, and she sought access to villages and refugee camps in the West Bank and Gaza where she might liaise with Palestinian groups – women whom the *intifada* had liberated from their traditional silence and subservience – and meet with foreign volunteers who ran institutions such as orphanages. She kept a record of the violence, the sado-masochism, the 'disappearances' and beatings about which she heard, and of the occasions where laws outlawing the PLO were employed by the army to stymie peaceful communication and cooperation. Armed with this information she then contacted the left-wing political party, *Ratz*, and was also put in touch with an Israeli institute that was building up a database on conditions in the West Bank.

Once she was convinced that, as she anticipated, I was not on the political right, Rachel also revealed to me how she had written letters to 'the President'. In the US she had placed herself on the mailing list of a Palestinian magazine that attempted impartially to report on the West Bank (when she moved to Israel she just gave them her new postal address). By now writing to the US President and also the Secretary of State and a number of newspapers – the *New York Times*, the *Globe* – about the violence in Israel, she could maintain a voice within the alternative Jewish-American lobby, getting America to see – through Jews – a different Israel. And if Israel then 'got what was coming to it', so be it.

At first Rachel was chary about putting her analyses of the mental illness and the violence in Israel into print. But once she saw that reprint of the

Amos Oz interview from an American newspaper, and also found that it had been taken up by *Ma'Arev*, a mainstream Israeli newspaper, she felt better about it. Entering these fields where others had spent so much more time and energy, Rachel confided that she sometimes felt like a child (she had when dealing with politics in the US too); and when she attempted to put her experiences in Israel on paper, to share what was in her head with a wider audience, it also usually sounded infantile. Nevertheless, her new Jerusalem flatmate, who had been politically active for far longer than she, had given Rachel material to read, and slowly Rachel felt she was 'improving'; a bit like when talking to me, she admitted, something 'resonated' and 'suddenly new doors open[ed]' for her.

The crucial point, Rachel elaborated, was that she could not bear being put in the position of 'oppressor'. And that was precisely what the Israeli government was making of her just by her being here; but now, at last, she could feel she was doing something about it. For you could not presume to say what was best for the Palestinians, as some Israeli commentators did, nor could you dismiss the situation, as did others, by recounting how much better off the Palestinians actually were living in Israel than they would be in an Arab country. That was irrelevant (two wrongs did not make a right). It was also irrelevant to compare Israel with the situations in Ireland or Russia – however much worse the latter may be. For here was a situation that she and others in Israel could possibly improve on. Indeed, she grew so incensed about the Israeli right-wing and their political leaders – mean, loathful people, as well as politically crazy (and running the country to boot, at present) – that she sometimes felt she would like to 'assassinate' 'their' prime minister, if she 'had the guts, or at least see him killed'.

A dialectics of personal growth

In my account of Rachel Silberstein, I have argued that her practice was continually to construe certain essentialized but contrastive aspects of the world – Judaism and morality; mental illness and alternative energy; her relations with her dogs and her movement round the world; the desert and the city; her pottery and her politics – and then to proceed to vacillate between these fixed points. Her vacillation freed her from the overriding influence of any one fixity – whether that influence was of an intellectual kind, or emotional, or physical, or cultural, or historical, or autobiographical. Her attempts to come to terms with and overcome the contrasts between these fixities, meanwhile, provided a tension, a dialectic, whereby she continued to give her life impetus and direction; her identification of extreme positions – 'psychic cesspool', 'Nazism', 'assassination' – gave onto the comparative moderation which her own journey eventually took. Rachel's life-project was to find the direction and the road to personal completion which she believed to be her proper, individual right, her interest and her need.

I was struck by Rachel's willingness and capacity for enunciating her own self-analyses. She knew she felt 'schizo' in Mitzpe and in Israel – also that this mirrored a duality that had brought her here initially – and that she was continuing to find experiences which were not 'clear-cut', not 'one thing or another'. She also knew how a juggling with difference was in her nature, and necessary for her equilibrium; as she put it on one occasion: 'I'm a political animal, Nigel, but I also need to touch the earth for my sanity'. Rachel recognized, too, how much individuality – individual thought and experience – was a value for her, and she conceived of this in terms of a cultural evolution from the traditional, communitarian Orient to the industrialized, developed West: from repression to self-expression.

There is much here, notwithstanding, that could be dismissed as reiterative, conventional and expectable. I have drawn attention to the way her various responses might be seen to mirror those to be anticipated from a new immigrant: questioning herself, her decisions and reactions, placing her life-course in analytical perspective, and so on. Likewise, her conceptualization of the world around her, the cognitive landmarks she identified in the social and cultural landscapes through which she moved – 'morality' versus 'Judaism', 'left-wing' versus 'right-wing', 'desert town' versus 'lively metropolis', 'Jew' versus 'Arab', 'bureaucrat' versus 'artist', and so on – these classifications and evaluations could be said to be hardly new to her ('a child of the 1960s'). Nor, again, might there be anything particularly novel in tying the individual/community distinction to a geographical and developmental evaluation concerning the West and the Rest. Said's popular *Orientalism* thesis (1978), at least some of which Rachel seemed to have taken on board, harangued against the purported injustices of this hierarchical and essentializing bifurcation said to be historically endemic to the West. Other commentators, meanwhile, have elaborated upon the Durkheimian thesis that the supreme valuation of the individual or self or *moi* in the West is merely the conventional way in which these societies have come to enculturate their members into a collective conscience – eliciting loyalty and control, justifying a derogation and, if necessary, subjugation of the person (Dumont 1986; Foucault 1977). In short, in her self-analyses (as I have recounted them), Rachel could be said to employ cognitive schemata which are anything but novel or hers own alone. In content they rehash stereotypical histories; in form they rehearse a binary dividing up of things into discrete essences which, it has been mooted, is the conventional Western ideational archetype (and fallacy) *par excellence* (Whitehead 1925); in application they reproduce Western solidarities and its traditional excuses for traducing the Other.

However, leaving aside the conventionality or otherwise of her cognitive schemata, what I would define as distinctly individual is the precise way Rachel dealt with these cognitions, navigating around and between extreme positionings as she charted a continuing life-course for herself. I would argue that she conjured up *her own* dialectics of personal growth – succeeded in plotting a way onward and upward always based on her personal reactions, and put into effect a progression whose logic stemmed from her own personal history. Rachel might have been lonely for company along the road, she might have sought congenial companions at each point along the way, but she did not make her decisions about moving on the basis of these relationships and she did not expect others' journeys and paths necessarily to overlap with hers. The cognitive landmarks with which Rachel dealt – morality versus Judaism, desert town versus lively metropolis – became personalized in her use of them, became something individual to her, then, not only by the way she set up often idiosyncratic oppositions between them and then vacillated between these – refusing the haven, the stasis and the limitation of any one landmark – but also by dint of the biographical history of vacillation and plotting which she brought to each ensuing encounter. She brought to the landmarks an understanding and a treatment which were equally her own.

Nietzsche writes at one point about how he esteems 'brief habits'; he fears the 'tyranny' of longer-standing ones for the way they might involve an arresting of experience and of the pursuit of authenticity (1960: 295). He can see the attractions of a search for stability and stasis – breaking habits takes courage and independence of mind, for it easily gives onto an individual journey and solitude – but he also believes more strongly that '[t]he will to a system is a lack of integrity' (1979c: 25). Approaching the complex wholeness of experience – putting oneself in a position to appreciate complexity – calls for a non-systemic and non-habitual apperception; Nietzsche, for one, would 'mistrust all systematizers and avoid them' (1979c: 25).

I do not think that Nietzsche would have seen fit to mistrust Rachel Silberstein on this score. She was brief in her habits and professed to having an enjoyable fullness to her life chiefly when she provided herself with a novel tension, an opposition, whose dialectical resolution would ultimately lead her further down the road of personal completion – if only by way of further tensions. She moved between essential features of a landscape but she herself seemed to claim none – except, perhaps, the individuality that carried her to the multiple, personal positionings and perspectives on life which she adopted as source of learning and fulfilment.

It was not always clear to Rachel in which direction she was going or to where; her world-view was that life was a quest, without a route or a destination known beforehand, and hence necessarily accompanied by experimentation, questioning and uncertainty. But she did consciously adopt a certain attitude towards this, namely a belief that partaking in the quest was an individual responsibility; no one could participate for her, no one should enter her 'head-space' and corrupt the individuality of her decisions, and no one should stop her – and she should not stop herself. Moreover, she appeared to me to practise largely an affirmative attitude towards the fate that this mindset brought about.

I have imagined Rachel's life-project as concerning travelling an individual road to personal completion. Her belief in this life-project gave her the confidence and the impetus, the compulsion, to travel between countries, identities, relationships, loyalties, social structures, institutions and habitations – all the time believing she was the same person on the same project. The strength of Rachel's relationship with her own life-project, and the logic of the decisions it provided her with (acting 'in order to'), all the time bolstered her and energized further travel.

Did, then, Rachel achieve control in her life? She professed to be 'in a ditch' financially, to find the backward parts of the human mentality (nationalism, violence and aggression) depressing, to find her dealings with bureaucracy distasteful, on occasion to feeling bored and alone; but then she also professed to finding these 'learning experiences', and they did eventuate from her own decisions to move. Over what she sought to – over what she found important in her life – I would say Rachel did exercise control; 'control', for Rachel, meant above all going her own way: a way forward that she independently conceived of, and that she experienced as right for her, as bringing personal growth.

6

STANLEY SPENCER AND THE VISIONARY METAPHYSIC OF LOVE

> I like my own life so much that I would like to cover every empty space on a wall with it.
>
> I don't want to lose sight of myself for a second.
>
> (Stanley Spencer)

In his 1991 biography of Stanley Spencer (1891–1959), Kenneth Pople offers an elaboration on the English painter's early pen-and-ink sketch, *The Fairy on the Waterlily Leaf* (Figure 3).

The sketch was drawn in 1910 when Stanley was eighteen, on the request of a Miss White whom he knew from the Berkshire village of Bourne End, to illustrate a fairy story she had written. But she was not pleased with the result and rejected it. Stanley was puzzled by the rejection and disappointed. Nine years later he again gave it as a gift, this time to his friend Ruth Lowy and her betrothed, Victor Gollancz (the publisher), and again was asked what it meant. He replied that it was a fairy on a waterlily leaf but that beyond that he did not honestly know what the picture was all about or what it was called. 'I was loving something desperately', Stanley later wrote of this time, 'but what this was I had not the least idea' (cited in Pople 1991: 21). What this something was, Pople suggests, was Stanley's dawning awareness of the miracle of love as such: his 'metaphysic of love' as it was to become. Drawn from deep personal feelings as yet unclarified, it was this that the sketch set out to honour: a depiction of love, whose depicting was in itself an act of love.

Pople elaborates (1991: 19–20): Stanley's fairy is a sturdy girl – no elfin – seemingly impossibly posed on two waterlily leaves above a pond. She is being courted by a prince in Renaissance dress (in the shape of a youth called Edmunds, a male model from Stanley's life class at the Slade School of Fine Art). The fairy figure is a representation of the village girl Dorothy Wooster, with whom Stanley had been a school pupil and to whom he had felt a boyish attraction. In order to imagine a prince's love for a fairy – the theme of Miss White's original story – Stanley had assembled images from his own experience; in this way he had sought to reproduce the emotion of the

ILLUSTRATIONS

Figure 3 Stanley Spencer, *The Fairy on the Waterlily Leaf* (41.9 × 30.5cm) 1910
Source: Stanley Spencer Gallery, Cookham.

theme. He draws Dorothy, therefore, beautiful and impossibly buoyant (physically speaking) because that is the sense his love for her translates as (metaphysically speaking): the physical logistics of the imagery become subservient to the emotion he feels for his subjects and imagines, therefore, for their relations one with another. As for the water, he chooses a little sandy beach by the bank of the Thames which he knew from his playing there as a boy. Finally, he adds scale to the central scenario by diminishing Dorothy's size relative to a row of wheatstalks on her right, and he adds perspective by way of three flowers or marsh plants which he draws in the top left-hand corner. On one view the plants seem to have been thrown up into the air by a juggling Dorothy (one of Stanley's older brothers became a professional juggler and entertainer). But on another, the marsh plants suggest that Stanley wishes us, like the prince, to be looking down on the scene as from above: as though Stanley had made the vertical height of the sketch into a horizontal expanse of smooth water. We and the prince are looking through the water of the pond at the fairy as through a window. The fairy's world is enchanting and lovable but also enchanted and intangible – as enchanted perhaps as the world Stanley associates with music (thus the crotchet-like shape of the plants), and as intangible as his (dawning) world of love still is for him. The fairy is an emanation of that world, but she must return there when the music stops; the prince cannot follow (any more than Stanley could follow the village girls into their world or find his visions in their mundane conversations). Nevertheless, in the picture there is the hint of love overcoming the boundaries between worlds: transcending the displacements of the physical and the spiritual, the everyday and the heavenly.

The picture comprises a visionary world, then, which brings together Stanley's personal everyday experience, grounded in local places and relations, with a transcendent theme: the dreams and hopes of a personal redemption through love. It was this theme, identifiable but mute in Stanley's early sketch, which was significantly and overtly to characterize his mature art. Art amounted to 'a parallel constructive order' to outward reality; through 'the spiritual framework of artistic desires', 'the everyday [could] be experienced as Edenic' (Spencer, cited in Patrizio and Little 1994: n.p.). As he matured, Stanley was to identify his artistic sense as his life-project; in pictures and in words he would compose and he would live a 'metaphysic of love'. It was a life-project which would issue in an artistic oeuvre of great originality and idiosyncrasy, and in a life-course which followed its own logic:

> My personal life is up-in-heaven life. My impersonal life is a separate-from-me thing, and my behaviour is quite difficult.

A brief biography

Stanley Spencer was born on 30 June 1891, at the village of Cookham-on-Thames, Berkshire (some thirty miles from London). He was the eighth surviving child of Anna and William Spencer, and grew up with six brothers and two sisters. The village was full of cousins, too, since Stanley's paternal grandfather had married twice and sired two large local families. The grandfather had been a builder who had moved to Cookham to benefit from the call for genteel, red-brick residences – for middle-class families who took advantage of the new railways to live outside London. Grandpa was also a musician and began a village choir, a tradition Stanley's father carried on in his role as a professional (peripatetic) music teacher and church organist. Christianity, for Stanley's father, was a poetic but all-embracing truth, as real and present as the immediate environment of Cookham village.

Stanley thus grew up in a large, noisy, musical and also literary household (the house was semi-detached and a family of first-cousins lived next door). There were musical recitations, debates, and frequent readings from the Bible. The family exhibited a close identity of scholarly interests and passions, maintaining a catholicity of tastes, a solicitude for the natural world and its moods, and detailed memories. 'The comprehension and the validity of experience' became something like the family lodestar (Pople 1991: 10).

Visual stimulation Stanley found in the form of Pre-Raphaelite pictures dotted around the family house, also in the large, illustrated family Bible and in pictorial books by Ruskin; and there were annual expeditions with Father and younger brother Gilbert to view the summer exhibitions at the London Royal Academy. While Stanley was taught initially at the dame school run by his sisters in a shed in their cousins' next-door garden, he always showed more interest in drawing than in his lessons; certainly he showed little early facility for the linear logic either of mathematics or of narrative form. He would also spend time wandering around Cookham – a village that he was to grow to love above all other places (indeed, to see as 'a village in heaven') – absorbing its atmosphere. If home was being cosily and contentedly tucked up in the family house, with those who loved him and shared his interests, then, like a child at a window gazing at the world beyond, Stanley was never to lose the sense of childhood fascination of venturing from home and being able, in a few steps, to feel an ambience at once familiar but also other-worldly. The relationship between the known situation and a new mysterious atmosphere, he was later to explain, seemed to him a vital interdependency between apparent opposites; it was like the musical inversions of a fugue, or like the house of his cousins on the other side of the dividing wall which separated their respective semi-detached homes: here was the known and here the other-worldly, here the outward truth and here the metaphysical.

While growing up to be himself an accomplished musician, able to reproduce melodies he had once heard by his keeping hearing them within himself – giving them an interior voice – Stanley announced, at the age of sixteen, his intention of becoming an artist. His father, supportive of his efforts as far as possible, arranged for him to have lessons with a local woman who painted watercolours. Shortly afterwards Stanley entered Maidenhead Technical Institute, and a year later, initially through the financial assistance of his father's sometime local patron, a Lady Boston, he went up to the celebrated Slade School, in London.

Stanley studied at the Slade from 1908 to 1912, gaining a scholarship, and enjoying among his contemporaries future luminaries of modern British art such as Paul Nash, Mark Gertler, David Bomberg, Ben Nicholson and Dora Carrington. But still, while other students were called by their surnames, Stanley was known by his fellows, half-affectionately, as 'our genius', or simply as 'Cookham' – so much his home that Stanley travelled to and from there, religiously, every day on the train, and so seemingly synonymous with his suburban, parochial world-view.

Cookham also remained Stanley's artistic inspiration. Even as his contemporaries were swept up in Continental art movements – Post-Impressionism, Cubism, Vorticism and Expressionism – and while friends such as Gwen Raverat (née Darwin, Charles' granddaughter) introduced him both to notions of political revolt against Victorian materialism and, later, to Bloomsbury-Group literary experimentation, Stanley remained enchanted by the validity of his Cookham experience. In Cookham he knew exactly where he was, what he had to do, and why; his spirit would soar and his imagination kindle, as he set out to explore, and then represent, the world of deep mysteries and 'miracles' he experienced around him.

In 1915, the First World War being a year in process, and having graduated from the Slade, Stanley enlisted in the Royal Army Medical Corps. He was stationed at a war hospital in Bristol as a medical orderly and then with the Field Ambulance in Macedonia. In 1917 he volunteered to join the 7th Battalion Royal Berkshires. On being demobbed, he again returned to Cookham and to painting. But short of money, and living and lodging with friends as he could, he also began the rather displaced existence among houses and villages which was to last much of his life: moving between Cookham and Bourne End, Durweston and Steep, Petersfield and Hampstead, Poole and Burghclere, St Ives and Swiss Cottage, Leonard Stanley, Port Glasgow and Epsom – and again Cookham.

In 1925 Stanley married Hilda Carline, a painter whom he had met at the New English Art Club in London; their first daughter, Shirin, was born the same year. The following years, 1926–7, he mounted his first one-man show, in London. Between 1927 and 1932 he was largely engaged in painting a First World War memorial to commission – Sandham Memorial Chapel, at Burghclere, Hampshire – while in 1930, a second daughter, Unity, was born. In 1932 Stanley was elected an Associate Member of the Royal Academy, but resigned in 1935 because of disagreements concerning his art. In 1937 he was divorced by Hilda, but he immediately remarried Patricia Preece. In 1940, the Second World War having begun, he was commissioned to paint the shipyards at Port Glasgow by the War Artists' Advisory Committee, working on this series of paintings until 1950, when he was made a CBE (Commander of the British Empire). In the same year he rejoined the Royal Academy and was elected to a Full Membership. Also in the same year, his ex-wife (and still closest friend) Hilda died, while protracted divorce proceedings with Patricia began. In 1950, too, he was threatened with prosecution on grounds of obscenity in his artistic works (uncompromising nudes and unconventional couplings) by retiring President of the Royal Academy, Alfred Munnings (who himself favoured rustic paintings of horses and gypsies), the case gaining some notoriety in the national newspapers. In 1955, notwithstanding, Stanley enjoyed a large retrospective exhibition of his work at the Tate Gallery, London, and in 1958 he was knighted and also received an Honorary D.Litt. from Southampton University. In 1959, Stanley Spencer died, of cancer of the colon; he was sixty-eight.

An artful autobiography

It was in 1938 that some friends (including Victor Gollancz) tried to encourage Stanley to write his autobiography. They argued that it would both help him make money towards his increasing domestic costs (one wife, one ex-wife and two daughters), and also explain himself to a public increasingly distanced by (what the critic John Berger would dub) the growing 'oddness' of his paintings' personal iconography (cited in Bell 1992: 232). At first Stanley was quite taken with the idea. In writing his autobiography, he reflected, he would see his life as a whole, identify the 'constant something in myself that I consider to be the essential me that I like' (cited in Collis 1962: 182). He would compose it not as a linear, chronological narrative but as if a stroll through his life, in different genres and styles, with digressions and pauses as the mood took him; chronological formality was less important to establish than sentimental development. He would write the story and at the same time illustrate it with drawing and painting; the whole would amount to a complex interchange of words and images. Neither stressing nor omitting anything, he would encapsulate all his thoughts, feelings and doings to date and thus 'redeem' them all.

Eventually, however, Stanley decided against it; if people would not understand his paintings, then why should they understand his writing about them? The paintings were clear enough – *Love Among the Nations* (1935); *Adoration of Old Men* (1937); *Sunflower and Dog Worship* (1937); *Women Going for a Walk in Heaven* (1938) – and his vision was not substitutable. Nevertheless, he did begin to write, and would thenceforth constantly be seen doing so. For the next twenty-one years he composed diaries, journals, extensive essays and unsent letters: some random jottings, some more formally styled; some directly accessible, some more nuanced and coded. It became an obsession and he kept every scrap he wrote: entreaties, memories and love-makings, philosophical, confessional, masturbatory and obsessional, about and to his paintings, wives, family, friends and himself. 'Writing', Stanley declared, 'is rejoicing' (cited in Collis 1962: 154), and another form of (sorting his thoughts and) making love to the world: something for which he demanded the emotional space to continue to practise, whether in public or private.

By the time of his death, his writing amounted to thousands of pages and millions of words. Collected in trunks, unordered, Stanley would dip into the storehouse as into a treasure chest, to re-read, reannotate, repaginate and rearrange. Indeed, familiarizing himself with the works of Shakespeare, Milton, Marlowe, Marvell, Blake, Keats and Dostoyevsky, he became a distinctive stylist. In the opinion of one of his biographers, Stanley may, with more formal training, have become as much a poet as a painter (Pople 1991: 15); and critic Tim Hyman concurs: the 'most fulfilled, courageous and irreplaceable British artist of the [twentieth] century' may have even been better with words than paint (1991: 33). Perhaps no other major artist since William Blake interwove his painting so closely with, and revealed himself so fully through, his writing: 'a stream-of-consciousness chronicle...unparalleled both in volume and intensity by any artist in the twentieth century' (Glew 2001: 13).

In seeking, then, a more nuanced appreciation of Stanley Spencer's art – the meaning he posited in it, and the place of his interpretation, reflection and revaluation, his vision, in the conscious control he exercised over his life – it is not inappropriate to include a selection of Spencer's own words in counterpoint. (All are taken from an extensive archive of Spencer's written materials, now housed at the Stanley Spencer Gallery, Cookham, and at London's Tate Gallery [cf. Glew 2001]; they are exracted here but are otherwise left unattributed.) Including his words also gives me some confidence that my largely verbal exposition of Spencer's visual expression may not be inappropriate.

Stanley Spencer's art, I shall argue, was something he used both to prescribe a general philosophy for earthly life and to describe – reflect, correct and redeem – his own life in particular. His personal vision amounted to the prosecution of a life-project through which he would succeed in dealing with the world on his own terms and in his own image.

A personal vision

Stanley surprised people in never knowing quite what to say when asked if he believed in God. Certainly he cherished no notions of an intimate figure, and he was appalled by those who made religion an excuse for dividing members from non-members, believers from non-believers, and for instituting a certain discipline on the world and its beings. This, he felt, was to parade an insensitivity to the fullness of experience and the need always to open oneself up to its complexity.

> *It is for me to go where the spirit moves me, and not to attempt to ally it to some known and specified religion.*

> *There is no-one saying no in my pictures all are saying yes.*

Nonetheless, an appropriate place to start an inside story of Stanley's art is with his Wesleyan Methodist upbringing – the ethos which, together with that of Gladstonean liberalism, permeated his childhood and represented the norms imbuing the domestic order of his family life. Here Stanley found a value placed on non-monetary things and a faith in perfect universal love, mediated by a one-to-one relationship with God, and attainable on earth. Its paradigm expression was the imagery of the Bible and the services in Cookham Wesleyan Chapel. It gave onto a coherent world order – homely, gentle, secure, comfortable, productive – in which, to an imaginative boy and youth, Cookham seemed to embody a 'sacred presence': a 'holy suburb of heaven'. Here, the natural and the supernatural commingled and other-worldly visions might be taken for granted; if the family home was, in major part, a manifestation of the terrestrial world, then domestic servants talking in attic rooms were likely to be communing with angels. Likewise, the swans on the Thames were metamorphosed angels, while on the field below Cliveden Woods, biblical shepherds watched their flocks, and Cookham churchyard was a way-station to Eden. The timeless stories of the Bible Stanley observed in his own personal childhood environment, translating their drama and other-worldliness into the everyday of his lived experience.

> *I like to take my thoughts for a walk and marry them to some place in Cookham.*

> *The thing which interests me and always has done is the way that ordinary experiences or happenings in life are continually developing and bringing to light all sorts of artistic discoveries.*

> *Religion (or love I don't mind) brings happiness & happiness brings gratitude & gratitude brings aspiration: the wish to express it in the best possible way....And this brings passion & passion brings & reaches to creative power. This is the way of Vision. It ends with me seeing this special, & to me crucial meaningfulness in ordinary appearance.*

Cookham simultaneously inspired Stanley and grounded him: allowed him to see universal truths and afforded him contact with, and bearings on, the here and now. And the sense of the village representing an earthly paradise stayed with him throughout his early adulthood. The experience of London and the Slade only made him more sure: everything in Cookham was cosy, innocent and of the eternal.

It was sitting in the family pew at church one morning in 1915, and hearing the activities of the village and the river going on outside, and again having the sense of the sanctity of the whole – church and village as one, so-called 'sacred' plus 'profane' – that Stanley recalled having the idea of taking his 'in-church' feeling 'out of church' and, in his art, transferring an act of worship to seemingly secular rituals, people and places.

> *[I wanted to take] the inmost of one's wishes, the most varied religious feelings...and to make it an ordinary fact of the street.*

> *I became aware that everywhere was full of special meaning and this made everything holy....I saw many burning bushes in Cookham. I observed this sacred quality in most unexpected quarters.*
> *What I saw was miraculous....Ever since these Cookham experiences, every tomorrow has seemed as the world to come.*

It was an idea (a unity and a stillness) that would initially be disrupted by his service in the First World War, but to which he would return thereafter with renewed inspiration and zeal.

To an extent, his experiences in the war provided a decisive rupture to Stanley's life, a displacement from an innocent vision. Thereafter, 'Cookham' represented a rapturous golden age he must now be intent on recapturing, through intervening experiences which he must redeem. As a medical orderly and latterly a soldier, he had succeeded in mentally escaping a detestable deindividuation and regimentation (courtesy of Augustine's *Confessions*) by finding a personal spirituality in menial tasks and everyday routines; but it was not until he began painting again that he was to achieve a full catharsis.

> *[Painting] redeemed my experience from what it was; namely something alien to me. By this means I recover my lost self.*

> *The first place an artist should find himself is in prison. The moment he realizes he is a prisoner, he is an artist, and the moment he is an artist, he starts to free himself.*

> *I have therefore thought that a great deal in this life was a key to the perfect life of heaven.*

Returning to Cookham and absorbing its atmosphere, then recording it in paint, was being again in heaven. Marrying his thoughts and feelings to people, places and events around the village – the divinity of their everyday occupations, the ritual of their parochial activities – was to create something holy.

Notwithstanding, the First World War was not the only disruption of a major, even tragic, kind in Stanley's life. His discovery of sex, his marriage to Hilda Carline, his polygamous desire for Patricia Preece, his divorce from Hilda, his feelings of terrible loss over Hilda, his estrangement from

Patricia, his relative poverty and homelessness (houselessness) – all of these precipitated crises of consciousness of a kind. The 'Stanley Spencer' whom he had understood himself to be, who was his life's guiding measure, was under threat. His encounter with, even persecution by, a small-minded, interfering and censorious public brought his encounter with himself to a head.

> *Existing laws and conventions interfere to a serious degree with my paintings. My art depends on emotions and wishes. If they are interfered with my work suffers. I know the excellence of these wishes. I know the powers these wishes have. It is ghastly that my art should be made subject to what vulgarity happens to lay down in law and morality. Such values, applied to my pictures, are quite inadequate to elucidate their true meaning. I am not against anything I know of. I will examine a religious scale of values as carefully as a non-religious scale. I am prejudiced to the religious side. But I am not going to have the religionist telling me what to worship. In all my sex experience I notice the same degree of emotion as in religious experience. But I feel lonely in finding myself the only worshipper when I am convinced the erotic side I am drawn to belongs to the very essence of religion. I feel that I am actually discovering a hoard of significant meanings to life, but am being hampered in my task.*

His action, however, was in each case to find himself again in his art-world (his writing as well as his painting); here, Stanley successfully and continually achieved equilibrium. Through his art he found a continuity and coherence to the narrative of his life, redemption for what had passed, joy in what was now and hope for what was to come; through his art he would build a monument not only to his everyday experience but also to his fantasy, and to the expression of his true needs.

Above all, his art, and the disciplined imagination with which Stanley approached it, replaced with order the disruption, the displacements and dissociations, of life. His art provided him with a wholeness and a fulfilment missing in other relationships – or, better put, made life and art one. Through living his art world, what Stanley found in the wider world reflected what he felt in his inner world.

> *I have always looked forward to seeing what I could fish out of myself. I am a treasure island seeker and the island is myself.*

> *I am aware that all sorts of parts of me are lying about waiting to join me. It is the way I complete and fulfil myself.*

> *Art is where I can find peace.*

But there was more. For, to this personally cathartic displacement and achievement of wholeness, Stanley came to marry an iconography (initially Wesleyan but increasingly pantheistic, even Buddhist, certainly idiosyncratic) of universal togetherness. Not only earth and heaven were unified in his art, but also men and women, races, nations and creeds, humans and animals, self and other; secular and numinous came together, but so did bodily desire and spiritual, the daily quiddities of village life and eternal innocence.

Comparison may be drawn between Stanley's personal metaphysic, the 'novel, hybrid architecture' of his 'visionary solipsism' (Hyman 1991: 31), and that of Blake (or Proust, or Dante).

Am reading Blake and Keats. I love to dwell on the thought that the artist is next in divinity to the saint. He, like the saint, performs miracles.

[T]he attractive thing about Blake is that God is found everywhere all the time.

While Stanley rejected the liturgical literalness of canonical religion, also its divisiveness and coercion, he still employed the paradigm of Christianity as a resource because it offered a sense and interpretation (one among many possible ones) of the disparate mysteries of the world, and the wonder of its experiencing. What Stanley asked his audience was not necessarily empathy, nor even sympathy, with his personal vision and representation, but an acknowledgement that existence is something whose awesomeness they experienced too.

Ultimately, Stanley's vision was also a parochial one: a sacred cult of the experiencing self which focused not on Jerusalem, Paris or Rome, but on the provincial world of Cookham. If the Christian Bible was an allegory of a great truth about the world, then Cookham was similarly allegorical if its 'pages' were read in the light of the vision that Stanley's art would provide. Like a medieval artist-craftsman-villager (a latter-day Piero della Francesca), Stanley would endeavour to capture for his audience the spiritual essence within ordinary local life. Happenings 'out of doors' in Cookham represented a pageant of revelations equivalent to those in the Bible, and Stanley's destiny was to identify the same wonder and awe in each, unite the two.

[C]ome to the realization that God is in everything and reach harmony ourselves.

[T]here is no division or separation between any part of one's make-up, and all of one's self is a vital part of any accomplishment or feeling.

Through the wholeness of his art, Stanley would not only celebrate everyday existence but also redeem it: make its conflicts, disorders and discords into ecstasies. His paintings would be a miraculous means by which he would transport what was represented to where all was holy, at peace, and truly itself.

Stanley was convinced that the spiritual harmony of redemption through his art was not only possible but imperative; it became so that his material existence and his artistic passion could not be separated. Like Christ's, his real triumph would lie not in a material kingdom but in a spiritual overcoming; like Christ, and despite the agonies of the inevitable and perpetual confusions and frustrations of existence, he would find both meaning and liberation in his creativity. By communing with God and nature, Stanley would become at home in the universe, identify with it; it was a state of joyful clarity and of solution to perplexity. Stanley would use his art to explain and reform his own life, while also providing signposts for others.

Beauty to me is expressiveness.

[T]o produce something which would make me walk with God.

It was as if people and events in Cookham were communicants of a church of which Stanley was the priest. He remained convinced of having been vouchsafed a miraculous insight in which the spiritual and everyday were fused in one meaningful whole: a deeper level of human consciousness which woke people to a new, true state of being, a more magnificent and beautiful way of life. From the random pieces which the world of the senses continually emptied into his brain, he would create art which would reveal the wonder and the identity of each thing on earth, at the same time transmitting something of the ecstasy that this led him to feel.

Stanley's vision amounted to a continuous procession in his mind: an unrolling pageant of material-spiritual sensations and expressions. It could overwhelm him but it also provided a magisterial transcendence, and he dedicated his life and art to its pictural reproduction. If Cookham was imbued with a divine truth, Stanley was too.

[A mass of] inward, surging meaning, a kind of joy, that I longed to get closer to and understand and in some way fulfil.

I felt moved to some utterance, a sense of almost miraculous power, and arising from the joy of my own circumstances and surroundings.

Nor was there any doubting the possessive individuality of the vision. Stanley might have seen himself in the role of priest or shaman, a Christ-like mediator, but his vision was his own: personal, idiosyncratic and, ontologically speaking, private.

My chief and only occupation is with my own thoughts. An empty room, a fire in the grate, are my chief need.

The most exciting thing I ever came across is myself.

The most unexpected thing I ever came across was myself.

A technical vision

This self-focus is the key to any deeper appreciation of Stanley Spencer's artistic production, and its technical features, namely:

(i)   a 'memory-feeling' which inspires a particular painting;
(ii) the personal quality of this memory-feeling;
(iii) a quality of connectedness that this personal memory-feeling comprises between Stanley and the scene portrayed and between its components;
(iv) a faithfulness to detail in the scene;
(v)   an emphasis on the scene portrayed being observed from a personal vantage-point;
(vi) a sense of place and placedness being celebrated in the portrayal;
(vii) also celebrations of nature, of love, and of individuality; and finally
(viii) a sense of spiritual wonder and joy concerning both the subject of the painting and the activity of its creation.

Let me deal briefly with each of these in turn.

What Stanley explained he was seeking in his painting was a visual expression of certain 'memory-feelings'. He made use of real places and people but he did not represent them exactly. Rather he painted a transfiguration of reality as experienced through a prism or filter of personal associations and feelings; his paintings were visionary effusions, manifestations of a personal phenomenology, through which he sought to present the *noumena* behind the *phenomena*.

[I]t is inward joy and emotion alone [which] direct me.

I am only concerned with the reality of what is in front of me insofar as it can and does assist me in revealing and expressing the reality of my thoughts and feelings.

Ideally, in a painting, the subject and Stanley's feeling for it became one; he portrayed a metaphysical alternative to the physical world, in an individual language of sentiment. For it was when people and place became subjective that Stanley believed they became open to the metaphysical, and it was, in turn, the transfiguration of the physical to the spiritually ecstatic that made the painting illuminating and meaningful.

To convey a concept of heaven in a picture Stanley would juxtapose, as in a collage, images of those places and relations in which he had felt the sanctity of ecstasy. Even placed and in relationships, however, Stanley's main subject was himself: the redemption of a past self, the affirmation of a present self in relation to (his) others. There is assiduous and intimate self-reference.

> *Usually, in order to understand any picture of mine, it means taking a seat and preparing to hear the story of my life.*

> *All my drawings are self-portraits, and no amount of 'abstract' or what-not will conceal from that.*

> *A picture is one's own likeness.*

Indeed, Stanley's art distinguished itself by the force and truthfulness with which the personal internal struggle of uncertainty, pain, needs, emotions and drives came to the fore and were realized in paint. The imagery was not obviously symbolic or emblematic, but Stanley presumed that all would have comparable memory-feelings for places and for people to his own, and that others may have recognized his as signposts to theirs. His perspective was as an individual among individuals, and the personal feeling he wished to capture was at the same time a universal one; others would be able to see in his art the kind of experiential phenomenon it represented. Through personal images he hoped to transcend the simply personal, and through personal exploration posit universal truths.

Stanley described his art as 'getting everything clear'. This meant primarily two things: clinging to detail, to a precise observation of the world and its component parts; and connecting those details, the world and its parts, with himself: the person responsible for identifying the world through this viewing (and loving). Meticulous precision in his art manifested a search for veracity of identity in the world, and from the minutiae of existence – including ephemera, scraps and waste – he would construct a cohesive whole: a unity in which truth arises from the relationship which the parts were made to reveal for each other, and from the whole to which the parts were seen to amount.

> *[W]hat is rubbish to some people is not rubbish to me, and when I see things thrown away I am all eyes to know what it is....These things were bits of the lives of people to whom they belonged and express their characters.*

> *I am always taking the stone that was rejected and making it the cornerstone in some painting of mine.*

Moreover, Stanley saw in these connections something emotional and spiritual, not simply mechanical. The physical depictions in his painting were expressions of the emotional involvement which the paintings' components had with each other and with him; what mattered above all was this emotional involvement and his ability to express it. This was why anatomical correctness had, on occasion, to be sacrificed. It was not that he set out to distort, but that the representation of emotional and spiritual connectedness took precedence over normal appearance, and this was how the subjects of his art, in their loving relatedness, 'really' looked. His art was the realization of a truthful spiritual and emotional identification.

Stanley's art meant objects depicted in relation to one another, but most importantly in relation to him. When this was achieved he found serenity. He also felt ecstasy: an ecstatic identification with the world and its spiritual wholeness as he had glimpsed it. The ecstasy was a form of fulfilment and also of possession; his desire to connect and to represent connectivity was a powerful longing, a need.

> *My life is a continual uniting and marrying a finding [of] my eternal state of union with everything I can feel this state with.*

> *I think an artist's life is very much a continual celebration of marriage between himself and what he wants to paint.*

> *An artist wishes to absorb everything into himself; to commit a kind of spiritual rape on everything because this converts all things into being or revealing themselves as lovable, worshipful things, snugly tucked up in the artist and his own special glory and delight....Every thing and person other than myself is a future potential part of myself, or a revealer of an agent in revealing unknown parts of myself.*

When he realized connection in a painting, it was like performing a miracle: achieving an equanimity, balancing and solving a puzzle of parts. Once achieved, moreover, the thought of its loss was terrifying. For it was not only a world of parts that he was assembling, but an identification of his place amongst them.

> *[T]he longer I stay in one place the nearer I get to life.*

> *[A] person is a place's fulfilment, as a place is a person's.*

Stanley claimed to be in love with his paintings, and with all the kinds of circumstances and persons in them; it was a possessive love and a protective one. His paintings expressed what he felt the world truly was, its true spiritual identity, and his own essential, human individuality within it. Not only did he identify with it but he wished others would too; his prophecy would be fulfilled when what he had depicted became the world for all.

> *Just as a book will absorb you into a world so I hope my paintings do so. They are parts of this idea I have…of life and what is to me significant in it….I wish people would 'read' my pictures.*

> *[Promenade of Women] form[s] a sentence, a statement of my feeling for women in general….I had great joy when painting this…because painting each girl was like suddenly meeting them and talking to them and living with them.*

> *These people, every one of them are the beloved of my imagination.*

Connecting with the world through his art, however, also gave his paintings a certain duality. They both depicted union and communion (and often figure Stanley himself in the act of connecting), and they were also markedly observational, even voyeuristic, and drew attention to themselves as paintings by placing the point of vision at an odd, usually elevated, angle. As a boy, Stanley recalled, much of what went on in Cookham did not include him; for reasons of age and of status, he was often observing social interaction from outside – from a house window, a tree, a bridge. And this perspective he retained as an adult (also retaining his small, child-like stature): detached, looking askance from a different height and distinctive vantage-point.

At the same time, his displacement was overcome and he did take part, as we have heard, belonging pictorially to the action and the emotion. Moreover, when he connected with the particular place and moment and people of a painting, he saw it as symbolic of connecting with a whole spiritual universe: a God which was everywhere and all times. He was a force of nature, and also of domestic spaces and the home. If God was outside (in Cookham and beyond) then he was also inside: to be found through introspection. And no one aspect was better or more important, even more moral, than any other; all was to be loved.

> *I loved it all because it was all God and me, all the time.*

> *[E]verywhere is heaven so to speak.*

Stanley's God of equality was also one of distinction and individuality. Hence, Stanley's dislike of uniformity, his distrust of authority and of any single, doctrinal viewing that would limit or discipline the infinite; hence, too, his impatience with shallowness.

An Englishman, when he is not washing, is shaving; and when he is not shaving, he is blacking his boots; and when he is not blacking his boots, he is cleaning his buttons, or putting his puttees on, or combing his hair down the middle. This last drives me to distraction. I want to shout: 'When are you going to THINK...?'

Stanley relished all the differences, in appearance and temperament, that distinguished people and things. He exercised, indeed, a predilection for these in his art to the point of caricature. For him the general truth about the world consisted of the sum total of its infinitively varied parts, and faith in human nature entailed a coming to terms with all its individually wonderful imperfections: loving it all.

Increasingly, Stanley's artistic vision, the memory-feelings he sought to express, with their emphasis on the personal, the detailed, the individual, the experienced, the natural and the spiritual, the connected, came together in this paean to love, and its emanation as sex. Sexuality, Stanley saw as the chief adult means of approaching God and achieving identification with all things. Sexual desire embodied the essence of all that was holy; sex was the essential transcendent and transformative experience.

A deep feeling in me longs to be made whole and where the longings are felt most is in these sex feelings which are the very essence of what I love in myself.

To me there are two joys, the joys of innocence and religiousness, and the joys of change and sexual experience; and while these two selves seem unrelated and irreconcilable, still I am convinced of their ultimate union.

I believe Christ talking is really me love-making to everybody.

Stanley came to see his mission as painting 'sexual sermons' which would preach, above all, the redeeming power of love. Love was the manifestation of God on earth, and love was humanity's 'joyful inheritance'. Love could bring about harmony and understanding, meaning and connectedness, between all people and all things; for while the things which constituted the world had a distinctly individual identity (independent of others and sensibly unknowable to them), love – 'giving and receiving' – was the force to bring things as close to perfect meeting as was possible on this earth. Sexual desire embodied an attempt to reconstitute an original and an ultimate unity. Seeing things as unconnected and apparently meaningless was unbearable, but love removed the barrier, to reveal the world redeemed and 'assembled now in sexuality'. Love was the route to that other-worldliness where the relationship between ordinary things is extraordinarily meaningful and wonderful.

[Love] reveals and more accurately describes the nature and meaning of things.... [I]t establishes once and for all time the final and perfect identity of every created thing.

Love finds the articulation and the rhythm.

Against 'the will of love', nothing could ultimately stand in the way.

The Resurrection with the Raising of Jairus' Daughter

Let me show how the above project and programme might manifest itself in one particular work of art. *The Resurrection with the Raising of Jairus' Daughter* was painted in 1947, while Stanley was still involved with his commission as a war artist to depict the naval shipbuilding at Port Glasgow. Resurrection was a favoured subject of his, and he entitled a number of paintings thus, throughout his life, that were set in places to which he felt he belonged, and which he loved. Hence he painted resurrections in Cookham, on the battlefields of the First World War, and in Port Glasgow itself. Thoughts of resurrection were never far from his mind, it seems, and that 'Last Day', on which resurrection would take place, became an all-encompassing theme, an umbrella concept for his artistic vision as a whole.

What Stanley conceived of in his version of the Christian theme was not a necessarily physical resurrection of the dead so much as a becoming-aware of the real meaning of life, and becoming alive to its enormous possibilities. Resurrections are displacements: awakenings to a state of realization of the potentialities of heaven-on-earth which sex and love, joy and oneness (as against cruelty, 'othering', hate, fear, suspicion and lust for power) brought about. Such an awakening or enlightenment could come to any person at any time, Stanley believed. Moreover, after this 'last judgement', all would be 'acquitted' without moral censure: '[a]ll things are redeemable in my opinion and I paint them in their redeemed state' (cited in Collis 1962: 163).

Stanley's ultimate goal through his art, was, as we have seen, human salvation *tout court*. What we see in his Resurrections, to begin with, is a redeeming of his own life. His various 'loves and longings' are 'made whole', seemingly ordinary circumstances combining with a spiritual happening as if *sub specie aeternatis*. Stanley draws together the varied strands of his life, religious and secular, his various associations with people and places, and his memories of their 'beloved ways and habits'. In particular we see a reunion between Stanley and the important women in his life: his wives Hilda and Patricia, Elsie the maid, and close friends Daphne Charlton and Charlotte Murray. A personal reconciliation with his first love (and continued closest friend) Hilda figures repeatedly; even though they were physically separated (by divorce and illness) for twenty years before her death, and for nine more years before his, Stanley continued 'conversing' with her in words and paint – his letters becoming longer and more frequent after their divorce – and he maintained the myth of their communication. A letter to Hilda written in the year after her death begins, with no change of tone: 'Come ducky and tread on the Moor with me' (cited in Collis 1962: 263); he described this posthumous letter-writing as 'a sort of getting my bearings' (cited in Glew 2001: 245). Indeed, since sex was the gate to heaven, and his sexual unity with Hilda (their 'you-me') was also one with God, and since God was now her everyday companion, Stanley continued thinking of Hilda sexually. An ultimate reconciliation between them was an act of faith for him.

Besides his own life and loves, Stanley envisaged in his Resurrections a general harmonizing of relations between people. Families and lovers, the quick and the dead, are reunited to engage in the heaven-on-earth of simple social and domestic activities, leisure and lovemaking. The resurrection is also an occasion of surprise and wonderment; people are inspired by the new meaning in their life and experience a 'beautiful wholeness' as the fulfilment of all life's hopes and wishes comes about. People feel and share joy at meeting again, and at the peace that this brings. It is a time of love's triumph over discord and adversity, and of sublime truth: a realization that, in love, people are in heaven.

Stanley's Resurrections are often in the form of triptychs, which was significant. First, here was a borrowing of Christian iconography, except that for Stanley the mystery of the trinity reproduced itself in all manner of seemingly insignificant everyday objects (in *The Dustman, or The Lovers* a teapot, an empty jam tin and cabbage stalks are held aloft in a rite of offertory). For Stanley, the triptych form also embodied the early memory-feeling of the mystery of individuality and connectedness: a duality of individual forms at once separated and connected by an overlapping intermediary. As he explained (cited in Pople 1991: 444):

> The emotion in the picture is dependent on there being two parts divided by a third part, and it is this kind of division which is important. It gives to each side section something similar to the meaning for me that subsists between the people who live in 'Fernlea' and next-door 'Belmont'.

Fernlea was Stanley's semi-detached childhood home, of course, and Belmont that of his cousins on the other side of the wall (where everything was familiar and yet reversed). At other times Stanley gave the example of the war hospital where he worked in Bristol – its male quarters on the right, and female on the left, separated from each other by a service block. In both there was the constitutive interdependency. In short, the triptych came to represent, for Stanley, the interrelationship between what was visible and known – Fernlea, the male quarters – and what was invisible and inverted – Belmont, the female quarter) – and their necessary coming together, and 'resolution', through an imagined, felt, loved, meeting and mediation.

Last, in the triptych can be seen Stanley's concern to represent the passage of time and the effects of change. The three panels assembled together depict a narrative in three episodes. Juxtaposed they offer a freeze-frame of crucial transformations. Perhaps moments of tension are revealed between a before, a during and an after; or perhaps, as the preceding is linked to the known present and the inevitable future, an otherwise hidden totality of meaning is displayed. Not only does the triptych draw attention to an act of redemption – the apparent discord of separation giving way to a comprehension of wholeness – but also its process.

The Resurrection with the Raising of Jairus' Daughter is one such triptych (Figure 4).

The painting is composed of three scenes, one urban, one rural, and one biblical, although, significantly, the three scenes and the three panels do not precisely coincide. The linkage of all three scenes within the one central panel emphasizes their unity, and suggests that any differentiation is a matter of convention, or narrowness of vision alone. With the vertical framing lines of the triptych recalling panels of glass, it is also as though one were looking at the scene through a window. It is perhaps implied that beyond this narrow view, the vantage offered by the window, an even more universal connectedness is to be espied.

Here too are some of the familiar features of Spencer's resurrection scenes that have been introduced above. The stylized figures, with their puppet-like bodies and extravagant gestures, draw attention to the rhythmic celebrations they are engaged in sharing. The life and action and movement of the scenes attest to the joy at redemption, and perhaps a wonderment or awe which overwhelms more subtle or graduated emotions such as might differentiate the protagonists. The packed composition, with its geometric arrangement of components, the density of colour, all speak to intensity and charged feeling. In the partial ignorance that the three scenes and their participants seem to have for one another, we find also Stanley's assemblage of episodes in the process of being transformed. We are privy to the scene in the moment of a great coming together of times, places, people and moods.

The high-angled viewpoint suggests Stanley's looking down on the world from an observational perch: a part of the scene yet detached, yet sharing in the consciousness of God. At the same time Stanley intimates his love for what his painting has brought him to know. Hence he and Hilda and Patricia figure in the foreground of the painting, bottom right, about to stride out of their semi-detached house (and/or garden and/or grave) to join the Cookham throng. Perhaps that is the three of them too, in an earlier, childhood manifestation, leaning on the wall of the house on the left of the painting, as they gaze onto the street-scene unfolding before them?

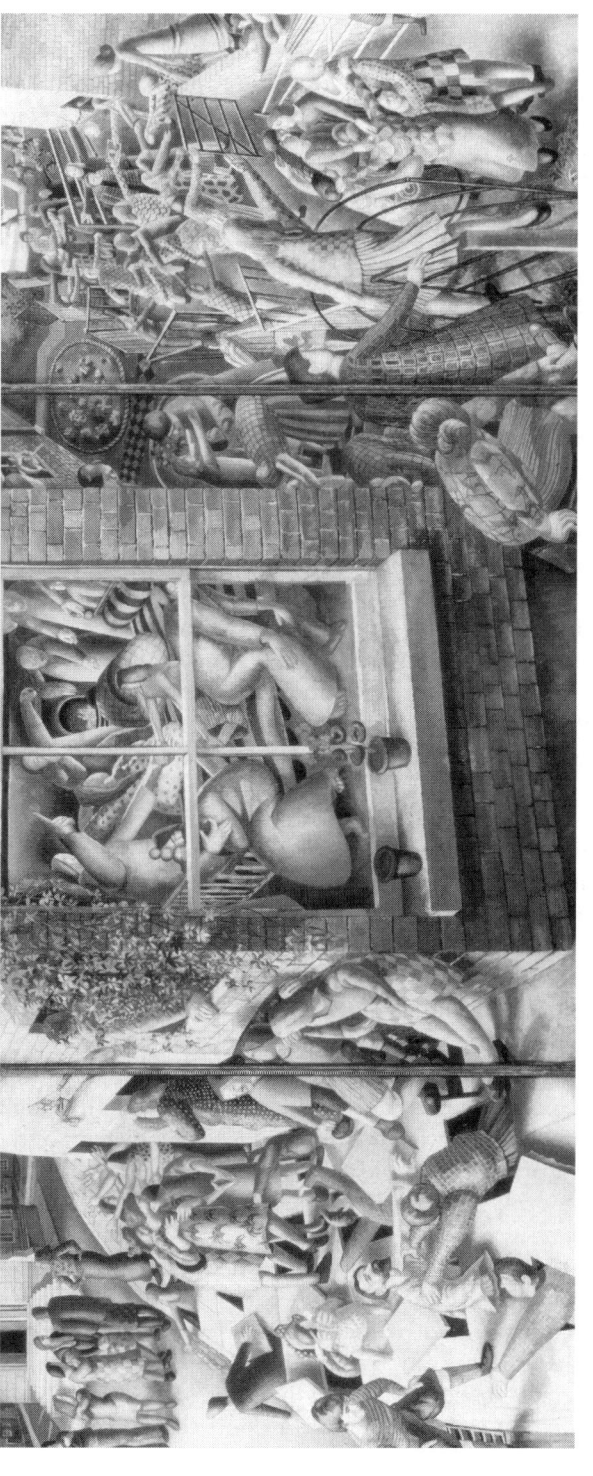

Figure 4 Stanley Spencer, *The Resurrection with the Raising of Jairus' Daughter* (centre panel 76.8 × 88.3cm; side panels 76.8 × 51.4cm) 1947
Source: Southampton Art Gallery.

Let me treat each panel separately for a moment. *The left panel* is set in Stonehouse, Gloucester, and drawn as early as 1940 (as was the sketch for the right panel). Visiting his friend Daphne Charlton in the Gloucestershire village of Leonard Stanley, Stanley had seen a wedding photograph in which there was a church built at the junction of two streets. The image struck him as significant and he kept it in his notebook before, seven years later, setting it in paint. Taking place before the church Stanley images a resurrection of townsfolk. They emerge from the paving stones as from their graves, or as workmen (or soldiers) from trenches they have dug, pushing back the stone covers with stiff limbs, and looking upward in wonderment. They are assisted by fellow wakers and by those who have awoken earlier or not been asleep: spouses, children, peers. A first instinct appears to be to hug and embrace, a second to stand relaxedly and chat. Three children (a boy and two girls) lean on the street corner, interested but somewhat blasé or bemused at the world. Between the children's feet is the metal shoe-scrape for cleaning mud off the feet of those emerging and about to re-enter their houses. With the Union Flag and the banner over the door, there is also the allusion to street-parties celebrating community events such as soldiers being welcomed back from war (the relaxed street life of town neighbourhoods was something Stanley found very poignant). As Stanley explained in a letter to a friend (Charlotte Murray 4/2/1947): 'in order to further make clear my feelings of happiness, I put over the door the usual "Welcome Home" signs and flags and bunting they put up for soldiers returning from war'.

Perhaps a developmental profile is intended by people's general positions in the scene, because as the younger children watch the pavement scene from its margins, older youths stand in the road with a seeming affectation of exaggerated nonchalance; they seem more interested in flaunting their lively potential before one another. Meanwhile, between the children and the youths, the pavement is full of adults with families greeting one another. Visual patterning also seems very significant in the painting. The plain or regular patterns of people's dress – squares, dots and lines – seem to reflect the design of the town: the regular shapes of the paving stones and the church stone walls and the brick houses. The people belong to their town and, in form, they are one, wearing the same design. Indeed, in a way people are grouped as though they were components in the structural fabric of the town, the adults' more complex embracing, on the pavement, reflecting the geometrics of the paving stones they stand on or replace, while the youths' looser grouping on the road reflects the more amorphous mass of the asphalt. In particular, people interrelate on the pavement as though embodying the paving stones they replace; and there is an angular quality, a predominance of squares and straight lines, in the scene as a whole.

A further predominance is of white light. This reflects off the walls of the house and church and asphalt and pavement, and, contrasts with the gaping blackness of the graves beneath the paving stones and the insides of the houses and the church; it is definitely out of doors that the light belongs and to which it pertains. Given the shadows, the light appears to come from the left and beyond the pictured scene. Perhaps it is the setting sun, which would make this panel more westerly than the other two; or else the rising sun from the east, the resurrection accompanying the new day; or else some miraculous light in the sky? Certainly, the difference in lighting between the scenes is one way in which Stanley suggests a temporal or otherwise transformatory relationship between the three.

The emphasis on either shade or light makes the human activity stand out as if that of actors on a stage. This also resonates with the theatrical gesturing that seems to be taking place, people stretching, embracing, waving, reaching, hoisting, pulling, leaning, slouching, arms akimbo. There is a curious mix of excited activity with domestic attitudes: Stanley's redemption takes place amid the parochial and everyday. Perhaps in the white light there is a further war allusion: anti-aircraft activity (spotlights and flak) lighting up the night sky. For there is a deserted and barren feel to the townscape, as if an unexpected gathering at night is taking shape – a meeting in the light in what had hitherto been thought of as a time of darkness – which would mean that the resurrection from the paving stones also alludes to the clearing of debris after a night of air-raids and a joyful discovery of people still alive. Here, in short, are people returning to their homes and bringing life to the town. Soon they will light up the dark church and house doorways, occupying perhaps the empty urban garden plots in the very top of the painting as they recently occupied their graves.

The central panel focuses on a lighted room inside a house, although a figure still leans out of the window of the house to look down on the scene in the left panel, and activity on both sides of the house further links the scene to panels on both left and right. The church at the junction of two streets (with the blackened doorway) in the left panel is echoed here by a house with a lightened window at the junction of two street scenes (and a junction of town and country). Inside the house, according to Stanley's title, we see the scene from the Christian Bible where Jesus causes Jairus' daughter to rise from the dead. According to the story (Mark 5: 22–4, 35–43), Jesus was asked by Jairus, a synagogue leader, to come and lay hands on his dying daughter. Before he could reach her, however (having been involved in another healing *en route*), people emerged from Jairus' house to announce that the girl was dead. Nonetheless, Jesus advised Jairus not to be afraid but to have faith. Taking his disciples Peter, James and John with him, Jesus approached the house, telling the crying and wailing crowd beside it that: 'The child is not dead but asleep'. When the people laughed at him, however, he bade them stay outside the house and entered it with the girl's parents and his disciples alone. Inside: 'He took the girl by the hand and said to her, "*Talitha koum!*" (which means "Little girl, get up!"). Immediately the girl stood up and walked around (she was about twelve years old). At this they were completely astonished'.

Presumably, the central figure with the raised finger and the white-light face, in Stanley's portrayal, is Jesus. Perhaps the parents are the couple sitting on the edge of the bed facing away from him, bent and distraught, head in hands; they wear spotted and chequered dress as do people in the left panel. Other figures in biblical dress (echoing a central bearded man resurrecting in the left panel) are then Jesus' disciples. They hug the spherical bedpost as a substitute doll or child, and sit or stand in tense prayerful poses. Other figures point to the central action of the scene, a girl sitting upright on a big bed, clutching Jesus' hand, calm amid the anguished, clenched adults. Her uprightness echoes that of Jesus' raised finger and contrasts with the generally bent postures of everyone else, while her calmness is a reminder of the disinterested and nonchalant poses of the non-adult in the left panel.

The scene is more singular and focused than in the left panel, however, while still dramatic and active. In fact, so much is happening that it exceeds the borders of the house window. The big bed is larger than the window aperture and we only get the snapshot of the scene, we cannot see it all. Our vision is further obscured by the cross of the sash window-frame (echoing the partial perspective which the 'window-frame' of the entire triptych can provide us). Furthermore, all this miraculous activity seems to be belied by the domesticity of the surroundings. Jesus in a contemporary English home, an inviting fire roaring in the grate, a homely striped bedspread, a spotted rug, Jairus' daughter transformed into a schoolgirl on a big modern bed, people in modern as well as biblical dress – all these seem strange juxtapositions, and the oddness is compounded by the ivy growing on the house wall, the flowerpots on the windowsill, and the suburban activities going on just outside the window. In many ways, the bed is the central feature of the panel – so frequent a trope for Stanley's memory-feelings of cosiness. Here it is a living space for the whole family and Jesus too, as well as being a spiritual altar; it combines homeliness with spirituality, and also perhaps thus links the essential spirituality of the lefthand (urban) scene with the homeliness of the righthand village (Cookham) scene. Just as people sit and lie across the striped bed, so they stand and lean across the lined walls and paving stones and the line separating road from pavement in the lefthand scene, and the lined walls and gates of the lefthand scene. Indeed, the frame at the foot of the bed is like a gate itself. The white light on Jesus, on the biblical dress and on the window-frame and sill also echo the whiteness of the left panel, while Jesus' raised arm is reflected by that of the women striding past the bed-like gate in the right panel. In short, the side panels, first conceived in 1940, and the central panel painted in Port Glasgow in 1947, are woven together by a number of overlapping visual echoes.

The right of the central panel begins the scene that takes up *the right panel*. Families hug, greet, wave handkerchiefs, exchange photographs and embrace, leaving houses and gardens to meet on the earthy lanes (in particular, The Pound) of Cookham village. Balancing the lefthand scene, there are people leaning out of windows for a better view and children leaning on walls to the side of the main action. What predominates is a sense of opening out and coming together. House and farm gates are flung open as are arms. As people emerge from beneath paving stones on the left so here they emerge from behind gates, and from windows and houses; they assist and attract one another into the open of Cookham Pound, just as they assist one another on the left into the light of day. There is the same stiffness of gesture of some people as in the left panel, as if they were stiff from sleep or death, or sleepwalking still, bumping into one another, draping themselves over one another, with their eyes as yet barely opened. What perhaps predominates is an emotion that people cannot contain; it takes over their bodies in exaggerated joy. Arms are another visual trope that link all three scenes, usually in raised positions; arms point skyward, they embrace or seek embrace, and sometimes they seem those of the once-crucified. Often, on the right, the reaching arms echo those of Jairus' daughter reaching out before the body.

As in the left panel, here, too, people seem to belong to their surroundings. On the left they took up the geometric structures of the townscape in their dress and posture. Now, the warm colours of their clothes merge with those of the country: the brown earth, the flowers, the red-tiled garden path, the ruddy brown fencing, the red-brick buildings, the green hedging and grass. One person's dress takes up the design of a house path, another's that of a flower bed. The townscape was as stark and bright, even sterile, as this village scene is muted, down-to-earth and dark – perhaps another reason for people to walk with arms outstretched. And while the cross-hatching of the intersecting lines of raised arms (and the circles of embracing people that the raised arms often make) link the right to the left, perhaps another difference is the emphasis on height. For while the town street on the left finds its echoes in the village path on the right, and the story narrated in both panels seems to take place in a vertical plane, still, on the right there seems to be more of a horizontal emphasis. In the left panel, we have the group on the road above those standing on the pavement, above those resurrecting from the pavement; in the right panel, there is more of a balance of different people coming out of different houses, each meeting in the middle, an equality that is then repeated in horizontal layers right up to the top of the frame and, by implication, beyond.

As he was painting the picture in 1947, Stanley spoke about it to his friend, the psychoanalyst Charlotte Murray. In his original 1940 sketch, he explained, the righthand scene in Cookham had included the figure of Daphne Charlton, the woman living in the Gloucestershire village of Leonard Stanley (where he had seen the photograph of the town church at Stonehouse) and with whom he was then emotionally involved. In the 1947 painted version, however, Daphne has been transformed into his first wife Hilda, with whom Stanley has effected an emotional reunion; she is seated, in a floral jumper and skirt, at the bottom of the scene perched on a piece of wood or stone (a tombstone, perhaps). Stanley paints himself standing beside her, somewhat uncertain, with his hand on a fence. And next to him there is what appears to be the figure of his second wife Patricia, marching forthrightly out into the throng as if a soldier or a traffic policeman (echoing Jesus' directing of Jairus' daughter to rise). She is as positive as Stanley and Hilda appear reticent, drawing attention to herself as the other two look on, their arms shielding themselves from attention (Stanley's coat has some of the quality of a covering of ancient Japanese armour). Interestingly, Stanley described to Charlotte Murray the figures of Hilda and himself as those of 'unbelievers who may have no logical connection with Jesus and the happy resurrecters in the room behind, although at least one of them (Hilda) looks up and seems aware of them'. But then through his painting Stanley achieves the duality of both representing himself and his multiple relationships – signalling the partiality and individuality of life on earth – and at the same time achieving the redemption of imagining a time of resurrection when all the parts will make a harmonious whole.

In sum, *The Resurrection with the Raising of Jairus' Daughter* brings together different parts of Stanley's life, different people, places and times, different moods and awarenesses, different ages and involvements, different memory-feelings, different kinds of reality, and makes a striking, full and cohesive visual tapestry of them all. The painting is a fine example of the way Stanley's life-project embodied an artistic movement from separation and dislocation to loving and harmonious order: from displacement (of time and travel) and death to re-placement, and via displacement (of individuality) to unity.

The church-house

Nowhere is the character of Stanley's artistic-metaphysic vision and life-project more clearly exhibited, in all its ambition and wholeness, than in his plans for what he dubbed a 'church-house'. After the successful completion of the memorial chapel at Burghclere in 1932, a commission he fulfilled by covering the entire chapel with murals depicting scenes from the First World War, Stanley envisaged something bigger again: 'I have done a small chapel now I wish to do a house' (cited in Bell 1992: 102). It would be a building capable of housing a series of paintings based on a common theme and maintaining a unity and coherence. It would be a 'church-house': 'A church and a house combined would perfectly fit the mixture' (*ibid.*). As ever, this would bring together the personal and domestic, everyday secular space and experience, with the universally spiritual, sacred emotions. After the disruption of the war and his memorial to it, he would return to Cookham, to his calling, and build a new memorial chapel – to peace and love.

Back in Cookham, however, Stanley found his ideas expanding further. He felt, as we have seen, that the tableaux he had witnessed in Cookham as a child were heavenly, but he also recognized that his adult experiences displaced him relative to them. Hence the necessity and, through his art, the capability, of resurrecting that past and redeeming the life that had been lived in-between times. But then the whole of Cookham village was already his church-house, his spiritual home, his heaven-on-earth; the whole village was his 'chapel out of doors and in the air'. The village street, then, could be imagined as a nave, the village cross-roads as a transept, the war memorial as an altar of love, individual houses as side-chapels, their fireplaces as mini-altars, and the back-gardens and river as side-aisles. Many of the events and paintings which Stanley went on to set in Cookham, portraying biblical characters and scenes, he envisaged as both taking place and hanging in this extended church-space.

More concretely, Stanley also imagined a large physical building which might house all of his paintings, and began planning its layout and its ambience, mundane-cum-spiritual. Its erection and architectural design would be as creative and visionary as its contents, and inculcate 'the imperturbable and right state of the human soul' (Spencer, cited in Alison 1991: 11). It would be a proper home for his paintings – and hence too for his life. The building would constitute a vast painted autobiography which would constantly expand as his life did, with new rooms being added and opened; it would be organic and endless, unfolding like his life coil. In it he imagined: 'that happy homely realm of thinking about myself and all my special brew of thoughts, when all the Stanleys, this me and that me, can come out like children coming out of school' (cited in Collis 1962: 231). This church-house would both duplicate the disposition of Cookham – the way Stanley had experienced its different areas, atmospheres and inhabitants – and also include separate chapels for his most significant relationships – with Hilda, Elsie, Patricia, Daphne and Charlotte. If individual paintings represented and realized different memory-feelings for Stanley, then the church-house would bring all together: an ongoing statement of his beliefs and a testament to all the people and elements in his life which were dear to him; a complete artistic representation of his life, embodying what he experienced, what he meant, what he ordained in the way of beauty, order and identity. Even as the world outside this spiritual-domestic space might appear superficially to be going its own way, his church-house would redeem all and provide a space in which one saw beyond appearance and lived in true identification with the world. Here would be living space and artistic representation coming together in one imaginative life-world. Here he would 'love to walk up to one of my past selves – "The Dustman", or the couples in "The Beatitudes" – which stand about in the land of me' (cited in Pople 1991: 396).

If anything, the obscure iconography, the fantasy, sexuality and caricature of his art, pertaining as it did to a personal iconography and projection of which only he was fully cognizant, served to distance Stanley ever more from the public and make his finding a sympathetic patron increasingly unlikely. The growing realization, as he aged, that he would not fulfil this dream left him despondent, and the joy of completing each painting was diminished by the knowledge that their ultimate meaning, their part in the whole of his life-world, might never become clear: '[I wish] to have all my real selves around me...like objects in a museum. My great losses are my pictures and Hilda' (cited in Alison 1991: 11). Nevertheless, the idea of an ever-expanding church-house in which he and his art would live remained extremely dear to him: a logic, a setting and a stimulant to his creativity. The church-house would amount to a unified, coherent whole, providing a narrative through which to come to terms with the complexity and change, the fragmentation and displacement of his life, each succeeding painting celebrating and illustrating 'the joy that followed the joy which the former painting illustrated' (Spencer 1955). The 'forest of rooms' – a total spatial and visual experience – would celebrate and record, re-place, relive and redeem Stanley's existence, sacralize and eternalize it, spiritually transforming all difficulties, discords and disruptions into harmony.

Even though Stanley failed to find a patron who would understand or even contemplate the endless ambition, the ambition of endlessness, which this project involved, and thus was forced to sell on his finished paintings, separating them from one another and from himself, the idea became the imaginative structure into which Stanley's artistic output fed. Thenceforth until his death, he painted with the image of his autobiographical, expanding church-house always in mind, living in the increasingly rich and coherent life-world which his artistic vision vouchsafed.

Fulfilment or compensation?

What may be said, then, in conclusion, of the relationship between Stanley Spencer's artistry, his creative vision and his consciousness of it, and the way he lived his life – the control he sought and was able to exert over it? Certainly, Stanley was happiest when he felt able to reconcile the two: life and vision. But this was not always – or easily, or immediately – the case. He suffered in the war, and with the regimentation of the army; he suffered the loss of Hilda and rejection by Patricia, and two stressful divorce proceedings; he suffered the censorial atmosphere of a buttoned-up English society which left him frustrated from having to hide a frank depiction of self-exposure and sexual fantasy, and also short of money; and he suffered from the dispersal of his art, a dependence on patronage and an inability to secure any for his grander projects. And yet, it seems that such was the force of his personal vision that Stanley was able overwhelmingly to reconcile life and artistry despite these sufferings, and thus to sustain his life-project. Hell, Stanley once declared, must be to exist in a state of unimaginativeness, and imperviousness to the spiritual. Surrounded by the imaginary world of his art and writings, this was something he never suffered; he lived his art and was happy in doing so ('sorrow and sadness is not me' were almost his last words).

Perhaps this is easiest to see in his relationship with Hilda Carline. Hilda was probably the person to whom he felt closest in the world; in her he saw the same mental attitude to things as himself. Hilda became his great 'hand-holder' and affirmer, the one who secured him so that his imagination and emotion might burgeon. Indeed, it might be said that his whole philosophy of love developed out of his love for Hilda, and at one point Stanley felt that any written autobiography would necessitate contributions from Hilda too: a collaborative hotch-potch intertwining 'both our journeys' (cited in Collis 1962: 181).

However, Stanley's 'self-intense' nature made him experience the relationship in a very personal way as a manifestation of his own spiritual vocation. His love for Hilda and his family appeared as much sublime – imagined – as mundane, and it was to become more so. 'Hilda was the love I felt for what I looked at', he wrote, 'she was the smoke coming from the factory chimneys. I want and need her in *all* my experience' (cited in Pople 1991: 453). His love 'for Hilda' united him not only to her but to all creation and to God too. It grew so that it was impossible for him to separate Hilda from his vision, he said, her presence in it seeming ancient and primordial, and it was 'through Hilda' that he bound all together, his existence and his art.

Increasingly, however, Stanley found himself and Hilda to be incompatible living partners. Their preferred lifestyles drew them apart and their actual worlds remained individual ones; each could only approach the other from their respective lives. Indeed, it is arguable that Stanley found he could live with Hilda happily and permanently only after divorcing her:

Hilda: You are too much of an artist to have satisfactory relations with any women. That is the price you have to pay for your genius.
(cited in Pople 1991: 174)

Stanley: In spite of all I feel for you and my need for you, somewhere in me is an absence of love. I never have fulfilled love for another.
(cited in Pople 1991: 195)

Hilda became his phantasm, his idea of her easier to love than her person; '[it is] incredible', he wrote to her at one point (1937), 'that you exist in the flesh!' (cited in Collis 1962: 127).

There was also the Patricia question. Stanley at one stage wanted them both, Hilda: domestic, thoughtful, considerate, sincere, complex, gauche, circumspect, intense; and Patricia: sophisticated, socially connected, elegant, stylish, vivid, lively, sexy, forceful, direct, superficial, teasing, opportunistic. The laws of England may not allow Stanley two wives, but he would have two all the same. He would behave as he felt proper, irrespective of how others did; whatever the law might say, he remonstrated, marriage was a private matter. Hilda and Patricia each gave him something necessary, but different, for the development of his artistic vision, and he could be passionate, sincere and wholehearted to both.

It might be argued that in constructing lovers (and others) largely in terms of his own imagination, Stanley Spencer's artistry served him primarily as compensation, a way to find refuge from his personal difficulties; and that the imaginary world of his art grew as his life's frustrations did, a means of vicarious living, self-justification and solipsistic fulfilment. Support for this view could indeed be drawn from Spencer's own words: 'my desire to paint is caused by my being unable – or being incapable – of fulfilling my desires in life itself' (cited in Robinson 1994: 68). Furthermore, some of Stanley's most poignant representations of domestic perfection – recreating his own marital harmony of the 1920s – were painted whilst attempting to divorce Hilda in the later 1930s. As his biographer Maurice Collis puts it, 'mad and noble', Hilda continued to bestride Stanley's life 'like an apocalyptic phantom' (1962: 224). Does this not demonstrate, then, that Stanley's artistic vision substituted for the failure of his real-life relationships?

This is not the conclusion I would draw, however. Stanley's artistry was not as contingent or strategic as this; above all it was not reactive, it was spontaneous. What he appreciated in Dostoyevsky above all other authors, Stanley once wrote was a 'vision which [was] the mover and creator of everything he [said]' (cited in Glew 2001: 230). Taking the measure of the person which this chapter has (largely verbally) appraised leads me to say likewise: Stanley Spencer was empowered by his vision; his art did not compensate for his life, it was its fulfilment.

One's real spiritual self, Stanley was fond of claiming, is present everywhere; through love one saw how there was an actual identification between individual self and entire world. One way he explained this was by saying that it was because one was part of God, and wherever God was you were too. Another way was by asserting that he, Stanley Spencer, was able and desirous to absorb everything in the world into himself, to make himself a 'treasure island'. 'The artist', we have also heard Stanley declaim, was someone who wished to tuck up everything snugly inside himself or herself – as 'his [or her] own special glory and delight' – but, equally, this was something of which all individuals were always capable; '[i]t was the privilege of the spirit [to be able to] find what it need[ed] anywhere' (cited in Harries and Harries 1983: 206). Stanley's own creative impulse, certainly, was all-embracing, possessed of a voracious enjoyment in looking at the world, dreaming it and re-creating it. However much he might dally with the trope of being insecure, in need of mothering, *au fond* Stanley was self-reliant. And he gained a fierce, wild happiness from his self-sufficiency in his art. In the 'impregnable castle of his imagination', as his biographer put it (Collis 1962: 197), Stanley had all that was necessary to him. He wished for people to be there when he wanted to unburden himself, but then for him to be left alone in order to 'live my inner self' (cited in Collis 1962: 154). Little that he really needed could be either taken from him or given to him.

The claim can be made that this included even Cookham. For all his nostalgia, the fact is that Stanley lived a peripatetic lifestyle after once leaving his natal village and going to war. There is no denying the love he had for the place, and its place in his vision, but there was an important sense in which ontologically the vision and Cookham — any particular place — were distinct. Cookham was his preferred visual trope, but his imagination was neither tied to nor circumscribed by the concrete place.

People generally make a kind of 'home' for themselves wherever they are and whatever their work which enables the more important human elements to reach into and pervade in the form of mysterious atmospheres of a personal kind the most ordinary procedures of work or place.

In all my ceaseless effort to cater for my own needs this landscape [Cookham village from Cookham Dene] came nearest to obliging me.

Stanley had faith, too, that his vision, his appetite and its fulfilment, represented achievements which were unique to him. Indeed, they were self-created: 'I know of nothing that I have ever done that I could say I did as a result of the love of God or because authorized by Him' (cited in Collis 1962: 184). This was also why he was keen to disavow suggestions of influence on his work: his creation was pure, his oeuvre individual. His ambition too was great. He was aware that, as one critic put it (Rothenstein 1945: 16), the 'almost frightening candour' with which, 'without reserve', he revealed his vision to a wider society was creating a personal iconography which challenged every contemporary English aesthetic norm; and, as Stanley once admitted, he was in danger of becoming ' "smug" on success' (cited in Bell 1992: 30).

As we have seen, it was Stanley's ambition, prophet-like, to represent and hence to realize a spiritual redemption of the entire everyday world. Looking round him, in Cookham and beyond, Stanley saw people, material objects and practices, possessed of 'the sacred'; in portraying this, pictorially and verbally, Stanley believed he could make the sacred presence not just more readily known to people but actually lived. For people seemed largely unaware of this sublime potential, and Stanley, too, experienced a sense of alienation and of dislocation. But through his art-works he could represent a transcendental, paradisiacal reality, and a means to reach that state: a vision of life in which people shared a happy and homely brotherhood with one another and their environment and were aware of their grace.

For Stanley to compose this portrayal was for him to become part: to live too in sacred, mysterious identification with the world. In other words, his art was actually, personally life-creating. To paint was to achieve union with the space of his canvas — which was the true world. In this union, all, everything phenomenal, might be overcome, rescued and redeemed: everything past and present, everything agreeable, disagreeable and mortifying, misfortuned, friendly and tragic; everything was absorbed, memorialized and transcended by its being imaginatively re-conceived 'in the land of me' (cited in Pople 1991: 396).

It was not by chance, then, that Stanley often pictured himself and his characters walking with Christ, and described himself as part of God. Stanley was a Christ-like prophet to himself: '[p]ainting with me was the crowning of an already elected king' (cited in Pople 1991: 86); '[I am] a new kind of Adam, and joy is the means by which I name things' (cited in Collis 1962: 184). (I am reminded of Nietzsche and his mystical alter-ego Zarathustra). In transposing his friends and lovers and himself, Cookham, Port Glasgow, Leonard Stanley, Stonehouse, Hampstead and so on, into the imagined worlds of his figurative art, he was able to displace, represent and re-place the whole world in a quasi-divine way. His message of love – ambitious, arrogant, certain, strange – might sit uneasily alongside English politeness and reserve but one day it would be acclaimed the truth.

This is not to say that Stanley's paintings did not also bring him more direct comfort, and immediate sought-after solutions to his life's setbacks; or that a desire for coherence in his work did not precisely mirror one for unity in his personal life; or that in his paintings he was able to make connections with people and places that effected a more mundane catharsis and bliss, even ecstasy. Rather, it is to say that Stanley was, and knew himself to be, an artist, a creator of worlds, first and foremost; and this was something with which his 'non-artistic projects', such as these were, had to come to terms: '[i]t has been my way to make things as far as I am able to – fit me' (cited in Arts Council 1976: 21). This was his impulse, and his need: to stay true to his own perceptions, to follow his imagination, even in the face of convention and the pressure of others:

> You [Stanley] would reckon to shape your own destiny, and therefore forcing things and riding right over them is part of your outlook. To you that seems right, to take the matter in your own hands and shape it as you will.
>
> (Hilda, cited in Pople 1991: 368)

Weighing up the evidence of his life, it would be my conclusion that this was something which Stanley Spencer succeeded in effecting. His artistic vision amounted to a life-project whereby he created the world, the social environment, to which he then related. The force of his imagination and the discipline with which he lived it made Stanley his own man. He related to otherness – his message was one of relatedness – but it was in his own terms, even in his own image. And though his relationships were largely his own creation, they were not necessarily one-sided:

Being with Stanley is like being with a holy person, one who perceives....he *is* the thing so many strive for and he has only to *be*....Stanley's home seems to be the whole world.

(Hilda, cited in Pople 1991: 463)

Part III

DISCUSSIONS

7

THE POWER OF ANY BODY-IN-ITS-ENVIRONMENT

> The word inside me I become it. The word slots my belly, my belly swells the word. New meanings expand from my thighs.
> (Jeanette Winterson, *Art and Lies*)

Winterson's is a striking image; it is also imagery beyond my experience – my possible experience as a man – and, to an extent, beyond my judgement. Am I to infer that bodily imagery is being employed here literally, or metaphorically, or both? Can it be that literary fecundity feels to Winterson like penetration and impregnation? Does she consider words to be phallic? Does she feel words in her belly? Winterson's sense of her own body is beyond me, and so too, to an extent, are the ramifications she would seem to draw from it regarding her world-view.

I am reminded of another exercise in what has been dubbed *écriture féminine*: the attempt to overcome what is felt to be the disempowering masculinity (phallocentrism and patriarchalism) of current linguistic structures and norms of expression, and to consciously attest in language to female experience (Rapport and Overing 2000: 126–9). Luce Irigary writes (1993, emphasis in original):

> [B]eyond the classic [masculine] opposites of love and hate…lies this perpetually *half-open* threshold, consisting of *lips* that are strangers to dichotomy.

Is this apprehension of a relationship of partial connection which is beyond dichotomy and opposition – as of a pair of 'lips', a 'perpetually half-open threshold' – something physically experienced by Irigary, something first felt and then intellectualized, or something rendered intellectual simply by analogy? Is this a bodily feeling of love-and-hate? As a man I am able to experience the possible appropriateness of the image as a metaphor but not its literal veracity.

But then the argument of *écriture féminine* could be taken a step further: to *écriture individuelle*. *Ecriture féminine* is strongly suggestive of the bodily nature of an essentially female experience, its power, and its possible consequences in interpreting the human condition. First, differences of anatomy and physiology would seem to suggest the existence of a radical 'insight barrier' for males to scale (Humphrey 1983: 72; cf. Raphael 1975: 111–15). Second, this insight is also empowering in a pan-human sense: '[w]e can use the transitional and creative nature of reproduction to transform our bodies and our selves' and hence overcome institutional 'oppression and objectification'; 'we can use our bodies to express our power, individuality, and creativity' (Counihan 1999: 214). This might mean that it is women and men both who can find in their 'innate bodily qualities' the empowering experience of 'extend[ing] themselves and their personal influence in physical and social space, as well as in time' (Comaroff 1985: 71). Female and male bodily experience alike provides a lived-in metaphor of supra-institutional freedom.

But then it must also be allowed that there will be essential aspects of *individual* embodiment and experience. What of the innate individual power of bodily creation and extension? Following on from the illustrative case-studies of Part II of the book, what I would now focus on is the embodied nature of individual experience: the close tie between life-project, world-view, an understanding of self and other, a way of engaging with the world; and an individual sense of embodiment which might be said to be responsible for empowering that life-project, 'bodying' it forth.

The body in anthropology

Reference to the body has played a significant part in the argumentation of this book, but the nature of the body has not been addressed directly. I have referred to the way that the body acts as a discrete yet permeable sensory mechanism, giving rise to an environing sensorium, a subjective phenomenology, to an individual life which is personal and unique. I have further contended that cognitive convictions may be grounded in an individual's bodily intuitions – that our world-views may be a version of our bodily experience – and that, specifically, the stance we adopt on questions of power (of 'in order to' motives *vis-à-vis* 'because'), or of irony (of our ability to make originary interpretations *ab nihilo*), may be a reflection of how we know ourselves as bodies. The body has appeared in this book as the first thing 'one' has a relationship with and at the same time an inextricable part of the *cogito*; the body plays host to a multitude of identities, of the changing essence of self, and yet is also the very means by which any sense of self is arrived at. The body has been described as 'the centre and periphery of knowledge' and yet at the same time as inextricably implicated in an environment that it is responsible for construing and is also 'responsible' for: an 'organism-plus-environment'. In this part of the book I want to address the phenomenon of the body in more depth and, by way of the particularities of Stanley Spencer, Rachel Silberstein, Ben Glaser and Friedrich Nietzsche, accord embodiment its proper social-scientific status.

THE POWER OF ANY BODY-IN-ITS-ENVIRONMENT

There has been a growing corpus of work, in recent years, in an anthropology which might broadly be termed 'existential' (Douglas 1977; Jackson 1981; 1996; von Uexkuell 1982; Kotarba and Fontana 1984; Csordas 1994; Stoller 1997) which has sought to recognize in bodily human experience a distinct phenomenology: a distinct, indeed fundamental, way of being-in-the-world. Bodily experience has been conceptualized apart from 'culture' so as to recognize certain congruencies and commonalities in the human condition over and against the specificities of formal cultural difference. Experience is asserted as being not the same as culture, then, not something that necessarily originates in culture nor something that culture perforce limits, or determines. Experience is understood as something which exists over and above a language of cultural norms and forms of expression and exchange, and as representing a potential human universal – in terms of capacity at least, if not substance – in the face of culture's spatial and temporal contingencies. It is a 'deception' to employ the concept of culture in order either to sidestep the subtleties of human being or becoming and claim an understanding of others' homogeneous (enculturated) state, or to claim for them an alien nature such that they are reachable only through a relativistic lens (Wilmsen 1999: xii–xiv). Whatever may be the specifics of culture, these are not enough to obviate the particularities of bodily experience or render them invisible or their disinterring impossible; the 'common embodiedness of our being-in-the-world' affords a common human ground (Jackson 1989: 135). It is the case, in short, that we experience beyond culture, and it is possible and necessary to access experiential commonalities and to recount and seek to account for these.

Of course, such insight begs a series of further questions: 'How is experience constituted? Of what does it consist and whence does it derive?'. At least two ways forward present themselves. One is to have further recourse to the concept of 'society'; to say that social structures and institutions encompass culture – or cultures, better, since any social milieu is likely to contain more than one set of cultural forms, more than one set of symbol-systems in whose terms people express themselves and meet with others in relationship – and that the social is responsible for mediating individual experience. Society is that institutional organization and aggregation of individuals whose quality of massification – of physically or, through technical means, distantly bringing together individual actors into some kind of juxtaposition of their life-trajectories – causes a determining and a coming together of individuals' experiences. Edmund Leach points us towards this sociological understanding when he describes the propensity of a social milieu for coherence despite its containing 'almost as many distinguishable systems of customary rules and conventions ["cultures"] as there are individuals' (1977).

However, in the same essay, *Custom, Law and Terrorist Violence*, Leach also points us towards another phenomenon in whose terms experience, its origination and possible sharing, may be elaborated: the 'body'. For, Leach emphasizes the individual 'creativity' from which social vitality derives, the way this creativity embodies a distinction from the institutional – indeed, a hostility from all that is customary and systemic – and how, for him, creativity and *ressentiment* instantiate 'the very essence of being a human being'. Creativity and resentment of the social-institutional are instinctual dispositions, 'part of our very nature' (1977: 19).

Elsewhere, Leach elaborates upon how creativity derives from 'imaginative operations of the human mind' which are poetic, non-logical and not rule-bound (1976: 5). Creativity amounts to an inventive capacity to take the world apart and make it to which Leach would happily give the appellation 'divine' (and only to this), a capacity inherent in all human beings (1969: 90). The primary thing that human beings create, moreover, is their own individual selves – generating their own consciousnesses and their own 'private languages' as they artfully employ and transform cultural forms (Leach 1969: 26).

The consequence of individual embodiment for social science is that the ethnographic writing of 'cultural differences' can be treated as proximally convenient only – and ultimately illusory (1989: 137). And since laws of cultural ontology, distinction and homogeneity – like those of historical process and of sociological probability (1961: 51–2) – are illusions amid a reality of endless diversity, the *only* certainty is the personality of the individual manifesting itself in the world, and knowing itself as an internal relation (Leach 1989: 137).

Positing the certain existence of the manifestations of an embodied personality (over and against that of 'history' or 'society' or 'culture') is, of course, not a small 'only'; seeing the body beyond culture and ontologically in lieu of society, indeed, is to find that one has only just formulated the problem. Individual embodiment may be a universal human modality, but this does not make the body a transparently sure, 'pure' or simple route to meaning or meaning-making; the capacity for 'personality', for being a human individual, to repeat, may be a far cry from its particular substantiation. As E. D. Hirsch avowed (1988: 258):

> [T]he distance between one historical period [or one sociocultural milieu] and another is a very small step in comparison to the huge metaphysical gap we must leap to understand the perspective of another person in any time and place.

Accessing and inscribing this 'metaphysical leap' continues to challenge the combined efforts of any number of scientific disciplines, and its celebration defines a venerable tradition of literary and liberal expression. Furthermore, setting up an embodied personalism over and against society and culture is a radical step for a discipline such as anthropology, a discipline that has traditionally promoted itself in the academic marketplace by extolling socio-cultural contextualization. (But then, according to Nietzsche, professionally denying the body, misunderstanding the role embodiment plays in knowledge and its expression, has been a characteristic Western-philosophical failing *tout court* [1979a: 6].)

Nietzsche, for one, expresses confidence that an account of the embodied nature of experience is feasible, notwithstanding, and that through it one might begin to 'learn anew': to inaugurate a new, existential understanding comprising the 'selfishness' of physiology, demeanour, nourishment, diet and climate (1979b: 66). Anthropological voices, moreover, can be found already fleshing out the new project. 'Our experience is anchored in our body', we have heard already from Jim Fernandez (1977: 478), while Paul Stoller encourages us to regard the sentient individual body and an environing world of forces, smells, textures, sights, sounds and tastes as aspects of one and the same existential phenomenon (1995: 7–8). The body becomes the site where individual cognitions, cultural codes, social practices and history, and ecological processes, meet; here is anthropology as a 'human ecology' (Milton 1993: 4).

So how should one set out to inscribe the deeper manifestations of an embodied personality: of individually embodied understandings of the world? Not, I would say, by way of substance – in terms of the particular (and diverse) things that individuals know of the world – but by way of capacity and disposition: the human capacity for bodily knowledge, the bodily human disposition to know. That is, one would not want, initially at least, to posit samenesses of bodily experiences, or even their range, between human individuals – and thus replace one determinism (cultural) by another (corporeal). Rather, one would want to say that there are species-limited (human-specific) capacities for experience, for perception and interpretation, which having a certain kind of nervous system enables. These shared capacities then give rise to great, substantive and ongoing diversities between people concerning what is 'meaningful': valuable, painful, routine, serendipitous, and so on. Individuals live in individually embodied worlds. And while there may be both individual desires and social pressures to experience the world alike – to claim experiential commonality for the validation of a social relationship – still, this must be distinguished from the individuality of experience *per se*; experience comes first, and analytically it can be differentiated from people's desires for their experience, their expectations and interpretations of it. (As R. D. Laing phrased it [1968: 81], a 'phantasy of groupness' [concerning the coherency and determinism of experiences among an assemblage of people] is something that people may imagine for themselves, but it is nonetheless a phantasy which each individual will be responsible for effecting [and continuing to effect] and which each will effect differently, even if in spatio-temporal conjunction with others.)

To begin, then, it is possible and necessary for analytical purposes, I would argue, to demarcate the different kinds of things which the human body and brain has the capacity to construct and know. First, then, might be identified the body's knowledge of itself. It is basic to our animal nature, according to physiologists, to know the difference between self and non-self (one's own body, one's own voice, from that of others), and it a manifestation of serious pathology (schizophrenia, for instance) when this is not the case. It is also true, however, that a human body's knowledge of itself plumbs depths of great complexity, subtlety and multiplicity. The body knows itself as a subject, then, an instrument of action and experience, and also as an object, a focus of others' attention and will; it knows itself to represent a surface on which self and world interact, and also a surface beneath which experience and interpretation of interaction takes place. Whatever one might want to say about the body's ability to deceive itself, it is surely true that no other knowledge matches the potential self-knowledge that the body possesses; the body cannot know something other with anything approaching the fullness, the immediacy and inescapability that it can know itself – and no other can know it in the same way.

Second might be identified the body's knowing of its environment. Through a purposive and experimental engagement with what surrounds it, the body develops a set of physical and intellectual habits: 'world-views'. These cause the body to form and know an environment as a series of expectations and anticipations, which it then seeks to have fulfil themselves (Rapport 1993). Third might be identified the body's knowing of others in its environment: things (people, objects) and events with which it is in interaction, and with which it continues to engage for the purposes of self-fulfilment.

It is important to reiterate that these three kinds of knowledge – self, world and other – are bound up together, mutually implicated. Also that these knowledges are personally embodied; they are the possession and creation of distinct individual organisms. Also that such mutually implicated, personally embodied knowledge is not a fixed or stationary phenomenon but one in continuous process of being and becoming. Finally, the identity of the organism and its environment – the organism-plus-environment – can be said to be dependent on the ongoing process by which that organism comes to know itself. The organism *is* its knowledge of the world, is the order it creates of and around itself.

The science of bodies-plus-environments

From the perspective of neurology, Gerald Edelman has recently argued that it is through activity-in-the-world from before birth onwards that the brain comes not only to structure itself, but also to structure, to know and form its bodily *hexis*, its habitual bodily dispositions and environment, in a particular, personal way. '[E]ach individual person [comes to be] like no other', for each is motivated by their own historical system of physiological 'values', of what has worked successfully for them in the past (Edelman 1992: 171). Brain-plus-body-plus-environment, we are to understand, amount to one phenomenal unit.

In different language, this echoes the Existentialist position that human identity is an ongoing interpretive project, and that what comes to be identified is *at once* self, other and environing world; these identities are implicated one with another, deriving from the same, ongoing acts of individual interpretation. In cybernetic terms (Bateson 1973), the identity of body and environment amounts to one cybernetic circuit: a unit of knowledge and of its evolution.

Significantly, this also echoes ongoing work in ecology which delineates the ways in which organisms do not so much adapt themselves to environments as create environments adapted to them. *The Extended Organism: The Physiology of Animal-Built Structures* is the title of a recent book by animal physiologist Scott Turner (2000) which contains the proposition that the edifices built by animals beyond the outer extents of their bodies can nevertheless be conceived of as (external) organs of their physiology. One finds in Turner's work stimulating possibilities for considering the ways in which human beings also extend themselves into environments in their appropriations of identities and life-projects. Juxtaposing Turner (and Edelman) against more Existentialist treatments of the power of interpretive organisms also helps offset a Gellnerian critique concerning the 'verbal hocus-pocus' of 'cheap Idealism': an interpretive social science which ignores the power of physical constraints in a fantasy of a 'concept-saturated' human world, 'the *Allmacht des Begriffes*' (Gellner 1988: 12).

Animal-built structures are ubiquitous, Turner begins, whether ephemeral in their construction and duration or more lasting. May it not be appropriate to consider these environmental mouldings as parts of the animals themselves, as much organs of their particular physiologies as what we are accustomed to thinking of as their 'internal' bodily workings? For here are things which likewise affect the flow of matter, energy and information to and through the organism, and between it and its environment. Are we justified, then, in delimiting organisms by the outer integument of their bodies: do 'they' not extend beyond them, into the environments they fashion?

What makes an organism distinctive, individual, Turner continues, is not the existence of its boundary or integument *per se* but the nature of what its boundary does. The boundary of an organism is best thought of as a process (not a thing) whereby certain internal conditions of life are maintained despite external conditions or variations. Most of an organism's major physiological functions operate to provide a degree of stability to its internal environment: the proper conditions of temperature, pH and solute concentration, and the organized delivery and distribution of nutrients, fuel, oxidant and wastes (a phenomenon physiologists term 'homeostasis'). Differently put, while the persistence of a particular organism's individual identity may be said to come about by way of the existence of a boundary between it and its environment, this boundary is in fact thoroughly permeable, causing matter and energy continually to pass through it. Organisms, Turner suggests at one point, are like hydroelectric plants in rivers: they stand in the middle of an energy flow which they channel through themselves and use to do work. (One is reminded of Nietzsche's image of power-quanta in constant flux and interaction.) Not that this channelling is to be envisaged as a passive process, Turner quickly adds, a mere sieving, for it is also the case that organisms exert adaptive control over the flows of matter and energy, thereby maintaining a homeostatic state in the face of changing conditions. But if, by virtue of its integumentary boundary, an animal comes to have a distinct internal physiology – structures and devices operating to maintain certain conditions of life – may not that animal also be said to have an external physiology responsible for a modification of the conditions 'beyond' its integument?

By structurally modifying their environments, organisms extend the range of homeostatic conditions necessary for their form of life from inside their 'bodies' to outside, adapting their environments to themselves (as themselves). If organisms manipulate and adaptively modify the ways energy and matter flow through environments as they do through themselves, we can say that they confer a degree of (their own) livingness to what is seemingly inanimate. '[T]he environment', for Turner, 'can [come to] have physiology' (2000: 7).

That this process is active and not passive is due to its being metabolically fuelled, initiated and maintained. Metabolism is the process whereby animals engineer the controlled combustion of fuel, usually glucose, channelling the energy through their bodies. This energy then serves animals for two fundamental purposes: to encode and transmit information about the making of copies of themselves – to procreate – and to create, to produce 'order' in the world. (Turner would describe physiology as essentially the study of 'how animals use energy to do order-producing work' [2000: 24]). 'Order' may be described in abstract terms as worldly conditions that require less information to describe them (than 'disorderly' ones). Order is an organization, a homogenization, a harmonization of the world from a particular point of view, for a particular purpose. If a large number of simple molecules are, for instance, reduced to a smaller number of more complex molecules, then the world has become more orderly. Less abstractly put, order means conditions that possess a stability, an organization and a predictability relative to an organism's ongoing needs: assembling a complex protein, say, from simpler amino acids. Through the metabolic process, animals use energy to produce homeostatic conditions, or the potential for these; that is, an environment they have ordered into a known and usable space (including a space used to store energy for later use). The amount of order an organism can create is dependent on the amount of energy acquirable to produce it – also on the inexorable inefficiency (entropy) of any order-producing process. Turner's point, however, is that animals use energy to do work on so-called 'external' environments precisely as they do on 'internal' ones to cause homeostasis. Both these domains are their 'physiology', and are maintained metabolically.

THE POWER OF ANY BODY-IN-ITS-ENVIRONMENT

Let me turn briefly to one of Turner's numerous examples from the animal kingdom: the construction, over the past 650–700 million years, by earthworms of soil burrows (2000: 81–119). Earthworm burrows build, aerate and fertilize soils; but their purpose in doing this, Turner explains, is a 'personal' one: to co-opt the soil so that it acts as an accessory kidney, ensuring the worms' survival in an otherwise uninhabitable environment. For, by their nature, earthworms evolved to be freshwater creatures. Their problem in living on land is keeping the right balance of water and salts in their bodies: maintaining a differential between the condition of the liquids inside their bodies and out, and offsetting a thermodynamic flux which would naturally tend towards equalization. If earthworms were animals simply adapted to their environments (and not vice-versa) then they would be severely limited regarding the soils they might inhabit. Earthworms, however, possess the energy and exercise the agency to change soil ecosystems, and to maintain them in the face of entropy.

Soil particles tend to weather and to decrease in size, becoming clay-like and soggy – a kind of liquidity earthworms cannot survive. The latter's practice, therefore, is to aggregate particles of soil together. This they do by secreting mucus from their body surfaces, by passing soil through their bodies so that mucus collects to it, and also by defecating calcite. These three processes act against soil erosion, keeping burrows open, and enabling the soil to absorb sufficient water but also to hold it weakly enough for earthworms to gain access to it. The result is vastly to expand the soil horizon where worms can live.

Earthworms have made a 'choice', Turner concludes; they have decided to employ energy to change the environment rather than themselves, co-opting the soil as an accessory organ of balancing bodily liquidity. It might be speculated that earthworms made this choice because, in evolutionary terms, it is far faster, and offers more flexibility, to change one's environment than to change one's internal bodily structure and chemistry; 'culture', one might (even) say, is a more rapid and also more flexible tool of adaptation than biochemistry.

In sum, Turner would have us see how interactions between organisms and environments result in the extension of physiological processes and conditions beyond what has come to be conventionally defined as the boundaries of those organisms – a physiology no different in principle from that going on 'inside' the body. Living organisms thus alter the random or entropic nature of energy- and matter-flows and impose an 'orderliness' on nature: 'the principles of thermodynamics don't stop at the organism's skin' (2000: 11). This imposition of orderliness, moreover, can be at a scale many times larger than the generating organisms. As 'architects and engineers of their environments' (2000: 7), animals can cause a physiological function to operate far beyond themselves such that their lives and projects ramify in time and space.

DISCUSSIONS

The extended body and its self

What kind of connection might we be willing to make between an animal-physiological and thermodynamic proposition and social science, between the world of the earthworm (Turner also instantiates termites' mounds transforming wind energy, crickets' burrows modulating, amplifying and directing sound, and spiders' webs operating as organs of respiratory gas exchange underwater) and the world of human being? What kind of coincidence, if any? The connection is not a new one, after all, nor need it be reductionist in application, as Bateson demonstrated in his drawing of quite direct links between the laws of thermodynamics and the symbolic construction of human environments. According to Bateson (after Norbert Weiner), our notion of 'information' about the world is a simple analogue of what physicists term 'negative entropy'; what we know about the world, the order we perceive there, is what we have arranged, willed and desired in the world: the 'randomness' we have managed to offset (Bateson and Ruesch 1951: 176–9). Our gathering of information about the world – the procuring of negative entropy in the world – instantiates the way that human beings are active participants in their universes: purposive entities, not mere conditioned components (Bateson and Ruesch 1951: 249–50).

A standard (positive) reaction to Turner's thesis might be to say that society and culture are the human equivalents of animal-physiological extensions. Here are 'non-natural' ecosystems (Tallis 2001: 4): engagements with the material world which are fostered by deliberate and active experimentation and change, are moved by possibility as well as actuality, and driven by senses of the world which are beyond physical senses. Through our clothes, our houses, our systems of production, our marriage preferences, our aesthetic traditions, our systems of alliance, exchange and reciprocity, we extend our physiological genotype so as produce a phenotype-plus-environment that enables us to co-opt the whole world to our adaptational advance. Jean Comaroff adopts similar terms to these to describe the symbolic practice among the Tswana whereby 'circulation of animals permitted the human persona *to extend beyond the spatio-temporal confines of physical being*' (1985: 126, my emphasis). In more general terms, Amos Rapoport describes how culturally distinct cognitive schemata 'underwrite', 'precede', the environments in which human beings live, so that the latter represent 'material expressions' of cultural organization (1998: 484, 488). Moreover, while it is the case that 'all living things organise space' (Rapoport 1998: 467) – distributing themselves within it in diverse, non-uniform and complex ways – it is also true that the more evolutionarily complex the organism, the more active a process this is, also the more symbolic the function of space becomes. Finally, the 'built environment' that is a human creation involves an organization of 'time, space, communication and meaning [which] add[s] up to a complete ecological system' (Rapoport 1998: 467).

But Rapoport also mentions, in passing, 'personal space' – a 'movable "bubble" of space surrounding an individual' (1998: 486) – and I believe Turner's data allow us to be more literal in our focus than the above social-scientific response, and also more microsocial, and to see individual organisms, not just species or groups, as 'architects and engineers of their environments'. In this vein, Raymond Tallis has recently depicted the ecological habitats of human societies as poolings of the 'individual environments' of their members, and of the latter's 'formulated accounts' of these (2001: 4). (In the same way, the traditional reified image of society and culture as cohesive and integrated large-scale wholes may more properly be replaced by an appreciation of social habitats as the multiple and ongoing aggregations of [possibly] loosely aligned actors, interests and institutions [Rapport and Overing 2000: 195–206].) Specifically, I would like to suggest that the human individual's life-project may be seen as a kind of environmental architecture, extending control of identity beyond the skin, conditioning an environment to which a person possesses a bodily adaptation. Pursuing a life-project may be conceived of as a practice which procures an extended environmental homeostasis: the maintenance of a set of life-conditions within which the self continues to flourish and has its objectives met.

More precisely, an individual's life-project may be seen to affect the choice of relationships, human and non-human, in which that individual engages and the way he or she conducts these: affording relations in one's own image. A life-project may affect the ways in which an individual attends to what is around him or her, and in this attention, this interaction, identity and environment are formed. (Existence, we know from Existentialism, gives rise to essence, and activity-in-the-world to identity.) A life-project may give rise to a particular bodily hexis: to the speed of one's life, one's patience and haste, to the discipline imposed on oneself, to one's engagement with time and space. A life-project may lead to specific reactions to events – to a recognition of certain things in one's environment as 'events' – and a life-project may lead to the recognition of certain things as resources towards effecting one's goals.

We might say, then, that through their life-projects, the four individuals whom we have met in Part II assured themselves of environmental milieux in which to proceed, to extend or project themselves, along their course. Stanley Spencer gave body to a poetic vision – a heavenly life of divine love, something embracing all the senses, both intellect and emotion, something realizing both the identity and the connectivity of all – by making his art into his personal and private life and living a metaphysical imaginary of physical togetherness in an English village environment. Rachel Silberstein embraced 'the other', through emigré transnationalism and political marginalism, so as to accede to a personal experience of environmental holism which guaranteed the authenticity of her road to completeness. Ben Glaser traversed nationalities, marriages and the finances of manufacturing companies so as to secure for himself that recreational environment where he might engage in private pursuit of the astrophysical secrets of the universe. Friedrich Nietzsche composed a philosophy of immortal movement and continual self-overcoming which manifested itself in an adult environment of solitary wandering, unconsummated relationships and passions most fully enjoyed on paper.

Let me go into a little more detail, considering these four life-projects as environments.

The bodies in question

Stanley Spencer's biographer, Maurice Collis, noted a tension which is, I feel, fundamental to an appreciation of Stanley's personality: he was physically a very small man – he often painted himself as small, almost child-sized and child-like, being escorted or loomed over by large, protective women – but he was also self-contained and self-sufficient. Stanley did not allow himself to be deflected from his main concern, his self-expression, and while he was bound up with three or four influential women, they did not, as Collis puts it (1962: 15), alter him in essentials. To return to Stanley's own words: 'Cooped up as I am in myself, I gaze out on my own chicken-run and feel I could write a chapter on each ridge of mud, or scratched hole or nettle or clawmark. I prefer to have no greater world'. He described his wife and best friend, Hilda Carline, as his 'hand-holder' but as the above comment (by which he accompanied a picture of a Cookham allotment and chicken-run) intimates, the body, the self and world which Stanley is most intent upon exploring in his art is represented in the 'ridge of mud, scratched hole, nettle and clawmark' of his own physical (bodily) sensorium. He is content to 'fish treasures' out of the 'island' of himself; at heart he remained reclusive.

A similar tension surrounds the seeming distantiations and displacements of Stanley's life. He espies Cookham village from outside – from a window, a tree, a bridge – while at the Slade he travels back and forth; after the First World War he enters upon a peripatetic existence outwith Cookham, while practising a form of art whose personal iconography disturbs the academy's norms of propriety and eludes a wider public understanding. And yet, the oddness and 'otherness' of this life grew out of a 'self-intense' nature (Pople 1991: 209), which demanded its own emotional space. The outside, indeed, was enticing in its mixture of strangeness and familiarity, and Stanley insisted on being able to go where and when the spirit moved him; he determined to stay open to the fullness and complexity of experience: doctrine, revelation, regimentation and closure were anathema. Even Cookham, Stanley's heaven-on-earth, was ultimately only a landscape, as he put it, which enabled him the nearest to cater for his inner needs – needs to find (painted and written) expression for what he felt. In the final analysis Stanley knew that his 'spirit' had the capacity to find what it needed anywhere; it dealt with the world on its own terms.

Stanley described the separation that existed between his 'personal' and his 'impersonal' lives; the former was 'heavenly' and he dwelt there whenever he could – even if this made his outward behaviour 'difficult'. For the personal was liberating and beautiful: a world of thought and feeling, emotion, sentiment and desire which amounted to a 'parallel spiritual order', and one which transformed the everyday, its regulations and chronologies (however prison-like), into beauty. 'I really feel that everything in one that is *not vision* is vulgarity', he wrote to a painter-friend.

Not that the impersonal, everyday world was an irrelevancy to Stanley. It was the means to demonstrate his power. 'Taking his thoughts for a walk' and 'marrying' them to a place, a scene, in Cookham or elsewhere was a way to make his inmost wishes an ordinary fact of life; assembling images from his mundane experience, absorbing (marrying) the whole world into himself, was the means by which Stanley provided himself with the medium to express that 'mass of inward, surging meaning, a kind of joy' he would 'in some way…fulfil'. Certainly, there was a mutuality here – the place, the scene, the mundane world and the person fulfilling each other – but it was also the case that Stanley regarded his art-work and the 'spiritual order' it manifested as transcendent. Art overcame the distinctions, limitations and partialities of the everyday, showing things complete and whole: sacred-plus-profane, seen-plus-felt, culture-plus-nature, self-plus-other.

Not only self-intense and self-sufficient, what characterizes Stanley Spencer's way of being, above all, seems to have been a drive towards self-expression whereby the phantasmagoria of his inner, personal, spiritual life would be not simply what he experienced but also what he made manifest as an environment in which to live. The church-house, never built, would have been the culmination of this – an alternative physical universe – but the paintings and the writings by themselves evidence the sense of awesomeness he successfully translated from the 'hen-coop' of his body out to chicken-run of the world.

There was an integrity which I found in *Rachel Silberstein*'s motivation, a purity, and a child-like innocence in her engagement with the world very reminiscent of how I would imagine Stanley Spencer. (It is notable, in considering the two lives in juxtaposition, while knowing them in different ways, the sense I have that here are distinct apprehensions of commensurate phenomena, similar phenomena found in different media.) The purposiveness and the intensity of Rachel's expression was diluted by no cynicism, affectation or facade – no 'worldliness' or sophistry. She took herself, she took others and she took the wider world as she found them.

'Found' is the operative word in Rachel's regard, indeed, for she was embarked upon a personal journey, charting an individual course towards knowledge and growth. She prided herself on her independence – financial, intellectual, affective, spiritual – and she knew herself to be in occupancy of a discrete 'head-space' and bodily sensorium. Her journey towards discovery, moreover, began with herself. What was she like? What did she like? She would come to know what made her happy, what she felt like, what her intuitions were, her desires (what 'bored her shitless') at particular times and places. She would 'get into' places, she would learn what organically grew out of 'the-individual-in-that-place'.

Having moved around, lived around, slept around for some fifty years, Rachel knew more now about who she was and where she found 'good vibes', but she was determined to remain open, to herself and to the world, and to keep on connecting experientially. Closed, 'Type-A' personalities turned her off, and 'repression' was the source of pain, both in the life of the repressed individual and in those with whom he or she came into contact. In her own engagements with others Rachel sought above all to respect the integrity of their otherness; she might endeavour to match herself – her characteristics, her capacities and skills – to others' needs, to cause a resonance between them, but she would take care never to interfere in their head-space and spoil their individual courses of development.

Matching herself up with others, in fact, was a significant part of Rachel's journey of discovery. She sought out a community of 'soulmates', a network of like-minded personalities with whom she could 'caucus'. These were people for whom 'normal interaction' would often not need words; supranational bodies among whom Rachel found she could discern those who shared world-views, those who occupied a commensurate head-space (cf. Wulff 1998).

And here exists a significant tension in Rachel's life, again reminiscent of Stanley Spencer's. On her journey towards discovery of herself, a journey taking her along an individual path, part of what Rachel ponders is whom is she the same as, and why. Is she Jewish, with similar genetic wiring and historic experience to a global diaspora, or is she American, a democrat? Is Jewishness something inside her or is she simply, morally human, and happier with those ('the [Israeli] Arabs') who do not practise forms of ethnic exceptionalism? Where and how does she feel at home?

This tension between individuality and belonging, and the questions it throws up, eventuates in Rachel maintaining her personal quest, and her physical journeying. At the age of forty-nine, moreover, and the formal ending of a significant chapter in her life – her marriage – it seems Rachel was seeking out more 'alternative' experiences from which to draw 'energy'. She charted a course to Israel, there to deserted Mitzpe Ramon, thence to the marginal and the downtrodden (the AACI, stray dogs, Peace Now, and Palestinians), in order to begin again: touch the earth, find herself, find love. But then Rachel also seemed inherently prone to brief habits, to knowing that every time and place had its fractures, its contrasts and oppositions, and that her personal environment was journeying in between. Her life was full, she exuded most purpose, when she had discerned a new alternative to connect with, and experience.

THE POWER OF ANY BODY-IN-ITS-ENVIRONMENT

What a woman needs in order to release her artistry, 'the freedom of her mind', Virginia Woolf famously opined in 1920s Cambridge, was 'a room of her own' (1963). Stanley Spencer's comment that his 'chief need' for the furthering of his 'chief and only occupation' – exploring 'his own thoughts' – was 'an empty room with a fire in the grate' (cited in Collis 1962: 15), bears a striking resemblance. The note on which I would leave Rachel Silberstein's story is not only her similar self-interest and self-knowledge – the internal focus on the self and its needs for self-expression – but also the balance or tension she embodies (like Spencer, like Woolf) between domicile and exploratory flight. 'I'm a political animal', Rachel found of herself, 'but I also need to touch the earth for my sanity'. Her journeying to and between possible futures was predicated upon the physical furnishings (the self-made furniture, the kiln, the pet's grave) to depart from.

Before *Ben Glaser* was out of his teens, he had moved from Vienna, his place of birth, to Cieszyn/Tesin on the Polish-Czech border, back to Vienna, and thence to Prague. It was a common enough Jewish trajectory in the late Habsburg empire, part of the way in which Jewish life was separate from – the experience of family connections and community distinct from – that of the grounded nationalities around them. This was to be followed, of course, by the often fatal disjunctions of the Second World War, the further movements and family dispersals as Jews fled the Nazis. Ben's interpretation of these circumstances meant initially a focus on his education (hastening to complete an engineering degree), then a focus on his physical survival (emigrating to Britain), and lastly a focus on earning a living (setting up and running a series of manufacturing companies).

Photographs of Ben as a young man show a handsome, stern and self-confident figure, physically assured. And yet, as evidenced by his early case of tuberculosis and his later rotundity, Ben also adopted a somewhat cavalier attitude to his body and its needs. He was a sensual man, enjoying bodily pleasures, especially food, sex and sunshine, but his body was above all a vehicle. It was his body that took him to university, to Britain, to self-employment – his body alone that he took with him on his journey from his family's erstwhile continental-European home – and yet what was far more important was what the body transported and contained: mind, memory, the passions. We have heard Stanley Spencer distinguish between his 'personal life' (an 'up-in-heaven life') and his 'impersonal life' (a 'separate-from-me thing'), and I find the differentiation useful too for apprehending Ben's behaviour. His more fundamental interpretation of his movements across the Habsburg empire and beyond, then, was to distinguish between what appeared on the surface of life – places, politics, fashions, bodies – and deeper, more significant, more lasting realities: it was the latter that were to be really valued as important for serious satisfactions. Nietzsche opined that '[t]he man with the *furor philosophicus* in him will no longer have time for the *furor politicus*', for 'reading newspapers or serving a party' (cited in Gane and Chan 2000: 69), and this was something Ben seemed to evidence. His home was in a recreational intellectualism – 'furious' (Nietzsche), 'heavenly' (Spencer), private in origin – which was utterly divorced from the immediate business of earning a living, even of surviving. His home was 'anywhere'.

His private passions made Ben and his life's work into a centre of conjunction in the world: a place where the 'conversation of mankind' (Oakeshott), as apprehended in its wider historical and spatial reaches, would crystallize and find enunciation, and also be taken onward. When Ben described the intention of his scientific papers 'Cosmos 1' and 'Cosmos 2', as 'the linking of all the parameters, relations and equations in the cosmos together' he might also have been describing his life-project as such.

Ben's work of conjunction involved him, first, in an intense engagement with the world, opening himself out to physics ('why things are made as they are'), to history (how the present looks *sub specie aeternatis*), to geography (what the worldly environment contains), and to aesthetics (how the world captivates the senses with beauty). Second, Ben would engage in diverse acts of self-expression – art-works, music, craft-works, scientific theorizations – by which a polymathic apprehension of the world would be concentrated into new forms of representation. This brought its own enjoyments and rewards, but was also a civilized act – the recalling of past advances in civilization and making them contemporary. It was also a social and pedagogic act, disseminating the knowledge of human civilization (of civilized minds such as Rembrandt, Beethoven, Ben-Gurion and Einstein) and assisting its appreciation by a new audience; Ben would therefore engage with whomsoever he could gain a hearing, in rapt terms and in as many languages as were available to him (pictorial as well as verbal), on whatever topics he was currently researching.

Ben's father was a Hebrew scholar and a rapporteur for Zionism, and it is tempting to see Ben himself in the Jewish tradition of fatherly guide and sage. If he did not immerse himself in holy scriptures and pass them on to pupils, garnished by his own interpretive commentaries, then he did immerse himself in the 'sacredness' of the material world and seek to transmit the wonder of it being interpreted. And yet I would stress instead the radical particularity of Ben's intense engagements. He may have sought out an audience for his accomplishments, but the latter derived from, made manifest and fed, an impetus that was his own; his interests, I would say, were individual in motivation and execution, also in their amalgamation, and they led Ben along an individual course. It was also the case that between places, times and relationships Ben's interests afforded his life a continuity, and a kind of purity or integrity too. Acting in furtherance of interests which were self-motivated and self-fashioned, he freed himself of proximate, merely fashionable, pursuits.

Ben might have acted on occasion *through* relationships – with his wives and children, with his wider family, with his business partners, with his Jewishness – but I do not believe that when it came to his interests and accomplishments he acted because of these. His life was given continuing force and direction because he supplied his own conviction, excitement, entertainment and vindication.

Nevertheless it is worth reminding ourselves of the many relations in which Ben did partake – the many conjunctions he caused to meet in himself – if only to be cognizant of the richness of the environment in which he enabled himself to act. Artistically, his courteous imitations of old masters of pictural and musical composition (from Rembrandt and Rubens to Bach and Beethoven) maintained relations between earlier artistic periods and the present. Scientifically, his respectful hagiography of the doyens of modern astrophysics kept alive the questions of the universe they had formulated and maintained a space for answers. Ethnically, he followed Jewish religious traditions – present-day freedoms evincing past sacrifices – and he supported the state of Israel (financially and with his frequent presence), loyally maintaining its good name amid the envy and ignorance of its vocal detractors. Familially, he maintained a role as loving elder of the Glaser 'clan', even as its members spread across Europe and beyond, and as the memorization of those who had died became a sad weight.

Due to the separation between the 'personal life' of his art-work and the 'separate-from-me thing' that was the 'impersonal life' of the everyday, we have found Stanley Spencer describing his behaviour with others as 'quite difficult'. The difficulty of living with Ben was perhaps attested to by the fact that he, like Spencer, underwent two divorces. But then his third marriage lasted nearly thirty years; Ben was demanding of my mother's attention but this was a passion for time in each other's company – and a jealousy in its absence – which he enjoyed as something mutual. I would see Ben's (earlier) failed relationships as matters of incompatibility, and note the great care Ben took when his private passions enjoyed a domestic reality.

One thing is plain, however: Ben knew the domestic arrangements which would suit him and put himself in position to acquire them. Like Stanley Spencer, like Rachel Silberstein, he determined to furnish 'his own room'. The materials for his art-work and his music-making, and his library of scientific texts, were literally laid out around him, the results of his artistic and scientific efforts likewise. Moreover, whether in his art-studio, his study, his library, even his kitchen, he placed himself among his artefacts – both temporally and spatially – in regular and habitual ways. While cavalier, then, in his attitude towards what was superficially, merely proximately, present – country, political fashions, even his own physique – Ben fashioned his points of conjunction with what was significantly, globally true, amid domestic milieux that physically reflected back his successful acts of self-expression: his 'synagogue-houses', one might say.

The nature of the breakdown which *Friedrich Nietzsche* suffered at the end of his life remains a mystery to his biographers: how literal was it and how metaphorical? After some eleven years of leading a wholly itinerant life, spending time more or less alone, receiving a tiny audience for his works – his voice becoming increasingly strident – and required ultimately to publish at his own expense, Nietzsche returned to the care of his mother and sister in a family household, retired to bed for eleven years and descended into incapacity and physical paralysis: gentle and childlike in demeanour, but seemingly incapable of coherent thought.

His last public gesture was the embracing of a beaten cart-horse on a Turin street. For some commentators, this was an act of psychological identification, showing Nietzsche too at the end of his tether, unable to proceed along the lonely path of working through a metaphysics which was founded upon a contradiction: a grand narrative which preached the end of grand narratives; an advocation of the will-to-power, self-overcoming, heroic morality, tragic art, the revaluation of values, a nuanced interpretation of life taken as a whole…when there was no truth, identity or integrity beyond language. For others, Nietzsche's breakdown was the aetiological endpoint of the congenital disease of the brain to which his father also succumbed, or else the culmination of the syphilis Nietzsche probably contracted as a student, coupled with the physical weaknesses brought about by his war experiences.

For a writer who described philosophy as inadvertent personal memoir, it is perhaps not surprising to observe how closely the tenets of Nietzsche's metaphysics are imitative of traits in his own life – but it is no less striking for that. Identities are ephemeral coalitions of power-quanta, Nietzsche prescribed, and even physical bodies can be conceived of as aggregations of contesting drives, instincts, affects and urges, orchestrated into tenuous and provisional alignment by intellect, reason and conscience; everything (and every thing) comes about 'in spite of'. Of himself, Nietzsche would say that his passions would kill him: tossed continuously to and fro, 'he' would eventually fall apart. He would not go back to God and yet he would adopt Zarathustra as his alter-ego and imagine descending from the mountain-tops with his prophecy: Nietzsche, the vicar of overman. Without God or spouse, home, job or nationality, he played the stranger-outsider *par excellence*, his engagement with others incidental to his purpose of charting his changing self and his self-knowledge; and yet, he suffered for being alone. He enjoyed his body physically – in exertion, sex, sport, food, music – and yet he also experimented with its diet (and calibrated results), playing with his bodily performance. As with Ben Glaser, his body was a vehicle: the site of his battle to know. Nietzsche attended a boys' boarding school, he enlisted as a cavalryman and then battlefield paramedic, he wrote a 'pitiless' masculinist prose, but then he returned to an all-female household as in his infancy (mother, grandmother, sister, maiden-aunts). In short, as Nietzsche himself put it, he was precisely 'a nuance', contrarieties meeting in him – 'entangled, ensnared, enamoured' – as they did in all things.

Philosophy should affirm, Nietzsche believed, and the significant distinction he posited in his own life between his writing and 'himself' ('another thing entirely'), might be read as Nietzsche exploring the potentialities of this affirmation. He sought to make writing into a dominating passion which might see him gaining vantage upon his bodily passions – upon his migraines, myopia and colic, his lovelessness, poverty and obscurity – thereby to know himself entire, and to revalue and transcend himself. Through his writing – from boyhood journals to twelve major works of philosophy in his final sixteen lucid years – he would spend a lifetime testing the limits of an individual's capacity to know, affirm, and fulfil his or her life.

To this task Nietzsche brought a relentless energy. In whatever he did, it seems, from battlefield nursing to philosophizing, he drove himself, even to excess. Maybe this was in compensation of the bodily infirmities, and the lack of time, with which he felt he was dealing. But then, as comprised of power-quanta, centres of force, Nietzsche also asserted that every thing in the world, organic and inorganic, was driven – its force reaching out beyond itself to colonize its environment and achieve pleasure. Of himself, Nietzsche spoke of a will which strode out, over obstacles and time, 'unburyable and uninjurable', finding joy in the worlds it created for itself.

What one could hope to achieve through one's exercise of will and the philosophical calibration (writing) of one's will, was a fullness of life. One was to be hungry for knowledge of self (and thus world), eat openly and richly, satisfy one's desires, sentiments and spirit, and hence come to experience many things in many ways. Reminiscent of the restless Rachel Silberstein, Nietzsche sought completion, and guarded against what he saw as the weakness of systematization and closure. If he worried himself continually with questions and contrasts, he could hope to rehearse the process of becoming of the whole world and survey the entire human scene.

To affirm all of life, to unite all into the vision and the knowledge that was willed by one individual, and to negate nothing, was also, Nietzsche believed (echoing Stanley Spencer) to 'redeem' all. The truth might be ugly, the reality of power-quanta unsettling, but an orchestration of this into a whole was beautiful, it was art-work. Whether enunciated as scientific fact, religious truth, mathematical statistic, or musical composition, an 'Apollonian' patterning of 'Dionysian' flux was an empowering illusion; indeed it could be life-saving.

Nietzsche described the overman as his gift to humanity: a greatness to aspire to, an example of perdurance, strength, responsibility and freedom. In writing about his life, in writing as his life, Nietzsche sought to transcend merely momentary embodiment – the body in the moment – and to achieve the integrity of an eternal return: describe an environment of eternal self-overcoming.

What kinds of embodied engagement with the world, what bodily understandings of self and other, do these four accounts of personal experience seem to have in common?

The word I come back to is that used by Leslie Chamberlain in her description of Nietzsche: *Machtgefuhl*, possessing a sense of what one could do, and therefore ought to do, with one's life, capacities, talents and powers. *Machtgefuhl* might be said to comprise first a certain 'self-intensity': an attention to oneself and interest in oneself, a coming to know oneself, and a belief that this is a proper activity for an individual. Second, the self-intense individual is interested in the fulfilment, the development and the expression, of what he or she knows of himself or herself; he or she believes that catering to the needs of the self is an appropriate priority and a valid pleasure. Third, the self-intense individual believes in this project of self-fulfilment single-mindedly: independently of others, of their judgements and their reactions (their hindrance and also, to an extent, their help). The individual's life-project of self-intensity is, ultimately, his or her business alone. Hence, the self-engagement of the self-intense individual translates into a coincidental disengagement from others. Fourth, however, and seemingly paradoxically, the self-intense individual also practises a certain disengagement from himself or herself, effecting a disjunction or displacement between different aspects of his or her life: the personal as against the impersonal, the experiential as against the conceptual, the spiritual as against the political, the recreational as against the occupational. Finally, the commonality of embodiment among the above self-intense individuals would seem to point to a displacement from their own bodies, a treatment of their bodies as vehicles for their life-projects but still as distinct from those projects. Even when embodiment figures centrally in their felt needs for self-fulfilment – that which experiences the joy of the mountains, the desert, music, sex – still the individual's life-project can in the final analysis be conceptualized separately from the body; the project's achievement represents a solidity, even fixity, in the face of the body's change and ultimate physical demise.

If life-project translates into how a self-intensity with which one attends to, interacts with, what is around one, including one's consciousness of oneself and one's body (thus giving rise to a kind of environmental architecture, to adaptational, homeostatic conditions which extend beyond the skin), then what, as architects or engineers of self-and-world, do the above four seem to have in common? As 'self-intense individuals', as actors with developed senses of who they are, what they need, and the importance of putting themselves in positions to satisfy their needs, they might be said to have expressed and sought to have fulfilled alike a sense of physical security: more exactly of domiciled groundedness. Spencer spoke openly of his favoured, heated empty room (even as he travelled between houses); Silberstein of a place where she could touch the earth; Glaser found homes in which he could physically spread out around him whatever he was crafting, while Nietzsche journeyed from and to the maternal milieu of his family home by way of a series of lodgings on a regular peripatetic route. In very different ways, each assured themselves of a 'room of their own'.

At the same time, all exhibited a pervasive restlessness, an unrootedness. They procured room for themselves, living space, but no place in particular. Place was more an incidental feature, a means or medium for other things; their focus was always beyond. This involved both a disengagement from immediate sociopolitical issues and also from proximate social relations. They lived *through* not *for* what was immediate and proximate, straddling and crossing the latter domains, and separating what they took to be the significant features of their 'real' lives from relations in the here and now; their real engagements were with their own visions of futurity. What they hoped for from others was not so much substantive agreement, or even understanding or cooperation, but the possibility of mutuality whereby the room they sought out for themselves might find an equivalence in others' practices; and the fulfilment they achieved might be reflected by others' – in their distinct ways.

It was not that they travelled quite alone, then. The life-project they maintained was, in part, physically represented: pictures, sketches, scraps of notepaper, journals, pencils, paints, books, pots, musical instruments, pets. Spencer, Silberstein, Glaser, Nietzsche – all made themselves artefactually secure, carrying with them memorable *materiel* which served as significant components in their maintaining personal habits of self-expression, of environmental engagement – channelling energy in routine ways – wherever they came to rest (as well as finding homes in transit as such). What characterized the environmental architecture that all four achieved in common, finally, was a kind of openness to the world. They set themselves up as points of conjunction for much if not all that they felt the world contained, seeking to take it into themselves and transform its diversity into an ordered – beautiful (Spencer), dialectical (Silberstein), logical (Glaser), redeemed (Nietzsche) – whole. It was, moreover, a conjunction, an assimilation, whose process, whose terms, whose energy and drive, they saw themselves as responsible for supplying; it was an openness in their own image. The *Machtgefuhl* of these four individuals led them into believing that it was their right, and their duty, to effect an environmental engineering for themselves.

The body in practice

- 'We commonly think of the external "physical world" as somehow separate from an internal "mental world"', Gregory Bateson comments (1973: 429), but it would be truer to say that '[t]he mental world – the mind, the world of information processing – is not limited by the skin'. There is a 'mental determinism' immanent in the universe (1973: 441).

- 'Places', the 'significant centres of our immediate experiences of the world', are 'fusions of human and natural order', according to Edward Relph (1976: 141). The identity of places bespeaks 'a complex and progressive ordering and balancing', an indissociable adaptation to each other of physical and observable features on the one hand and 'personality, memories, emotions, and intentions' on the other. The whole amounts to a 'unique set of moments of space-time' in those individuals doing the experiencing (1976: 56–9); however they might vary in range (from rooms to continents), places become 'whole entities, syntheses of natural and man-made objects, activities and functions, and meanings given by intentions' (1976: 141).

- Human beings have a 'social intelligence', as Nicholas Humphrey describes it (1983), which means they seek out transactions with the world, forcing such transactions, indeed, upon whatever they are able. Over human evolution, therefore, the transactional potential of countless things has been explored, and, by way of this process, 'things have come alive' (1983: 27). It is through these relationships that human beings have advanced their security, and lessened indeterminacies in their environments: putting themselves in situations where their own knowledge has a determining effect on what there is in their environments to know.

- Like other higher organisms, but more so, human beings have a repertoire of behaviours at their disposal, and make a choice regarding which behaviours they put forward into the world as interactional means with their environments, Karl Popper and John Eccles expound (1977). Furthermore, since their choice of behaviour makes the world into a certain sort of place, human beings' active subjectivity and cogitation can be said to alter their natural-selective chances and affect evolution. Natural selection thus takes the form of an evolving relationship between external forces and human products and purposes, human consciousness. One can describe human beings as active creators of their environments and their contents, indeed, creating by way of action. Moreover, this is something that each human being, as an individual organism, is responsible for doing (well or badly) for itself: '[by way of] individual action, the organism may "choose", as it were, its environment.... Thus the activity, preferences, skill, and the idiosyncrasies of the individual animal may directly influence the selection pressures to which it is exposed, and with it, the outcome of natural selection' (Popper and Eccles 1977: 12).

A number of theses can be seen to resemble the argument put forward in this section of the book concerning an embodied engagement with the world. The individual, I have contended, actively, continually and idiosyncratically extends himself or herself into the world, and thereby constitutes his or her identity and that of his or her milieu as a mutual pair: self-plus-environment. My particular emphasis has, of course, concerned power. A certain kind of extension, of activity-in-the-world, namely the construction of identity and milieu in terms of an individual life-project, affords individual actors the capability of proceeding along their own path in their own way: securing a life lived in reflection of their intentions and will. I take encouragement from the resemblances to be found, above, in animal physiology, in cybernetics, human geography, neurology and philosophy of self, to an existential-anthropological thesis concerning the individual life-project. Here perhaps is a truth of the human condition that different human sciences each access in their own terms (cf. Devereux 1978: 1–3).

Other seeming resemblances, however, I would continue to decry. For instance, there is the culturological thesis that might define the individual life-project as a kind of social-structural necessity or symbolic inevitability, and there is the sociological thesis that would construe individuals in pursuit of life-projects as measures of historical opportunity or necessity. An example of the former might be Louis Dumont's apprehension of Hindu 'world-renouncers' (*sadhus*) (1966) – those who eschew the proximate demands of Indian caste society in order to adopt an alternative life-style centring on more fundamental spiritual concerns – as individuals manoeuvred into a position beyond social relations in order for the wider society to be able to maintain a symbolic opposition between what is individual and asocial on one side and an everyday majoritarian social life of hierarchical structures and collectivist values on the other. Far from agents exercising existential power, world-renouncers *à la* Dumont are framed as cultural pawns through whose displacement and seeming individuality the symbolico-structural order and interdependence of society proper – of collective Man – is properly identified, validated and assured. A version of the sociological thesis might point out how the individuals on whom I have chosen to focus in this book operated within a historical period in the West (1850–2000) when traditional communities and lifestyles were being overtaken by modernizing forces – industrialism, urbanism, capitalism, nationalism, globalism – and modernist processes – the democratization of education, health and bureaucracy, the enfranchisement of women, the emancipation of the Jews – such that the movement of people in search of their own life-projects, and destiny and fulfilment across national, institutional and other borders became normative: a right and a duty (cf. Berger and Kellner 1973; Lukes 1990).

Notwithstanding the superficial concordances that might be drawn between the practice of life-projects by Spencer, Silberstein, Glaser and Nietzsche and the above theorizations, the kind of phenomenon I am identifying in this book is not compassed within these kinds of discourse; I would want to claim for it a different order of existence. In the same way that Max Weber located his notion of charisma over and against the particularities of socio-cultural milieux – whether traditional or modern – and allowed for the charismatic individual operating decisively upon those normative and structural arrangements willy-nilly (1946), or the way that Kenelm Burridge's idea of individuality exists as an existential modality to which people might be expected everywhere to have potential recourse, irrespective of socio-cultural conditions and of the notions of personhood which provide the outward form of their everyday lives (1979), my sense of the operating of life-projects is of a capacity that individuals possess apart from and even despite cultural and societal immediacies and contingencies.

Important questions remain, nonetheless, regarding the conditions under which the capacity becomes an habitual practice. I have spoken of *Machtgefuhl*, of self-intensity and the 'genius' of single-mindedness, and while it is not the overriding concern of this book to locate the source of such traits – so much as illustrate their existence and consequence – it behoves me to consider at least briefly what kind of a phenomenon *Machtgefuhl* might be.

The obvious points of departure to suggest themselves are 'nature', and 'nurture'. *Machtgefuhl* can be conceived of as a form of natural force of character – 'good ego strength', as psychology puts it, 'ontological security', an instinct for self-preservation and self-love (*amour de soi*), self-confidence and resilience in the face of obstruction – considered to be an innate quality of the individual actor. Alternatively, *Machtgefuhl* can be approached as something elicited by one's environment – adapted from 'mentors', copied from 'role-models' – and taken on by the individual actor as an aspect of his or her 'social intelligence' and maturity. These approaches are not mutually exclusive, of course, and perhaps it is a mistake ever to imagine the given and the revaluated, being and becoming, as ever existing outside a dialectic of mutual constitution. I have defined my stance in this book as a pragmatic one – wanting to encompass in its humanistic project both those who would define individuality as an ontological form of subjective consciousness, and those for whom individuality is an instrumental ethos, a means of ensuring equal treatment and rights – and my conclusion here regarding the phenomenal nature of *Machtgefuhl* will be equally open-ended and pragmatic; for the purpose of recognizing the existence of individual life-projects, for respecting their practice and celebrating their possibilities, it is unimportant whether they are considered innate or learned.

Genius, Nietzsche wanted to prescribe as something to be acquired, something one grew into. My stress too would be on the developmental aspects of self-intensity or single-mindedness: they are matters of positive feedback. The practice of pursuing a life-project bestows certain qualities of character on its exponents, such that having one and maintaining one, expecting to see a life-project through to completion, are essential components in its continuing effects; 'hope', in Humphrey's phrasing (1983: 208), 'will create its own object'. In dialectical fashion, the practice of life-projects can be responsible for the continuing disposition. Such a conclusion also accords with the emphasis this book has given to activity-in-the-world, to the intentioned and ongoing exploratory practices whereby individuals create and recreate the meaningful environments in which they live. Life-projects come to be understood as fundamentally *forms of intentioned undertaking*: ways of being active, ways of attending to the world which have certain significant consequences for their executors.

In writing about the way in which 'action/body/consciousness' represents 'a unity' in human lives, Mark Harris (2000: 8–9) appropriates Herman Melville's literary motif of the 'confidence-man'. The confidence-man (or -person), Harris explains, is a tricksterish figure whose practice is to blend self-fashioning, changeability, recoverability and opportunism in such a way as to instantiate an identity which is 'free' from the collective conventions of cultural classification and social differentiation, and to embody an indifference to what lies beyond his or her own projects. Disdaining to become entangled in other worlds than his or her own, the confidence-person practises an 'anarchic sociality' and thus 'avoid[s] control and domination', even becoming invisible to others' gaze (Harris 2000: 196). It is not that the confidence-person is 'marginal', nor that his or her behaviour is a matter of 'resistance'; rather it is that, practising movement as a form of ongoing activity-in-the-world, he or she accedes to an environmental positioning beyond the provenance of others' objectifying markers. The 'creative pulse' for the 'confident' life is provided instead by 'rhythms' that inhere in its own environmental praxis (Harris 2000: 212–14).

In fulfilling themselves as confidence-persons, one might say that the practice of *Machtgefuhl*, of single-mindedness and self-intensity, is more important for Stanley Spencer, Rachel Silberstein, Ben Glaser and Friedrich Nietzsche than the mere ontological truth of *Machtgefuhl*. Here are self-interested and self-involved individuals who want to know themselves, who act as though they know themselves, and who take seriously the project of pursuing an idea of themselves (an idea through themselves and for themselves) which they value. Formulating this sense of who they are and where they wish to go – of their environmental status – is the vital factor in their acceding to a successful embodiment of environmental extension and control.

8

TOTAL INSTITUTIONS AND THE VIOLENCE OF SOCIETY: THE DEATH OF POWER?

> It must be remembered that each of us, both objectively and subjectively, lived the *Lager* in his own way.
> (Primo Levi, *The Drowned and The Saved*)

A thesis concerning individual life-projects has been illustrated by way of four particular lives. Stanley Spencer, Rachel Silberstein, Ben Glaser and Friedrich Nietzsche have each manifested a bodily force, a practical will, which I have called 'existential power'. Each, I have argued, leads his or her life in terms of 'in order to' motives which impart to those lives a certain directionality, velocity and projection, in an environment of their own constitution and experience, and which deny the social-scientific validity of imposing 'because' motives (cf. Gray 2000: 8).

There remains, however, a question which cannot be sidestepped if the thesis is to have general validity, and which this concluding section of the book takes up. Bluntly put: what of the will of the individual within a totalitarian regime or totalizing institution – under slavery, despotism, religious fundamentalism, amid the witch-hunt, the Stalinist gulag, the Nazi concentration camp – which would seem to do intentional violence to individuals' freedom of expression, sense of self and environment for manoeuvre? What occasion for *Machtgefühl* here?

Erving Goffman described a 'total institution' as a setting where a number of people 'together lead an enclosed, formally administered round of life' (1961: 11). Encompassed by the institution, they find a world provided for them, and their time and interests captured; every aspect of their lives is overwritten. Here are individual bodies, in Foucault's words, 'totally imprinted by history' (1977). For Foucault, of course, there is never a place where 'the laws of individual desire, the forms of individual language, the rules of individual actions, and the play of individual mythical and imaginative discourses' are not overwritten and over-determined in this way (1972); the best to be hoped for is a playing off one coercive-discursive episteme/regime against another, ending up possibly with some relatively rule-less space (or place of anti-rule) in the interstices of 'governmentality' (1991b: 102–3). For a more humanistic Goffman, a total institution is something which one can imagine people entering and leaving. Notwithstanding, on arrival in the institutional domain Goffman depicts individuals as 'mortified', their habitual conceptions of self no longer supported by ambient social structures: 'the boundary that the individual places between his being and the environment is invaded and the embodiment of self profaned' (1961: 32). Institutionalized individuals embark upon new and radically re-fashioned 'moral careers', ordinarily ones of curtailment, dispossession, disfigurement and violation (Goffman 1961: 24).

Goffman's words resonate strongly with accounts of those who have lived through periods of totalitarianism, where the institutional rationale is the control of persons as much as space (Shore and Wright 1997: 30). What I would turn to now is one such famous account, that of Primo Levi in Auschwitz, the Nazi concentration and death camp (*Lager*), in order to examine the question of individual will and wilfulness. It might seem offensive even to posit the suggestion, but in order to round out the thesis that this book has explored concerning an individual's life-project and existential power, the estimation that Levi's experiences in a Nazi concentration camp were in a sense freely interpreted and self-willed must be broached, as an extreme case.

The *Shoah*

Michael Bernstein (1998) has noted how often the Nazi Holocaust of the Jews, or *Shoah*, is employed as an extreme or limiting case (a reflex Leo Strauss dubbed the 'reductio ad Hitlerum'). At a time when other absolutes and universalizing claims have come to be eschewed, this catastrophe seems to maintain its imaginative grasp, in a variety of discourses, as *telos*: an ultimate negative truth by which human experience can be subjected to an all-encompassing standard, a 'moral marker of absolute evil' (Aschheim 2001: 29). I do not mean for it to play this kind of role here. I might concur with Bernstein that, '[a]s an actual historical project, devised and carried out by a modern industrialized nation...the *Shoah* was, in an almost primal sense, without parallel or precedent' (1998: 6), but it can also be said, as does Zygmunt Bauman (1989), that historically the Holocaust was continuous with, part and parcel of, recognizably quotidian or domestic socio-cultural domains. Bauman talks of the Holocaust as a window throwing an especially bright light onto certain features of modernist social life, rather than a distinct thing-in-itself.

What should also be stressed, however, is the unique, extreme, primal effects that feeling caught in the Holocaust spotlight may have had on the individual. '[A]fter Auschwitz, a new shape of knowing invades the mind', Terrence des Pres explains (cited in Bernstein 1998: 8), and in Primo Levi's account of '*Lager* life', we find the process by which an individual descends into abysmal depths and rises from them again, portrayed 'in an almost primal sense'. But what is the precise nature of that 'primal', 'invading' shape, and what does it tell us about the existential nature of individuals' wills in social milieux? Can there be individual life-projects in the *Lager*?

In the testimonies of a wide array of Holocaust survivors (Langer 1997), personal narratives bespeak atrocities whose impact collapses conventional identities and distinctions (living and dying, human and inhuman nature); '[n]othing is true outside the context of the *Lager*', Levi wrote (1987). Perhaps the primal effects which the Holocaust had on those individuals who lived through 'it' lends to their accounts a means for the reader to decipher personal experience amid collective forms of traumatic memory. So that one can accede to existential evidence of radical displacement – of individual world-views, of personal life-narratives, paradigms, *Gestalten* – without understanding the trauma of the *Lager* as a necessarily collective experience of violation; the individual testimony makes ego-syntonic truths which begin as 'individualized passions' (Jackson 2002).

Primo Levi, the *Lager*, and the reprieve of writing

"[I]n the sad event that one of you should survive me, you will be able to say that Leon Rappoport got what was due him, left behind neither debts nor credits, and did not weep or ask for pity. If I meet Hitler in the other world, I'll spit in his face and I have every right to ..." A bomb fell nearby, followed by a roar like a landslide. One of the warehouses must have collapsed. Rappoport had to raise his voice almost to a shout: "because he didn't get the better of me."...

I have reason to believe that Rappoport did not survive [the frightful situation surrounding the evacuation of the *Lager*]. So I considered it my duty to perform as best I could the task with which I was entrusted.

(Primo Levi, *Moments of Reprieve*)

The significance of death in life – of the idea of death for a consciousness of the significance of life – has been expounded from many vantage-points. 'Death destroys a man: the idea of Death saves him', E. M. Forster has his character, Helen Schlegel, assert in the novel *Howards End* (1950. 213). 'Without the idea of suicide, I would have killed myself from the start', E. M. Cioran claims (1987: 16) to be 'his most positive philosophical formula', through which he is able to 'tolerate anything'; reminiscent of Nietzsche describing 'the thought of suicide [as] a great consolation' through whose help 'one has got through many a bad night'. For Cioran and Nietzsche as for Forster, the idea of death, of actively courting its apprehension, is a route to affirm life.

In the writings of E. M. Forster as a whole, indeed, an explicit connection can be found between revaluating death and arriving at an ethic of life (cf.

Furbank 1982; Rapport 1994a: 59ff.). For Forster, an ongoing (ironizing, transcending) awareness that life is finite and might be short can be a person's salvation. Amid the warring principles in human life, amid war as such, the positive value of death is that it may accompany a directing of human thoughts and energies towards more appropriate objects and concerns: love, friendship, creativity and beauty, a spiritualization of life and an eschewal of narrow materialism. The fact of death, furthermore, affords the best vantage upon individuals' 'I'-ness, upon their seeing themselves and being seen as distinct and as whole. Reflecting upon death leads one to see how, amid life's passing, one's thoughts, feelings and actions are all connected together in and through the same mortal, embodied consciousness; also how one's experiences of self – of saying 'I', of objectifying one's life – best provides the connection of one with others (cf. Wilde 1913: 156).

At first blush, Forster and the gentilities of the English social milieux that made up his public (and literary) life, may seem distantly removed from the exigencies of life, and the death-in-life, that was Nazi Europe for Primo Levi. However, one must recall how Forster (like Nietzsche) suffered the death of his father in infancy, how he worked for the Red Cross in Egypt during World War One, how he disseminated libertarian and anti-Nazi pamphlets during the 1930s (such as *Nordic Twilight* [1940]), and how he served more than once as President of the (British) National Council for Civil Liberties and campaigned against censorship and totalizing notions of sedition and obscenity. More significantly, Primo Levi was to describe his experiences in Auschwitz as his 'education' as a writer:

> [T]he *Lager* was [my] university....[B]y living and then writing about and pondering those events, I have learned many things about man and about the world.
>
> (1987: 398)

> [I]f I had not lived the Auschwitz experience, I probably would never have written anything. I would not have had the motivation, the incentive, to write.
>
> (1987: 397)

Levi's life as a writer (e.g. 1987; 1994; 1996) embodied a testifying, a bearing witness, to the experiences of death which his being in Auschwitz afforded him.

To reduce the infinite, undefined tangle of the world to a schema, Levi begins, may represent a simplification which is necessary for orienting ourselves in complex environments and deciding upon courses of action, but such working hypotheses should not be mistaken for knowledge of reality. For to know is to embrace ambiguity. It is ambiguity which will thus colour Levi's descriptions when he introduces life in the *Lager* as a set of complex relations which do not reduce to 'victims' and 'persecutors', 'righteous' and 'reprobates', 'good' and 'evil'. This he disparages as the world of children – or of *Lager* newcomers.

The totalitarian state can exert a frightful pressure over the individual, Levi continues: the ideologizing of socialization, enculturation and everyday life, the control of information, the inculcation of terror. 'Nevertheless, it is not permissible to admit that this pressure is irresistible' (1996: 16). But what is the precise intent of Levi's phrasing, 'permissible to admit'? That it is true but not ethically enunciatable? That it may be made true or made false according to one's behaviour, but that for the sake of humanity's moral advance it should not be admitted as even possibly true? Or that it is simply not true in any circumstance?

In any event, life in the *Lager* and under totalitarianism are not quite synonymous, Levi next advises. For while, in one respect, the Nazi *Lager* reproduced the hierarchical structure of the totalitarian state – inasmuch as 'all power is invested from above and control from below is almost impossible' – nonetheless 'there never existed a state that was really "totalitarian" from this point of view'; even in the larger Third Reich, or in Stalin's Soviet Union, '[s]ome form of reaction, a corrective of the total tyranny has never been lacking' (1996: 31). However, in the *Lager*, any such reaction was impossible (at best suicidal), any such a corrective was non-existent, and the power of the representatives of the institution absolute; oppression was extreme and enforcement utterly efficient. After the laceration of family ties, the forced migrations, segregations, humiliations, and malnutrition, individuals were too demoralized to resist; ignorant of where geographically they were, who they worked for and for what reasons, why frequent selections and 'disappearances' occurred, and manacled by day-to-day needs and happenstance, individuals were unable to form representations of anything bar an enormous edifice of violence and menace which overwhelmed them. Vulgarly put, people in the *Lager* lived animal lives: without sense of culture, family or country, without their clothes or hair, and confined to the present by feelings of hunger, fatigue, cold and fear; they lived without reasoning, reflecting, observing, comparing, remembering, or expressing themselves. They lived neither by acts of their own will, acts for which they were responsible, nor even by way of their own cowardice. It is for this reason too, Levi concludes, that suicides were more common after the *Lager*s were liberated than before: in the *Lager*s, individual freedom did not extend even to such acts of choice as suicide.

Levi gives a totalizing account of non-humanity and deindividuation (*If This Is a Man*), and of the non-existence of free will – or any will. However, other details of Levi's recounting, including his own reactions, ameliorate – at the least ambiguate – such a conclusion. It becomes apparent that the mortification processes of the *Lager* do not necessarily, or so easily, reduce to nothingness individuals' senses of self, or their acts of personal sense-making.

Admittedly, these senses of self appear in largely dismal vein, initially: Levi and others feeling shame at witnessing crimes against which their will is too feeble to put up a defence; their feeling guilt at not having enough will to resist being absorbed into the totalizing system; their feeling pain at the diminishment wrought by their being regularly drilled (before work, before sleep, during air-raids) and marked not in terms of who they were but of impersonal, categorial assignments.

More positively, however, there is the will and capacity to react against the tyranny, even to rebel, which Levi witnessed in a few individuals who differentiated themselves in this way from 'the anonymous, faceless, voiceless mass of the shipwrecked' (1994: 10). Usually, these were not among the most oppressed individuals in the system, the least well off, 'the persecuted, predestined victim, the prostrate man' (1994: 10), but those who possessed what Levi calls 'valour' or 'virtue'. This possession, which 'allows them to survive and makes them unique', and which is most important for our purposes here, Levi is careful to distinguish from the understanding of those qualities normally 'approved of by common morality' (1994: 10). In terms of the latter, it sometimes seemed to Levi that 'the worst survived, the selfish, the violent, the insensitive, the collaborators' (1996: 63). And there is a further ambiguity. For while 'valour' and 'virtue' can be understood as both referring to an individual's 'worth', Levi makes a subtle distinction between them. For while it is true that both those with valour and with virtue exhibited the power to react against the mortifications of the *Lager* and, in a sense, to continue to exist as themselves within it, those with valour died. For they insisted not only on maintaining an identity, but also a dignity; they insisted on 'trading blows' with 'the entire world' that the *Lager* represented, seeking to give as good as they got, and in achieving this dignity they paid a high price: they were 'defeated' and killed (1996: 110). The 'virtuous' lived, meanwhile, 'found reprieve', because, while losing their dignity, they still managed to exert leverage upon their present hell so as to gain perspective on it, contextualize it and look at it ironically. As Levi puts it, they drew strength from elsewhere: from a feral vitality, from love, from cunning, from legend, from music, from superstition and belief. Faith in a wider, comprehensible universe, for example, whether Jewish, Zionist, Humanist or Marxist, helped situate the *Lager* and put its experiences in their place. (This brings to mind the title of a poem by Philip Larkin, 'The Importance of Elsewhere', whose last line bemoans the lack of natal displacement the poet feels able to exert upon his sad life in England: 'Here no elsewhere underwrites my existence' [1990: 104].)

Moments of Reprieve was the title Primo Levi gave to the volume where he recounted the stories of those with the valour or the virtue for self-survival: 'Tischler', 'Grigo', 'Wolf', 'Cesare', 'Rumkowski', 'Bandi' and, as in the extract above, 'Rappoport'. But what of his own survival? Here, Levi is as ambiguous as before. 'Each individual is so complex an object', he wrote (1996: 43), 'that there is no point trying to foresee his behaviour, all the more so in extreme situations; and neither is it possible to foresee one's own behaviour'. '[O]ur future depends heavily on external factors, wholly extraneous to our deliberate choices, and on internal factors as well, of which we are, however, not aware' (1987: 397). Certainly, Levi had no religious faith, and he resisted the one occasion he was tempted to pray (before a final selection process at Auschwitz) because he did not feel, as an atheist, he could 'change the rules [by which he had lived his life and played his game] at the end of the match', or without feeling shame later were he to survive (1996: 118). After the war, he was incensed by any suggestion of providential intercession; he survived, Levi concluded, largely by luck (by his having scarlet fever, and being unable to walk, when the *Lager* remnants were force-marched away by the Nazis just before the arrival of Allied troops); also by his interest in the human spirit, by his stubborn insistence on always recognizing his companions as people not things, and by his will to survive and to recount what he had witnessed and endured.

To elaborate somewhat — since it is important for the discussion that Levi be heard out as fully as possible — when he first published *If This Is a Man* in 1947 and *The Truce* in 1963, he felt he had performed the only 'task' which he found clearly defined for him to undertake. Here were accounts of things he had experienced which seemed imperiously to demand of him that he tell them. Thus he had 'testified', assuming thereafter that he would return 'home', and to his profession as a chemist. Moreover, he had written in the style of a chemist: the lucid scientific witness, filing his weekly report, on a monstrous experiment to which he found himself an unwitting survivor, with precision and concision (cf. Mallett 1995: 3–4).

Thereafter, however, Levi found that a host of further details kept returning to his mind concerning the fundamental features of Auschwitz which he had described; of his 'two years of life outside the law' (1994: 11) it seemed he had not forgotten a single thing. People especially kept coming to mind, asking him to grant them 'the ambiguous perennial existence of literary characters' (1994: 10). Hence, as the years passed, writing made a space for itself in his life, eventually taking over completely.

But then Levi's words also give onto another understanding, besides the testimonial, of the place of writing in his life. For he explains that his need to write the story of his experiences was so strong that he began it during his time within the *Lager* itself; despite the dangers, and even though he had to destroy his notes immediately, he found himself working towards a refined scriptural receptivity to all he experienced — including sentences in languages he did not know. This receptivity was not only a symptom of the time, he explains (of culture-shock, we might say), but also a vital factor in his salvation. 'The aims of life are the best defence against death' (1996: 120), and intending to write, to remember and to testify, gave him a goal, a life-project which cognitively displaced him from the deathly totality of the *Lager*; writing afforded him an elsewhere. Hence Levi even concludes that the sum total of his brief but tragic *Lager* experiences, and the longer, complex writer-witness ones, is 'clearly positive' (1987: 398). Overall, he is richer and surer than he would otherwise have been, and through his writing he had 'challenged and defeated Auschwitz and loneliness' (1997: 154). Levi's words clearly resonate with those he describes as 'Rappoport's Testament' (1994). In their affirmation they also have a Nietzschean ring: 'What does not kill me makes me strong' (1979c).

Even here, however, the ambiguity does not go away. In order to resist an infernal order such as the Nazis, Levi counsels, one needs a very solid moral foundation: this is the 'elsewhere' of valour and virtue which displaces the self of the individual from the present. Without this, one succumbs; even as a victim one becomes corrupted and part of the system. In writing his narrative (of self and world), therefore, Levi always attempted to repress hatred in himself, seeing it as a Nazi way; instead, he counted upon reason and discussion as supreme instruments by which progress and justice might be effected. And yet, there is a sense in which one cannot, indeed must not, wholly understand or rationalize what happened, Levi knows, for this is to explain it, contain it and in part justify it; here are inhuman words and deeds, counter-human (Dionysian, Nietzsche would say), which are without precedent and without rationality, and which must remain so. The violence of Hitlerian Germany, Levi concludes, was useless and without logic, succeeding in causing pain for its own sake and in effecting a schismogenesis of violence which continues unabated into the present. Reason, art and poetry are of little use for understanding a place where they have been eradicated. Levi himself committed suicide in Turin in 1987 (cf. James 2002).

What kind of text, then, do these ambiguous details of Primo Levi's life and writings represent in the discursive focus of this book? In one reading, they amount to a rather conclusive indictment of the thesis that: 'there are only "in order to" motives and to claim otherwise is bad faith; "because motives" are what we formulate in order to pretend that something or someone other than ourselves is responsible for what we feel, think, say, or do'. In the *Lager*, according to Levi at one point, totalitarian control was so complete that people were mostly reduced to animals: robbed not only of the will to act but even the capacity to react. Those few who did manage to react almost committed suicide: they were up against a totalizing system and were summarily extirpated. Those few who survived did so by chance, but then had to live with their shame.

What defences can I mount against this reading? First to remember the words from Levi that serve as epigraph to this section: both objectively and subjectively, individuals lived (and died) the *Lager* in their own way. Only *post facto* and in certain essentialist constructions do 'World War Two', and 'Auschwitz', become singular things-in-themselves. And this defining of them as singular is, in an important sense, a limiting of them if it obscures the countless individual activities and circumstances that went to make 'them' up and the manifold ways in which 'they' were experienced. Within the place 'Auschwitz', then, hundreds of thousands of different lives were led and lost, made up of countless experiences and interactions (cf. Young 1988). To amass these is to continue the Nazis' dehumanizing process of massification; each individual, in other words, lives his or her own tragedy of dehumanization, makes their own sense of it, and dies their own death from it (cf. Soekefeld 1999).

But then, 'it' is not really an 'it' either; one does not get very far if one replaces an institution, 'Auschwitz', by a process, 'dehumanization', if it is still something that all individuals go through, even if it is in their own individual ways. And from the Nazi point of view, the difference is negligible, irrelevant. To the extent that the Nazi desire is to exterminate a group or category of people whom they designate as the same, it is irrelevant if the individuals placed within that category feel themselves different, and continue to experience such difference up to the point of their extermination. Hence the importance of Levi's recounting of those in Auschwitz who exhibited 'valour' and 'virtue': those who refused to be dehumanized or refused to give in. Among these people, will is most easily witnessed still. More precisely, here were individuals able to look askance on the immediate present, on their immediate contexts, by viewing them ironically, in the light of a broader, ongoing life-narrative or 'project', which provided them with an 'elsewhere' (a means of removing themselves cognitively from the world, the total institution which the Nazis would impose on them). Levi's acts of testimonial writing, beginning immediately in the *Lager*, represent one kind of this self-promise of futurity. Others' strategies (which may seem in terms of contemporary morality to be signs of selfishness, duplicity, insensitivity or violence) allowed them to do likewise: to get the better of the selection processes and those administering them. Here were individual acts and frames of mind by whose virtue survival was achieved.

And yet, Levi insists that such valour and virtue, while representing inner qualities of the individual – and within the grasp also of those who let themselves become 'anonymous, faceless, voiceless, prostrate' by the 'loss of their family ties, the forced migrations, segregations, humiliations, and the malnutrition' – are qualities beyond individual awareness and control. But this insistence, I would insist, is a rhetoric on Levi's behalf, a trope: a modesty through which to explain his own survival and that of others, in the context of the enormous loss of life, without claiming any special intentionality for the survivors or passing judgement for their lack on the dead. Hence Levi's depiction of unconscious determinism, of 'internal factors of which we are not aware', is belied by his own extreme self-consciousness, both at the time and after, and that of numerous others whom he describes. Of course, Levi could still argue that how one person comes to be self-aware (and another not) is beyond his or her awareness, but this seems to be a path to possible infinite regress and without final resolution; either one accepts that — insofar as we understand the roots of human consciousness at all — the fact that we are self-aware means that we can make ourselves aware of how we come to have that self-awareness (as I would), or one posits an initial unawareness or unconsciousness beneath which no awareness can reach (as Levi seems to). These are different givens. Suffice it to say that, at least for my case here, and whatever his protestations to the contrary, it is arguable that the individuals whom Levi describes as valorous and virtuous knew how their valour and virtue, their strength, their will to preserve their integrity, their dignity, or their lives, came about: they knew what their qualities could be used for, and did so with intentionality.

But I am still faced with Levi's broader insistence that individual futures are determined — influenced at least — by 'external factors, wholly extraneous to their deliberate choices'. Whatever the valour or the virtue of particular individuals, the conditions of the *Lager* — the possibly random selection procedures, the caprice of the absolutely powerful *kapos* and other *Lager* satraps — were non-rational, unfathomable and ungainsayable, and hence represented circumstances beyond the reach of individual intention and outside their control. The inmates of the *Lager* were 'helpless before a catastrophe that had no more relation to their characters, motives or actions than an earthquake', their experience more akin to a natural 'horror' than human 'tragedy' (Dwight Macdonald, cited in Wheatcroft 2000: 10). Here, as Levi concludes, was violence beyond logic.

Such violence, it seems to me, is *a limiting case*: where the act of suicide (rather than the idea of suicide) represents the only 'in order to' motivation whereby the individual can escape the clutches of encompassing circumstances and will his or her own way on. Where interaction between people is such that one party treats another in a completely arbitrary way, even to the extent that their life might be forfeited, then the only possible intentioned action still available to the threatened individual (the *Lager* inmate, the slave-labourer, the dehumanized subaltern) is to take their own life before that possibility eventuates. These are extreme circumstances, I would say.

Janina Bauman (2000) has argued that one should recognize in the suicides of the *Lager* (and the ghetto) the exerting of a will which makes all the difference in the world to the process of dehumanization; to choose the way and time of one's dying is to resist the oppressor, escape humiliation and insist on one's dignity. Nevertheless, what damage does the possibility and the practice of some human beings subjecting others to murderous events of dehumanizing randomness do to the wider thesis of this book? If one can envisage — indeed, read accounts of — conditions where individuals are free to commit suicide but nothing besides, then this seems as if a tremendous amount in their lives *does* occur *because of* the intentions of others — however the oppressed individuals might see themselves and the projects of their lives.

Moreover, if one allows for 'because' motives here, as one seems to – this individual lives his or her uncertain life in Auschwitz, on a Roman galley, as a colonized 'subaltern', as a battered wife, because of the whim of their various gaolers' – then when is it definitively not the case that ' "because" motives' do not at least represent a component in individuals' decisions?

To counteract this line of argument I have to defend the position that individuals are always responsible for the sense they make of their lives, for the meanings they live by, and that what is special, and unique, about the limiting case – the extreme circumstance – of 'violence beyond logic' described above – is that this is *the only circumstance* in which the sense, the meanings, which individuals make of their lives and by which they intend to lead them, to order them, is irrelevant. In all other circumstances, interaction amounts to a formal negotiation (a negotiation in terms of symbolic forms) by which individual meanings and orders come to be aligned one with another. In the Nazi *Lager*, exceptionally, it was not symbolic negotiation or exchange to which one (powerful) party to the interaction was interested, but physical negation, obliteration.

'Democratic' as against 'nihilistic' violence

The further suggestiveness contained in Levi's phrasing, 'violence beyond logic', is its adverting to a violence 'within logic'. Violence *per se* was not what made the circumstance of the *Lager* extreme, so much as a kind of violence which was indiscriminate and random. What is the relationship, then, it should now be asked, between individuals seeking to live in terms of 'in order to' motives and life-projects and 'logical violence'? This is a significant question not least because of the possibility of life-projects themselves being defined as 'violent', in the sense of selfish, exploitative, autocratic. In arguing that furthering a life-project is not necessarily a violent act in the latter sense, but also that Levi is right to draw attention to different circumstances of violence in human life, I would employ a distinction between 'democratic violence' and 'nihilistic violence': between a violence potentially contained within the logic of everyday life and exchange, and violence which explodes the possibility of any negotiated routine (cf. Rapport 2000).

For Anthony Wallace (1964), the best term to describe the relationships between individuals which make up the day-to-day routines of ongoing socio-cultural systems is 'equivalence structures'; elsewhere I have referred to them as 'talking-partnerships' (1987: 170–7). Individuals manage to organize themselves, align their behaviours into reliable and joint systems of interaction, without developing uniform cognitive maps or possessing equivalent motives, by virtue of their behaviours' 'equivalency': by coming to possess sets of behavioral expectancies of one another which coincide (cf. Devereux 1978: 125–9). Individuals learn to trust that in certain routine situations, others' behaviour is predictable, and can be habitually and confidently interrelated with actions of their own. Wallace calls such joint systems 'contracts': habitual social interactions which individuals establish for the mutual facilitation of their separate strivings and which give onto social groups.

What is vital for the success of these behavioural contracts, to repeat, is not so much agreement between individuals concerning what is taking place – or any such mutual understanding or homogeneity of this kind – as coincidence and expectability. However different and diverse may be the interpretations of individuals who partake of the contractual relations of exchanging common social forms, so long as each can predict, each can expect, certain behaviours from the other, then the relationship is able to continue – as can the underlying diversity. Hence Wallace defines the socio-cultural systems constituted by these behavioural contracts as 'organizations of diversity'. (Wallace argues, indeed, that it is difference that is likely to be a *necessary* feature – differences of opinion concerning what the relationship is about and why it is taking place – for the relationship to continue. Whether 'necessary', in a functional sense, or not, I would argue that such difference – a diversity of individual world-views which are maintained by the exchange of 'the same', shared symbolic forms – is the social norm [Rapport 1993].)

Expectability means that each individual is able to continue to find the behaviour of the other(s) understandable, meaningful, trustworthy. This is true even to the extent that had each understood the actual meanings of the other, then each might have felt violated: felt that the sense each was making of their regular exchange, and the way each was using the relationship towards the fulfilment of an individual life-project, amounted to doing violence to the other's sense of self and world. Ordinarily, however, this does not become apparent. The 'friendly ambiguities' of language, as Sapir puts it (1956: 153), are such that it is normally the case for each individual to manage to 'reinterpret the behaviour which he has under observation in terms of those meanings which are relevant to his own life'. This violence, therefore, I should like to describe as 'democratic': the mutual, interactional norm.

For, if the *sine qua non* of the social contract is individuals' possession of coincident expectations which allow them mutually to orient their behaviour to one another in a particular relationship (or kind of relationship), then the stability of such expectations is not threatened by a violent diversity of individual interpretations which do not breach the civil surface of the exchange. 'Democratic violence' recognizes the norm of individual difference – of an individual construction of a diversity of possibly incompatible and mutually contradictory life-projects and world-views – living beneath an ambiguous surface of social-structural calm, within behavioural contracts that individuals continue to share.

'Democratic violence' thus amounts to an appreciation of the 'ordinary violence' of everyday life and exchange as 'a sort of constant' around which the social is organized (Aijmer 2000: 9). There always is such violence in the everyday inasmuch as there always is individual diversity and creativity existing within, beneath and through symbolic forms and institutional structures. While the very term 'violence' may be commonly associated with the breakdown of civil order and exchange – with extreme breaches of civility between people (Stanage 1974: 232) – by distinguishing, nonetheless, between the outward *form* of civil exchange and its inward *content*, one can reach a point of analytical accommodation between the violence of universal and ubiquitous individual creativity on the one hand and the civility of social structure on the other; 'beliefs and blindnesses', in the novelist's phrasing (Compton-Burnett 1969: 30), are the substance of interpersonal relations which individuals manage by way of 'kindness and lies' (Greene 1974: 58). (Edmund Leach, drawing on Existentialist notions [after Camus, Sartre and Nietzsche], we have heard defining doing violence by way of social-structural norms as fundamental to the imaginative workings of the individual mind, and the latter's creativeness and gratuitousness as representing 'the very essence of being a human being' [1977:19].) Distinguishing between symbolic form and individual interpretation, in short, there is a way in which one may become reconciled to violence and violation as mundane and routine, even 'democratic'; democratic violence is defined as behaviour which does not deny or negate the possibility and ability of fellow-interactants to go on interpreting and meaning as they choose, even while the meanings which each construes in the interaction might be found to violate others'.

A 'nihilistic violence', on the other hand, I would describe as behaviour which disorientates fellow-interactants such that the latter's acts of prediction and interpretation are made impossible or irrelevant. Nihilistic violence breaches the surfaces of civil exchange, nullifies the shared forms of behaviour, such that orientation towards them by others, and their development of stable expectations of trust with regard to them, are prevented (cf. Johnson 1982: 8). Violence of a nihilistic kind is that to which others cannot adapt, behaviour which others cannot expect or predict and find meaningful.

Nihilistic violence, in short, makes mutual expectation and a diversity of individual interpretation impossible; it denies the possibility of a civil relationship of mutual predictability and orientability by violating any practicable norms of exchange. This denial or negation may take a variety of forms and degrees. Random sounds, silences and actions, which preclude viable interactions of a routine and ongoing kind through their very gratuitousness, deny others the opportunity of making sense, of making meaningful interpretations of particular interactions. But then maiming or killing will preclude viable interaction and meaningful interpretation henceforth and in general. Hence, a sliding-scale of nihilistic violence may be conceived of, the severity adjudged in terms of the intended and/or received injury to others' present and future ability to make sense, to create meaning.

In this depiction, violence *per se* might be morally neutral, a fact of the individual (creative) interpretation of social exchange even within the ambit of the apparently orderly, habitual and routine (cf. Marx 1976: 110). Furthermore, violence should not be tied, analytically, to particular forms of behaviours and excepted from others (violence does not correspond to brutality or physicality or the absence of empathy; violence is not precluded by the presence of empathy or intimations of concern [cf. Rapport 1987: 191–3]). Rather the emphasis is on violence as an 'experienced reality' (Aijmer 2000: 3): as that which gives onto, or negates, a diversity of meaningful experiences. Democratic violence is that which encompasses a diversity of individually created meanings, nihilistic violence is that which precludes these.

The definition of 'goodness' in a moral society, Iris Murdoch offers (1970), may less concern doing good to others than abstaining from doing others harm: abstaining from visiting one's own desires onto them so that they may come into their own. The immoral horror of the Nazi *Lager* was precisely its extreme negation of the possibilities of its individual victims 'coming into their own'.

A personal view of the morality of self/other relations

> We must make deliberate efforts to acknowledge the subtleties, inflections and varieties of individual consciousness which are concealed by the categorical masks which we have invented so adeptly. Otherwise, we will continue to deny people the right to be themselves, deny their rights to their own identities.
>
> (Anthony Cohen, *Self Consciousness*)

Echoing Edmund Leach, Anthony Cohen argues (1994: 180–1) that individuals routinely resist the imposition upon them of identities by others. These are both heroic and mundane battles against deindividuation, against being treated in terms of how others would have them seem not how they are. They occur amid the purportedly universalizing procedures of bureaucracies in modernist democracies (Herzfeld 1993), and they occur, *in extremis*, in the concentration camp.

Nor have social scientists been innocent of these massifying practices, Cohen continues, in their attempts to colonize and occupy individuals' consciousness so that the latter become pressed, willy nilly, into the matrices of perception of certain socio-cultural (religious, ethnic, local, economic, occupational) categories or groups. They are perpetrated every time a classificatory label, a collectivizing identity, is caused to stand for the meaning of an individual life, and the particularities of its praxis and environment. (Perhaps it is to excuse themselves this generalizing that social scientists have seen fit to emphasize individuals' vulnerability to external forces and to downplay their resilience.)

For at least two reasons, however, Cohen concludes, social scientists should work towards 'giving people back' their individual consciousnesses, their selfhoods. First, inasmuch as this contributes to a broader decolonization of the human subject, a democratization and liberalization of the social-institutional forms (social scientific writings as much as polities) within which individuals lead their lives. Second, inasmuch as this makes for better social science: a better comprehension of the workings of social institutions, their formations and evolutions, and the way they are inexorably informed by the consciousnesses of the individuals who animate them in particular situations and at particular times. To privilege the social-institutional over the individual, the formal over the experiential, the public over the personal and private motivation, is to misconstrue and corrupt the nature of the former.

By way of an Existentialist framework, and 'ethnographies of the particular', I have attempted in this book to portray individual lives in personal and individual terms. I have argued for this methodologically: that such lives cannot properly be understood, and the consequences of those lives for others (for broader socio-cultural milieux) except through an appreciation of the interpretations, meanings, intentions, of their individual 'owners', their construers and creators. I would further argue for this morally: that seeing individual lives in individual terms is to afford them dignity, both from the vantage-point of the social-scientific observer and the individual owners of those lives. To derive a 'plan of life', a life-project, from one's own faculties rather than mere imitation, John Stuart Mill proposed (1972), is to exercise one's moral potential as a human being; there is moral value in recognizing responsibility for one's own life, in defining where one has come from and where one would go to, in seeing one's life as a life-work, even a work of art.

Centring on living one's own life need not be regarded as a selfish matter. Indeed, self-interest, in the form of self-knowledge and self-motivation can be viewed as a positive and a necessary thing (not only a dignified thing) for the enabling of equitable social relations. Reflecting upon the project of one's life, respecting that project, controlling one's resources in the direction of its fulfilment, affords the possibility of partaking intentionally in symmetrical (as distinct from merely habitual or rote) relations with others. Respecting one's own life puts one in a position to recognize the moral value of individuality as such: in others' life-projects as well as one's own.

Individual life-projects, of course, need not run along these lines, and one can easily imagine individuals negating life on the one hand and engaging with it autocratically on the other, as means to further themselves irrespective of others or at others' expense. The individuals (and life-projects) I have chosen as illustrations in this book, however, have not only become and remained 'their own persons', I would argue, but also provide moral examples to follow; my writing about them is an attempt to employ social-scientific scholarship in the pursuit, as Stoller phrases it (1997: xvi), of 'an enriched quality of life'.

I am reminded of a character from Auschwitz whom Levi names 'Alberto'; Alberto who was much loved in the *Lager* for the way in which 'miraculously he had remained free', sentimentally speaking (1997: 142). Here was an individual 'of good and strong will', whose 'words and acts were free: he had not bowed his head, he had not bent his back'. For Alberto, 'renunciation, pessimism, discouragement were abominable and culpable: he did not accept the concentration camp universe, he rejected it both instinctively and with his reason, and he did not let himself be tainted by it'. In an important sense, moreover, Alberto's strength was a moral act, Levi concludes, for:

> A gesture of his, a word, a smile had a liberating virtue, they were a rip in the rigid fabric of the *Lager*, and all those who had contact with him felt this, even those who did not understand his language.
> (1997: 142)

Being 'one's own person' can set a moral example, inspire others likewise to become the individual ends, the work, of their own lives without inveigling others as their means.

I also admire the way in which the individual lives I have focused upon in this book have come to 'contain multitudes' within them. They have contrived their own variety and diversity, their own elsewheres, and have maintained journeys, through ironic displacements, between spaces and selves. In the process of their cognitive and physical movement through life, they have achieved their own knowledge, acceded to Nietzsche's 'general economy of the whole'; whether this whole has been visual-metaphysical (Spencer), migrant-experiential (Silberstein), logical-positivist (Glaser), or poetical-philosophical (Nietzsche), it has not been derived from convention, nor contingent upon external validation, or negation. Finally, it has been on their own terms that they have come to relate to others; their relations too have been part of their self-expression. And while none of these individuals can be said to have contracted exactly conventional relationships, I feel they did not use others dishonestly. Rather, there was an openness in the relations, an interest and frankness, which reflected the individuals' self-interest in their own lives. Spencer, Silberstein, Glaser, Nietzsche did not exploit others underhandedly, and they did not retreat from them; rather they paid them the compliment of being open about themselves and their individual life-projects while expecting their consociates likewise to be writers and players in distinct, ongoing life-narratives. Might not these journeys be undertaken for a while side by side, in conscious alignment even in collaboration?

Identifying the moral potential in self-centredness and self-knowledge – positive and necessary aspects of social relations built upon mutuality – has a respectable and varied recent history:

- It is self-centredness which enables the individual to be broadly benign, 'good nature [being] the most selfish of all virtues', William Hazlitt surmised (1826).

- Personality should be recognized as 'an element of revelation', Oscar Wilde argued (1913: 156), since it is only by looking inward, knowing oneself, that one can hope to see outward to individual others.

- In order for there to be a 'We-relationship', Alfred Schuetz averred, there must first be an 'I'; '[e]verything I know about your conscious life is really based on my knowledge of my own lived experience' (1972: 106). It is an individual's individuality, and his or her appreciation of it, which is thus the means of possible connection. On this basis, individuals can achieve 'sympathetic participation' in one another's lives, through an awareness of their different streams of consciousness, their 'subjective contexts of meaning', proceeding side by side (1972: 166). Even granting the 'bodily givenness' of face-to-face interaction, any such mutuality of perspectives will be subject to a great variety of coincidence, but there is still the possibility of what Schuetz termed 'true' and 'pure' meetings.

- In Darwinian terms, Nicholas Humphrey (1983) describes introspection – the individual's reflexive examination of his or her own conscious experience – as the adaptive means human beings employ to equip themselves with a framework (conceptual, emotional, volitional) for modelling others' behaviour. It is 'an intimate of his own consciousness [who can catch] the intimations of consciousness in others', adjudging outer effects as signs of inner causes, and so reason from analogy with oneself to an accommodation of alterity (1983: 63).

- In 'self-ishness' and 'self-fulfilment' can be lodged an intrinsic moral respectability, Alan Gewirth asserts (1998), because an endorsement of one's own rights to a prospective and purposive agency – to developing one's potentialities and satisfying one's desires free from arbitrary restriction – endorses the rights of others, and commits one to universalist standards; individuals grant inherent dignity to the lives of others and accord them respect because they do so to their own. Being on their own journeys of transvaluation – of self-overcoming, of becoming other to themselves – individuals imagine themselves as the others they meet and treat them accordingly. Hence, an interpersonal morality of individual agents living under conditions of mutual entitlement can be seen to derive from an inner-oriented fulfilment as much as from outer-influenced denial.

'[T]he kind of people I like', E. M. Forster confessed, 'can put themselves in another person's place and not do harm because they know how much it hurts to be hurt' (cited in Jones 1959: 12). What self-centred individuals claim for themselves (their capabilities for feeling exhilaration as for pain) they also concede to others; they take others seriously as other potential versions of themselves ('I could become or could have been something like what others are...I am potentially all personalities' [Kateb 1992: 247]). The individuals I have focused upon in this book have reached out to others with a message of self-knowledge whose logic is that of symmetry: 'We can empathetically meet, you and I, and mutually benefit from an appreciation of what individually we have come to know – about love (Spencer), about growth (Silberstein), about the cosmos (Glaser), about wilfulness (Nietzsche)'.

Emerson was especially sensitive to the issues of self-centredness in relationship. 'Solitude is proud and society vulgar', he begins (1981: 393–4), 'solitude is impracticable, and society fatal'; to effect the morality of self-centredness it is necessary to work at both not treating others instrumentally, as one's means, and not treating oneself disrespectfully, irresponsibly, as if the life of another. What is important, therefore, is for us to 'keep the diagonal line' between solitude and society: 'keep our heads in the one and our hands in the other. The conditions are met, if we keep our independence, yet do not lose our sympathy'. There is something of my understanding of 'dignity' in Emerson's notion of 'proud solitude'; while losing sight of one's individuality and acceding to the superficial forms, categories and classes by which others would 'vulgarly' define and limit one, is 'fatal'. And yet, turning one's back on others – and on their individuality – is 'impracticable' and the attempt selfish; there is no way out of socio-cultural milieux. Hence the need for the diagonal line – the 'zigzag' (Rapport 1994a: 30–6) – between head and hand, between autonomy and sympathy: between living one's own life and making space for others living theirs.

Emerson's trope of head versus hands resonates appositely with Wallace's notion of contractual 'equivalence structures' (1964). Individuals in socio-cultural milieux meet in formal practice, via habitual behavioural contracts, while maintaining their own meaningful environments (and projects). Having one's 'hands' at work in socio-cultural milieux, interacting with others in an 'equivalent' fashion, physically and sentimentally assisting them in the furtherance of their lives, is distinct from the more nuanced and embodied way in which one knows oneself and works towards advancing one's life along chosen routes. We have hands-on experience of the lives of others but a 'hands-in' participation only in our own embodied environment; we possess an internal phenomenological relationship only in the praxis that makes up our personal sensorium.

This is not to ignore or downplay the significance of the moral role individuals might play in one another's lives. Primarily, that role is to make space for the other to construct his or her own life-projects. This can be a large role to play. Indeed, acknowledging the potential of nihilistic violence to disrupt the pursuit of life-projects, making it impossible for others to see their environments as orderly and meaningful, or making interpretations of meaning irrelevant to their projects by subjecting them to random injury, forcefully delineates the role of the other in individuals' dignified fulfilment of themselves. Individual human beings can but live alongside others.

Perhaps it is not stretching the point too far to describe the exercise of this book, from one perspective at least, as an account of the roles individuals play in making space for one another's life-projects. I have done my best to describe Stanley Spencer, Rachel Silberstein, Ben Glaser and Friedrich Nietzsche in their own terms, to elaborate upon the circumstances in which they placed themselves and caused themselves to act. There is a glaring misprision in this accounting, however; in narrating others' lives, it is inevitable that I write from a perspective which is distinct from that of those leading the lives. What is more, I undertake the exercise with a definite purpose in mind. I have conscripted the lives of these four individuals to make my own argument, arriving at conclusions that I claim to be true. In this sense the writing in this book may be described as 'autobiography', my narrating ('plagiarizing') others' lives becoming a resource in the advancing of a life-project of my own. Notwithstanding, I would argue that the 'violence' done to the authenticity of Spencer's, Silberstein's, Glaser's and Nietzsche's individual lives in this process is of the democratic rather than the nihilistic kind. I cannot know these four as they knew or know themselves, and I do not approach them innocent of self-interest. Nevertheless, I would hope to have provided them the space, and to have accorded them the respect, whereby my account does not overwrite their right to have 'written themselves' – and is reflected partly in the distinct presentational style of each illustrative account. With each I lay claim to a certain distinctive (Schuetzian) we-relationship, so that even though I write from my own perspective I produce that social-scientific-cum-literary alchemy (empathy, intuition, imagination) whereby their individual perspectives are elucidated.

My confidence in the possibility of this, indeed, is entirely necessary to my conceiving of the project of this book and to construing its argument. It has meant that even though 'life-project' is my own term, and in spite of the very different lives Spencer, Silberstein, Glaser and Nietzsche have determined for themselves, in different historical and socio-cultural milieux, and the different ways I have known them, I have felt warranted in claiming that their lives manifest a common quality. I have referred to this quality as *Machtgefühl*, and described its characteristics of single-mindedness and self-intensity, its display of energy, confidence, toughness and endeavour. A common quality has enabled Spencer, Silberstein, Glaser and Nietzsche to project themselves similarly along a life-course delineated and defined by their own consciousness and will. Here is Stanley Spencer achieving ecstasy through portraying loving, eternal unions in a earthly 'suburb of heaven', against a background of day-to-day relations of compromise, transience and sexual yearning. Here is Rachel Silberstein pursuing personal growth and completion along a road that takes her continually between the partial and partisan solutions of others, and away from where she currently is: confident that she can always discover the way and benefit from the passage. Here is Ben Glaser at home in the cultivating of interests of ultimate worth – music, art, knowledge of the origins of the universe – while passing through mundane situations of only proximate significance: escaping persecution, earning a living, maintaining familial relations. Here is Friedrich Nietzsche inscribing himself prophetically into the future history of Existential philosophy, by writing a reflexive phenomenology of embodied existence, and rejecting a common life in slave to abstractions, diversions and obfuscations.

Machtgefuhl affords the lives of these four a corresponding coherency, a projective force and an end; they show themselves alike to be cognizant of the individuality and finiteness of their lives, and able and willing to maintain themselves in 'the centre of their spheres' (Cohen 1992: 235). It is not that their life-projects necessarily and always evince a clear plan or graduation, as I have said, it is that what is undertaken in present and future is seen to build on what has been undertaken in the past, maintaining a cumulative line of endeavour, in order to achieve an individually formulated end; and the endeavour is effected with a continuing drive, with single-mindedness and self-intensity, and with the force to circumvent obstructions.

Machtgefuhl, I have further argued, is a human capacity, part-and-parcel of our existential power, and the potential 'genius' of us all. Apprehending these individual lives in individual terms does not preclude my writing them at the same time from my own perspective; while my perspective and their perspective might also stand for those of Everyperson.

Enshrining 'in order to'

What do I say, then, finally, about the book's questions: about the relationship between self-consciousness and an individual's control over his or her life, about the balance of 'in order to' motives and 'because'? Self-knowledge, self-motivation, self-centredness, may enable one to resist deflection in one's life-course, to react against external pressures with 'valour' or 'virtue', but does it allow one to transcend what is beyond oneself – a wider milieu of prior conditions, socio-cultural circumstances, and of others – and inhabit an environment coterminous with one's own embodiment? Yes and no. Yes, inasmuch as the meaning of this beyond is not given and not essential: the individual decides what these forms (words, norms, people, objects, actions) mean. No, inasmuch as the individual can be forced into taking account of, and attempting to make meaning out of, certain forms which are directed at him or her. If he or she is arbitrarily imprisoned or enslaved, labelled and ghettoized, infibulated and married off, herded into a concentration camp and gas chamber, then such things are not to be ignored. But still, they are experienced within the life-world of the interpreting individual.

It is in this way that I understand Sartre's summary that: 'the secret of a man is...the limit of his own liberty, his capacity for resisting torture and death' (1947: 499). That is, between form (social structures, cultural symbologies) and individual there always exists an 'internal relation' (Winch 1970: 107). External forms impinge on the individual's life-world, but there is no necessary, direct, singular or essential effect that they have within it. Their significance remains subjective, and for this reason, I would conclude, their nature is significantly subjective too. Or again, to adapt Levi's words, since external forms (say, circumstances in the *Lager*) come to be subjectively experienced and lived, the forms (the *Lager*) can be said to become objectively distinct in each experiencing. This is what enables individuals to assert a sense of humanity (concerning both themselves and others) even in the most dehumanizing of situations; this is why, as Michael Jackson has put it (1998: 203), individuals are not themselves reduced to nothingness even when their capacity to affect the external world has been rendered negligible: they are still responsible for constructing and reconstructing the reduced world in their imaginative interpretations of it. This is their 'secret', the extent of their 'liberty'. There are, in sum, no (essential, singular, necessary, direct) ' "because" motives' because the affecting forms, the conditions and circumstance, only take shape, only become particular things with particular effects, when particular individuals apprehend them.

The Schuetzian-Sartrean formulation of 'in order to' that I have been employing as trope throughout this book to form my argument concerning life-projects and existential power, brings me to the conclusion, however, that, *in extremis*, in the case of the nihilistic violence of the totalizing institution, the claim that only 'in order to' motives exist (and that 'because' motives are bad faith) must take into account the power of others to force themselves on an individual's attention and elicit a reaction – however subjective or idiosyncratic, or imaginative, or constructive, or negatory, this latter comes to be. Individuals are always responsible for their acts of interpretation, for the ways their lives become meaningful – and hence come to be *per se* – but violent others have the power to force such acts upon them – or to kill them and make further acts of becoming impossible (perhaps Nietzsche reached this point already, in his formulation that 'everything decisive comes about "in spite of"' [1979b: 100]).

What I was seeking in enshrining 'in order to' motives and denying 'because' was, in part, an escape from the necessity of the relational: the understanding common in social science that intention is always comparative, that identity is consequent upon 'playing the *vis-à-vis*', and everything is therefore 'beside itself' (Boon 1982: 230–1); hence nothing can arise *ab nihilo*, from the 'nothing' of the monadic individual self, from the singularity of the body-in-its-own-environment, and be 'self-existent' (Emerson 1981: 95). It seemed to me that this was precisely wrong; that however mysterious-sounding, matter and meaning, consciousness and intention, in human life did well-up from within the body of the individual (and from there alone), and that it was a crucial issue for social science to accommodate this truth. It had to be recognized that individuals were the possible sources of gratuitous, 'free' meanings, and instruments for putting these into effect in the world. Existence really did precede essence, and the power of existence was continuously to give rise to essence: absolutely new and individual, possibly, bearing no relationship to what had been before (cf. Rapport 2001a).

I would stand by this thesis still, and accommodate myself to Schuetz's distinction by claiming that a mistake resides in the use of the term 'motive'. Distinguishing 'in order to' motives from 'because' motives, as Schuetz does, suggests that these are phenomena of the same order or type; but they are not. 'In order to' is a description of an intentional and embodied consciousness in the process of making meaning; 'because' is a description of power external to that embodied consciousness which may be responsible – *in extremis* – for forcing acts of meaning-making upon it or denying the future possibility of such acts. 'Because' is the nihilistic 'in order to' motive of another.

'In order to' and 'because' do not originate in or relate to the individual body in the same way, then. There can be no ' "because" motives' because acts of meaningful interpretation are the preserve of the individual. Individuals do what they do in accord with the logic and the development of their worldviews: in accord with the ongoing history of their intentional activity-in-the-world, the history of organism-plus-environment that their interpretations take forward. They can be forced into making an interpretation – others can force their attention upon them – and through force they can be denied interpretation – others can maim or kill them, or subject them to gratuitous acts – but individuals are not forced into particular meanings or motivations; these remain a personal preserve. When 'darting to an aim' (Emerson 1981: 152), moreover, the individual-as-projectile has more chance than otherwise to elude others' machinations. When they conjoin personal interpretations with a life-project, individuals embody and exercise the power to make their own circumstance.

BIBLIOGRAPHY

Abu-Lughod, L. (1991) 'Writing Against Culture', in R. Fox (ed.) *Recapturing Anthropology*, Sante Fe: School of American Research Press.
Abrams, M. (1995) 'What is a Humanistic Criticism?', in D. Eddins (ed.) *The Emperor Redressed*, Tuscaloosa: University of Alabama Press.
Adams, R. (1977) 'Power in Human Societies', in R. Fogelson and R. Adams (eds) *The Anthropology of Power*, New York: Academic Press.
Aijmer, G. (2000) 'Introduction', in G. Aijmer and J. Abbink (eds) *Meanings of Violence*, Oxford: Berg.
Alison, J. (ed.) (1991) *Stanley Spencer: The Apotheosis of Love*, London: Barbican Art Gallery.
Althusser, L. (1997) *Lenin and Philosophy*, London: New Left Books.
Amit, V. and Rapport, N. (2002) *The Trouble with Community: Anthropological Reflections on Movement, Identity and Collectivity*, London: Pluto.
Amit-Talai, V. (1994) 'Urban Pathways: The Logistics of Youth Peer Relations', in V. Amit-Talai and H. Lustiger-Thaler (eds) *Urban Lives*, Toronto: McClelland and Stewart.
Anderson, B. (1972) 'The Idea of Power in Javanese Culture', in C. Holt (ed.) *Culture and Politics in Indonesia*, Ithaca NY: Cornell University Press.
Ansell-Pearson, K. (1994) *An Introduction to Nietzsche as Political Thinker*, Cambridge: Cambridge University Press.
Appadurai, A. (1991) 'Global Ethnoscapes: Notes and Queries for a Transnational Anthropology', in R. Fox (ed.) *Recapturing Anthropology*, Sante Fe: School of American Research Press.
Archetti, E. (1994) 'Introduction', in F. Archetti (ed.) *Exploring the Written*, Oslo: Scandinavian University Press.
Aronoff, M. J. (1973) 'Development Towns in Israel', in M. Curtis and M. Chertoff (eds) *Israel: Social Structure and Change*, New Brunswick: Transaction.
Arts Council of Great Britain (1976) *Stanley Spencer*, Glasgow: Maclehose.
Aschheim, S. (2001) 'A Review of the *Journal of Genocide Research*', *Times Literary Supplement*, 5145: 29–33.
Ashley, K. (1990) 'Introduction', in K. Ashley (ed.) *Victor Turner and the Construction of Cultural Criticism*, Bloomington: Indiana University Press.
Auden. W. H. (1951) *The Enchafed Flood, or The Romantic Iconography of the Sea*, London: Faber.

BIBLIOGRAPHY

Augé, M. (1995) *Non-places: Introduction to an Anthropology of Supermodernity*, London: Verso.
Avruch, K. (1981) *American Immigrants in Israel*, Chicago: University of Chicago Press.
Babcock, B. (1993) 'At Home, No Women are Storytellers: Ceramic Creativity and the Politics of Discourse in a Cochiti Pueblo', in S. Lavie, K. Narayan and R. Rosaldo (eds) *Creativity/Anthropology*, Ithaca NY: Cornell University Press.
Bachelard, G. (1994) *The Poetics of Space*, Boston MA: Beacon.
Bachrach, P. and Baratz, M. (1968) 'Two Faces of Power', in M. Swartz (ed.) *Local Level Politics*, Chicago: Aldine.
Bailey, F. (2001) *Treasons, Stratagems and Spoils*, Boulder: Westview.
Bailey, F. (ed.) (1971) *Gifts and Poison*, Oxford: Blackwell.
Barthes, R. (1968) 'La Mort de l'Auteur', *Manteia*, 5.
——(1982) 'Introduction to the Structural Analysis of Narratives', in S. Sontag (ed.) *A Barthes Reader*, London: Cape.
Bateson, G. (1936) *Naven*, Cambridge: Cambridge University Press.
——(1959) 'Anthropological Theories', *Science*, 129: 294–8.
——(1973) *Steps to an Ecology of Mind*, Frogmore: Paladin.
——(1980) *Mind and Nature*, Glasgow: Fontana.
Bateson, G. and Ruesch, J. (1951) *Communication*, New York: Norton.
Bauman, J. (2000) 'Moral Choices at the Time of the Gas Chambers', mimeo.
Bauman, Z. (1989) *Modernity and the Holocaust*, Ithaca NY: Cornell University Press.
Bell, K. (1992) *Stanley Spencer: A Complete Catalogue of Paintings*, London: Phaidon.
Benedict, R. (1932) 'Configurations of Culture in North America', *American Anthropologist*, 34: 1–27.
Berger, J. (1969) *Art and Revolution*, New York: Pantheon.
——(1975) *A Seventh Man*, Harmondsworth: Penguin.
——(1988) *The White Bird*, London: Hogarth.
Berger, P. (1963) *Invitation to Sociology*, Harmondsworth: Penguin.
——(1970) 'Identity as a Problem in the Sociology of Knowledge', in J. Curtis and J. Petras (eds) *The Sociology of Knowledge*, London: Duckworth.
Berger, P. and Kellner, H. (1973) *The Homeless Mind*, New York: Random House.
Bergson, H. (1975) *The Creative Mind*, Totowa: Littlefield & Adams.
Bernstein, M. (1998) 'Homage to the Extreme: The Shoah and the Rhetoric of Catastrophe', *Times Literary Supplement*, 4953: 6–8.
Beteille, A. (1965) *Caste, Class and Power*, Berkeley: University of California Press.
——(1977) *Inequality Among Men*, Oxford: Blackwell.
Blake, W. (1975) *The Complete Poems*, London: Longman.
Blau, P. (1967) *Exchange and Power in Social Life*, New York: Wiley.
Bloch, M. (1997) *Ritual, History and Power*, London: Athlone.
Bloom, H. (1975) *The Anxiety of Influence*, Oxford: Oxford University Press.
Blumer, H. (1969) *Symbolic Interactionism*, New Jersey: Prentice-Hall.
Boon, J. (1982) *Other Tribes, Other Scribes*, Cambridge: Cambridge University Press.
Boswell, S. (1973) *The Book of Boswell*, Harmondsworth: Penguin.
Bourdieu, P. (1977) *Outline of a Theory of Practice*, Cambridge: Cambridge University Press.
Bridgwater, P. (1978) 'English Writers and Nietzsche', in M. Palsey (ed.) *Nietzsche: Imagery and Thought*, London: Methuen.

BIBLIOGRAPHY

Brodsky, J. (1988) 'The Politics of Poetry', *The Sunday Times*, 10 January.
Bruner, J. (1990) *Acts of Meaning*, Cambridge MA: Harvard University Press.
Bruner, J. and Weisser, S. (1991) 'The Invention of Self: Autobiography and its Forms', in D. Olson and N. Torrance (eds) *Literacy and Orality*, Cambridge: Cambridge University Press.
Burridge, K. (1979) *Someone, No One: An Essay on Individuality*, Princeton: Princeton University Press.
Carrithers, M. (2000) 'Hedgehogs, Foxes, and Persons: Resistance and Moral Creativity in East Germany and South India', in N. Roughley (ed.) *Being Humans*, Berlin: de Gruyter.
Carus, P. (1972) *Nietzsche and Other Exponents of Individualism*, New York: Haskell & House.
Chamberlain, L. (1996) 'A Spoonful of Dr Liebig's Beef Extract', *Times Literary Supplement*, 4871: 14–15.
——(1997) *Nietzsche in Turin*, London: Quartet.
Chambers, I. (1994) *Migrancy Culture Identity*, London: Routledge.
Cheater, A. (1999) 'Power in the Postmodern Era', in A. Cheater (ed.) *The Anthropology of Power*, London: Routledge.
Chesterton, G. K. (1936) *Stories, Essays and Poems*, London: Dent.
Chodorow, N. (1994) 'Reflections on Personal Meaning and Cultural Meaning', paper delivered at the workshop 'Anthropological Perspectives on Psychoanalytic Theory and Practice', American Anthropological Association Meetings, Atlanta.
——(1999) *The Power of Feelings*, New Haven: Yale University Press.
Cioran, E. M. (1987) 'E. M. Cioran's Vision of Universal Doom', *International Herald Tribune*, 20 July, 16.
Cohen, Abner (1974) *Two-Dimensional Man: An Essay on the Anthropology of Power and Symbolism in Complex Society*, London: Routledge & Kegan Paul.
Cohen, A. P. (1992) 'Self-conscious Anthropology', in J. Okely and H. Callaway (eds) *Anthropology and Autobiography*, London: Routledge.
——(1994) *Self Consciousness*, London: Routledge.
Cohen, A. P. and Comaroff, J. (1976) 'The Management of Meaning', in B. Kapferer (ed.) *Transaction and Meaning*, Philadelphia: ISHI.
Cohen, A. P. and Rapport, N. (eds) (1995) *Questions of Consciousness*, London: Routledge.
Cohen, E. (1970) 'Development Towns – The Social Dynamics of "Planted" Communities in Israel', in S. Eisenstadt, R. Bar-Yosef and C. Adler (eds) *Integration and Development in Israel*, Jerusalem: Israel University Press.
Collins, P. (2002) 'Both Independent and Interconnected Voices: Bakhtin among the Quakers', in N. Rapport (ed.) *British Subjects: An Anthropology of Britain*, Oxford: Berg.
Collis, M. (1962) *Stanley Spencer*, London: Harvill.
Comaroff, J. (1985) *Body of Power, Spirit of Resistance*, Chicago: University of Chicago Press.
Compton-Burnett, I. (1969) *Mother and Son*, London: Panther.
Comte, A. (1951) *Système de Politique Positive*, vol. II, Paris: Mathias.
Counihan, C. (1999) *The Anthropology of Food and Body: Gender, Meaning, and Power*, New York: Routledge.

Crews, F. (1995) 'The End of the Poststructuralist Era', in D. Eddins (ed.) *The Emperor Redressed*, Tuscaloosa/London: University of Alabama Press/Phaidon.
Csordas, T. (ed.) (1994) *Embodiment and Experience*, Cambridge: Cambridge University Press.
Culler, J. (1981) *The Pursuit of Signs*, Ithaca NY: Cornell University Press.
Dawkins, R. (1996) *God's Utility Function*, London: Orion.
Devereux, G. (1978) *Ethnopsychoanalysis*, Berkeley: University of California Press.
Dewey, J. (1981–90) *The Later Works, 1925–53*, Carbondale: Southern Illinois University Press.
Dilley, R. (1999) 'Introduction: The Problem of Context', in R. Dilley (ed.) *The Problem of Context*, Oxford: Berghahn.
Donadio, S. (1978) *Nietzsche, Henry James and the Artistic Will*, New York: Oxford University Press.
Douglas, J. (1977) 'Existential Sociology', in J. Douglas and J. Johnson (eds) *Existential Sociology*, Cambridge: Cambridge University Press.
Dreitzel, H. (1970) 'Introduction', in H. Dreitzel (ed.) *Patterns of Communicative Behaviour*, London: Collier-Macmillan.
Drury, M. O'C. (1981) 'Conversations with Wittgenstein', in R. Rhees (ed.) *Ludwig Wittgenstein: Personal Recollections*, Oxford: Blackwell.
Dumont, L. (1966) *Homo Hierarchicus*, Chicago: University of Chicago Press.
——(1986) *Essays on Individualism*, Chicago: University of Chicago Press.
Durkheim, E. (1915) *The Elementary Forms of the Religious Life*, London: Allen & Unwin.
Earle, T. (1998) 'Political Domination and Social Evolution', in T. Ingold (ed.) *Companion Encyclopedia of Anthropology*, London: Routledge.
Edelman, G. (1992) *Bright Air, Brilliant Fire*, Harmondsworth: Penguin.
Efrat, E. (1984) *Urbanization in Israel*, London: Croom Helm.
Eley, G. (1994) 'Nations, Publics and Political Cultures: Placing Habermas in the Nineteenth Century', in N. Dirks, G. Eley and S. Ortner (eds) *Culture/Power/History*, Princeton: Princeton University Press.
Emerson, R. W. (1981) *The Portable Emerson*, ed. C. Bode, Harmondsworth: Penguin.
Epstein, A. (1968) 'Power, Politics and Leadership: Some Central African and Melanesian Contrasts', in M. Swartz (ed.) *Local Level Politics*, Chicago: Aldine.
Eves, R. (1998) *The Magical Body: Power, Fame and Meaning in a Melanesian Society*, Amsterdam: Harwood Academic.
Fardon, R. (1987) 'Introduction: A Sense of Relevance', in R. Fardon (ed.) *Power and Knowledge*, Edinburgh: Scottish Academic Press.
Feld, S. (1982) *Sound and Sentiment*, Philadelphia: University of Pennsylvania Press.
Fernandez, J. (1971) 'Persuasions and Performances: Of the Beast in Every Body…and the Metaphors of Everyman', in C. Geertz (ed.) *Myth, Symbol and Culture*, New York: Norton.
——(1977) 'Poetry in Motion: Being Moved by Amusement, by Mockery and by Mortality in the Asturian Countryside', *New Literary History*, VIII(3).
——(1982) *Bwiti*, Princeton: Princeton University Press.
——(1992) 'What it is like to be a Banzie: On sharing the experience of an Equatorial Microcosm' in J. Gort, H. Vroom, R. Fernhout and A. Wessels (eds) *On Sharing Religious Experience*, Amsterdam: Rodopi.

——(1993) 'Ceferino Suarez: A Village Versifier', in S. Lavie, K. Narayan and R. Rosaldo (eds) *Creativity/Anthropology*, Ithaca NY: Cornell University Press.
——(1995) 'Amazing Grace', in A. P. Cohen and N. Rapport (eds) *Questions of Consciousness*, London: Routledge.
Fernandez, J. and Huber, M. (eds) (2001) *Irony in Action*, Chicago: University of Chicago Press.
Forster, E. M. (1940) *Nordic Twilight*, London: Macmillan.
——(1950) *Howards End*, Harmondsworth: Penguin.
Foucault, M. (1972) *The Archaeology of Knowledge*, New York: Harper.
——(1977) *Discipline and Punish: The Birth of the Prison*, New York: Pantheon.
——(1980) *Power/Knowledge*, ed. C. Gordon, Brighton: Harvester.
——(1981) *The History of Sexuality*, vol. 1, London: Pelican.
——(1991a) 'What is an Author?', in P. Rabinow (ed.) *The Foucault Reader*, Harmondsworth: Penguin.
——(1991b) 'Governmentality', in G. Burchell, C. Gordon and P. Miller (eds) *The Foucault Effect*, Chicago: University of Chicago Press.
Furbank, P. (1982) 'The Philosophy of E. M. Forster', in J. Herz and R. Martin (eds) *E. M. Forster: Centenary Revaluations*, Basingstoke: Macmillan.
Gane, L. and Chan, K. (2000) *Introducing Nietzsche*, Cambridge: Icon.
Gatheru, R. M. (1965) *Child of Two Worlds*, New York: Doubleday.
Geertz, C. (1971) *Islam Observed*, Chicago: University of Chicago Press.
——(1973) *The Interpretation of Cultures*, New York: Basic Books.
——(1995) *After the Fact*, Cambridge MA: Harvard University Press.
Gellner, E. (1988) *State and Society in Soviet Thought*, Oxford: Blackwell.
——(1993) *Postmodernism, Reason and Religion*, London: Routledge.
——(1995) 'Anything Goes: The Carnival of Cheap Relativism Which Threatens to Swamp the Coming *Fin de Millenaire*', *Times Literary Supplement*, 4811: 6–8.
——(1998) *Language and Solitude*, Cambridge: Cambridge University Press.
Gewirth, A. (1998) *Self-Fulfilment*, Princeton: Princeton University Press.
Giddens, A. (1990) *The Consequences of Modernity*, Stanford: Stanford University Press.
Gilman, S. (ed.) (1987) *Conversations with Nietzsche*, Oxford: Oxford University Press.
Gitelman, Z. (1982) *Becoming Israelis*, New York: Praeger.
Glaser, A. (1993) 'Jewish Refugees and Jewish Refugee Industries', in U. Henriques (ed.) *The Jews of South Wales*, Cardiff: University of Wales Press.
Gledhill, J. (2000) *Power and its Disguises*, London: Pluto.
Glew, A. (ed.) (2001) *Stanley Spencer: Letters and Writings*, London: Tate.
Goffman, E. (1961) *Asylums*, Harmondsworth: Penguin.
——(1972) *Encounters*, London: Allen Lane.
——(1978) *The Presentation of Self in Everyday Life*, Harmondsworth: Penguin.
Golomb, J. (1995) *In Search of Authenticity*, London: Routledge.
Goodman, N. (1978) *Ways of Worldmaking*, Hassocks: Harvester.
Gramsci, A. (1971) *Selections from the Prison Notebooks of Antonio Gramsci*, London: Lawrence & Wishart.
Gray, J. (2000) *At Home in the Hills*, Oxford: Berghahn.
Greenberg, M. (1986) *The Hamlet Vocation of Coleridge and Wordsworth*, Iowa City: Iowa University Press.
Greene, G. (1974) *The Heart of the Matter*, Harmondsworth: Penguin.
Grimm, R. (1977) *Nietzsche's Theory of Knowledge*, Berlin: de Gruyter.

BIBLIOGRAPHY

Hallowell, I. (1974) *Culture and Experience*, Philadelphia: University of Pennsylvania Press.
Handler, R. and Segal D. (1990) *Jane Austen and the Fiction of Culture*, Tucson: University of Arizona Press.
Hannerz, U. (1980) *Exploring the City*, New York: Columbia University Press.
Harries, M. and S. (eds) (1983) *The War Artists*, London: Michael Joseph.
Harris, M. (2000) *Life on the Amazon*, Oxford: Oxford University Press.
Hazlitt, W. (1826) *The Plain Speaker*, London: Colburn.
Heidegger, M. (1981) *Nietzsche*, 2 vols, London: Routledge & Kegan Paul.
Heikkinen, A. (1997) 'Vocational Education as a "Life-Project": Reflections from the Case of Finland', *Journal of European Industrial Training*, 21(67): 213–9.
Heller, E. (1988) *The Importance of Nietzsche*, Chicago: University of Chicago Press.
Helms, M. (1993) *Craft and the Kingly Ideal: Art, Trade, and Power*, Austin: University of Texas Press.
Hendry, J. (1996) *Wrapping Culture: Politeness, Presentation and Power in Japan and Other Societies*, Oxford: Oxford University Press.
Henriques, U. (ed.) (1993) *The Jews of South Wales*, Cardiff: University of Wales Press.
Herzfeld, M. (1993) *The Social Production of Indifference*, Oxford: Berg.
Hirsch, E. D. (1988), 'Faulty Perspectives', in D. Lodge (ed.) *Modern Criticism and Theory*, London: Longman.
Hobart, M. (1985) 'Texts est un con', in R. Barnes, D. de Coppet and R. Parkin (eds) *Contexts and Levels*, Oxford: JASO.
Hollingdale, R. (1965) *Nietzsche: The Man and his Philosophy*, Baton Rouge: University of Louisiana Press.
Horton, R. (1967) 'African Traditional Thought and Western Science', in B. Wilson (ed.) *Rationality*, Oxford: Blackwell.
Humphrey, N. (1983) *Consciousness Regained*, Oxford: Oxford University Press.
Hunter, F. (1970) 'Community Power Structure', in E. Keynes and D. Ricci (eds) *Political Power, Community and Democracy*, Chicago: Rand-McNally.
Hutcheon, L. (1994) *Irony's Edge*, London: Routledge.
Hyman, T. (1991) 'Stanley Spencer: The Sacred Self', in J. Alison (ed.) *Stanley Spencer*, London: Barbican Art Gallery.
Ions, E. (1977) *Against Behaviourism*, Oxford: Blackwell.
Irigaray, L. (1993) *An Ethics of Sexual Difference*, Ithaca NY: Cornell University Press.
Irwin, A. (2002) 'The Social Organization of Soldiering: A Canadian Infantry Company in the Field', Ph.D. thesis, University of Manchester.
Isaacs, H. (1966) *American Jews in Israel*, New York: Day.
Jackson, M. (1981) 'Knowledge of the Body', *Man* (n.s.) 18: 327–45.
——(1989) *Paths Toward a Clearing*, Bloomington: Indiana University Press.
——(1996) 'Introduction: Phenomenology, Radical Empiricism and Anthropological Critique', in M. Jackson (ed.) *Things As They Are*, Bloomington: Indiana University Press.
——(1998) *Minima Ethnographica*, Chicago: University of Chicago Press.
——(2002) *The Politics of Storytelling*, Copenhagen: Museum Tusculanum Press.
Jacobson, D. (1978) 'Scale and Social Control', in F. Barth (ed.) *Societal Scale and Social Organization*, Oslo: Greig.
James, A. (1995) 'On Being a Child: The Self, the Group and the Category', in A. P. Cohen and N. Rapport (eds) *Questions of Consciousness*, London: Routledge.

James, C. (2002) 'The Unmysterious Suicide', *Times Literary Supplement*, 5177: 3–4.
Jenkins, R. (1983) *Lads, Citizens and Ordinary Kids*, London: Routledge & Kegan Paul.
——(1992) *Pierre Bourdieu*, London: Routledge.
Johnson, C. (1982) *Revolutionary Change*, Stanford: Stanford University Press.
Jones, D. (1959) 'An Interview with E. M. Forster on His Life and His Books', *The Listener*, 1 January.
Jones, E. (1955) *Sigmund Freud: Life and Work*, vol. 2, London: Hogarth.
Kapferer, B. (1988) *Legends of People, Myths of State*, Washington: Smithsonian Institution Press.
Kateb, G. (1991a) 'Introduction: Exile, Alienation and Estrangement', *Social Research*, 58(1) (special issue: 'Home: A Place in the World', ed. A. Mack).
——(1991b) 'Democratic Individuality and the Meaning of Rights', in N. Rosenblum (ed.) *Liberalism and the Moral Life*, Cambridge MA: Harvard University Press.
——(1992) *The Inner Ocean*, Ithaca NY: Cornell University Press.
Kearney, R. (1988) *The Wake of the Imagination*, London: Hutchinson.
Kelly, G. (1969) *Clinical Psychology and Personality*, New York: Wiley.
——(1970) 'A Brief Introduction to Personal Construct Theory', in D. Bannister (ed.) *Perspectives in Personal Construct Theory*, London: Academic Press.
Kerby, A. P. (1991) *Narrative and the Self*, Bloomington: Indiana University Press.
Kierkegaard, S. (1958) *The Journals of Kierkegaard 1834–1854*, Glasgow: Fontana.
Kohn, T. (1995) 'She Came out of the Field and into My Home: Reflections, Dreams and a Search for Consciousness in Anthropological Method', in A. P. Cohen and N. Rapport (eds) *Questions of Consciousness*, London: Routledge.
Kotarba, J. (1984) 'A Synthesis: The Existential Self in Society', in J. Kotarba and A. Fontana (eds) *The Existential Self in Society*, Chicago: University of Chicago Press.
Kotarba, J. and Fontana, A. (eds) (1984) *The Existential Self in Society*, Chicago: University of Chicago Press.
Kundera, M. (1990) *The Art of the Novel*, London: Faber.
Kurtz, D. (2001) *Political Anthropology: Paradigms and Power*, Boulder: Westview.
Laing, R. (1968) *The Politics of Experience*, Harmondsworth: Penguin.
Lame Deer (J. Fire) (1980) *Lame Deer*, London: Quartet.
Langer, L. (1997) 'The Alarmed Vision: Social Suffering and Holocaust Atrocity', in A. Kleinman, V. Das and M. Lock (eds) *Social Suffering*, Berkeley: University of California Press.
Langer, S. (1964) *Philosophical Sketches*, New York: Mentor.
Larkin, P. (1990) *Collected Poems*, London: Faber.
Lavie, S., Narayan, K. and Rosaldo, R. (eds) (1993) *Creativity/Anthropology*, Ithaca NY: Cornell University Press.
Lavrin, J. (1971) *Nietzsche*, London: Studio Vista.
Law, J. (1991) 'Power, Discretion and Strategy', in J. Law (ed.) *A Sociology of Monsters*, London: Routledge.
Leach, E. (1954) *Political Systems of Highland Burma*, London: Bell.
——(1961) *Rethinking Anthropology*, London: Athlone.
——(1969) *A Runaway World?*, London: Oxford University Press.
——(1976) *Culture and Communication*, Cambridge: Cambridge University Press.
——(1977) *Custom, Law and Terrorist Violence*, Edinburgh: Edinburgh University Press.
——(1984) 'Glimpses of the Unmentionable in the History of British Social Anthropology', *Annual Review of Anthropology*, 13: 1–23.

——(1989) 'Writing Anthropology: A review of Clifford Geertz's *Works and Lives*', *American Ethnologist*, 16(1): 137–41.
——(2001) *The Essential Edmund Leach, Volume Two: Culture and Human Nature*, eds S. Hugh-Jones and J. Laidlaw, New Haven: Yale University Press.
Leman, G. (1970) 'Words and Worlds', in D. Bannister (ed.) *Perspectives in Personal Construct Theory*, London: Academic Press.
Levi, P. (1987) *If This Is a Man* and *The Truce*, London: Abacus.
——(1994) *Moments of Reprieve*, London: Abacus.
——(1996) *The Drowned and The Saved*, London: Abacus.
——(1997) *The Periodic Table*, London: Abacus.
Lévi-Strauss, C. (1962) *Totemism*, Harmondsworth: Penguin.
——(1963) *Structural Anthropology*, New York: Basic Books.
——(1966) *The Savage Mind*, Chicago: University of Chicago Press.
——(1975) *The Raw and the Cooked*, New York: Harper Colophon.
Lewis, H. D. (1973) *The Self and Immortality*, London: Macmillan.
——(1982) *The Elusive Self*, London: Macmillan.
Louch, A. (1966) *Explanation and Human Action*, Berkeley: University of California Press.
Lukes, S. (1990) *Individualism*, Oxford: Blackwell.
Lyman, S. (1984) 'Foreword', in J. Kotarba and A. Fontana (eds) *The Existential Self in Society*, Chicago: University of Chicago Press.
Mair, J. (1977) 'The Community of Self', in D. Bannister (ed.) *New Perspectives in Personal Construct Theory*, London: Academic Press.
Mallett, P. (1995) 'Primo Levi', paper presented at the Open Association, University of St Andrews, 17 February.
Mann, T. (1947) *Nietzsche's Philosophy in the Light of Contemporary Events*, Washington: Library of Congress.
Martin, G. (1983) 'The Bridge and the River. Or The Ironies of Communication', *Poetics Today*, 4(3): 415–35.
Marx, E. (1976) *The Social Context of Violent Behaviour*, London: Routledge & Kegan Paul.
——(1990) 'Editorial Introduction', in E. Peters, *The Bedouin of Cyrenaica*, Cambridge: Cambridge University Press.
Marx, K. (1887) *Capital*, London: Sonnenschein.
Maslow, A. (1968) *Toward a Psychology of Being*, New York: van Nostrand.
Mauss, M. (1979) *Sociology and Psychology*, London: Routledge & Kegan Paul.
May, R. (1958) 'The Origins and Significance of the Existential Movement in Psychology', in R. May, E. Angel and H. Ellenberger (eds) *Existence*, New York: Basic Books.
Mill, J. S. (1972) *'Utilitarianism', 'On Liberty', and 'Considerations on Representative Government'*, London: Dent.
Milton, K. (1993) 'Introduction: Environmentalism and Anthropology', in K. Milton (ed.) *Environmentalism*, London: Routledge.
Mises, L. von (1949) *Human Action*, London: Hodge.
Moore, B. (1958) *Political Power and Social Theory*, Cambridge MA: Harvard University Press.
Morris, B. (1997) 'In Defence of Realism and Truth: Critical Reflections on the Anthropological Followers of Heidegger', *Critique of Anthropology*, 17(3): 313–40.

Murdoch, I. (1970) *The Sovereignty of Good*, London: Routledge & Kegan Paul.
Nehamas, A. (1985) *Nietzsche: Life as Literature*, Cambridge MA: Harvard University Press.
Neisser, U. (1976) *Cognition and Reality*, San Francisco: Freeman.
Nietzsche, F. (1911) 'On Truth and Falsity in their Ultramoral Sense', in *'Early Greek Philosophy', and other Essays*, London: Foulis.
——(1957) *The Use and Abuse of History*, Indianapolis: Bobbs-Merrill.
——(1960) *Joyful Wisdom*, New York: Ungar.
——(1967) *The Birth of Tragedy*, New York: Random House.
——(1968) *The Will to Power*, New York: Random House.
——(1973) *On the Genealogy of Morals*, New York: Random House.
——(1979a) *Beyond Good and Evil*, Harmondsworth: Penguin.
——(1979b) *Ecce Homo*, Harmondsworth: Penguin.
——(1979c) *Twilight of the Idols*, Harmondsworth: Penguin.
——(1980) *Thus Spoke Zarathustra*, Harmondsworth: Penguin.
——(1991) *Daybreak*, Cambridge: Cambridge University Press.
——(1994) *Human, All Too Human*, Harmondsworth: Penguin.
——(1997) *Untimely Meditations*, Cambridge: Cambridge University Press.
Oakeshott, M. (1962) 'The Voice of Poetry in the Conversation of Mankind', in *'Rationalism in Politics', and other Essays*, London: Methuen.
Ong, W. (1977) *Interfaces of the Word*, Ithaca NY: Cornell University Press.
Oppenheimer, P. (1989) *The Birth of the Modern Mind*, New York: Oxford University Press.
Ortega y Gasset, J. (1956) *The Dehumanization of Art, and other Writings on Art and Culture*, New York: Doubleday.
——(1961) *Meditations on Quixote*, New York: Norton.
Overing, J. (1987) 'Translation as a Creative Process: The Power of the Name', in L. Holy (ed.) *Comparative Anthropology*, Oxford: Blackwell.
Oz, A. (1992) 'Israeli Literature', The Raymond Williams Lecture, Hay-on-Wye Book Festival.
Pareto, V. (1966) *Pareto: Sociological Writings*, ed. S. Finer, London: Pall Mall.
Parsons, T. (1937) *The Structure of Social Action*, New York: McGraw-Hill.
Patrizio, A. and Little, F. (1994) *Canvassing the Clyde: Stanley Spencer and the Shipyards*, Glasgow: Glasgow Museums.
Percy, W. (1958) 'Symbol, Consciousness and Intersubjectivity', *Journal of Philosophy*, 55.
Peters, E. (1990) *The Bedouin of Cyrenaica: Studies in Personal and Corporate Power*, eds J. Goody and E. Marx, Cambridge: Cambridge University Press.
Polsby, N. (1968) 'How to Study Community Power: The Pluralist Alternative', in M. Swartz (ed.) *Local Level Politics*, Chicago: Aldine.
Pople, K. (1991) *Stanley Spencer*, London: Collins.
Popper, K. (1975) *Objective Knowledge*, Oxford: Oxford University Press.
——(1980) *The Open Society and its Enemies*, 2 vols, London: Routledge.
——(1997) *The Myth of the Framework*, London: Routledge.
Popper, K. and Eccles, J. (1977) *The Self and Its Brain*, Berlin: Springer.
Pospisil, L. (1971) *Kapauku Papuans and their Law*, New Haven: Human Relations Area Files Press.

Preston, J. (1991) 'The Trickster Unmasked: Anthropology and the Imagination', in I. Brady (ed) *Anthropological Poetics*, Savage: Rowman & Littlefield.
Putnam, H. and Putnam, R. (1996) 'What the Spilled Beans Can Spell: The Difficult and Deep Realism of William James', *Times Literary Supplement*, 4864: 14–15.
Ray, W. (1989) *Literary Meaning*, Oxford: Blackwell.
Raphael, D. (1975) 'Women and Power: Introductory Notes', in D. Raphael (ed.) *Being Female: Reproduction, Power, and Change*, The Hague: Mouton.
Rapoport, A. (1998) 'Spatial Organization and the Built Environment', in T. Ingold (ed.) *Companion Encyclopedia of Anthropology*, London: Routledge.
Rapport, N. J. (1986) 'Cedar High Farm: Ambiguous Symbolic Boundary. An Essay in Anthropological Intuition', in A. P. Cohen (ed.) *Symbolising Boundaries*, Manchester: Manchester University Press.
——(1987) *Talking Violence: An Anthropological Interpretation of Conversation in the City*, St John's: ISER Books, Memorial University of Newfoundland.
——(1993) *Diverse World-Views in an English Village*, Edinburgh: Edinburgh University Press.
——(1994a) *The Prose and the Passion: Anthropology, Literature and the Writing of E. M. Forster*, Manchester/New York; Manchester University Press/St Martin's Press.
——(1994b) 'Trauma and Ego-Syntonic Response. The Holocaust and the "Newfoundland Young Yids", 1985', in S. Heald and A. Duluz (eds) *Anthropology and Psychoanalysis*, London: Routledge.
——(1997a) *Transcendent Individual: Towards a Literary and Liberal Anthropology*, London and New York: Routledge.
——(1997b) 'The "Contrarieties" of Israel. An essay on the Cognitive Importance and the Creative Promise of "both/and"', *Journal of the Royal Anthropological Institute* (n.s.) 3(4): 653–72.
——(1997c) 'Edifying Anthropology. Culture as Conversation: Representation as Conversation', in A. James, J. Hockey and A. Dawson (eds) *After Writing Culture*, London: Routledge.
——(1998) 'Coming Home to a Dream: A Study of the Immigrant Discourse of "Anglo-Saxons" in Israel', in N. Rapport and A. Dawson (eds) *Migrants of Identity*, Oxford: Berg.
——(1999) 'Context as an Act of Personal Externalization: Gregory Bateson and the Harvey Family in the English Village of Wanet', in R. Dilley (ed.) *The Problem of Context*, Oxford: Berghahn.
——(2000) '"Criminals by Instinct": On the "Tragedy" of Social Structure and the "Violence" of Individual Creativity', in G. Aijmer and J. Abbink (eds) *Meanings of Violence*, Oxford: Berg.
——(2001a) 'Random Mind: Towards an Appreciation of Openness in Individual, Society and Anthropology', *The Australian Journal of Anthropology*, 12(2): 190–220.
——(2001b) 'Communicational Distortion and the Constitution of Society: Indirection as a Form of Life', in W. Watson and J. Hendry (eds) *An Anthropology of Indirect Communication*, London: Routledge.
——(2001c) 'Bob, Hospital Bodybuilder: The Integrity of the Body, the Transitiveness of "Work" and "Leisure"', paper presented at the American Anthropological Association Meetings, Washington DC.
Rapport, N. J. (ed.) (2002) *British Subjects: An Anthropology of Britain*, Oxford: Berg.

Rapport, N. J. and Dawson, A. (1998) 'Home and Movement: A Polemic', in N. Rapport and A. Dawson (eds) *Migrants of Identity: Perceptions of 'Home' in a World of Movement*, Oxford and New York: Berg.
Rapport, N. J. and Overing, J. (2000) *Social and Cultural Anthropology: The Key Concepts*, London and New York: Routledge.
Rawls, J. (1971) *A Theory of Justice*, Cambridge MA: Harvard University Press.
Redfield, R. (1952) 'The Primitive World View', *Proceedings of the American Philosophical Society*, XCVI: 30.
Relph, E. (1976) *Place and Placelessness*, London: Pion.
Robinson, D. (1979) *Stanley Spencer: Visions from a Berkshire Village*, Oxford: Phaidon.
——(1994) *Stanley Spencer*, London: Phaidon.
Rorty, A. (1986) 'Self-deception, *Akrasia* and Irrationality', in J. Elster (ed.) *The Multiple Self*, Cambridge: Cambridge University Press.
Rorty, R. (1979) *Philosophy and the Mirror of Nature*, Princeton: Princeton University Press.
——(1992) *Contingency, Irony and Solidarity*, Cambridge: Cambridge University Press.
Rothenstein, E. (1945) *Stanley Spencer*, Oxford: Phaidon.
Rubinstein, R. (1998) 'Collective Violence and Common Security', in T. Ingold (ed.) *Companion Encyclopedia of Anthropology*, London: Routledge.
Sacks, H. (1974) 'On the Analysability of Stories by Children', in R. Turner (ed.) *Ethnomethodology*, Harmondsworth: Penguin.
Said, E. (1978) *Orientalism*, London: Penguin.
Samuel, R. (1975) 'People's History', in R. Samuel (ed.) *Village Life and Labour*, London: Routledge & Kegan Paul.
Sapir, E. (1956) *Culture, Language and Personality*, Berkeley: University of California Press.
Sartre, J-P. (1947) *The Republic of Silence*, New York: Harcourt Brace.
——(1956) *Being and Nothingness*, New York: Philosophy Library.
——(1972) *The Psychology of Imagination*, New York: Citadel.
——(1975) 'Existentialism is a Humanism', in W. Kaufman (ed.) *Existentialism from Dostoevsky to Sartre*, New York: New Arena Library.
Schuetz, A. (1972) *The Phenomenology of the Social World*, London: Heinemann.
Scott, J. (1985) *Weapons of the Weak*, New Haven: Yale University Press.
——(1990) *Domination and the Arts of Resistance*, New Haven: Yale University Press.
Sermons by Artists (1934) London: Golden Cockerel.
Shelley, P. B. (1954) 'A Defence of Poetry', in D. Clark (ed.) *Shelley's Prose*, Albuquerque: University of New Mexico Press.
Shore, C. and Wright, S. (1997) 'Policy: A New Field of Anthropology', in C. Shore and S. Wright (eds) *Anthropology of Policy: Critical Perspectives on Governance and Power*, London: Routledge.
Shostak, M. (1993) 'The Creative Individual in the World of the !Kung San', in S. Lavie, K. Narayan and R. Rosaldo (eds) *Creativity/Anthropology*, Ithaca NY: Cornell University Press.
Simmel, G. (1971) *On Individuality and Social Forms*, ed. D. Levine, Chicago: Chicago University Press.
Simpson, A. (1998) 'Memory and Becoming Chosen Other: Fundamentalist Elite-making in a Zambian Catholic Mission School', in R. Werbner (ed.) *Memory and the Postcolony: African Anthropology and the Critique of Power*, London: Zed.

Skalnik, P. (1999) 'Authority versus Power', in A. Cheater (ed.) *The Anthropology of Power*, London: Routledge.
Smith, G. (1999) *Confronting the Present*, Oxford: Berg.
Soekefeld, M. (1999) 'Debating Self, Culture in Anthropology', *Current Anthropology*, 40(4): 417–47.
Sontag, S. (1967) *Against Interpretation, and other Essays*, New York: Farrar, Strauss & Giroux.
Spencer, S. (1955) *A Retrospective Exhibition*, London: Tate Gallery.
Spengemann, W. (1980) *The Forms of Autobiography*, New Haven: Yale University Press.
Stagl, J. (2000) 'Anthropological Universality: On the Validity of Generalisations about Human Nature', in N. Roughley (ed.) *Being Humans*, Berlin: de Gruyter.
Stanage, S. (1974) 'Violatives: Modes and Themes of Violence', in S. Stanage (ed.) *Reason and Violence*, Totowa: Littlefield & Adams.
Steiner, G. (1975) *After Babel*, London: Oxford University Press.
——(1978) 'The Distribution of Discourse', in *'On Difficulty' and other Essays*, Oxford: Oxford University Press.
Stern, J. P. (1978) 'Nietzsche and the Idea of Metaphor', in M. Palsey (ed.) *Nietzsche: Imagery and Thought*, London: Methuen.
——(1981) *A Study of Nietzsche*, Cambridge: Cambridge University Press.
Stocking, G. (1992) *The Ethnographer's Magic, and other Essays in the History of Anthropology*, Madison: University of Wisconsin Press.
Stoller, P. (1989) *The Taste of Ethnographic Things*, Philadelphia: University of Pennsylvania Press.
——(1995) *Embodying Colonial Memories*, New York: Routledge.
——(1997) *Sensuous Scholarship*, Philadelphia: University of Pennsylvania Press.
Strong, T. (1975) *Friedrich Nietzsche and the Politics of Transfiguration*, Berkeley: University of California Press.
Tallis, R. (2001) 'The Truth about Lies: Foucault, Nietzsche and the Cretan Paradox', *Times Literary Supplement*, 5151: 3–4.
Tanner, M. (1994) *Nietzsche*, Oxford: Oxford University Press.
Tawney, R. H. (1931) *Equality*, London: Allen & Unwin.
Tonkin, E. (1992) *Narrating our Pasts*, Cambridge: Cambridge University Press.
Torres, G. (1997) *The Force of Irony: Power in the Everyday Life of Mexican Tomato Workers*, Oxford: Berg.
Turner, J. S. (2000) *The Extended Organism: The Physiology of Animal-built Structures*, Cambridge MA: Harvard University Press.
Turton, A. (1986) 'Patrolling the Middle Ground: Methodological Perspectives on Everyday Peasant Resistance', *Journal of Peasant Studies*, 13: 36–48.
Uexkuell, J. von (1982) 'The Theory of Meaning', *Semiotica*, 41(1): 25–82.
Vaihinger, H. (1924) *The Philosophy of 'As If'*, London: Routledge & Kegan Paul.
Vauvenargues, Marquis de (1997) *Des Lois de L'Esprit*, Paris: Desjonquères.
Vincent, J. (1990) *Anthropology and Politics*, Tuscon: University of Arizona Press.
Wagner, R. (1991) 'Poetics and the Recentering of Anthropology', in I. Brady (ed.) *Anthropological Poetics*, Savage: Rowman & Littlefield.
Wallace, A. (1961) 'The Psychic Unity of Human Groups', in B. Kaplan (ed.) *Studying Personality Cross Culturally*, New York: Harper & Row.
——(1964) *Culture and Personality*, New York: Random House.

Watson, C. W. (1992) 'Autobiography, Anthropology and the Experience of Indonesia', in J. Okely and H. Callaway (eds) *Anthropology and Autobiography*, London: Routledge.
Watson, G. (1991) 'Rewriting Culture', in R. Fox (ed.) *Recapturing Anthropology*, Santa Fe: School of American Research Press.
Weber, M. (1946) *From Max Weber: Essays in Sociology*, London: Routledge & Kegan Paul.
——(1947) *Theory of Social and Economic Organization*, New York: Oxford University Press.
Werbner, R. (1991) *Tears of the Dead*, Edinburgh: Edinburgh University Press.
Wheatcroft, G. (2000) 'Horrors Beyond Tragedy', *Times Literary Supplement*, 5071: 9–10.
White, H. (1973) *Metahistory*, Baltimore: Johns Hopkins University Press.
Whitehead, A. (1925) *Science and the Modern World*, New York: Macmillan.
Wilde, O. (1913) *Intentions*, London: Methuen.
Williams, R. (1963) *Culture and Society 1780–1950*, Harmondsworth: Penguin.
Williksen-Bakker, S. (1994) 'The Moulding of Identity in South Pacific Poetry and Prose', in E. Archetti (ed.) *Exploring the Written*, Oslo: Scandinavian University Press.
Wilmsen, E. (1999) *Journeys with Flies*, Chicago: University of Chicago Press.
Winch, P. (1970) *The Idea of a Social Science, and its Relation to Philosophy*, London: Routledge & Kegan Paul.
Winterson, J. (1995) *Art and Lies*, London: Vintage.
Wittgenstein, L. (1978) *Philosophical Investigations*, Oxford: Blackwell.
——(1980) *Culture and Value*, Chicago: University of Chicago Press.
Wolf, E. (1974) *Anthropology*, New York: Norton.
——(1998) 'Anthropology among the Powers', keynote address, European Association of Anthropologists conference, Frankfurt.
——(1999) *Envisioning Power*, Berkeley: University of California Press.
——(2001) *Pathways of Power*, Berkeley: University of California Press.
Woolf, V. (1963) *A Room of One's Own*, Harmondsworth: Penguin.
——(1972) *A Writer's Diary*, London: Hogarth.
——(1980) *Orlando*, Frogmore: Granada.
Wulff, H. (1998) *Ballet across Borders*, Oxford: Berg.
Yelvington, K. (1996) 'Flirting in the Factory', *Journal of the Royal Anthropological Institute*, 2(2): 313–33.
Young, J. (1988) *Writing and Rewriting the Holocaust*, Bloomington: Indiana University Press.

INDEX

Abrams, M. 55–6
Abu-Lughod, L. 19–20, 89
activity-in-the-world 75, 79–81, 109, 220, 225, 236, 238–9, 261
Adams, R. 80
aesthetics xii, 34
agent and agency 14–15, 19–20, 22, 28, 42, 52, 56, 58–9, 66, 72, 75–6, 78, 81, 110, 223, 237, 256; *see also* creativity
Aijmer, G. 251, 253
alienation xii, 52, 71, 108, 116, 210
Alison, J. 205–6
Althusser, L. 86
ambiguity 3, 40, 43–4, 68, 87, 89, 243–7, 251
Amit, V. 19, 53, 59
Anderson, B. 79–80
anomie 52, 71, 114, 116
Ansell-Pearson, K. 9
Appadurai, A. 44
Archetti, E. 29
Arendt, H. x–xi
Aronoff, M. 154
'as if' 12–14, 89
Aschheim, S. 241
Ashley, K. 32
Auden, W.H. 74
Auge, M. 66
Augustine 40, 127, 187
Auschwitz xiv, 21, 134, 241, 243, 246–8, 250, 254; *see also* Nazis
Austen, Jane 44–5
authenticity 20, 35, 50, 53, 55, 73, 105, 124, 128, 177, 225, 258; *see also* bad faith
authority 83, 85
auto-anthropology 36
Avruch, K. 156

Babcock, B. 45
Bachelard, G. 41–2
Bachrach, P. 83
bad faith xiii, 52–6, 247, 260
Bailey, F. 85, 87
Baratz, M. 83
Barthes, R. 14, 64–5
Bateson, G. 17–18, 24, 27, 29, 75, 82, 221, 224, 235
Bauman, J. 249
Bauman, Z. 241
'because' motives *see* 'in order to' and 'because' motives
Beethoven, L. 122, 132, 145, 150, 230–1
being and becoming 35–6, 41, 47, 49–52, 67, 82, 99–100, 217, 220, 238, 260; *see also* emergence
Bell, K. 184, 204, 210
Benedict, R. 45, 74
Benjamin, W. x
Berger, J. 15, 27, 41, 54, 184
Berger, P. 17, 52, 64–5, 237
Bergson, H. 27
Bernstein, M. 241
Beteille, A. 75, 83
Bhabha, H. 52
biography and autobiography 5, 14–16, 74, 89, 177, 184, 205–7, 258; *see also* narrative
biology 10, 18, 22, 34, 60–1
Blake, W. 6, 185, 188
Blau, P. 77
Bloch, M. 83,
Bloom, H. 14, 15
Blumer, H. 38
body 23, 30–2, 35, 40, 54–6, 59–61, 75–6, 78, 80, 87, 90, 96–7, 99–101,

INDEX

128–30, 215–27, 229, 232–4, 239–40, 260–1; body-plus-environment 24, 75, 82, 89–90, 216, 219–23, 236, 260–1; *see also* embodiment
Boon, J. 260
Boswell, S. 45
Bourdieu, P. 51, 62–3, 65, 86
Bridgwater, P. 10
Brodsky, J. 46, 51
Bruner, J. 30, 33
Burridge, K. 47, 70–1, 79, 237

Carrithers, M. 71–2
categorization 16, 19, 48–50, 70, 73, 107, 149, 239, 248, 253, 257; *see also* stereotype
causality 11–12, 42, 45, 52, 54, 60, 65–6, 69–70, 78, 82, 84, 88
Chamberlain, L. 94, 97, 99, 101, 128, 234
Chambers, I. 43
Chan, K. 230
charisma 237
Cheater, A. 83
children 19, 46, 73–4
Chodorow, N. 73–4
Cioran, E.M. 242
circumstance xi, xiv, 3, 27, 34, 36, 48–9, 67–8, 73–4, 149, 248–50, 258–61; *see also* conditions, socio-cultural
class 16, 66, 76
classification 25, 27, 82
cognition 20, 25–6, 28–33, 35, 40, 42–8, 55, 71, 73, 78–9, 149, 171, 176–7, 216, 219, 246, 248, 250, 255
Cohen, Abner 82–3
Cohen, Anthony P. 23, 28, 39, 41, 69–70, 86, 88, 253, 259
Cohen, E. 154
collective representations 61, 66, 68–70
Collins, P. 59
Collis, M. 8, 184, 196–7, 205, 207–10, 226, 229
Comaroff, Jean 216, 224
Comaroff, John 88
communication 3, 37–8, 44, 56, 76–7, 83, 208
community 3, 8, 14, 19, 26, 47, 52, 237
Compton-Burnett, I. 252
concept 33–4, 43–4, 47, 50, 52, 54, 58, 61, 64, 71–2, 76, 79, 87, 103–7, 112, 121, 127, 217, 221, 234, 256; *see also* categorization

conditions, socio-cultural 3, 17, 47–50, 54, 59, 61, 65, 67–8, 74, 149, 238, 249, 259–60
conscience collective 60–1, 176, 237; *see also* collective representations
consciousness x–xi, 3–6, 10–15, 18–34, 38–42, 46–7, 50–3, 58, 60, 66–71, 76, 78, 80–1, 84–9, 101, 129–30, 149–50, 177, 185, 187, 206, 218, 234–9, 242–3, 248–9, 253–61; *see also* cognition
context 29, 31, 38, 65–8, 74, 83–4, 245, 248, 256
control: human 17, 100, 222; individual 3, 5–6, 12, 14, 21, 32, 34, 50, 65, 86, 89, 101, 128–30, 149, 178, 185, 206, 225, 239, 248–9, 259; institutional 3, 7, 52, 77, 84, 86, 176, 239, 244, 247
convention 28, 35, 42, 44–7, 49–50, 57, 63–5, 68–74, 76, 78–9, 83, 217, 239, 242, 255
conversation 36–7, 41, 144, 208, 230
conversion 46–7
Counihan, C. 216
creativity xi, 6, 15–20, 23, 26–9, 35–6, 41–7, 51, 66, 70, 74–8, 106, 108, 190, 206, 209–11, 216, 218, 222, 236, 238–9, 243, 251–2, 254
Crews, F. 66
Csordas, T. 217
Culler, J. 65
cultural relativism 18–19, 217
culture xi–xii, xiv, 13–14, 17–21, 26, 28, 32, 38–9, 42–5, 47–9, 52–4, 57–9, 61–3, 66, 69, 71–4, 78, 81, 83–4, 217–19, 223–5, 237–9, 254, 257–8
cybernetics 221, 237

Darwin, C. 10, 114, 120, 128, 145, 183, 256
Dawkins, R. 10
Dawson, A. 51
death xiv, 24, 85, 242–3, 246, 248–9, 259; *see also* suicide
deconstruction 18–19, 48–9
Descartes, R. 40, 63–4, 110, 127
determinism xi, 4–5, 12, 19, 21, 28–9, 34, 36, 42–3, 52, 57–8, 63–71, 78, 83, 88, 219, 235–6, 240, 248; *see also* causality
Devereux, G. 40, 88, 250
Dewey, J. 75, 84, 87

INDEX

diaspora 228
dignity xii, xiv, 4, 12, 14, 17–20, 57, 245, 249, 254, 256–7
Dilley, R. 65, 88
discourse 4, 7, 16, 18–19, 37, 42, 46, 56, 61–2, 65–6, 72, 76–7, 84, 87, 237, 240
displacement 7, 42–7, 50–1, 54–5, 71, 80, 88, 181, 183, 187–8, 194, 196, 204–6, 210, 226, 234–5, 237, 242, 245, 247, 255; *see also* movement
'dividuals' 81
Donadio, S. 10, 12
Dostoyevsky, F. 185, 208
Douglas, J. 26, 31, 217
Dreitzel, H. 38
Drury, M. 39
Dumont, L. 71, 176, 237
Durkheim, E. 23, 52, 60–1, 65–6, 73, 176

Earle, T. 77
Eccles, J. 236
ecology 90, 219, 221, 224–5
eco-system 224
Edelman, G. 25, 36, 220–1
Efrat, E. 154
ego-syntonism 88, 242
Einstein, A. 131–2, 135, 142–7, 150, 152, 230
embodiment 11–12, 15, 19, 21–5, 30, 54–5, 75, 80, 90, 100, 216–19, 234, 236, 241, 243, 257, 259, 261
emergence 29, 38, 67–9, 74
Emerson, R.W. xiv, 12, 25, 27–8, 42, 50–1, 55, 74–6, 82, 128, 257, 260–1
emotion 12, 40, 51, 59, 73–4, 79, 99, 106, 146, 171, 175, 179–80, 184, 188, 207, 225, 227, 236, 256
empathy 58, 89
empowerment 15, 51, 79, 86, 209, 215–6
enculturation *see* socialization
energy xi, 4, 6–7, 9, 33, 35, 48–9, 56, 69, 75, 78, 80, 82–3, 89–90, 129–30, 153, 178, 221–3, 233, 235, 243, 258; metabolic 75, 222; *see also* passion
Enlightenment, The 17, 40
entropy 222–4; *see also* randomness
environment 3, 7, 21–2, 27, 31, 40, 54, 57–8, 67–8, 74–5, 80, 82, 90, 132, 149–52, 157, 186, 210–11, 216, 220–8, 231–41, 253, 257, 259; and homeostatic order 221–3, 225, 234–5, 257; *see also* body, body-plus-environment
Epictetus, 34–5
Epstein, A. 82
essence and essentialism 13, 16, 19–20, 25, 29, 35, 42, 67, 81, 177, 225, 247, 259–60; *see also* being and becoming
ethics xii, 244
ethnicity 16, 19, 47, 57, 73, 76, 156, 164, 231, 253
ethnomethodology 36
Everyperson 6, 15–16, 20, 55, 89, 259
Eves, R. 52
Existentialism 7, 11–12, 16–19, 36, 50, 53–4, 58, 67, 69, 77, 79–82, 89, 129, 221, 225, 237, 242, 252, 254, 259; in anthropology 217–18
experience xi, 12, 15, 19–29, 36, 40–1, 49, 51–8, 65–8, 72–9, 84–7, 177–83, 186–9, 206–7, 215–20, 225–8, 234–6, 241–9, 253–6, 259–60

Fardon, R. 5
Feld, S. 40
Fernandez, J. 40, 43, 45–6, 55–6, 70, 75, 219
Fontana, A. 28, 217
force 7–8, 26, 42, 53, 75–8, 82, 89–90, 100–1, 150, 206, 211, 233, 238, 240, 253, 259
form and content 3, 14, 26, 28, 38–40, 43–4, 56–9, 67–70, 72, 76–9, 82–3, 87–8, 100, 149, 176, 217–18, 237, 250–2, 254, 257, 259–60; *see also* public and private
form of life 13, 39, 165, 222
Forster, E.M. 242–3, 256
Foucault, M. 18, 61–2, 65, 176, 240
freedom 17–18, 21, 29–30, 34–5, 42, 46, 49–50, 53, 55, 59, 65, 68, 84, 89, 110, 150, 216, 229, 239–41, 244, 255, 260; *see also* transcendence
Freud, S. 9, 46, 52, 65
Furbank, P. 243

Gane, L. 230
Gatheru, R. 45
Geertz, C. 6, 18, 69, 71, 83
Gellner, E. 17, 47, 133, 221
gender 16, 19, 44, 57, 73, 76, 215–16
Gewirth, A. 256

ghetto xiv, 249, 259
Giddens, A. 43
Gilman, S. 93, 130
Gitelman, Z. 156
Glaser, A. 134
Glaser, Ben xii, xiv, 4, 11, 15–16, 21, 34, 89, **131–52**, 216, 225, 229–32, 234–5, 237, 239–40, 255, 257–8
Gledhill, J. 87
Glew, A. 185, 197, 208
globalization 44, 237
Goethe, J. x, 84, 97, 100, 122, 126, 132
Goffman, E. 64–5, 240–1
Golomb, J. 29, 50
Goodman, N. 14
governmentality 240
Gramsci, A. 86
Gray, J. 240
Greenberg, M. 33
Greene, G. 252

habit 38–9, 44, 46–7, 49, 59, 66, 68–9, 75, 177–8, 220, 228, 231, 235, 238, 241, 250–2, 257
habitus 32, 51–2, 57–8, 61, 63, 65–6, 72, 76
Hallowell, I. 32
Handler, R. 44–5
Hannerz, U. 38
Harries, M. 209
Harries, S. 209
Harris, M. 239
Hawking, S. 142, 146–7
Hazlitt, W. 255
hegemony 16, 28, 32, 52, 71, 78, 86–8; *see also* determinism
Heidegger, M. 9, 52
Heikkinen, A. 35
Heller, E. 10, 127
Helms, M. 79, 81
Hendry, J. 5
Henriques, U. 136
Herzfeld, M. x, 253
Herzl, T. 133
hierarchy 19, 45, 52, 78, 83, 85, 237, 244
Hobart, M. 66
Hollingdale, R. 94
Holocaust, the (*Shoah*) xiv, 136, 158, 162, 241–2; *see also* Nazis
home 16, 43, 51–2, 99, 119–20, 136, 140, 147, 150, 165–6, 169, 182–3, 190, 205, 209–11, 228–30, 232, 234–6, 258; *see also* displacement
Horton, R. 7
Huber, M. 43
human nature 32, 44, 50, 89, 218, 220, 252
human rights xii, 17, 57, 61, 235, 237–8, 253, 256, 258
humanism xii, 11, 14, 17–20, 56–8, 238, 240, 245
Hume, D. 26, 105
Humphrey, N. 41, 216, 236, 238, 256
Hunter, F. 80
Husserl, E. 25
Hutcheon, L. 46
Hyman, T. 185, 189

ideal-type 12–13, 45
identity 18, 31–3, 35–7, 51–2, 55–6, 69–76, 78, 81–3, 89, 150, 156, 175, 178, 205, 216, 221, 225, 236, 239, 242, 245, 253, 260; categorial xii, 16, 69, 245, 248, 253, 257; *see also* categorization
identity politics 19
ideology 4, 22, 42, 65, 71–2, 77, 86–8, 244; *see also* hegemony
imagination xi, 14–15, 20, 22, 26–9, 31, 36, 42–6, 50, 53–7, 68–9, 87, 89, 101, 149, 179–80, 183, 188, 206–11, 218, 252, 256, 258, 260; *see also* creativity
individual x–xi, xiv, 3–7, 12–29, 32–4, 37–8, 45–61, 65–6, 69–81, 84, 87–90, 129, 150, 153, 176, 215–21, 225, 234–61; as permeable 75, 216, 221; as projectile 7–9, 149–50, 225, 240, 258–9, 261
individualism xi, 10, 22, 35, 46, 60, 71
individuality xi–xii, 3, 6, 11–12, 14, 16, 19–20, 22–3, 35, 41, 46, 48–9, 54, 67, 70–2, 75, 89 149, 216, 219, 237–8, 254, 256–7, 259; democratic 4, 253–8
Ions, E. 66
'in order to' and 'because' motives 52–8, 65, 67, 74, 84, 87, 89, 150, 178, 216, 240, 247, 249–50, 259–61; *see also* intention
institution xiv, 4, 8, 21–2, 26, 38, 44–5, 48, 52, 58–60, 64, 68–70, 76–9, 83–4, 87, 90, 153, 164, 178, 216–18, 225, 237, 240–1, 248, 252–4, 260; *see also* totalization

INDEX

intention 6, 22, 26, 34, 37–8, 52, 57, 78, 81, 87, 230, 236, 238, 248–50, 254, 260–1
interaction 6, 10, 20, 37–9, 59, 73–4, 78–9, 85–6, 143, 220, 225, 234, 236, 249–51, 256–7; *see also* talking-relationship
interpretation 5–6, 14, 30–1, 38–9, 44–5, 48, 53, 56–7, 67–8, 70, 72–4, 78, 80, 82–9, 129, 149–50, 185, 216, 219, 221, 229, 241, 251–2, 254, 259–61
intersubjectivity 37, 41
introspection 24–5, 32, 129, 163, 256
Irigaray, L. 215
irony xi, 10–11, 42–9, 55, 70, 77, 79–80, 86, 88–9, 107–8, 113, 116, 216, 243, 245, 248, 255; defined 42–3; *see also* transcendence
Irwin, A. 45, 86
Isaacs, H. 156

Jackson, M. 20, 52, 58, 66, 68, 72–4, 217, 242, 260
Jacobson, D. 77
James, A. 47
James, C. 247
James, I. 54, 58
James, W. xiii
Jenkins, R. 57, 66
Jewry 99, 133–7, 140, 144, 149–50, 153, 156–7, 161–6, 170, 172–7, 228–31, 237, 241, 245
Johnson, C. 252
Jones, D. 256
Jones, E. 9
journeying 93, 149–50, 152–3, 160–1, 164, 166, 172, 175, 177, 207, 227–9, 234, 255–6

Kant, I. 12–13, 24–6, 40, 102–3, 105, 116, 127–8
Kapferer, B. 65
Kateb, G. 4, 51, 256
Kearney, R. 65
Kellner, H. 52, 237
Kelly, G. 27–8
Kerby, A. 29
Kierkegaard, S. 34–5, 46, 127
knowledge 12–13, 17, 19, 23–6, 30–3, 41, 43, 49, 51, 58, 65–6, 128–9, 216, 218–21, 227–8, 233–4, 236, 239, 241, 243, 254–8; *see also* truth

Kohn, T. 40
Kotarba, J. 26, 28, 217
Kurtz, D. 76

Lacan, J. 65, 74
Laing, R. 40, 74, 219
Lame Deer 45
Langer, L. 242
Langer, S. 26
language xii, 22, 28, 30, 37, 39, 45, 56–7, 61, 65–6, 68–9, 72–4, 76–8, 80, 215, 217, 240, 251
Larkin, P. 245
Law, J. 62, 65
Leach, E. 12–13, 30, 49, 55, 79–81, 217–18, 252–3
Levi, P. xiv, 21, 240–50, 254–5, 260; 'valour' and 'virtue' 245, 248–9, 259
Levi-Strauss, C. 63–5
Lewis, H.D. 18, 23–4, 32, 40
liberalism 11, 17, 65, 254
life-course 4, 7–8, 76, 149–50, 176, 181, 258–9
life-policy 34, 164
life-project 3–5, 9, 12, 14–16, 21, 33, 39, 42, 49–50, 78, 88–90, 129, 132, 144, 149–50, 153, 160, 175, 178, 181, 185, 204, 206, 211, 216, 221, 225–6, 230, 234–42, 246, 248–51, 255, 257–60; defined 6, 34–5, 259; as environmental architecture 225, 234–5
life-world 14, 39, 52, 76, 206
literariness 11, 42–5, 218, 239, 242–3, 246, 258; *see also* biography and autobiography
Little, F. 181
Louch, A. 66
Lukes, S. 237
Lyman, S. 36

Machtgefühl 4, 99, 234–5, 238–40, 258–9; *see also* self-intensity
Mair, J. 31
Mallett, P. 246
Mann, T. 9
Martin, G. 45, 77
Marx, E. 83, 252
Marx, K. xi, 52, 60, 65, 67, 86, 124
Maslow, A. 27
Mauss, M. 61, 65, 71
May, R. 67

INDEX

meaning 3–5, 16, 26, 28–30, 37–41, 45, 53, 56–9, 65–9, 73–5, 78, 81, 84, 86, 88, 185, 205–6, 218–19, 227, 236, 238, 250–4, 256–7, 259–61; *see also* form and content
Melville, H. 239
'meta' 42, 45, 48, 71, 77
methodological pluralism 58, 254
migrancy 93, 120, 137, 145, 147, 150, 152–78, 209, 225–6, 229, 232, 234–5, 255; *see also* movement
Mill, J.S. 65, 254
Milton, K. 219
mind 20, 22, 26, 33, 40–1, 52, 55, 59, 61, 70, 218, 229, 235, 241, 252
Mises, L. von 66
modernity 43, 52, 237, 241, 253
moments of being 13, 27, 29, 31, 43, 51, 65, 74–6, 79, 83–4, 236
momentum 7–9, 29, 59; *see also* force
Moore, B. 83
morality 13, 16, 19, 29, 33, 40, 48, 54, 60, 66, 70–2, 77, 100, 160, 244–5, 247–8, 252–7; *see also* ethics
Morris, B. 56
movement 35, 46–8, 51, 55–7, 71, 75, 82, 87, 118, 128, 150, 177–8, 183, 226, 229, 234, 237, 239, 255; *see also* journeying
Murdoch, I. 253

narrative xi, 4, 14, 20, 29, 31, 33, 35, 38–9, 51, 73, 88–9, 100, 149, 184, 206, 242, 247–8, 255, 258
nation xii, 16, 76, 146, 153–4, 163, 178, 225, 228–9, 232, 237, 241
Nazis xii, xiv, 11, 16, 21, 134, 136–7, 149, 160, 171, 175, 229, 240–1, 243–8, 250, 253; *Lager* (concentration camp) 90, 240–50, 253–5, 259–60; *see also* Auschwitz
Neisser, U. 27
Neurath, O. 24
Nietzsche, Friedrich xi, 4, 6–7, 9–13, 15–16, 21, 24, 26, 28, 32, 34–5, 42 3, 49, 55, 66–7, 75, 82, 87, 89, **93–130**, 132, 177, 210, 216, 219, 222, 226, 229–30, 232–5, 237–40, 242–3, 247, 252, 255, 257–60; his 'anthropology' 100, 123; 'in spite of' 115, 125–6, 232, 260; on aesthetics 103, 108, 114–15, 117, 125–7; on art 4, 30, 35, 42, 44, 100, 109, 111–12, 116–17, 121, 124–7, 130, 233; on causality 105, 107, 112–13; on consciousness 110; on fiction 9, 11–13, 15, 43, 73, 103–14; on genius 6–7, 9, 12, 16, 49, 99, 238, 259; on individuality 102–4, 109–10, 119, 121–6, 128, 232; on interpretation 108–14; on knowledge 99–100, 106, 112, 115, 117–19, 124; on language 106–7, 111–12, 118, 121, 127, 232; on 'masters' and 'slaves' 123–4; on power-quanta 101–5, 122–3, 126, 128, 130, 222, 232–3; on science 107–8, 120, 123, 127, 233; on self-overcoming 118–27, 129, 232–3; on tragedy 115–17, 121, 232; on truth 105–9, 112–13, 116–18, 120, 125, 128, 232; on values 117–24, 126, 128, 232; on will-to-power 11, 28, 35, 49, 82, 87, 101–5, 108–9, 111, 113–20, 123–4, 127, 129, 232–3; on writing 96–7, 99–100, 126–8, 130
noumena *see* phenomena and noumena

Oakeshott, M. 144, 230
objectivity 20, 27, 32, 53, 58, 63–4, 66, 69, 73–4, 87, 240, 247, 260
Ong, W. 32, 41
Oppenheimer, P. 43
organism-plus-environment *see* body, body-plus-environment
Ortega y Gasset, J. 33, 41, 43, 47, 51
otherness 17, 36, 42–3, 54, 73, 76, 81, 182, 216, 220–1, 226, 234, 251–2, 255–7, 259
Overing, J. 20, 22, 35, 43, 59, 75, 77, 215, 225
Oz, A. 163, 171, 175

Pareto, V. 53, 60, 85–6
Parsons, T. 85
passion 13, 102, 129, 132, 139–40, 143–7, 149, 152, 226, 229–33, 242; *see also* energy
Patrizio, A. 181
perception 40–1, 56, 60, 70, 74, 219
Percy, W. 37
performance 78, 232
personalization 39, 68, 77–8, 84, 90, 149, 177, 218, 220, 223, 225, 227, 236

280

personhood 22, 47–8, 70–1, 79, 81, 237
Peters, E. 74
phenomena and noumena 13, 24–6, 28, 32, 67, 102–4, 112, 116, 191
phenomenology xi, 24, 67–8, 73, 75, 78, 81, 84–5, 89–90, 191, 216–20, 238, 257–8; *see also* sensorium
physiology 11, 24–5, 55, 61, 216, 219–24, 237
Plato 40, 59
poetry x, 14–16, 23, 41, 54–5, 57–8, 99–100, 112, 185, 218, 225, 245, 247
Polsby N. 83
Pople, K. 9, 179, 182, 185, 197, 205, 207, 210–11, 226
Popper, K. 14, 19, 36, 59, 236
Pospisil, L. 45
poststructuralism 18–19, 22, 32, 56–7, 65–6, 76–7, 81
power: artistic 10; collective 3, 65–6, 77, 260; economic 77, 83; embodied 54, 75, 80, 215–16; existential 3, 5, 12–14, 16, 20–1, 36, 42, 52–3, 55, 74–6, 78–84, 88–90, 221, 237, 240–1, 260; (defined xi, 75, 89); experiential 84–5, 88–9; Foucauldian 62, 66; impersonal 3, 5, 53, 62, 64, 67, 76, 83–4, 87; imaginative 54, 87; individual xiv, 9, 13, 16, 26, 35–6, 51–2, 76,; 80–2, 99, 216, 227, 234, 236, 240, 245, 261; institutional 3, 5, 21, 53, 74, 76–9, 83, 85, 244; political 52, 55, 74, 77, 83–4; relational 79–81; structural 3, 5, 14, 19, 66, 74, 76–7, 84, 86, 244; *see also* empowerment
pragmatism xii, 11–13, 20, 238
Pres, T. des 241
Preston, J. 28
psyche 73–4
psychology 73–4, 78, 84–5, 88, 149, 232, 238
public and private xi, 3, 6, 30, 37, 39, 41–2, 64, 69, 72–3, 77–8, 88, 149, 181, 184, 205, 208, 225–7, 229, 231, 251–7, 259, 261; *see also* personalization
Putnam, H. 10
Putnam, R. 10

race 16, 19
randomness 66, 76, 87, 223–4, 249–50, 252, 257

Raphael, D. 216
Rapoport, A. 224–5
Rapport, N. 3, 6, 15, 18–20, 22–3, 26, 27, 30, 35, 38–9, 42, 49, 51, 53, 59, 6, 68, 75–8, 80, 84, 86–8, 215, 220, 225, 243, 250–1, 253, 257, 261
rationality xi, 17–19, 24, 31, 47, 55, 71, 247
Rawls, J. 33, 35
Ray, W. 56–8, 77
redemption xii–xiii, 181–211, 233; *see also* reprieve
Redfield, R. 32
reductionism 16
reflexivity 11, 33, 36, 43, 163, 256, 259; *see also* irony
religion 16–17, 44, 46–7, 53–4, 56, 60–1, 66–7, 86, 156, 165, 240, 246, 253; fundamentalism 46, 240; *see also* conversion
Relph, E. 235–6
reprieve 242, 245
rhythm 61, 239; *see also* interaction
Rilke, R. 42
Robinson, D. 208
role 60–1, 64, 70, 72, 77, 79, 81, 83
Rorty, A. 31
Rorty, R. 13, 19, 43
Rothenstein, E. 210
Rubinstein, R. 85
Ruesch, J. 224

Sacks, H. 63, 65
Said, E. 161, 176
Samuel, R. 6
Sapir, E. 251
Sartre, J.-P. 17, 25, 27, 29–30, 35, 40, 53–4, 67, 82, 252, 259–60
scale 6
schismogenesis 247
Schuetz, A. 52, 256, 258, 260–1
science 13–14, 17, 19, 23, 40, 44, 100, 145, 148, 218, 220, 237, 246
Scott, J. 86
Segal, D. 44–5
self xi, 4, 15, 21–37, 41, 50–6, 60, 67–70, 74, 80–1, 87, 89, 100, 128, 147, 150, 160, 176, 189, 206, 209, 216, 218–21, 225–6, 229, 234, 240–7, 251, 254–7, 260; *see also* emergence
self-intensity 4, 7, 9, 16, 50, 149, 207,

226–7, 234, 238–9, 258–9; *see also* single-mindedness
sensorium 10, 40–1, 70, 75, 80, 90, 115, 216, 226, 228, 257
Shakespeare, W. 53, 185
Shelley, P.B. 22–3, 54
Shore, C. 241
Shostak, M. 45
Silberstein, Rachel xii, 4, 11, 15–16, 21, 34, 89, **153–78**, 216, 225, 227–9, 231, 233–5, 237, 239–40, 255, 257–8
Simmel, G. 60, 76–9
Simpson, T. 47
single-mindedness 4, 6–7, 9, 12, 16, 34–5, 129, 150, 234, 238–9, 258–9; *see also* self-intensity
Skalnik, P. 85
Smith, G. 86
social fact 23, 57, 60–1, 64, 66, 84
social relations 4, 6, 71, 75, 79–83, 89, 150, 177–8, 181, 188, 207–8, 211, 217, 219, 225, 231, 235, 250–2, 254–5, 257, 260
social science xi, 75, 218, 221, 224, 253–4, 258, 260
social structure 3–4, 7, 11–12, 19, 28, 38–9, 42–5, 52, 56–7, 60–1, 63–6, 71–2, 74, 76, 81, 83, 86, 178, 217, 237, 241, 244, 251–2, 259
socialization 14, 22, 60, 66, 176, 217, 244
society xi, xiii, 3, 8, 17, 19, 26, 28, 32, 37–9, 43–9, 52–66, 69, 72–3, 78, 83, 88, 176, 206, 210–11, 217–8, 224–5, 237–9, 251–4, 257–8; as aggregation 7–8, 38–9, 59, 69, 217, 225, 250–1; *see also* community
Soekefeld, M. 248
Sontag, S. 40
Spencer, Stanley xii, 4, 8, 11, 15–16, 21, 34, 89, **179–211**, 216, 225–31, 233–5, 237, 239–40, 255, 257–8
Spengemann W. 15
Spinoza, B. 145, 147, 196, 230
Stagl, J. 44
Stanage, S. 252
Steiner, G. 37, 78, 80
stereotype 19, 36, 69, 176
Stern, J. 94, 130
Stocking, G. 18
Stoller, P. 19–20, 40, 217, 219, 254
Strathern, M. 5

structuralism 16, 18–19, 22, 31, 56–8, 65–6, 68, 77
structuration 22, 38, 43–4
subjectivity xiii, 5, 20–1, 24–9, 31–3, 40–1, 57–8, 66, 69, 73, 89–90, 216, 236, 238, 240, 247, 256, 260; *see also* personalization
suicide xiv, 242, 244, 247, 249
symbology, cultural 26, 28, 39–40, 46, 55, 59, 65, 68–70, 77, 217, 237, 251–2, 259; *see also* form and content

talking-relationship 250
Tallis, R. 224–5
Tanner, M. 9, 123
Tawney, R. 80, 85
technology 43, 62, 76, 217
text 30
tolerance 4
Tonkin, E. 88
Torres, G. 88
totalization 57, 59–61, 66, 73, 86, 90, 240–1, 243–4, 246–8, 260
transcendence xi, xiv, 3, 11, 18, 20, 27, 34, 36, 41–2, 44–5, 48, 54, 57–8, 70–1, 87, 89, 99, 115–17, 145, 181, 190, 210, 227, 233, 243, 259; *see also* 'meta'
translation 43, 69, 106, 180
trope 55–5, 69, 121, 128, 153, 202–3, 209, 248, 257, 260
truth 9, 11, 13–14, 17–18, 31, 42–4, 46–50, 55, 70–1, 84, 89, 148, 237, 241–2, 244, 258, 260
Turner, S. 221–4
Turner, V. 32, 44
Turton, A. 86

Uexkuell, von 217
unconsciousness 18, 28, 32, 44, 53, 63, 65–6, 76, 79, 84, 248–9

Vaihinger, H. 12
Vauvenargues, M. de 6
Vincent, J. 86
violence 21, 45, 59, 240–1, 244, 247–53, 260; democratic 250–1, 258; nihilistic 88, 250, 252, 257–8, 260–1

Wagner, R. 24, 32, 41
Wallace, A. 38, 41, 250–1, 257
Watson, C. 20

INDEX

Watson, G. 87
Weber, M. 23, 60, 75, 79–80, 83, 237
Weiner, N. 224
Weisser, S. 30, 33
Werbner, R. 88
Wheatcroft, G. 249
White, H. 42
Whitehead, A. 22, 53, 176
Wilde, O. 10, 243, 256
will xi, 6–7, 17, 19–20, 28, 34, 46, 49–50, 52, 54, 57, 70, 75–80, 82–3, 85, 93, 99, 129, 224, 236, 240–2, 244–5, 247–9, 255, 258; *see also* energy
Williksen-Bakker, S. 47
Wilmsen, E. 217

Winch, P. 259
Winterson, J. 215
Wittgenstein, L. 11, 39, 127
Wolf, E. 17, 77, 82, 88
Woolf, V. 31, 36–7, 229
world-making 13
world-view xi, 6, 26–34, 38–9, 42, 45, 68–9, 78, 84, 86, 88–9, 106, 114–15, 150, 183, 215–16, 220, 242, 251, 261; *see also* context
Wright, S. 241
Wulff, H. 228

Yelvington, K. 88
Young, J. 248